Hollywood
Goes
Shopping

Commerce and Mass Culture Series
Edited by Justin Wyatt

Hollywood Goes Shopping
David Desser and Garth S. Jowett, Editors

Screen Style: Fashion and Femininity in 1930s Hollywood
Sarah Berry

Active Radio: Pacifica's Brash Experiment
Jeff Land

Hollywood Goes Shopping

David Desser
Garth S. Jowett
Editors

Commerce and Mass Culture Series
University of Minnesota Press
Minneapolis • London

"Hollywood Exoticism: Cosmetics and Color in the 1930s," by Sarah Berry, was originally published in *Screen Style: Fashion and Femininity in 1930s Hollywood,* by Sarah Berry (Minneapolis: University of Minnesota Press, 2000).

Published by the University of Minnesota Press
111 Third Avenue South, Suite 290
Minneapolis, MN 55401-2520
http://www.upress.umn.edu

Printed in the United States of America on acid-free paper

Library of Congress Cataloging-in-Publication Data

Hollywood goes shopping / David Desser and Garth S. Jowett, editors.
        p.   cm. — (Commerce and mass culture series 3)
    Includes index.
    ISBN 0-8166-3512-9 (hc) — ISBN 0-8166-3513-7 (pb)
    1. Motion pictures—Social aspects—United States.   2. Consumer behavior—United States.   I. Desser, David.   II. Jowett, Garth.   III. Series.
PN1995.9.S6 H65 2000
302.23'43'0973—dc21   99-056290

11 10 09 08 07 06 05 04 03 02 01 00   10 9 8 7 6 5 4 3 2 1

THESE ESSAYS ARE DEDICATED

TO

NINA C. LEIBMAN

Contents

Acknowledgments

This book is dedicated to the memory of Nina C. Leibman, an important voice in contemporary film scholarship that was taken from us all too soon. The project grew out of a panel Nina conceived and organized for the Society for Cinema Studies annual conference held in Dallas, Texas, in the spring of 1996. The title of this book is taken from the title Nina gave to the panel. She had intended to deliver a paper as well as chair the panel, and she had chosen Garth Jowett, Murray Pomerance, and Rick Worland as the other participants. That panel was accepted by the program committee. Tragically, Nina was killed in the fall before the conference, before she could finish the paper she was working on; David Desser requested of the program committee that the panel be allowed to continue. Garth, Murray, and Rick presented their papers to honor Nina's memory. At the time of the conference, Garth Jowett thought that the entire subject of consumer culture and Hollywood cinema would make a worthy anthology, and he suggested that he and Desser work on bringing that to fruition.

The intention was to publish only original essays, and a call for papers was issued through a variety of Internet listservs and discussion groups as well as through the Society for Cinema Studies. We received a large number of submissions and had to make some difficult choices as to what could fit and which essays would work well together. We are grateful to the many authors who graciously submitted essays and can only apologize to those we could not accommodate. We hope this book inspires others to continue the work started here. In particular, we need to see more scholarship dealing with African American, Latino/a, and Asian American audiences as consumers and creators. We are hopeful that future work will build from this foundation and continue the efforts that Nina began.

It is a tribute to Nina's originality of thought that this is the first work to probe in depth the multifaceted array of issues surrounding the links between consumer culture and Hollywood cinema. Indeed, Nina's own research, only at the beginning stages at the time of her death, is not represented in this volume: the images of and links between Hollywood films and the major Los Angeles department stores in the postwar era. Yes, there was a personal element to her work: before embarking on graduate work in film at the University of California, Los Angeles, Nina worked as a buyer for one of the big L.A. retailers. But it was typical of Nina to bring her scholarly brilliance to the things she knew and loved. We can only lament the loss of her own contribution to this volume, the loss of her unique and special take on these issues so close to her heart and soul.

As we dedicate this book to Nina's memory, we would like to thank all our authors, who graciously declined any honoraria or royalties for their contributions in order to honor Nina's work. We would also like to thank Debbie Beeson of the Unit for Cinema Studies at the University of Illinois for her help with this volume. And to Murray Pomerance, who not only participated in the original panel, but whose friendship and humor brought much pleasure to Nina in the last months of her life, we offer a special thank-you. To Gorham (Hap) Kindem we offers thanks for his gracious and astute comments on many of the essays in this volume. We must also thank Hilary Radner, who suggested that Justin Wyatt, newly editing a series at the University of Minnesota Press, might find this manuscript of interest. And we are especially grateful to Justin Wyatt, series editor at the University of Minnesota Press, who breathed new life into this project when it almost faded away, and to Jennifer Moore at the Press for her efforts to put this volume on the fast track and to help make it that much better, too. Nina's loss is an incalculable one to the world of film scholarship. But even more, so many of us in film studies lost a true, loving, and genuine friend. This volume can do little to ease the pain of this loss, but we hope that it is a worthy monument to a woman whose love for film was matched only by her love for her friends and family.

Introduction

David Desser and Garth S. Jowett

In their famous study of the community of Middletown (in reality Muncie, Indiana), undertaken in 1924, the sociologist Robert S. Lynd and his social psychologist wife Helen Merrell Lynd emphasized the important role that the new forms of communication and transportation played in decreasing social and cultural isolation in the United States. In particular, they noted the increasing ubiquity of a nationwide media-created culture, and that "indeed, at no point is one brought up more sharply against the impossibility of studying Middletown as a self-contained, self-starting community than when one watches these space-binding leisure-time inventions imported from without—automobile, motion picture, and radio—reshaping the city."[1] Thus even in the first quarter of the century the fact that life in the United States was changing rapidly was a topic of considerable interest and some apprehension. We can now more fully appreciate that the massive changes in economic, political, social, and cultural life that Americans have undergone in the twentieth century are almost too numerous to calculate or comprehend. This has not stopped historians and others from attempting to catalog the sources and nature of these changes. However, it is only in relatively recent times that the media of communication, and popular culture in general, have been identified as potent sources of social and cultural change, affecting in turn every aspect of modern society, from economics to politics, from aesthetics to language, and from mores to religion.

It is particularly gratifying for film specialists to note the increasing interest on the part of social historians in the role of the motion picture in the shaping of twentieth-century American society and culture. Scholars in many disciplines are now beginning to examine and explain how the cinema may both serve as a primary resource to begin to comprehend these changes, to trace them, to visualize them, and is itself implicated in helping bring about these monumental shifts. The profound reconceptualizations of American society around the turn of the century were brought about, to begin with, by industrialization, urbanization, and immigration (emigration from Europe and Asia and migration from South to North, and from the rural to the urban), factors intimately linked to the growth and development of the cinema, itself an industrialized, urbanized art and entertainment form hugely appealing to and produced by immigrants and migrants. The well-known stories of the rise to power in the film industry and the formation of what we now know as Hollywood on the part of immigrant Jews from Central and Eastern Europe, for instance, reveals this profound relationship between the new medium of cinema and America's new citizens.[2] Cinemagoing was both a new medium and a new activity for newly urbanized and/or Americanized immigrants and refugees and was part and parcel of the landscape of change the United States itself was undergoing.

Cinema provided more, of course, than entertainment, but even as an entertainment medium it inaugurated vast shifts in social life. Among other things, within the cinemas and on the screen itself, educational lessons were imparted about what it means to be American while America itself was transformed in the process. One such transformation was the ever-increasing emphasis on consumption, on consumerism not only as a public good but as a political, commercial, and individual necessity. This represented, at the very least, a profound difference from nineteenth-century ideals of production, thrift, savings, and the entrepreneurial spirit within the realm of the family and the town. Such a shift not only had impacts on the ideals of family and labor, but spoke to the very heart of issues of gender, sexuality, and the public realm. It is arguable that at the very heart of the cinema may be found the contradictions and paradoxes of twentieth-century consumerism and thus the very basis of so much of modern and postmodern life.

A focus on consumerism and the cinema, then, allows one to explore some fundamental ideals, issues, and problems of twentieth-century American life and, by extension, much of industrial and postindustrial society around the globe. A focus on consumerism and the cinema, alternately, allows one to think anew about the growth and development of the cinema—how, when, and why its appeal proved so strong, so powerful, and so lasting. One comes through this lens to a better understanding of how cinema developed its commercial base, not only as an "industry" but as an institution, one with profound ideological as well as economic impacts. Cinema's implications for other industrial modes of production and its relationship to other consumer activities and ideologies help us to understand more clearly cinema's impacts on daily life and culture. This anthology, then, addresses issues of broad cultural import while seeking to understand better the growth, development, and even the decline of cinema itself. From the influence of cinema on society to the influence of society on the cinema, the contributors to this book seek to highlight these relationships through the lens of consumerism and consumer culture.

Perhaps among the most important issues within consumer culture have been that culture's effects on women and how women are particularly implicated in and targeted by consumer culture.[3] This anthology brings together a number of essays that deal specifically with this aspect of consumer culture. The growth and development of the motion picture industry itself is owed largely to its appeals to women, at least in the cinema's first half century, and the growth and solidification of consumer culture has always found women right at the center of this development. The imbrication of women and consumer culture has been a central concern of the contemporary feminist movement, especially given the implications of consumerism for women's domestic roles and women's self-images. The cinema, too, has been an important site of examination and critique of mass culture. A look at cinema and its relationship to consumer culture, then, offers a wealth of possibilities for the ongoing feminist understanding and critique of cinema and its interconnections with consumerism and contemporary culture.

A focus on consumerism and the cinema also allows, perhaps even mandates, an understanding of how issues not only of gender but also of race and class have been structured into, worked through, and, often, remain problematic in contemporary culture. Although more work remains to be done in these areas, especially perhaps concerning how subcultural groups have been specifically addressed as consumers or how such groups have subverted mainstream attempts to suppress or co-opt their own images and identities, the present volume highlights a number of instances in which race and class take a prominent, if sometimes covert, pride of place.[4]

Many of the essays gathered here present new information, new components to our understanding of the rise of cinema and the concomitant rise of consumer culture. A number of essays, for instance, show how current trends in cinema and culture, such as the concern with body type and body shaping and a focus on youth, actually occurred much earlier than previously thought. Similarly, the cinema's relationships with other media, especially publishing (newspapers and novels in particular), are shown to have been part and parcel of the cinema's growth and of the cinema's attempts to broaden and legitimate its appeal.

This volume is divided into three parts, although readers will see that these divisions are not hard and fast. Still, the overall design allows a focus on three distinct areas of cinema and its relation to consumer culture. Part I, "Creating Consumers," deals with two interrelated issues: how the cinema built its audience—that is, created consumers for its own product, the movies—and how the cinema created a consumer culture where other products, such as newspapers, books, makeup, and fashion, and other lifestyle issues created a climate encouraging the largely female audience to consume goods, services, and images. Part II, "Consuming Creators," deals with developments within the star system that show how the importance of movie stars greatly enhanced the power of the cinema to influence consumerism, and how, over time, shifts in the culture at large affected the idea and ideals embodied in movie stars. Part III, "Hollywood: The Dreamscape," revolves around the significance of a place, a specific geographic locale (variously, Hollywood or Los Angeles or, more generally, "California") in creating an identity that could be consumed—visualized, imagined, created—by its audience.

Heather Addison, in "Hollywood, Consumer Culture, and the Rise of 'Body Shaping,'" points out the tremendous increase in consumerism after World War I and the recognition of just how deeply the cinema was implicated in this shift. A quote from *Photoplay Magazine* speaks of the effect of movies: "New desires are instilled, new wants implanted, new impulses to spend are aroused." Among these new desires instilled and implanted was the desire for a "fit" body. The ability to possess such a body gave rise to a movement then known as "body shaping." Hollywood was not, of course, alone in instilling this new image of and desire for the shaped body. But what was new to both Hollywood and the linked mass media was the manner in which they addressed their insistence that women's self-improvement arose from a sense of profound self-dissatisfaction. Although it has been the case at least since the 1960s that the mass media have promulgated specific images of the female body as the most desirable, Addison notes that this perhaps unfortunate feature of the cinema arose much earlier than previously realized.

The address of the motion pictures to women was a component of early cinema's rise not only to respectability (a well-acknowledged and documented aspect of cinema history) but to commercial viability.[5] Barbara Wilinsky's "Flirting with Kathlyn: Creating the Mass Audience" documents the importance of the serial. *The Adventures of Kathlyn* (1913) was a coproduction of the *Chicago Tribune* and the Selig Polyscope Company, which created this first ever of the cinema's serials in order to boost the paper's circulation among women and, in turn, boost women's attendance at the pictures. The *Tribune's* support for women's suffrage, for instance, had endeared it to a female readership. The success of the relationship between the paper and the cinema in serializing the adventure story also predisposed the paper to increase its coverage of motion pictures (although it was not the first newspaper to do so, as a later essay in this volume reveals). Other newspapers followed, leading to the creation of such serials as *The Perils of Pauline* and *The Exploits of Elaine*. Similarly, this successful cross-fertilization between the *Tribune* and Selig led to greater coverage of film and related consumer enterprises in mass-market magazines.

The woman-centered address of movies continued throughout the 1920s, perhaps most spectacularly through the famous figure of "the flapper." Sara Ross, in "The Hollywood Flapper and the Culture of Media Consumption," demonstrates how the film industry had to concern itself with the details of creating, legitimating, and maintaining a culture of media consumption. It did so by utilizing the figure of the flapper, a popular media construct who, the cinema itself demonstrated, was not only a consumer but a savvy consumer of the cinema itself. A focus on the film *Flaming Youth* (1923) demonstrates not only a profound relationship at this stage in cinema's development between film and publishing, but also how film justified a concern with film itself— the educational value of the cinema became a prime component of the cinema's appeal to its female audience.

Cynthia Felando's "Hollywood in the 1920s: Youth Must Be Served" also takes up the image of the flapper. Felando maintains that it was not in the 1950s when Hollywood first targeted the youth market, but in the 1920s. But this image of "youth" did not include young people in general, but, more specifically, young women. This led to a significant cycle of films focusing on college life and another cycle of films devoted to the flapper. The flapper was something of a frightening figure to some audiences—young, free, perhaps delinquent. Similarly, women at college were perhaps envisioned as free, loose, out of control. The films worked to shift the image, then, from "youth as a delinquent class" to "youth as a consumer class." In the cinema's focus on youth, we see a concomitant focus on consumerism.

Moving on from the 1920s, Sarah Berry's "Hollywood Exoticism: Cosmetics and Color in the 1930s" looks at the rise of makeup in film and culture and Hollywood's attempts to construct something like a "multicultural beauty." The significance of Max Factor and the rise of Technicolor photography are detailed here, as the movies and supporting discourses such as fan magazines attempted to teach women the art and craft of makeup. If the 1920s had "body shaping," the 1930s had "the makeover." Hollywood's stars represented idealized types for emulation and demonstration of cosmetic self-transformation. In describing these developments, Berry also details Hollywood's attempts to come to terms with the vexing issues of race. Her explication of Hollywood's Latina stars in particular provides a fascinating glimpse into the contradictions of Hollywood's constructions of whiteness.

Rick Worland and David Slayden bring the chronology of Hollywood's development and its imbrications with consumer culture into the 1950s as they provide an entirely new look at and interpretation of one of the cinema's best-remembered science fiction classics. In "From Apocalypse to Appliances: Postwar Anxiety and Modern Convenience in *Forbidden Planet*," the authors make the compelling case that for all the pop-Freudian interpretations of this vaguely derived Shakespearean adaptation, the real meaning of the film may be found in the images of postwar consumer culture the film subtly and not-so-subtly highlights. Again, the appeal to women, to the female audience constructed as consumers, is notable. Worland and Slayden make the case that the film represents something of a transition between Rosie the Riveter and a new image: Robby the Robot. Robby the Robot, surely the best-remembered figure in the film, functions as a servant, a worker, and a homemaker. He is something like the ultimate postwar labor-saving device, a mirror for 1950s automobiles, television sets, household furnishings, and newfangled appliances. In this manner, the popular media, especially the cinema, played a significant role in selling consumer-based technology—a technology that stemmed significantly from wartime advances in science and weaponry. Thus films such as *Forbidden Planet* played off of fears of apocalyptic destruction in favor of consumer abundance.

The first essay in Part II finds Gaylyn Studlar taking Audrey Hepburn's star appeal and her relationship to haute couture as the basis of her essay, "'Chi-Chi Cinderella': Audrey Hepburn as Couture Countermodel." Hepburn's onscreen and offscreen costuming by Givenchy complicates the nature of the cinematic gaze, with Hepburn's films functioning as much as fashion shows as narratives. The "new look" in fashion that Hepburn represented in the postwar era was an important democratization of haute couture, while Hepburn herself was a countermodel to the "mammary madness" embodied by the likes of Jane Russell and Marilyn Monroe. A reading of *Sabrina* (1954) highlights these linked issues. Studlar relates the decline of Hepburn's film career to the decline of the influence of Paris haute couture in the 1960s in favor of more off-the-rack and casual clothes.

Rebecca L. Epstein's "Sharon Stone in a Gap Turtleneck" takes as its starting point Charles Eckert's early and influential look at the cinema and consumerism, "The Carole Lombard in Macy's Window," originally published in 1978. Epstein surveys the terrain of movie stars as fashion icons and sees important shifts from the height of such iconography in the 1930s to a totally different set of relations in the contemporary era. Perhaps the biggest change may be described as a move from actress-based to character-based fashion trends. Whereas the "looks" of such stars as Gloria Swanson, Mae West, and Joan Crawford carried over from film to film and in extratextual discourse, more contemporary trends may be found in specific characters, such as the "Annie Hall" look from Woody Allen's 1977 film of that name or the "Rachel" look of the character from the television show *Friends*. Another such shift in the relationship between audience and star may be seen in the move from something like a "best dressed" to a "worst dressed" list—the latter occupying more clout than the former since the advent of the notorious Mr. Blackwell and his commentary on "fashion failures." In the contemporary era, the designer has become as much of a star as the star herself, and the award show occupies the specular view of the audience far more than the films themselves. Epstein notes that Audrey Hepburn was perhaps the last of the fashion stars; the cultural changes of the 1960s, the advent of television, and the increasing importance of gossip and the tabloids shifted the balance of power.

Continuing with a focus on the meaning and significance of stars, Aida A. Hozić, in "Hollywood Goes on Sale; or, What Do the Violet Eyes of Elizabeth Taylor Have to Do with the 'Cinema of Attractions'?" views the decline of classic Hollywood and the rise of postmodern consumer culture through the lens of Elizabeth Taylor, perhaps the last of the true "movie stars." Hozić understands Hollywood as moving from an era in which it was "the dream factory" to one today that is closer, in a certain way, to the primitive "cinema of attractions." Relying on Tom Gunning's foundational essay on early cinema, Hozić notes that in contemporary cinema, narrative is often devalued at the expense of spectacle, and the transition from classical to postclassical Hollywood led to the triumph of "merchants"—agents, distributors, marketers. Within this new cinema of attractions, the ownership of imagery is paramount. For Hozić, Elizabeth Taylor's notorious yet commercially successful film *Cleopatra* (1963) is both the end of an era and a harbinger of things to come.

Taking us right up to the present with an examination of very recent films, the concluding essay of Part II puts into question perhaps hoaried notions of the progressiveness of "art" and the retrograde tendencies of "entertainment." Angela Curran's "Consuming Doubts: Gender, Class, and Consumption in *Ruby in Paradise* and *Clueless*" puts into question old-style Frankfurt School notions that viewers are passive consumers of the products of the "culture industry," but also questions cultural-studies cliches of "resisting" readers reacting to and "re-reading" conservative texts to posit the possibility that some films themselves might engage in questioning the role consumption plays in American society. *Ruby in Paradise* and *Clueless* are exemplars of this possibility and in particular also raise issues relating to feminism and consumer culture with their focus on young women who are implicated in and resistant to an economy and a cinema structured around consumption.

In Part III, the exploration of consumerism and the cinema shifts a bit to take into account not just films' overt displays of consumerism or the consumption of movie stars and movie characters, but the importance of place, of grounding cinema in a sense of space. Jeffrey Charles and Jill Watts detail this importance in "(Un)Real Estate: Marketing Hollywood in the 1910s and 1920s." They begin with the well-known image of the Hollywood sign in the Hollywood Hills. Perhaps most film scholars know that once the sign said "Hollywoodland," but few may realize that the sign was part and parcel (so to speak) of an attempt to carve out a new, vital subdivision from the Los Angeles landscape. *Los Angeles Times* publisher Harry Chandler was particularly influential in attracting film folk to L.A. and in promoting the movie business, in turn, in his newspaper. The *Los Angeles Times* was the first paper in the country to assign a regular columnist to the movies. As the film industry gradually settled in Hollywood, a complex interrelationship developed between the text of the film and the context of place: the marketing and consumption of real and unreal visual space. Charles and Watts note in a new way the significance of movie-related discourse surrounding the "actual" home lives of movie stars. The making of movies could be grounded in an actual space, a real place, "Hollywood," and the stars' homes—particularly the glamorous, opulent mansions of the likes of Mary Pickford and Douglas Fairbanks (their famous estate Pickfair) and Harold Lloyd—became intimately connected to the consumption of cinematic images. "Maps to the stars' homes" and movie tours became popular extrafilmic discourses in the 1920s. The actual place called Hollywood was hardly the location for all of the studios, and virtually none of the stars lived there, but the internationally recognized symbol of "Hollywood" was born in this era.

If early Hollywood is the focus of Charles and Watts's essay, then contemporary, postmodern Hollywood is the site of Josh Stenger's analysis in "Lights, Camera, Faction: (Re)Producing 'Los Angeles' at Universal's CityWalk." If early Hollywood created an ambiguous relationship between the site of movie production and the sights on view in the cinema, contemporary Hollywood plays even more strongly on the simulacrum. Universal Studios' CityWalk is part shopping mall, part theme park, part homage to the movies, and all tourist attraction. It sits between Universal Studios and the site of its famous tour and the eighteen-screen Cineplex Odeon Multiplex theater high above the San Fernando Valley, sufficiently far from the L.A. streets it partly reproduces. It both avoids and reproduces what Stenger calls L.A.'s "spatial apartheid," providing a safe shopping experience far from the city's mean streets. While the real, the actual, Los Angeles exists some few miles away, shoppers and tourists can engage in sight-seeing and souvenir buying as if they are in a movie about an idealized Los Angeles, safely ignoring or blocking out the nearby city itself.

A "real" L.A. locale is utilized in the highly successful film *Pretty Woman* (1990): Beverly Hills's Rodeo Drive, known for its hugely upscale shops. Thomas E. Wartenberg, in "Shopping Esprit: *Pretty Woman*'s Deflection of Social Criticism," acknowledges the significance of Rodeo Drive and sees how the film attempts, on one level, to reject the consumerist values the street itself seems to signify. Yet, for Wartenberg, the film is ultimately unsuccessful in criticizing its consumer basis. Although it rejects wealth as a standard of value, it substitutes "beauty," a different kind of wealth, as naturalizing and legitimating the fit between the film's seeming low-class prostitute heroine (Julia Roberts) and her eventual rise to the upper class, her "suitability" to shop on Rodeo Drive. Most critics have seen *Pretty Woman* as a variant on the story of Cinderella, certainly a useful recognition. For Wartenberg, however, a more useful and revealing intertext is George Bernard Shaw's *Pygmalion*, and a comparison to Shaw's play (although

xx David Desser and Garth S. Jowett

less so to the musical film version, *My Fair Lady*) reveals just how and why *Pretty Woman* falls short of a genuine social critique.

The anthology's concluding essay is by Larry W. Riggs and Paula Willoquet-Maricondi. Their "A Wild Child Goes Shopping: Naturalizing Commodities and Commodifying Nature in *Nell*" focuses on the popular 1994 film starring Jodie Foster. The authors maintain that *Nell* identifies the consumption of processed commodities in general and of commodified cinema in particular, with intelligent consciousness itself. The film's visual strategies are similar to a recent trend in product advertising wherein the use of nature, the bucolic, enhances the cultural, manufactured item. Moreover, such commercials, along with the film, assert that happy social connections, as well as enjoyable opportunities for solitude, are created and preserved by manufactured commodities. Ultimately, the story of Nell, the character and the film, is that of the inescapable obedience to the law of consumption. In a sense, with *Nell*, we come full circle—from early cinema's implication in the growth and development of commodity culture, of educating audiences to the nature and value of consumption, to the postclassical cinema of the postmodern era, where the consumption of images *is* the product.

The essays in this volume show that cinema was never a discreet entity. Whether films derived from novels or short stories or magazine exposés, were advertised in and written about in newspapers and journals, showcased stars onscreen and off, set or responded to fashion trends and styles, or implicated themselves in the very landscapes in which they were shot, the cinema exists in a complex network always in need of explication and exploration. The cinema's links to consumerism and consumer culture, perhaps the defining substratum of twentieth-century life and culture, make it imperative that further study be undertaken along these lines. This book is only the continuation, we hope, of important and exciting forays into the ever-fascinating and seductive world of mass media and popular culture.

Notes

1. Robert S. Lynd and Helen Merrell Lynd, *Middletown: A Study in American Culture* (New York: Harcourt, Brace, 1929), 5.

2. The works of Lary May and Neil Gabler tell these stories well. See Lary May, *Screening Out the Past: The Birth of Mass Culture and the Motion Picture Industry* (New York: Oxford University Press, 1980); Neil Gabler, *An Empire of Their Own: How the Jews Invented Hollywood* (New York: Crown, 1988).

3. For a very useful survey of the theoretical terrain of consumer culture, and in particular the implications for women's issues, see Celia Lury, *Consumer Culture* (New

Brunswick, N.J.: Rutgers University Press, 1996), esp. chap. 5. For a useful perspective on women and consumerism vis-à-vis the cosmetics industry, see Kathy Peiss, "Making Up, Making Over: Cosmetics, Consumer Culture, and Women's Identity," in *The Sex of Things: Gender and Consumption in Historical Perspective*, ed. Victoria de Grazia, with Ellen Furlough (Berkeley: University of California Press, 1996).

4. For further work in the area of race and consumer culture, see, for instance, Sharon Willis, "I Want the Black One: Is There a Place for Afro-American Culture in Commodity Culture?" *New Formations* 10 (spring 1990): 77–97. See also Lury, *Consumer Culture,* chap. 6. On class and consumer culture, see, for instance, Susan Porter Benson, "Living on the Margin: Working-Class Marriages and Family Survival Strategies in the United States, 1919–1941" in *The Sex of Things: Gender and Consumption in Historical Perspective,* ed. Victoria de Grazia, with Ellen Furlough (Berkeley: University of California Press, 1996).

5. Readers unfamiliar with issues connected to the cinema's appeal to women and to the middle class sifted through the lens of consumerism should see Sumiko Higashi, *Cecil B. DeMille and American Culture: The Silent Era* (Berkeley: University of California Press, 1994).

PART I

CREATING CONSUMERS

1.
Hollywood, Consumer Culture, and the Rise of "Body Shaping"

Heather Addison

> The agrarian economy is out. Truth is still truth but human relations have changed. . . . The result of . . . thrift today is merely nonbuying in an economic order which depends upon mass buying and ever greater and greater mass buying, for the welfare of all.
>
> Edward Filene, *The Consumer's Dollar,* 1934

> Being beautiful isn't easy. Overcoming fat or building yourself up is a hard, hard job. But you *can* if you *will.* . . . You must give yourself the works, and not complain. I pledge you my word that if you will string along with me and do what I tell you to do, you will be as lovely as the stars of Hollywood—and lovelier!
>
> Sylvia of Hollywood, *No More Alibis,* 1934

My broad aim in this essay is to theorize the interrelationship of early consumer culture, Hollywood, and "body shaping." (I use the term *body shaping* to refer to those activities, such as "reducing," that attempt to increase or decrease the size of the body or to sculpt the body through the creation of musculature.) I will argue that both Hollywood and consumer culture emerged in the 1910s and 1920s, enriching one another in a convenient symbiosis. Body shaping—as an imperative, as an activity in which consumers were admonished to engage—developed as a by-product of the symbiotic relationship between Hollywood and consumer culture.

Hollywood and Consumer Culture

A consumer culture is a culture in which "consumerism" is a prevailing ideology. Robert Bocock defines consumerism as "the active ideology that the meaning of life is to be found in buying things and pre-packaged experiences."[1] Consumerism is a particular kind or degree of consumption; it is consumption that is based upon perceived (psychological) need rather than actual (physical) need. This kind of consumption is prompted by an excess of production. Manufacturers seek consumers to absorb this excess; they use advertisements to urge consumers to buy. Such advertisements attempt to convince consumers of the satisfaction consumption brings—happiness, success, youth, beauty, and so on. Prior to the late 1910s, the United States was not a consumer culture. This is not to say that goods were not produced and consumed or that ads were not printed before World War I, but rather to suggest that "consumerism" was not a prevailing ideology in pre–World War I America, where the Puritan values of hard work and thrift predominated.

After the war, a new atmosphere of production and consumption emerged. The advent of scientific management in the 1910s, pioneered by such figures as Frederick W. Taylor, allowed manufacturing to be done more efficiently. In *Our Master's Voice: Advertising,* a 1934 book about the nature and development of American advertising, James Rorty cites statistics that indicate that per capita production advanced twice as fast in the post–World War I era as in the prewar era.[2] This created a new pressure to sell goods, and advertising increased dramatically.[3] In the more recent *Captains of Consciousness,* Stuart Ewen identifies the 1920s as the crucial period for the advent of consumer culture. Of that period, he says:

> With a burgeoning productive capacity, industry now required an equivalent increase in potential consumers of its goods. . . .
>
> . . . In response to the exigencies of the productive system of the twentieth century, excessiveness replaced thrift as a social value. It became imperative to invest the laborer with a financial power and a psychic desire to consume. . . .
>
> . . . Foresighted businessmen began to see the necessity of organizing their businesses not merely around the production of goods, but around the creation of a buying public.[4]

Industry's new productive capacity prompted a reevaluation of the role of workers. Instead of being viewed simply as producers, they were now seen as potential consumers of the goods they created. Consumption was identified as a crucial activity of the production process. Factory owners began to be less resistant to shorter hours and higher wages, because such apparent "concessions" to workers offered those workers the time and the financial means to be better consumers.

In their quest to "manufacture consumers," industry leaders turned to advertisers, who promised to wear down Victorian notions of thrift and to habituate the public to buying. "Modern advertising must be seen as a direct response to the needs of mass industrial capitalism," claims Ewen. "In the 1920s, advertising played a role of growing significance in industry's attempt to develop a continually responsive consumer market."[5] Ewen's use of the term *modern advertising* is significant, for a new breed of advertisements emerged in the 1910s and 1920s. This new advertising formed the backbone of consumer culture. Prior to World War I, advertisements had extolled the individual merits of products, noting their usefulness, sturdiness, and so on. But in the 1910s that began to change. Instead of talking about *products,* ads began to talk about *consumers.* Advertisements fostered and preyed upon consumers' fears and insecurities. Robert S. Lynd and Helen Merrell Lynd, who in 1924 conducted a field investigation to "study synchronously the interwoven trends that are the life of a small American city,"[6] recognized this shift in tone:

> In place of the relatively mild, scattered, something-for-nothing, sample-free, I-tell-you-this-is-a-good-article copy seen in Middletown a generation ago, advertising is concentrating increasingly upon a type of copy aiming to make the reader emotionally uneasy, to bludgeon him with the fact that decent people don't live the way *he* does. . . . This copy points an accusing finger at the stenographer as she reads her *Motion Picture Magazine* and makes her acutely conscious of her unpolished finger nails.[7]

In order to "bludgeon" readers in this fashion, advertisers enlisted the aid of social psychologists, who recommended "the use of psychological methods . . . to turn the consumer's critical functions away from the product and toward himself. The determining factor for buying was self-critical and ideally ignored the intrinsic worth of the product."[8] This was particularly true for body improvement products. For example, a 1925 advertisement for Odorono deodorant in *Motion Picture Magazine* warned women that excessive perspiration can be "a real threat" to romantic happiness. "After all, the greatest dangers are not always big and overwhelming. Often they are really little things that wedge their stealthy way between you and happiness" (see figure 1).[9] Men's bodies did not escape scrutiny, either. In a 1925 issue of *Motion Picture Classic,* the headline on an ad for the Allied Merke Institutes Home Treatment system for stopping hair loss asked, "Could She Love Him Were He Bald?" and advised men not to "let thin, scanty hair ruin *your*

It comes creeping in—and you do not know it!

—a real threat to happiness

After all, the greatest dangers are not always big and overwhelming. Often they are really little things that wedge their stealthy way between you and happiness.

And sometimes the saddest thing about it is—you do not see it coming; you do not even know it's there!

Such a danger is one kind of personal neglect. It flashes no danger signal; but uncorrected, it is a real threat to happiness.

It is that neglect of which the woman is guilty who says, "Oh no, I am never bothered with perspiration."

The great mistake which so many women make is to think that because they do not suffer with excessive perspiration *moisture*, they cannot offend with its unpleasant *odor*. Because they are fastidious about daily bathing, they think their personal daintiness is assured!

Soap and water alone cannot protect you. You know how you often notice perspiration moisture under the arms shortly after a bath. Excitement or nervousness brings it out instantly.

Women who best know the secrets of daintiness take no chances. They care for the underarms as regularly as for the teeth and fingernails. And 3 million of them have found their one *sure* dependence in Odorono, the Underarm Toilette.

A physician formulated Odorono as a scientific corrective of *both* perspiration moisture and odor. It is a clear, clean liquid, antiseptic in action. Doctors and nurses make constant use of it in hospitals.

Twice a week is often enough to use Odorono. Each application *assures* 3 days freedom from unsightly, uncomfortable moisture and from that repellent odor which is so deadly to feminine daintiness.

And you do not need to bother with other precautions! Odorono keeps your lingerie and blouses dry, fresh and unstained; free from those ugly, wet "half moons" under the arms.

Are you taking a chance on this danger? Personal daintiness is too prized a quality to risk neglecting. Keep it safe with the twice-a-week Odorono habit. *Know* you are altogether above reproach. You can get Odorono at all toilet counters, 35c, 60c and $1 or sent prepaid.

RUTH MILLER
The Odorono Company, 130 Blair Avenue, Cincinnati, Ohio
Canadian Address: 107 Duke St., Toronto

—Send for Sample Set of the complete Underarm Toilette—

RUTH MILLER
130 Blair Avenue, Cincinnati, Ohio

Please send me sample set of Odorono, Creme Odorono, (for odor only) and Odorono Depilatory with booklet, for which I enclose 10c.

Name..

Address..

(Note: Sample of any one, 5c)

Figure 1. Advertisement for Odorono deodorant in *Motion Picture Magazine*, 1925.

personal appearance" (see figure 2).[10] If consumers could be convinced to be dissatisfied with themselves, they would have a general urge to buy. Such an urge is the engine of a consumer culture, and it is this engine that advertisers of the 1910s and 1920s attempted to build.

In this endeavor, they were aided and abetted by the motion picture

Could She Love Him Were He Bald ?

ON what a slender thread hangs interest—Affection—*Love!*
    She notices, for the first time, some tell-tale specks of dandruff on his coat, and that his hair is getting thin on top. What if he should lose it! Could she love him then—*if he were bald*—bald as Uncle Charley?
    The very thought is a severe shock to her, for she has always been so proud of his personal appearance—and her own. Wherever they have gone together, the verdict of their friends has been, "What a good-looking couple."
    But if he should lose his hair—if he had a shiny, bald head—she just couldn't stand it. Anything but that. She wouldn't mind a sweetheart or a husband, whose hair was gray, or even one with a red head—but a bald head . . .
    Could any girl's romance survive *that* blow?

New Hair For You In 30 Days
—Or No Cost!

Don't let thin, scanty hair ruin *your* personal appearance.
It isn't necessary.
If you are worried over the condition of your hair
    —if it is falling out
    —if it is getting thin on top
    —if your bald spot is growing larger every day
send at once for our free booklet, which gives you full particulars of an easy, simple home treatment that has grown new hair in one month's time for hundreds of people.
    Don't say "It's too good to be true." Don't be skeptical. Don't doubt. Investigate. That's the only wise thing to do. It costs you nothing to find out what this treatment has done for others—what it can do for you.
    So, mail the coupon now. Learn all about this marvelous, new treatment that produces such amazing results.

Proof of Success

    You are not asked to take our word in this important matter. We can refer you to hundreds of delighted people for whom we have grown new hair, after all other remedies failed. Read these brief extracts from a few of the hundreds of grateful letters, which are on file in our offices, open to your personal inspection:
    "Your treatment so far is nothing short of wonderful. New growth started after three weeks. My fears of baldness are gone forever."—Angus McKenzie, Lakeview, N. J.
    "The top of my head is almost covered with new hair. I have been trying for last five years, but never could find anything that could make hair grow until I used your treatment, and now my hair is coming back."—Tom Carson, Ohio.
    "Hair stopped falling out and quite a lot of fine new hair is coming in where my head was bald. Can highly recommend it."—F. L. W., San Francisco, Cal.
    "Lots of hair is growing where I was bald. It was just as bare as the palm of my hands. New hair is coming again."—C. Fitzgerald, New York.
    "I have gained remarkable results. My scalp now is all full of fine new hair. I am well pleased with results."—A. W. B., Maywood, Ill.
    "A new growth of hair has shown on each side of temple where I have been bald for years."—Chas. Barr, New York.
    If you want just such results as these people are getting—if you want to stop your falling hair—cover up your bald spots—improve your personal appearance—let us hear from you at once.

Free Booklet Tells All

    All you need do, to obtain full details of this easy, pleasant, home treatment, that grows new hair in thirty days or costs you nothing, is to sign and mail the coupon at the bottom of this page.
    This interesting, 32-page booklet, not only fully explains our simple, scientific system of growing new hair, but it gives you positive proof of what we have done for others, together with photographs showing what can be accomplished.
    Act promptly. The sooner you get this informative little book, the sooner you can stop your hair from falling out—start to cover up the bald spots—begin to improve your personal appearance.

ALLIED MERKE INSTITUTES, Inc., Dept. 501
512 Fifth Avenue   New York

ALLIED MERKE INSTITUTES, Inc.,
Dept. 501, 512 Fifth Avenue, New York.
    You may send me, in plain wrapper, without cost or obligation, a copy of your new booklet telling all about the Merke Institute Home Treatment for stopping hair from falling out, growing new hair and improving one's personal appearance.

Name..
                (State whether Mr., Mrs. or Miss)
Address...
City.. State...............

7

Figure 2. An advertisement for the Merke Institute Home Treatment system from the January 1925 issue of *Motion Picture Classic*.

industry. During the 1910s and 1920s, the American motion picture industry flourished. Production became centered in and around Hollywood, California; the vertically integrated studio system emerged; and by 1928, attendance at movie theaters had reached sixty-five million people per week.[11] The precise nature of the relationship between Hollywood and consumer culture is uncertain. (Here I use the term *Hollywood* to refer to both the multifaceted institution that includes films, stars, and promotional media and the geographic area where films are produced and industry profits are conspicuously consumed.) Mike Featherstone argues that motion pictures, along with other media, allowed consumer culture to emerge. Mass-circulated images promoted the new standards of behavior, appearance, and lifestyle to which the public began to aspire. "In the 1920s the foundations of a consumer culture became established with the new media of motion pictures, tabloid press, mass circulation magazines and radio extolling the leisure lifestyle, and publicising new norms and standards of behaviour."[12] According to this paradigm, consumer culture depends upon the mass media to create desire and to promote consumption. Indeed, in the early 1930s, a promotion booklet for advertisers in *Photoplay,* a motion picture fan magazine, emphasized the "longings" inspired by the screen:

> *Photoplay* . . . is outstandingly tributary to the great sales-making, want building influence of the screen.
>
> . . . During that hour or two in the romantic world of make-believe, potent influences are at work. New desires are instilled, new wants implanted, new impulses to spend are aroused. These impulses may be at the moment only vague longings, but sooner or later they will crystallize into definite wants.
>
> . . . *The motion picture paves the way. Photoplay carries on, renewing the impulses caught on the screen.*[13]

Obviously, consumer culture did depend upon the mass media to promote new lifestyle standards and to advertise new products. But the cinema occupied a unique position in the media realm because, unlike newspapers, magazines, or radio, it did not rely upon advertising revenue for its existence. Newspapers, magazines, and radio *had* to promote the ideology of consumerism. They were explicitly part and parcel of consumer culture. American motion pictures contained no explicit advertising messages. They were under no direct obligation to promote the values of consumer culture, and yet they did. Why? James Rorty offered one possible theory in 1934:

Why does the motion picture with a high content of "romance," "beauty" and conspicuous expenditure represent the standard movie product of maximum salability? Because the dominant values of the society are material and acquisitive. And because the masses of the population, being economically debarred from the attainment of these values in real life, love to enjoy them vicariously in the dream world of the silver screen. The frustrations of real life are both alleviated and sharpened by the pictures.[14]

In other words, both Hollywood and consumer culture had the same goal: inspiring *want*, either to watch films or to purchase products. As Annette Kuhn has noted, films tend to offer an unattainable fantasy life to bring viewers back again and again.[15] This fantasy lifestyle provided rich fodder for advertisers, who urged consumers to pursue it. Motion pictures and consumer culture were thus the perfect complements for one another. Movies inspired wants that advertisers could exploit, and advertisements incited wants that movies could vicariously satisfy, establishing a cycle in which these phenomena tended to reinforce each other in a symbiotic fashion. (Of course, this is not to say that the sole function of films was to inspire wants and/or to vicariously satisfy wants inspired by advertisements; clearly, the film-viewing experience is a multilayered, complex one.)

The interrelationship of consumer culture and Hollywood provided fertile ground for the growth of a body shaping trend. First, as Featherstone argues, consumer culture bases its appeal primarily upon the visual media, and such media tend to emphasize physical appearance: "Images make individuals more conscious of external appearance, bodily presentations and 'the look.' . . . A culture dominated by words tends to be intangible and abstract, and reduces the human body to a basic biological organism, whereas the new emphasis upon visual images [in the 1920s] drew attention to the appearance of the body, clothing, demeanour and gesture."[16] As a "moving" visual medium, Hollywood cinema called attention to the body. It also allowed standards of appearance to be disseminated on a mass scale.

Second, the body provided an ideal arena of consumption. Each consumer had a body, each body was constantly changing (aging, losing or gaining weight, and so on), and each body had a nearly infinite number of features that could be "improved." If consumers could be convinced to be continually critical of their bodies, manufacturers and advertisers would benefit. They took note of Hollywood's emphasis on the body, recognized the potential for profit, and began to produce and promote body improvement products. Consumers who absorbed the messages in body improvement ads began to crave thin, muscular, wrinkle-free bodies; one way they could "have" such bodies was by watching them on the silver screen. Movies with slender, well-toned bodies therefore became even more appealing. Again, this is not to suggest that consumers went to films only to view attractive bodies. In regard to body shaping, however, it is likely that Hollywood and consumer culture reinforced one another.

By virtue of its status as *the* mass visual medium of the first half of the twentieth century, Hollywood produced, distributed, and exhibited millions of images of the body. In the 1910s and 1920s, Hollywood films began to present more glamorous bodies. Lighting techniques improved and close-ups were used more frequently. Sets and costumes became more elaborate. Star personalities such as Mary Pickford, Douglas Fairbanks, Gloria Swanson, Greta Garbo, John Gilbert, Colleen Moore, and Clara Bow emerged. During this period, advertisements promoting physical perfection began to hammer away at consumers. Hollywood films offered consumers the means of vicariously achieving the physical perfection that ads urged them to seek. Such films also made consumers more receptive to the arguments in advertisements for body shaping products.

This cycle began with Hollywood's emphasis on physical appearance. Directly or indirectly, advertisements for body shaping products and methods that emerged in the 1910s and 1920s based their appeal on standards established by Hollywood. Ads for body shaping products appeared much more frequently in motion picture fan magazines than in other popular magazines. Many ads and/or body shaping guides specifically cited Hollywood stars or lifestyles as a means of establishing the value and desirability of losing weight or building muscles. Furthermore, 1920s commentary on the body shaping craze frequently attributed its rise to the influence of Hollywood.

Body Shaping

Body shaping is the term I am using to refer to activities that attempt to alter permanently the size or shape of the body, as opposed to modifying it temporarily through the use of clothing or other cosmetic devices. Body shaping activities include "reducing" or losing weight, gaining weight, muscle building, and attempting to increase or decrease the size of particular body parts, such as the bust, neck, or ankles. Of course, body shaping activities were not unknown before the 1910s,[17] but a new, identifiable body shaping trend did emerge in the 1910s and peak in the mid- to late 1920s.

The hallmark of this trend was an aversion to fat and a subsequent urge to reduce, for both women and men. (For women, the ideal was rounded slenderness; for men, the ideal was a well-sculpted body with no superfluous fat.) Between 1910 and the late 1920s, fat became physically, socially, and aesthetically offensive. This is evident in the popular literature of the period. In a 1927 piece in the *Saturday Evening Post,* a formerly fat man described the new imperative to reduce and his own attitudes toward fat:

> Back in the year 1912, or thereabouts, I noted the interesting fact that the world seemed to be populated mostly by persons belonging to one of two classes—fat persons who were trying to get thin and thin persons who were trying to get fat.
>
> I discover, in my examination into this problem in 1927, that the basic situation has changed radically. . . . Now I find that the world is populated largely by fat people trying to get thin and by thin people trying to get thinner. Fat seems to have gone out of fashion all along the line. . . .
>
> Consequently, this is the period of reduction, especially the period of female reduction. . . .
>
> I know, as a layman who has made a study of the matter for years, what every dietitian, doctor, chemist and physical expert knows, if he knows anything—that fat is fatal, that it is dangerous, that it is a physical crime.[18]

If the number of articles in popular periodicals is any indication, Americans did become more aware of fat between 1900 and 1930. In the periodicals indexed in the *Readers' Guide to Periodical Literature,* only eleven articles under the heading of "Corpulence" were published in the years 1900 to 1909; from 1910 to 1919, there were twenty-six such articles, and from 1920 to 1929, forty-five articles about corpulence appeared. Many of these articles were personal "reducing stories" accompanied by diet plans. All of the articles acknowledged a new standard of slenderness:

> The slim figure is in the ascendant. . . .
>
> Fat is now regarded as an indiscretion, and almost as a crime. . . . Yet within living memory it was no disgrace to depress the scales to the extent of twenty stone or more. . . . Fat . . . was indulgently tolerated, and even respected.[19]

> One of the greatest bugaboos in the world, so far as modern men and women are concerned, is *fat*. Probably half the people in this country are worrying about their weight. . . . A few of them want to add more pounds, but with most of them the pressing problem is one in subtraction.[20]

In 1926, *Photoplay Magazine* ran a series of extensive, sensational articles on the dangers of "Reduceomania" and noted that the American Medical Association had called a special conference on weight reduction to address the dangerous health risks of quack reducing methods. The results of this conference were published in *Your Weight and How to Control It,* a volume edited by Dr. Morris Fishbein, then editor of the *Journal of the American Medical Association.* One of the book's contributors notes that the people who tend to engage in the reducing craze are "young girls, older women who wish to be considered young, and middle-aged men who want to increase their business efficiency."[21] Another strongly criticizes the "fad for slenderization":

> All the doctors agreed in condemning the craze for the boyish form and the barber-pole figure at any cost. Men and women, especially women, in their eagerness to reduce, have not stopped to consider whether it was wise or safe to take off the "pound of flesh." . . . Women have pounded and rolled, dieted and drugged themselves, and submitted to tortures rivaling those of the Inquisition—all in the search for beauty.[22]

Despite its denunciation of extreme reducing methods, however, the American Medical Association seemed to endorse the position that excess fat is generally undesirable: "Abhorrence of undue fat is today a characteristic American vogue. . . . Whether obesity is due to laziness and overnutrition or to some obscure derangement of the endocrine glands . . . the American of today is likely to reject its advances as far as he comfortably can."[23]

The proliferation of body shaping ads in the 1910s and 1920s, particularly in motion picture fan magazines, also provides evidence of a body shaping trend. The number of body shaping ads in motion picture magazines increased tenfold between 1915 and 1925. It is reasonable to assume that such ads proliferated because they were successful in prompting consumers to buy. For reducing, the ads offered pills (often containing thyroid extract), eating plans, creams, soaps, bath salts, foams, gums, teas, and various machines (including vibrating belts, suction cups, and rolling pins designed to massage fat

Figure 3. Dr. Jeanne Walter advertised her Rubber Garments for Men and Women in 1917.

away). For building muscles, the ads offered development "systems" (usually consisting of several booklets) and various machines designed to build up the chest and arms. The form and content of body shaping ads also evolved during this period, becoming larger and more strident and focusing more specifically on the elimination of excess fat.[24] In 1917, Dr. Jeanne Walter advertised her Rubber Garments for Men and Women by simply announcing that her product could "Reduce Your Flesh!" (see Figure 3).[25] By the early 1920s, more humiliating ads had begun to appear. "When Marriage Is a Crime!" trumpeted an ad for the Strongfort System. This ad explained that any man who is less than physically perfect commits a crime if he marries (see Figure 4).[26] The headline on an ad for SAN-GRI-NA tablets (i.e., thyroid pills) asked, "Why Are You Fat?" and pointed out that "there is no need today for any fat man or woman to remain so, and keep on being the target for jokes. . . . A French scientist has found a new way to dissolve 'fat-forming elements' in the system" (see Figure 5).[27] Such body shaping ads tried to convince readers that plump, flabby flesh was a significant hindrance to social acceptance, especially love.

Thus there is considerable evidence that a body shaping trend emerged in the 1910s and 1920s. Advertisements for body shaping products appeared with unprecedented frequency. Popular writers of the 1910s and 1920s, as well as the medical community, seemed to agree that the nation was in the midst of a reducing craze. Although men were affected by this craze, women apparently participated with greater frequency and intensity. Because women's social and economic worth often depended in large measure upon their appearance, they may have been more susceptible to such a trend.

It is worth noting that body shaping advertisements, articles, and books of this period, judging by the physical images they present, addressed a white audience. Therefore my conclusions in this essay will apply chiefly to white Americans of the 1910s and 1920s. Americans of color may have also been affected by the reducing craze, but the evidence currently available prevents my drawing any conclusions as to the extent of their involvement.

Hollywood and Body Shaping
Advertisements

Around 1910, body shaping ads began to appear in general popular magazines such as the *American Magazine, Ladies' Home Journal,* and

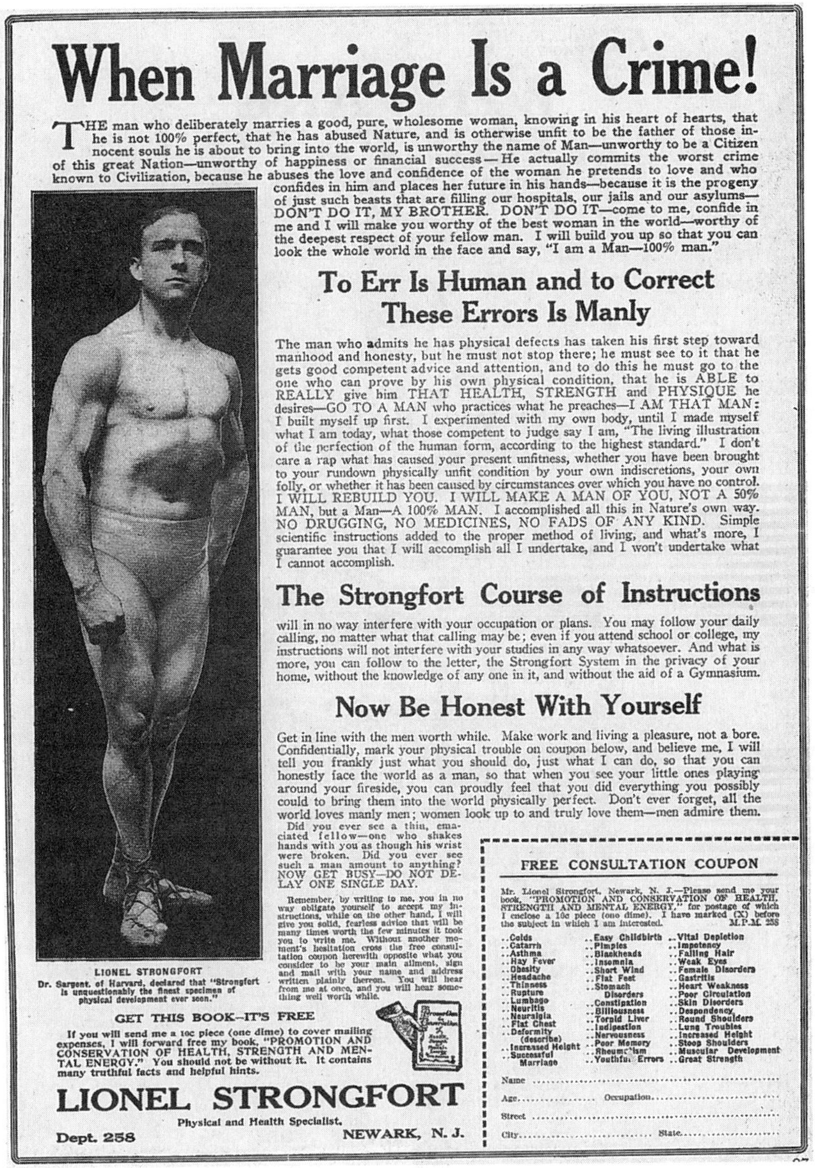

Figure 4. Humiliation escalates with the advertisement for the Strongfort Course of Instructions, 1921.

WHY ARE YOU FAT?

WHEN IT'S NOW SAFE AND EASY TO LOSE 5 TO 6 POUNDS A WEEK

Simple New French Discovery Does Away With Diets, Creams or Drugs

She used to be so Stout

There is no need today for any fat man or woman to remain so, and keep on being the target for jokes. If you are ashamed of your figure, especially in a bathing suit, where fat cannot be concealed; if you cannot find clothes to fit you—if your friends call you "fatty," and if you are not popular, cheer up! NOW YOU CAN BE HELPED. A French scientist has found a new way to dissolve "fat-forming elements" in the system and to transform any fat man or woman into a normal, slender person. No longer should you suffer from high blood pressure, dizziness, rheumatism, weak heart and tired feeling. Thanks to "SAN-GRI-NA" it is now within your reach to possess the figure you have been longing for, and at the same time improve your health. "SAN-GRI-NA" is the easiest and safest way known to reduce, and hundreds of people write in every day, telling what it has done for them. Mrs. Pasquale, of Worcester, lost 63 pounds; Mrs. Mae Busque, of Ware, Mass., writes: "I have lost 29 pounds." Mrs. Bellssner, of Chicago, writes: "I have lost 10 pounds." Mrs. Marqua, of Paris, France, writes: "From 250 pounds I am down to 175." Madame Elaine, of New York City, explains that she lost fifty pounds in eight weeks with "SAN-GRI-NA," after she had tried everything known to reduce, without success. She is a living example of the wonderful transformation that any fat person can go through by simply taking two small tablets of "SAN-GRI-NA" before each meal. Go to your druggist today and get a package of "SAN-GRI-NA"— sold at a price within the reach of all. "Be sure to get 'SAN-GRI-NA,' as it is the only thing I ever found to reduce me, and which I can truthfully recommend to any fat man or woman," says Madame Elaine, of New York City.

If your druggist does not carry "SAN-GRI-NA" in stock he can get it from his wholesaler, or you can send a money order or check for $1.50 direct to the Scientific Research Laboratories, 1841 Broadway, Dept. 271, N. Y. C., and one full sized box of "SAN-GRI-NA" will be mailed you direct.

Figure 5. An advertisement for SAN-GRI-NA tablets, which were thyroid pills, 1925.

Good Housekeeping, as well as in motion picture fan magazines such as *Photoplay, Motion Picture Magazine,* and *Motion Picture Classic* (which began as a supplement to *Motion Picture Magazine*). Around 1915, the incidence of such ads began to increase significantly, at least in some of these publications. I have examined advertisements that appeared in these publications from 1915 through the early 1930s. These magazines were some of the most popular of their era, with circulations of a few hundred thousand to more than two million.[28] Although I have examined mostly "women's" magazines, my list includes the *American Magazine,* which chiefly addressed men and "male" interests, such as business. Motion picture fan magazines may have had a predominantly female readership, but ads that addressed men often appeared in these publications.

The increased frequency of body shaping ads in the 1910s and 1920s not only provides evidence for a body shaping trend, but also links its emergence to Hollywood. Ads for body shaping products were scarce and sporadic until approximately 1915, when their frequency began to increase markedly in motion picture fan magazines.[29] Other popular monthly publications, such as the *American Magazine, Good Housekeeping,* and *Ladies' Home Journal,* showed no such increase in body shaping advertising,[30] and by the mid-1920s, the apparent peak of the craze, body shaping ads appeared ten times more frequently in motion picture fan magazines than in other monthly magazines I examined.

If, as authorities of the period suggested, women were the primary participants in the body shaping craze, women's magazines would be a logical place for body shaping ads to target a female audience. But clearly, advertisers promoted their body shaping products more heavily in motion picture fan magazines than in other women's magazines. Reaching women was not enough; the ads had to reach a particular audience of women. Apparently, readers of motion picture fan magazines were the most receptive to the arguments offered in body shaping ads, perhaps because they had absorbed the standards of physical perfection offered in Hollywood films and maintained by Hollywood stars.

In terms of ad prominence, motion picture fan magazines also led the way. At this time, magazines usually presented a few pages of advertisements at the beginning of an issue, followed by the body of the magazine. Ads again appeared toward the end of the publication, interspersed with feature items. In general popular magazines, body shaping ads did not appear in front advertising sections, whereas in motion picture magazines full-page body shaping ads appeared in front advertising sections as early as 1915. Beginning in 1920, one or more body

shaping ads routinely appeared in the front ad section of *Photoplay.*
In the *American Magazine, Good Housekeeping,* and *Ladies' Home
Journal,* body shaping ads, when they appeared at all, were always
published in the rear advertising sections.[31]

In addition to appearing prominently in motion picture fan magazines, some body shaping ads explicitly cited Hollywood standards of
physical perfection or Hollywood stars to establish an appeal for their
products. Hollywood stars provided examples of physical perfection
that readers could envy and attempt to emulate. As early as 1915,
swimmer and motion picture star Annette Kellermann advertised her
physical culture system in *Photoplay,* declaring, "My motion picture,
Neptune's Daughter, and my own exhibitions on the stage, show what
my course of Physical Culture has done for me. . . . Devote but fifteen
minutes daily to my system and you can weigh what nature intended."[32]
In 1925, an ad for Form-O-Youth Reducing Foam announced, "From
Hollywood Comes This Wonderful Reducing Foam. . . . How natural
that they should find the secret of the youthful figure in this famous
community of beauty!"[33] A 1928 ad for Marmola prescription tablets
offered an endorsement by Constance Talmadge (see Figure 6):

> Constance Talmadge says: "The demand for slender figures is so uni-
> versal that movie stars must have them. Not only beauty, but good
> health and vitality argue against excess fat." . . .
> This is to women—and to men—who admire and desire the slen-
> der figures shown by movie stars. . . .
> . . . Note how slenderness prevails wherever you look today. . . .
> Anyone can see that overweight is generally inexcusable. . . .
> Anyone who suffers excess fat, in any part, should try Marmola.[34]

A 1929 ad for the Battle Creek Health Builder (a machine with a belt
to vibrate fat away) advised readers:

> Keep Fit the Battle Creek Way. For radiant health, alluring beauty—
> [try] this easy new method that famous screen stars use and recom-
> mend. Screen favorites must keep trim and vigorous. Back-breaking
> exercises are too exhausting. "Starvation" diets are inadvisable, often
> dangerous. How, then, do they solve this important problem? Easily.
> They use the Battle Creek Health Builder.[35]

This ad included endorsements by Edmund Lowe of Fox, Joan Crawford of MGM, Reginald Denny of Universal, Renée Adorée of MGM,
and Sue Carol of MGM. Finally, a 1930 ad for Kellogg's All-Bran declared Laura LaPlante of Universal one of "the most envied Women

Constance Talmadge

Says: *"The demand for slender figures is so universal that movie stars must have them. Not only beauty, but good health and vitality argue against excess fat."*

The Pleasant Way to Banish Excess Fat

This is to women — and to men — who admire and desire the slender figures shown by movie stars.

There are several ways in which millions now attain them. One is self-denial in the diet, one is excessive exercise. Both require discretion, both stamina, and both must be continued long. Excess fat was very common when these were the only ways to end it.

The Modern Way

Twenty years ago another method was developed, based on wide research and scientific tests. The purpose is to aid the natural process of turning food into fuel and energy, rather than into fat. It supplies an addition to the substance which does that in the body.

This discovery was embodied in Marmola Prescription Tablets. People have used them for 20 years — millions of boxes of them. And delighted users have told the results to others.

The use has grown to very large proportions. Now note how slenderness prevails wherever you look today. Excess fat, once so common, is the exception now. Anyone can see that overweight is generally inexcusable.

No Starvation

Users of Marmola are not required to adopt abnormal exercise or diet. Moderation aids results, but extremes are not advised. Users depend for the main results on the factors in Marmola.

Take four tablets daily until the right weight is attained, then stop. If again you start to gain weight take a little more Marmola. Simply use Marmola to supply lacking factors, until Nature keeps the slenderness you desire.

Picture shows Miss Talmadge as she appears in her latest European farce-hit "Breakfast at Sunrise."

No Secrets

Marmola is not a secret prescription. The factors are known and recognized by authorities everywhere. The complete formula comes with every box, also an explanation of results. This is done to avoid any fear of harm from what Marmola does.

Anyone who suffers excess fat, in any part, should try Marmola. Test it because of what it has done for so many. Also because of the scientific reasons told in every box. Learn why it has held for so many years the top place in its field. Watch the results for a month, then tell others your decision. You can do no greater kindness to friends who overweigh.

Start now. Order a box before you forget it. You cannot afford to stay fat. Beauty, health and vitality forbid it. Learn now how easily Marmola corrects this ill condition.

Marmola prescription tablets are sold by all druggists at $1 a box. If your druggist is out, he will get them at once from his jobber.

MARMOLA
Prescription Tablets
The Pleasant Way to Reduce

Figure 6. An advertisement for Marmola prescription tablets, endorsed by the actress Constance Talmadge, in 1928.

today" and recommended that readers use All-Bran if they wished to achieve a "rounded slimness" similar to Ms. LaPlante's (see Figure 7).[36]

The connection between Hollywood and reducing was usually not an explicit one, however. Body shaping advertisements that specifically cited Hollywood were actually rather rare, constituting less than 1 per-

The most envied Women today

In dieting for the slim figure, be sure your diet is well balanced with a regular supply of roughage

LAURA LA PLANTE
Universal Star

You KNOW THEM—the women who wear fashion's latest clothes with such stunning effects. To be sure they are slim, but you would never think of calling them thin. "Rounded slimness" seems to describe them perfectly.

Some women are naturally willowy and graceful. But for every one within this charmed circle there are hundreds—yes, thousands—who are dieting . . . almost starving themselves to achieve the figure they'd give the world to have.

Some succeed. But unfortunately too many pay the penalty of too strenuous diets. Weight may be lost but years of age are often added to the face. The skin becomes sallow. The eyes tired. There is a lack of stamina. And if the one dieting told the truth *she would say she is often dizzy* . . . often suffering from a dull headache.

What can be the matter? You may be surprised when we tell you. The diet that produces such unhappy results frequently lacks roughage. And no matter how light a diet may be, the symptoms and evils of irregular elimination are inevitable if roughage is not included in each menu.

By including Kellogg's ALL-BRAN in a reducing diet, you keep fit as you take off weight.

ALL-BRAN does not add fat to the body. Its calory content is low. But its abundant bulk sweeps the intestines clean of poisonous wastes. It relieves and prevents internal congestion safely. It helps supply your body with minerals and vitamins as well as with roughage.

You will like the appetizing, nut-sweet flavor of ALL-BRAN. Eat it in clear soups. On salads. Soaked in orange, prune or fruit juice. As a cereal with milk or cream. Delicious with honey added. Just eat two tablespoons daily—in chronic cases with every meal.

How much better to eat and enjoy ALL-BRAN and relieve congested condition than to depend upon pills for the same result. Kellogg's ALL-BRAN is an important and vital addition to any reducing diet. Made by Kellogg in Battle Creek.

SEND FOR THE BOOKLET
"Keep Healthy While You Are Dieting to Reduce"

It contains helpful and sane counsel. Women who admire beauty and fitness and who want to keep figures slim and fashionable will find the suggested menus and table of foods for dieting invaluable. It is free upon request.

KELLOGG COMPANY
Dept. MC-1, Battle Creek, Michigan

Please send me a free copy of your booklet "Keep Healthy While You Are Dieting to Reduce."

Name_____

Address_____

83

Figure 7. An advertisement for Kellogg's All-Bran, 1930.

cent of all body shaping ads. Most body shaping ads included lean and/or well-muscled images of the creators of the products or "before and after" pictures of satisfied, "ordinary" customers. It may be that the cost of securing endorsements by Hollywood stars discouraged most body shaping advertisers from pursuing them. Or perhaps such explicit endorsements weren't necessary. Merely placing the ads in motion picture fan magazines may have been enough to invoke Hollywood standards of attractiveness implicitly. Motion picture fan magazines were closely linked with Hollywood, providing moviegoers with star interviews, star photos, and sometimes even articles written by stars. Such magazines served as extensions of star personas and general discourse about Hollywood. As readers associated the information in these magazines with Hollywood, so they would associate the advertisements with Hollywood. Advertisers of body shaping products preferred motion picture fan magazines over other popular magazines by a margin of more than ten to one, indicating that the effectiveness of body shaping ads was maximized in fan magazines.

Body Shaping Advice

Body shaping advice articles demonstrated a similar affinity for motion picture fan magazines. By the 1920s, Hollywood had clearly become a symbol of physical culture. Most body shaping advice articles appeared in motion picture fan magazines and/or cited Hollywood in some fashion. A mention of Hollywood served to authenticate the body shaping advice being proffered and to imply that anyone could achieve Hollywood standards of attractiveness (with the purchase of the right products). For example, "Merrily We Roll Along," a 1929 advice article published in *Collier's,* notes that motion picture stars provide examples of the physical ideal that Elizabeth Arden helps women achieve: "She [Elizabeth Arden] has shown the recipe in the movies—illustrated by tantalizing glimpses of lovely slim creatures who sway about like white birches dipping to a breeze . . . who show us what we were once and may be again."[37]

Fan magazines articles that offered body shaping advice were often written by Hollywood stars. In 1921, *Photoplay* ran a series titled "How I Keep in Condition," with monthly installments by such stars as Corinne Griffith and Marion Davies. The preface to these articles declares, "The motion picture star who cannot work ninety per cent of the time and look her best, will soon be 'out.' . . . The film star, more than any other woman of any other time, has to guard her greatest asset: her good looks. She has to keep in perfect condition always—for if she doesn't, the camera's cruel eye calls attention to her shortcomings."[38] An extensive 1924 article, "The Stars Tell How They Keep Those Girlish Lines," provides detailed descriptions of the diet plans of fifteen screen stars, including Bebe Daniels, Nita Naldi, Gloria Swanson, Billie Burke, and Agnes Ayres. Of the diets suggested, the "pineapple and lamb chop diet" recommended by Nita Naldi is apparently the most popular. In a small section at the beginning of the article, E. W. Bowers, M.D., endorses this diet: "These beauties of Hollywood and other favored cities who have adopted the pineapple and lamb chop diet have done well. . . . The lamb chop provides the lean meat necessary for maintaining the strength. It supplies sufficient protein to repair the waste of body. Yet it contributes no fat. The pineapple supplies enough of sugar to keep the fires of strength burning."[39] Of this diet, Naldi is quoted as saying, "Yep, I have adopted the lamb chop and pineapple diet. Up to now I've been taking it for a month. . . . The old saying that one must suffer to be beautiful is true, but it doesn't tell all the truth. One must suffer Hades to be thin."[40] None of the diets is described as a pleasurable experience; rather, dieting seems to be a kind of martyrdom that film stars must endure in order to retain their positions as objects of fame.

Physical culturists offering advice took care to associate their names with Hollywood. In "You Can Keep a Youthful Figure If You Treat Your Muscles Right," an advice article in the *American Magazine,* a physical fitness expert explains how to prolong the endurance of youth and lose fat by exercising the muscles. There is no reference to Hollywood in the article itself, but beneath a photo of the fitness expert, the caption reads: "For over twenty-five years Milton H. Berry, of Hollywood, California, has been studying the muscles of the body. He is not a physician nor a physical culturist. He terms himself a physical re-educator."[41] Here, the mention of Hollywood lends credibility to Berry, making him a more "authentic" expert. In a similar but more explicit fashion, Sylvia, a popular physical culturist of the period, also had a Hollywood pedigree. *Photoplay* refers to her as "Sylvia Ulbeck, masseuse extraordinaire of Hollywood, the flesh sculptor who pounds, beats and curses the stars into shape."[42] Ulbeck published a series of reducing articles in *Photoplay* in the early 1930s. In these articles and in a body shaping book she published in 1934, she bases her authority and reputation on the fact that she has worked in Hollywood. "The list of stars who have Sylvia to thank for miraculous aid is too long to mention here," reads the introduction to her book. "Gloria Swanson, Constance Bennett, Norma Shearer, Ruth Chatterton, Ronald Colman and Ramon

Novarro are but a few of the hundreds of Hollywood players who swear by Sylvia."[43] Clearly invoking Hollywood standards of attractiveness, Ulbeck promises to make her readers "as lovely as the stars of Hollywood—and lovelier!"[44]

Body Shaping Commentary

While body shaping advertisements and advice articles demonstrate a clear link between body shaping and Hollywood, they do not address the question of causality. It is therefore useful to examine historical materials that analyze the origin and development of the reducing craze. Although such speculations can be no more conclusive than contemporary hypotheses on the origins of the late-twentieth-century "waif ideal," their close chronological relationship to the craze affords them a certain legitimacy.

Articles in the 1920s that discussed the reducing phenomenon produced varying opinions as to its cause. In general popular magazines, the new standard of slimness and the urge to reduce were usually attributed to "fashion":

> Even the great of the earth cannot afford altogether to disregard the dictates of the fashion which decrees that all men and all women shall present to the world the outlines of spare severity.[45]

> But of late, Fashion . . . has . . . decreed that henceforth slimness and leanness and flatness are to be the order of the day in youth as well as in middle life; that our girls and boys, our youths and maidens, are to be rid of all roundness and plumpness of figure . . . that the figures of our flappers and subdebs shall be slender and slinky and lathlike, and the line of grace no longer the curve, but the prolonged parallelogram.[46]

In one sense, the word *fashion* refers to the newest cuts and styles of clothing. In the 1910s and 1920s, clothing became long, thin, and straight, resembling, as one author noted, a golf bag. *Fashion* in a more general sense can refer to new trends, attitudes, and expectations. In both senses, it is not a stretch to describe Hollywood as an arbiter of fashion. Clothing fashions of Hollywood stars such as Gloria Swanson were frequently emulated by fans. Furthermore, Hollywood films and stars were synonymous with the new "modern" age, and were subsequently in an ideal position to influence—and perhaps instigate—new trends, such as reducing.

Articles in motion picture fan magazines openly explored the relationship between Hollywood and reducing. Such articles did not promote this connection as though it were something of which those in Hollywood should be proud. Rather, they acknowledged the connection as an unfortunate development. In "Wholesale Murder and Suicide," the first article in the *Photoplay* series on the dangers of quack reducing methods, author Catherine Brody considers the possibility that Hollywood may be responsible for cultivating a desperate urge to reduce:

> Reducing is not a new idea nor are dangerous reducing methods new. . . . In these days of the boyish figure, however, reducing has come to be more than an idea. It is even more than a fad, doctors say. It is a mania.
>
> Just how reduceomania has come to be is a hopeless question. Did the popularity of the straight up and down, one-piece frock in America make the boyish figure an ideal for women of all ages? Was it envy and the desire to emulate the corsetless, pliant, bob-haired flapper? Many people blame the movies for this as for other sins. They say that the movies, which set standards of beauty for more people and to a far greater degree than the stage, have emphasized slightness, thinness, to such an extent that any other kind of figure looks strangely overnourished to American eyes.[47]

A 1925 article in *Motion Picture Classic* baldly asserted Hollywood's relationship to the diet craze: "'Oh, that this too, too solid flesh would melt, thaw, and resolve itself into a dew.' This is the cry which is heard round the world. . . . The eighth industry of the world, viz. the movies, is directly responsible for this state of affairs."[48] *Photoplay* followed suit in 1929:

> Diet! It has put the one world famous star in her grave [this is a reference to Barbara La Marr, who actually died of a drug overdose], has caused the illness of many others, has wrecked careers and has become, largely through its practice in Hollywood, the Great American Menace!
>
> For as Hollywood does so does the rest of the world.
>
> The stars have set the styles in slim figures. The correct weight for a girl five feet two inches tall is 119 pounds. The average screen player of this height weighs only 108 pounds.[49]

These articles also asked an important question: "Why must the stars starve themselves?" That is, why did Hollywood require a slender bodily ideal that was so difficult to achieve? Both articles blamed motion picture technology:

If a practical stereoscopic camera lens were perfected these all too rigid diets would be unnecessary. When a woman steps in front of the camera she adds from five to twenty pounds to her figure. The camera photographs but two dimensions. This tends to flatten a round object.[50]

If the stars wish to look like normal human beings instead of elephants on the screen, they must face the world with figures which are reed-like. And so everybody is doing it; for the normal human being insists on looking starlike.[51]

If screen performers believed they had to be extra slender to appear "normal" weight before the camera, one might ask how such a circumstance might influence motion picture fans to reduce. If stars appeared "normal" or "average" weight on screen, how would this inspire viewers to pursue a new slender ideal? First, most stars reduced to the extent that they still appeared slender on screen, even with any added "camera weight."[52] Second, what viewers knew about stars did not end with motion pictures. In fan magazines, many articles detailed actors' and actresses' struggles to maintain perfect forms. Readers of these articles may have dreamed of becoming stars themselves; in the 1910s and 1920s, young Americans, particularly women, began to journey to Hollywood in droves, hoping to become stars.[53]

Fan magazine readers looking for helpful hints to make the wand of stardom someday work its magic for them were confronted by articles such as "She Rolls Her Own Fat Away":

[This is] the story of how Clara Bow . . . beat the Brooklyn department stores out of another tubby ribbon clerk and gave to Hollywood a rollicking gaiety that has stirred the pulse of its languid social realm.

[As a high school student, she read fan magazines and dreamed of being a star.]

She'd be a star some day . . . but first off, she'd get thin.

"Roll on the floor and grow thin," she read somewhere.

She locked herself in her bedroom, pushed her bed against the wall, lay down on the floor and rolled. "I'd roll around the room like a rubber ball until I was so dizzy that I couldn't move," she said. "Then I'd jump up and stagger to the looking glass to see if I'd lost any fat. Once I fell against the dresser and bumped my head awfully."

One day she skipped school and visited the New York studios. She learned that Elmer Clifton wanted a girl of her type for a part in "Down to the Sea in Ships."

> . . . Her work was praised but she was told that she was still too
> fat. She went home and rolled some more on the bedroom floor.[54]

Losing weight was not the only factor in Clara Bow's rise to stardom, but the article implies that it was certainly a requisite one. In a 1928 article, "Starving Back to Stardom," we are told the "sad" story of Molly O'Day, "whose career was blighted by ice cream and candy." Apparently, First National Pictures refused to give O'Day another motion picture role until she lost twenty pounds. The article concludes, "She's in Hot Springs, Arkansas, when this is written. And she not only has a dietitian but a physical instructor. Hot baths every morning and evening. And three times a day, spinach and lamb chops and pineapple."[55]

Although the focus of such articles was mostly on female stars, male stars were subject to physical standards as well. For example, the caption of a full-length 1923 photo of Rudolph Valentino (clad only in shorts) in *Photoplay* read, "Rudolph Valentino keeps trim all the time. It's a habit with him. . . . He knows that an actor can retain his ability and hold his place in the limelight only so long as he remains in good physical condition."[56] Similarly, 1925 snapshots of Ramon Novarro in *Motion Picture Classic* were presented as evidence of one of the "penalties" of being a screen star: "The avoirdupois [fat] must be kept just right."[57] Fan magazine readers with dreams of stardom—however slight—were given the message that stringent dieting and physical conditioning were necessary ingredients of that dream. A 1930 ad for Bonomo's Physical Culture course emphasized the connection between physical perfection and Hollywood stardom, claiming, "No matter how much talent or beauty you have, you can't succeed [in Hollywood] unless you're physically fit!"[58]

Conclusion

The historical evidence cited above documents a connection between Hollywood and body shaping and suggests a plausible cause-effect relationship between Hollywood-inspired consumer culture and the emergence of the reducing craze of the 1910s and 1920s. This relationship, which I have described in some detail in this essay, can be summarized as follows: By virtue of its status as a mass visual medium, Hollywood cinema called attention to the body in a way that had not been possible before the advent of "moving pictures." Camera lenses were believed to add weight to the body, prompting actors and actresses to diet in order to appear "normal." Beginning in the 1910s, fans could read about the lifestyles (including the physical regimens) of their favorite stars. Manufacturers and advertisers, recognizing the potential for profit, began to exploit Hollywood's physical standards. In the emerging consumer culture of the late 1910s and 1920s, strident advertisements urged readers to buy body shaping products. Such advertisements, which appeared most frequently in motion picture fan magazines, intensified consumers' new concerns about physical appearance. This established a cycle in which Hollywood's standards of attractiveness were reinforced by advertisements that urged consumers to reduce.

I do not wish to mitigate the importance of other factors that may have contributed to the emergence of the reducing craze. Wartime sentiment, feminism, and science were at least partially responsible for a new awareness of body size. During World War I, it was considered unpatriotic to carry around extra calories that someone else—such as a soldier—might need.[59] A popular 1918 diet book took overweight Americans to task for their selfishness:

> In war time it is a crime to hoard food. . . . Yet there are hundreds of thousands of individuals all over America who are hoarding food. . . . *They have vast amounts of this valuable commodity stored away in their own anatomy.*
>
> . . . Instead of being looked upon with friendly tolerance and amusement, you [fat individuals] are now viewed with distrust, suspicion, and even aversion! How dare you hoard fat when our nation needs it?[60]

Such wartime sentiment, although intense, was relatively brief; historian Frederick Lewis Allen notes that the bubble of "Spartan idealism" surrounding the war burst soon after its conclusion in late 1918.[61]

The 1910s and 1920s were also a period when women's roles underwent radical changes; women won the right to vote, moved into the workplace in greater numbers, stayed single longer, smoked cigarettes, and drank. Feminist scholars have argued that periods of change in female roles tend to produce a slender feminine ideal,[62] and clearly the feminine ideal of the 1920s was slimmer than in the preceding decades. A 1922 *Photoplay* article described this "New American Beauty":

> The statuesque and fulsome pulchritude of a generation ago has given way to the fragile, girlish type.
>
> In spite of the 19th Amendment [women's suffrage], the last ten years have seen the American beauty softened, feminized, and reduced to an amazing extent.

. . . the American beauty was big, athletic, stately.

Today we find beyond question that the new and reigning American beauty is small—the tiny, childish, girlish type.[63]

When the Nineteenth Amendment passed, women may have felt some pressure to "prove" that they could still be feminine. Thus they adopted a diminutive, youthful ideal that was distinctly nonthreatening to male power.

Feminism cannot account for male participation in the reducing craze, however. Although the craze did center on women, it was not devoted exclusively to them; men were urged to become fit and to shed excess fat as well. A 1924 *Saturday Evening Post* article that lamented the pressures on women to slim down also declared that "of recent years little less than a regular propaganda of slander has been directed against fat. The charges are that it overloads our muscles, clogs our heart action, packs our livers, spoils our figures—and nobody loves a fat man."[64] Perhaps one reason men failed to escape the net of the reducing craze lies in reducing's association with science—for example, principles of nutrition, the new field of endocrinology, and life insurance statistics indicating that overweight shortened life expectancy. Because the male gender has traditionally been associated with reason and rationality, men may have been more likely to face mockery or self-doubt if they disregarded the pronouncements of science, especially in the 1920s, when science, along with business, enjoyed incredible prestige.

Despite the significance of World War I, feminism, and science, it is likely that this craze, characterized as it was by a pronounced aversion to fat and a widespread urge to reduce, would not have been possible without the twin phenomena of Hollywood and consumer culture. Hollywood offered new standards of attractiveness that were distributed on a mass scale and exhibited in a visual, "moving" medium. A burgeoning consumer culture, hungry for potential avenues of consumption, latched onto these new standards of physical perfection and continually exhorted consumers to pursue them. Had either of these institutions been absent, any reducing trend that may have emerged would probably not have been as prolonged or as intense.

Ultimately, the reducing craze of the 1910s and 1920s was curtailed by two factors: reducing "sanity" and the Great Depression. When *Photoplay Magazine* ran its series of articles on the dangers of "Reduceomania" in 1926, declaring that it "refuses to admit to its advertising columns any internal reducing preparations or questionable methods," body shaping advertising in that publication did decline sharply for a time, although it began to rebound within a couple of years.[65] *Photoplay* quickly broke its promise not to advertise any "internal reducing preparations" or "questionable methods," but more articles and advertisements did mention the need for "sane reducing." The surge in body shaping advertising in 1928 and 1929 seems to indicate that the cautionary *Photoplay* articles (as well as similar articles that appeared in other publications) dampened but did not dissipate the desire for reducing products. This desire was further dampened by the Depression, which probably made it less attractive for people to starve themselves for "fashion" when so many were facing real starvation. From a peak of more than one hundred ads per year in motion picture fan magazines, the number of body shaping ads stabilized at forty to eighty per year in the early 1930s. Reducing was no longer a craze, a fad, or a mania, but it did not go away. Advertisements for body shaping products continued to appear. Interestingly, perhaps as a result of the Depression, ads for methods to gain weight began to outnumber ads for reduction methods. But although standards of attractiveness evolved, consumers were still exhorted to spend money on molding their bodies. The relationship between consumer culture and Hollywood had been established and continued to exert its influence even during the Depression—and beyond.

Notes

1. Robert Bocock, *Consumption* (New York: Routledge, 1993), 50.

2. James Rorty, *Our Master's Voice: Advertising* (New York: John Day, 1934), 29.

3. Rorty notes that in 1909, advertisers spent $54 million placing ads in periodicals; in 1929, the figure was $320 million (ibid., 24). Stuart Ewen offers the following figures: "In 1918, total gross advertising revenues in general and farm magazines was $58.5 million. By 1920 the gross had reached $129.5 million; and by 1929, $196.3 million." Stuart Ewen, *Captains of Consciousness: Advertising and the Roots of the Consumer Culture* (New York: McGraw-Hill, 1976), 32. (It is not clear which periodicals these authors included or excluded in their statistics or which figures may be more accurate, but it is clear that advertising revenues were dramatically on the rise in the 1910s and 1920s.)

4. Ewen, *Captains of Consciousness,* 24–26.

5. Ibid., 31–32.

6. Robert S. Lynd and Helen Merrell Lynd, *Middletown: A Study in American Culture* (New York: Harcourt, Brace, 1929), 3.

7. Ibid., 82 n. 18.

8. Ewen, *Captains of Consciousness,* 37–39.

9. Advertisement, *Motion Picture Magazine,* October 1925, 89.

10. Advertisement, *Motion Picture Classic,* January 1925, 7.

11. Attendance figure from Richard Koszarski, *An Evening's Entertainment: The Age of the Silent Feature Picture* (Berkeley: University of California Press, 1990), 26.

12. Mike Featherstone, "The Body in Consumer Culture," in *The Body: Social Process and Cultural Theory,* ed. Mike Featherstone, Mike Hepworth, and Bryan S. Turner (London: Sage, 1991), 172.

13. *Photoplay Magazine* promotion booklet, quoted in Rorty, *Our Master's Voice,* 252, 254.

14. Ibid., 256.

15. Annette Kuhn, *The Power of the Image: Essays on Representation and Sexuality* (London: Routledge, 1985), 13.

16. Featherstone, "The Body in Consumer Culture," 179.

17. For example, *Physical Culture,* a magazine published by Bernarr Macfadden and dedicated to the ideal that diet and exercise could cure any illness, first appeared in 1899. According to Theodore Peterson, *Magazines in the Twentieth Century* (Urbana: University of Illinois Press, 1956), *Physical Culture* had a circulation of approximately 150,000 from 1902 through 1919. By 1954, under the name *Bernarr Macfadden's Journal,* it had a circulation of approximately 20,000.

18. Samuel G. Blythe, "Get Rid of That Fat," *Saturday Evening Post,* 23 April 1927, 10–11.

19. "The Cult of Slimness," *Living Age,* 28 February 1914, 572–73.

20. Dudley A. Sargent, "Are You Too Fat, or Too Thin?" *American Magazine,* November 1921, 13.

21. Harlow Brooks, "The Price of a Boyish Form," in *Your Weight and How to Control It,* ed. Morris Fishbein (1926; reprint, Garden City, N.Y.: Doubleday, Doran, 1929), 30.

22. Wendell C. Phillips, "Introduction," in *Your Weight and How to Control It,* ed. Morris Fishbein (1926; reprint, Garden City, N.Y.: Doubleday, Doran, 1929), x.

23. "Penalties of Obesity" (editorial), *Journal of the American Medical Association* 27 (August 1927): 694–95.

24. Advertisements for the Corrective Eating Society provide an interesting example of this evolution. In an ad that ran in the *American Magazine* in October 1915, the Corrective Eating Society offered "Eugene Christian's Course in Scientific Eating," promising that purchasers can "Eat to Live 100 Years" (93). The tone of this ad was merely informative; the ad did not attempt to humiliate readers or bludgeon them into buying the course. Indeed, the ad was not a "body shaping" ad at all; it only recommended a particular course of eating in order to maintain health. Soon, however, the tone of the ads began to change. In the July 1916 *American Magazine,* the tag line of a Corrective Eating Society ad read, "The Crimes We Commit Against Our Stomachs" (69). Later in the ad, readers were told, "A man's success in life depends more on the co-operation of his stomach than on any other factor." In an April 1919 ad in the same publication, the tag line was: "Why Some Foods Explode in the Stomach" (143).

Meanwhile, in *Photoplay,* where no ads for the Corrective Eating Society had previously appeared, a full-page ad in the August 1921 issue announced, "New Discovery Takes Off Flesh Almost 'While You Wait'!" (7). The Corrective Eating Society was still offering a course by Eugene Christian, but it was now titled "Weight Control—the Basis of Health." The ad noted that by taking off "useless fat," women can wear attractive clothing styles and men can enjoy a miraculous return of youthful energy. In April 1922, a full-page ad for the Corrective Eating Society appeared in the *American Magazine* (169). As in *Photoplay,* the ad was now about weight control instead of merely eating for health. "Doctor's Wife Takes Off 40 Pounds through New Discovery," read the tag line. In 1922, some of the society's ads in *Photoplay* began to adopt a forceful tone: "It's a Crime to Be Fat—When It's So Easy to Be Slender" (December 1922, 7).

25. Advertisement, *Motion Picture Magazine,* March 1917, 156.

26. Advertisement, *Motion Picture Magazine,* March 1921, 87.

27. Advertisement, *Motion Picture Magazine,* December 1925, 108.

28. For example, both the *Ladies' Home Journal* and the *American Magazine* had circulations of more than two million throughout most of the 1920s, and *Photoplay Magazine,* a leading motion picture periodical, had a circulation of more than 200,000 by 1918 and more than 600,000 by the early 1930s. According to information I received via e-mail from the *Ladies' Home Journal,* circulation figures for that magazine were as follows: December 1916, 1,604,903; June 1927, 2,498,310; and December 1934, 2,545,857. The *American Magazine* announced circulation of more than two million on the cover of several issues throughout the 1920s. Koszarski notes that *Photoplay*'s circulation in 1918 was 204,434 (*An Evening's Entertainment,* 193), and Rorty cites a 1930s promotion pamphlet for *Photoplay* that lists a circulation of more than 600,000 (*Our Master's Voice,* 252).

29. In 1915, *Photoplay Magazine* averaged one body shaping ad per monthly issue; in 1920, it carried more than 3 body shaping ads per issue, or more than 35 per year, and in 1925, the apparent peak of the body shaping trend, *Photoplay* averaged 11 body shaping ads per issue, or more than 135 body shaping ads per year. These figures represent my tally of the number of body shaping ads for the periods cited. I counted only those ads that promoted body shaping activities, per the definition of such activities noted earlier. I counted all body shaping ads, irrespective of their size, which ranged from a fraction of a page to a full page. Because it is often difficult to draw the line between cosmetic devices and body shaping products, others may arrive at slightly different statistics.

Motion Picture Magazine and *Motion Picture Classic* echoed the *Photoplay* trend. Here are some representative figures for *Motion Picture Magazine*: 1917, 16 body shaping ads published; 1921, approximately 59 body shaping ads; 1925, 116 body shaping ads; 1930, 76 body shaping ads. *Motion Picture Classic* began publication in 1915 as *Motion Picture Supplement,* a supplement to *Motion Picture Magazine.* In 1916, it became *Motion Picture Classic.* Based on the issues I have been able to examine, I offer the following statistics for body shaping ads in *Motion Picture Classic*: November 1915–August 1916, 13 ads; March 1921–February 1922, 60 ads; 1925, 64 ads; 1930, 59 ads. *Motion Picture Classic* published fewer body shaping ads than *Photoplay* or *Motion Picture Magazine*, but this may have been because the advertising sections in *Motion Picture Classic* were twenty-five to fifty pages shorter than those in *Photoplay* or *Motion Picture Magazine.*

30. In 1915, the *American Magazine* carried eight body shaping ads; in 1920, eleven; and in 1925, five. *Good Housekeeping* had no body shaping ads in 1915, ten body shaping ads in 1920, and seven body shaping ads in 1925. The *Ladies' Home Journal* carried ten body shaping ads in 1915, ten in 1920, and only three in 1925.

31. For example, from 1921 through 1924 the Corrective Eating Society advertised a weight control course in both *Photoplay* and the *American Magazine.* During this period, sixteen ads appeared in *Photoplay*; thirteen of those were full-page ads in the front advertising section. In contrast, in the *American Magazine* only two ads for the Corrective Eating Society's weight control course appeared, both in the rear advertising section. Although the messages of the ads were similar in both publications, the ads clearly appeared more frequently and more prominently in *Photoplay.*

32. Advertisement, *Photoplay Magazine,* June 1915, 170.

33. Advertisement, *Photoplay Magazine,* October 1925, 92.

34. Advertisement, *Motion Picture Classic,* February 1928, 81.

35. Advertisement, *Photoplay Magazine,* March 1929, 113.

36. Advertisement, *Motion Picture Classic,* January 1930, 83.

37. Betty Thornley, "Merrily We Roll Along," *Collier's,* 7 December 1929, 19.

38. Preface to "How I Keep in Condition," *Photoplay Magazine,* September 1921, 45, and November 1921, 33.

39. "The Stars Tell How They Keep Those Girlish Lines," *Photoplay Magazine,* September 1924, 28.

40. Ibid., 30.

41. Milton H. Berry (as reported by Magner White), "You Can Keep a Youthful Figure If You Treat Your Muscles Right," *American Magazine,* August 1927, 43.

42. Lois Shirley, "The Enemy of Beauty—Over-Exercise," *Photoplay Magazine,* August 1931, 30.

43. Carolyn Van Wyck, "Introduction," in Sylvia of Hollywood, *No More Alibis* (New York: Macfadden, 1934), 9.

44. Sylvia of Hollywood, *No More Alibis* (New York: Macfadden, 1934), 12.

45. "The Cult of Slimness," 572.

46. Woods Hutchinson, "Fat and Fashion," *Saturday Evening Post,* 21 August 1926, 64.

47. Catherine Brody, "Wholesale Murder and Suicide," *Photoplay Magazine,* July 1926, 30–31.

48. Harriette Underhill, "The Movies Give the World a Boyish Form: Motion Pictures Have Transformed the Public Taste in Feminine Pulchritude," *Motion Picture Classic,* November 1925, 30.

49. Katherine Albert, "Diet—the Menace of Hollywood," *Photoplay Magazine,* January 1929, 30.

50. Ibid., 31.

51. Underhill, "The Movies Give the World," 73.

52. For example, *Photoplay* published a chart in 1929 that lists 125 pounds as the healthy weight for a woman five feet, four inches, in height. A 1931 article, "Who Has the Best Figure in Hollywood?" lists heights and weights for about twenty actresses. Clara Bow, Joan Crawford, and Constance Bennett, who were all five feet, four inches, weighed 112 pounds, 110 pounds, and 100 pounds, respectively. Adele Whitely Fletcher, "Who Has the Best Figure in Hollywood?" *Photoplay Magazine,* March 1931, 35.

53. A 1923 article in the *New York Times* noted that Mary Pickford is "adding her voice to the warning of the Hollywood Chamber of Commerce to the movie-mad boys and girls who are swarming into the film studio city at the rate of 10,000 a month. . . . The Chamber is endeavoring to spread . . . information about how few the chances are for cinema glory and how many are the trials and privations on the path to such an ambition." "Hollywood Warns Film-Struck Girls," *New York Times,* 12 December 1923, 23.

54. Glenn Chaffin, "She Rolls Her Own Fat Away," *Photoplay Magazine,* June 1925, 78, 112.

55. Lois Shirley, "Starving Back to Stardom," *Photoplay Magazine,* August 1928, 80, 120.

56. "Gossip—East and West," *Photoplay Magazine,* April 1923, 68.

57. *Motion Picture Classic,* November 1925, 24.

58. Advertisement, *Motion Picture Magazine,* March 1930, 10.

59. Hillel Schwartz, *Never Satisfied: A Cultural History of Diets, Fantasies and Fat* (New York: Macmillan, 1986), 141–142.

60. Lulu Hunt Peters, *Diet and Health—with Key to the Calories* (Chicago: Reilly & Britton, 1918), 12–13.

61. Frederick Lewis Allen, *Only Yesterday: An Informal History of the Nineteen-Twenties* (New York: Harper, 1931), 25, 77.

62. Contemporary feminist scholar Susan Bordo explains that "female hunger is especially problematized during periods of disruption and change in the position of women. . . . dominant constructions of the female body become more sylphlike—unlike the body of a fully developed woman, more like that of an adolescent or boy (images that might be called female desire unborn)." Susan Bordo, *Unbearable Weight: Feminism, Western Culture, and the Body* (Berkeley: University of California Press, 1993), 206.

63. Adela Rogers St. Johns, "New American Beauty," *Photoplay Magazine,* June 1922, 26–27.

64. Woods Hutchinson, "A Defense of Fat Men," *Saturday Evening Post,* 7 June 1924, 8.

65. In 1925, *Photoplay* published more than 135 body shaping ads; in 1926, that number declined to 74, and in 1927, to only 39 ads. But then it began to climb again: in 1928, 74 body shaping ads appeared, and in 1929, 88.

2.
Flirting with Kathlyn: Creating the Mass Audience

Barbara Wilinsky

During the early part of the 1900s, industrial development in the United States and the resulting shifts in the country's economic structure led to changes in the leisure style of the American population, particularly in urban areas. As the economy became increasingly centered on consumer culture, leisure in the United States became to a greater extent commodified, relying—like other aspects of industry—on the mass market to achieve profits. Financial success became dependent on the ability to attract the greatest number of possible customers. Courting a mass market encouraged commodified leisure to break down the class and gender separations that were prominent in leisure activities. An example of this effort to enlarge the leisure audience can be seen in the creation of the film and newspaper serial *The Adventures of Kathlyn*.

The Story of *Kathlyn*
A 1913 motion picture serial coproduced by the Selig Polyscope Company and the *Chicago Daily Tribune, The Adventures of Kathlyn* has earned its place in the footnotes of many film history books as the first motion picture *serial* (with holdover endings) produced in the United States.[1] However, it is the attempt of the *Chicago Tribune* and Selig Polyscope to expand their publics through the creation of *The Adventures of Kathlyn* that truly lends insight into the relationship between consumer culture and commodified leisure in the United States at this time. Motion pictures were associated mostly with a working-class audience, whereas the *Tribune* was seen as having a "largely white, native-born, middle-class readership."[2] The *Tribune* and Selig attempted to blend their class-based audiences to attract men and women from all classes. As Miriam Hansen writes, "The new leisure culture was demonstratively inclusive, allowing for the public mixing of genders,

classes and ethnic (though not necessarily racial) constituencies. This inclusiveness no doubt was illusory insofar as it pretended to a social homogeneity; it did, however, make a certain difference for people who had hitherto been excluded from public life, especially women and recent immigrants."[3] This unification of the mass audience required the negotiation of different cultures, styles, prejudices, and traditions in order even to attempt to attract consumers from different classes and from both genders. Because Selig and the *Tribune* were seen as having different initial audiences, a joint venture appeared to be a sensible way for them to attract new readers/viewers who would be pulled from the other medium while maintaining their original publics. The desire to increase the audience for both the *Tribune* and Selig resulted in a negotiation of different values and styles that became apparent in the creation, promotion, and content of *The Adventures of Kathlyn.*

The story line of the serial focuses on Kathlyn Hare, a twenty-four-year-old American whose father is bequeathed the mythical monarchy of Allaha, which is located in India. The father, Colonel Hare, travels to Allaha to look into the matter and is taken captive by Umballah, the deceased king's protégé, who himself wants to be king. Umballah, who was a "street rat" before the king took him in and educated him, tricks Kathlyn into traveling to Allaha, convinces her that her father is dead, and names her queen of Allaha. Because it is one of the country's laws that no woman can rule unmarried, Umballah announces, to Kathlyn's horror, that she will marry him. The rest of the serial involves events that put Kathlyn's life in danger and exhibitions of her bravery and strong will as she attempts to evade marriage and get out of India. Many of the incidents within the serial involve wild animals, making use of both the serial star's reputation for making animal films and William Selig's extensive collection of wild animals (which are, of course, themselves interrelated).[4] Although it is not certain whether the *Tribune* or Selig came up with the initial idea for this joint venture or for the story line of *Kathlyn*, the inclusion of wild animals in the plot does suggest that Selig's zoo was considered when the story was written.[5]

The first of the thirteen filmed installments of *The Adventures of Kathlyn* was released in Chicago on Monday, 29 December 1913.[6] This three-reel premiere episode was followed biweekly by two-reel installments. Every Sunday, beginning 4 January 1914, the *Chicago Daily Tribune* printed serialized installments of *The Adventures of Kathlyn.* The serial attempted to draw people back to the theaters and to the newspapers for each new episode by withholding closure, resulting in the first filmed serial.[7] The twenty-six written segments of the serial

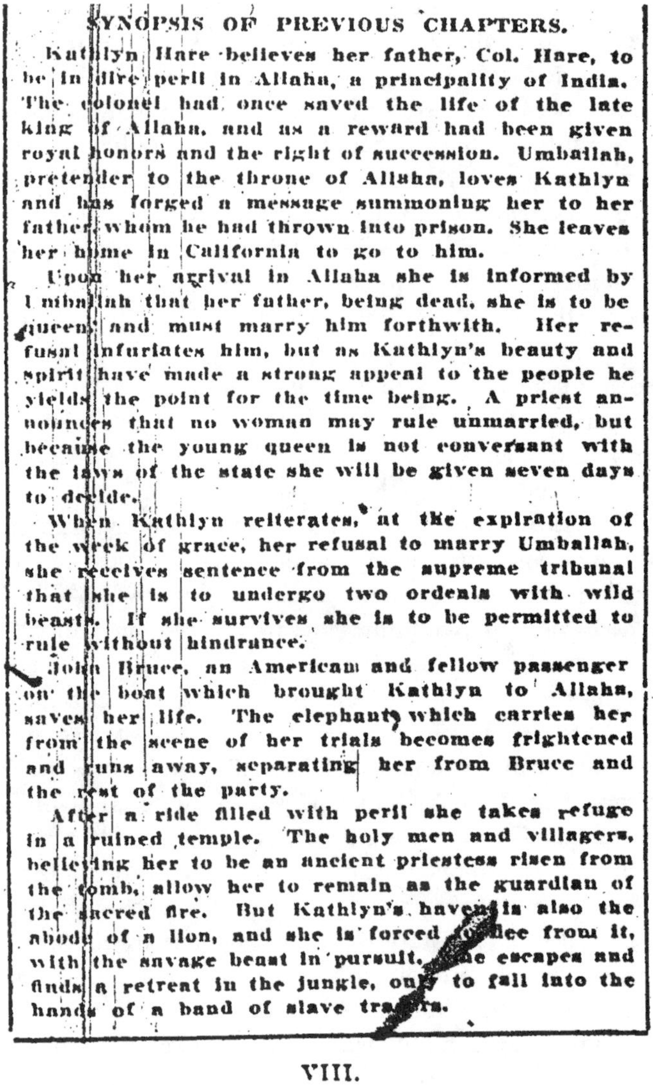

SYNOPSIS OF PREVIOUS CHAPTERS.

Kathlyn Hare believes her father, Col. Hare, to be in dire peril in Allaha, a principality of India. The colonel had once saved the life of the late king of Allaha, and as a reward had been given royal honors and the right of succession. Umballah, pretender to the throne of Allaha, loves Kathlyn and has forged a message summoning her to her father, whom he had thrown into prison. She leaves her home in California to go to him.

Upon her arrival in Allaha she is informed by Umballah that her father, being dead, she is to be queen and must marry him forthwith. Her refusal infuriates him, but as Kathlyn's beauty and spirit have made a strong appeal to the people he yields the point for the time being. A priest announces that no woman may rule unmarried, but because the young queen is not conversant with the laws of the state she will be given seven days to decide.

When Kathlyn reiterates, at the expiration of the week of grace, her refusal to marry Umballah, she receives sentence from the supreme tribunal that she is to undergo two ordeals with wild beasts. If she survives she is to be permitted to rule without hindrance.

John Bruce, an American and fellow passenger on the boat which brought Kathlyn to Allaha, saves her life. The elephant which carries her from the scene of her trials becomes frightened and runs away, separating her from Bruce and the rest of the party.

After a ride filled with peril she takes refuge in a ruined temple. The holy men and villagers, believing her to be an ancient priestess risen from the tomb, allow her to remain as the guardian of the sacred fire. But Kathlyn's haven is also the abode of a lion, and she is forced to flee from it, with the savage beast in pursuit. She escapes and finds a retreat in the jungle, only to fall into the hands of a band of slave traders.

VIII.

Figure 1. The *Adventures of Kathlyn* synopsis preceding chapter 8, *Chicago Daily Tribune,* 22 February 1914.

appeared in the *Tribune*'s "Special Features/Color Section" accompanied by film stills and sketches of scenes from the story.[8] *The Adventures of Kathlyn* was not simply a Chicago phenomenon. According to the *Motion Picture News,* the serial was also published in the *New York Sun, Boston Globe, Philadelphia Record, Baltimore Record,* and fifty-four other newspapers.[9]

Although the release of the films prior to the publication of the stories indicates that the film serial was expected to be the bigger attraction that would pull people to the *Tribune* serialization, it is probable that the exchange of audiences was expected to be reciprocal.[10] Before each installment of *Kathlyn,* the newspaper included the line, "It is possible not only to read the novel but to see the photo drama at the moving picture theaters." This promotion encouraged those people who had only read the serial and not yet seen the film to go to the theaters. Although I have not found information about the screening practices for *Kathlyn,* it is also probable that some mention of the *Tribune*'s printed installments was made at the showings of *Kathlyn*—within the film itself, on magic lantern slides, or on flyers.

This lack of information about the filmic experience of *The Adventures of Kathlyn* is certainly one of the most problematic aspects of researching this serial. Although reviews of the film serial confirm that it had the same plot structure as the printed installments, visual information about the actual film installments and the way they were filmed and screened is sorely missed. Much of the research that is available must also be considered in relation to its function as promotion for the *Tribune* and the film serial. Written for the *Tribune* by Harold MacGrath, who was a successful popular novelist,[11] with the film scenario adapted by Gilson Willets, *The Adventures of Kathlyn* starred Kathlyn Williams, then known as the "Selig Girl."[12] Williams began working in motion pictures with Biograph in 1909 and had moved to Selig by 1910.[13] She was known for making films featuring wild animals and earned the name "Kathlyn the Unafraid."[14] In his book *Those Fabulous Serial Heroines,* Buck Rainey describes Williams's screen persona as "that of an unspoiled girl as natural and genuine as a child, keenly alive and with a diversity of absorbing interests."[15] The narrative of *The Adventures of Kathlyn* certainly reinforced this image.

Kathlyn and the Desire for Larger Markets

According to Rainey, Selig had very definite plans when he produced the filmed version of *Kathlyn*: "Selig's idea was to pull even more fans to the theater (and subscribers to the paper) by making an adventure film filled with wild animals and thrills that would act as a magnet to draw the masses hungry for vicarious adventure."[16] If Selig was trying to create an exciting film, the *Motion Picture World* review suggests that he succeeded. The trade journal reported, "One thrill succeeds another so rapidly that the spectator is out of breath, mentally, in trying to keep abreast of them."[17] This appeal to action and adventure within

Kathlyn was in keeping with the early-twentieth-century focus on excitement within working-class leisure.[18] Additionally, the serial's connection to the popular form of melodrama (which in its traditional definition refers to action, thrills, and adventure) associated these films with a more "lowbrow" audience.[19] Kenneth Macgowan, who was a film critic at this time, supports the idea that serials were considered inferior when he tells of how film critics attended serials to laugh at them, not review them.[20]

Aside from being frequently derided as a lower-class form of entertainment, motion pictures were also considered (by the middle and upper classes) morally dubious. In the early 1910s, attacks on the moral propriety of the motion picture industry led to an interest in "uplift" of the motion pictures, their theaters, and their audiences.[21] The coproduced serial was a way for Selig to appeal to the "mass" audience (the melodramatic film) and make the motion picture appear respectable (by association with the *Tribune,* which was supposedly the most "upstanding" newspaper in Chicago).[22] Not only did the connection of the serial with the newspaper help assuage the moral reformers, it also offered Selig a great deal of publicity that reached a more upscale audience.

Although at this time the motion picture industry was looking for coverage in the newspapers, there was a time when this coverage was usually negative. During the *Tribune*'s 1907 editorial effort to "clean up" Chicago, nickelodeons were targeted among those institutions that were said to be destroying the wholesomeness of the city.[23] An editorial in the *Tribune* from that year stated that nickelodeons were "ministering to the lowest passions of children . . . influence wholly vicious. They cannot be defended. They are hopelessly bad."[24] The change of position that led the *Chicago Tribune* to enter into a venture with a motion picture company can be traced to the fierce circulation war in which the Chicago newspapers were engaged during the 1910s. Two major figures at the *Tribune* in 1913 can be connected to the development of *The Adventures of Kathlyn*: Joseph Medill Patterson (who coedited and copublished the *Tribune* with his cousin Robert Rutherford McCormick) and James Keeley, the newspaper's daily editor. The interests and policies of these two men fostered an atmosphere in which a project like *The Adventures of Kathlyn* could be conceived.

James Keeley, as the daily editor, was mostly concerned with increasing advertising and circulation by providing services to readers and advertisers.[25] He told a group of students at Notre Dame University in 1912, "The newspaper that not only informs and instructs its readers but is of service is the one that commands attention, gets circulation and also hold its readers after it gets them."[26] A full-page advertisement in the *Tribune* on 31 January 1914 featured a bold, capitalized headline: "SERVICE." The ad read: "Through the news, editorial and special features departments, service to the readers. Through the advertising and promotion departments, service to the advertiser." This ad illustrates the importance that Keeley placed in the *Tribune*'s providing benefits to its "audiences." Keeley wanted to make the newspaper a part of the "every day" lives of its readers.[27] Home delivery became one of the major focuses of the drive to increase circulation. Advertisements for *Kathlyn* often pushed home delivery, telling readers that because so many people wanted to read the printed episodes of *Kathlyn,* the newsstands would sell out quickly. Many of the *Kathlyn* ads included the text: "Whatever else you do, *don't miss* TOMORROW'S SUNDAY TRIBUNE. Don't wait till the last minute and have your paper man tell you there are 'no *Tribunes* left.' Phone your news dealer tonight . . . and *order* TOMORROW'S SUNDAY TRIBUNE *delivered at your door.*"

Kathlyn Faces the Female Consumers

This focus on getting the newspaper into the home and the desire to raise advertising revenue, which came mostly from department stores and consumer goods, led the *Tribune* to express an interest in increasing its female readership. As Hansen explains, "The shift from a production-centered economy to one of mass consumption crucially depended upon the female shopper whose numbers had increased ever since the Civil War."[28] To attract these female consumers, Keeley instituted columns such as "How to Keep Well" and others that gave advice to the lovelorn and beauty tips.[29] Special advertising directories, such as "Shops You Ought to Know," were directed at women. In response to criticism of these departments, Keeley told the same group of students at Notre Dame in 1912, "I believed that there were hundreds, yes, thousands of girls in and around Chicago who had no one to whom to go with their personal troubles. I felt there was an opportunity to stretch a helping hand, and I was right."[30] It is more likely that Keeley believed that there were "hundreds, yes, thousands" of new readers to attract to his newspaper. The *Tribune* also featured advertisements that both encouraged female readership and suggested to advertisers that the newspaper had female readers. An example of one such ad tells the story of how a woman found, through the *Tribune*'s lost-and-found section,

$1500 worth of jewels that she had lost. The inclusion of a "woman's" story acted as an impetus for women to read the newspaper, and the woman's use of the lost-and-found section suggested to advertisers that women turned to the *Tribune* for information. This focus on women began a drive that eventually led to the publication of books by the *Chicago Tribune* such as *Why Women Read the World's Greatest Newspaper* (a 1928 book seemingly directed toward potential *Tribune* advertisers).

These efforts to appeal to female readers probably also increased the *Tribune*'s popularity among the working-class population. As Kathy Lee Peiss notes in her book *Cheap Amusements,* fashion was very important to working-class women within the workplace, and they would often read newspaper columns to keep up with the latest styles.[31] Additionally, advice columns in newspapers sometimes helped working-class readers to negotiate their two worlds of ethnic tradition and twentieth-century wage earning.[32] The inclusion of these columns in the "upscale" Chicago newspaper may have helped to increase the columns' (and the newspaper's) popularity among working-class women. As Peiss suggests, working-class women were interested in and often played with "the culture of the elite."[33]

Kathlyn Cuts across Class

Joseph Medill Patterson, the coeditor and copublisher of the *Tribune,* while certainly interested in selling newspapers, had political interests that may have influenced his involvement with *Kathlyn.* In 1907, when his family's newspaper was attacking nickelodeons for their lack of morality, Patterson wrote for the *Saturday Evening Post* what was probably one of the most thoroughly researched articles on the film industry published up to that time; it was titled "The Nickelodeons: The Poor Man's Elementary Course in the Drama."[34]

Despite approaching motion pictures from an elitist, bourgeois position, in this editorial Patterson expressed an appreciation of the medium that "enlisted itself on special behalf of the least enlightened, those who are below the reach even of the yellow journals."[35] In his discussion of the medium that attracts the "least enlightened" audience, Patterson wrote, "Today the moving-picture machine cannot be overlooked as an effective protagonist of democracy. For through it the drama, always a big fact in the lives of the people at the top, is now becoming a big fact in the lives of the people at the bottom."[36] Patterson's interest in seriously researching the film industry and his relatively progressive position toward motion pictures indicate that he might have been interested in utilizing motion pictures to reach the "people at the bottom."

Furthermore, it has been speculated that Patterson had been a member of the Socialist Party.[37] However, when he began to run the newspaper, he could not express these political interests publicly, particularly since his cousin and coeditor/copublisher did not believe that the newspaper should act as a political force.[38] Patterson chose to redirect his editorial power to support the women's suffrage movement that was growing at the time.[39] The *Tribune* featured many articles on suffrage, and occasionally even included suffrage as a section within the table of contents.

Patterson was most interested in the Sunday edition of the *Tribune*. According to one account, Patterson, working with assistant Sunday editor Mary King, turned the Sunday edition "strongly toward a light feminine appeal."[40] To increase circulation, Patterson built up a strong comics section and increased the amount of fiction published in the newspaper.[41] That these features were intended, at least partly, for women becomes clear in the *Books of Facts* published by the Tribune Company about the newspaper. Within this book, the comics and the fiction offerings are listed under the heading "Some Reasons Why Women Like the Tribune."[42]

The *Adventures of Kathlyn,* which was part of the Sunday paper's "Special Features" section, was one means by which the newspaper sought to attract new readers. The *Tribune,* considered the more "respectable" newspaper in Chicago, was not seen as having the nickelodeon audience as its readers.[43] Because it was believed that people who attended nickelodeons were part of the lower classes, it seemed as though *Tribune* readers (who were supposedly of the middle to upper classes) did not attend motion pictures at these sites. Therefore, by coproducing a film that was expected to appeal to the nickelodeon audience and printing a fictionalized version of the film, the *Tribune* hoped to draw nickelodeon patrons to the newspaper as new readers.[44] The 1922 book *The WGN,* published by the Tribune Company, explains the way the *Tribune* won the circulation war of the teens by increasing the circulation and advertising: "The first step was to capitalize the soaring motion picture craze for Tribune benefit."[45] Several years later, the *Tribune* also promoted the way that it had "obtained mass circulation without losing a practical monopoly of better class readers."[46] Clearly, the *Tribune* considered itself to have a high class of readers; however, through ventures like *The Adventures of Kathlyn,* the newspaper also managed to build a mass appeal.

Promoting *Kathlyn*

That *Kathlyn* was important to the *Tribune* is clear from the amount of promotion the newspaper invested in the film and the story. Many large ads were run in the newspaper proclaiming that "thousands" stood in line to see *Kathlyn* and promoting the exorbitant expense of the serial (see Figure 2). For weeks after the *Tribune* began featuring MacGrath's story, a box was placed on the front page of the Sunday *Tribune* containing a very brief summary of the story and telling readers on what page they could find *Kathlyn* (see Figure 3). A listing of locations at

Figure 2. *Kathlyn* ad, *Chicago Daily Tribune*, 4 January 1914.

SUMMARY OF THE NEWS.

SUNDAY, JANUARY 11, 1914.

WEATHER FORECAST.

Chicago and vicinity—Cloudy and unsettled Sunday and probably Monday, not much change in
temperature, light variable winds.
Illinois—Generally fair Sunday, and Monday,
slightly warmer Sunday in north portion, moderate northwest winds becoming variable.
Sunrise, 7.18; sunset, 4.42. Moonrise, 5:07 Sunday.

TEMPERATURE IN CHICAGO.
[Last 24 hours.]

Maximum, 3 n. m. Saturday....25
Minimum, 2 a. m. Sunday....20

3 a. m.....25	11 a. m.....24	7 p. m.....23	
4 a. m.....24	12 noon.....24	8 p. m.....23	
5 a. m.....24	1 p. m.....24	9 p. m.....22	
6 a. m.....22	2 p. m.....23	10 p. m.....22	
7 a. m.....24	3 p. m.....22	11 p. m.....21	
8 a. m.....24	4 p. m.....22	Midnight.....20	
9 a. m.....24	5 p. m.....24	1 a. m.....20	
10 a. m.....23	6 p. m.....24	2 a. m.....20	

Mean temperature, 23; normal for the day, 24.
Excess since Jan. 1, 85.
Precipitation for 24 hours to 7 p. m., .01. Defi-
ciency since Jan. 1, .18 inch.
Wind, W.; max., 21 miles an hour at 7:47 p. m.
Relative humidity, 7 a. m., 57%; 7 p. m., 60%.
Barometer, sea level, 7 a. m., 29.99; 7 p. m., 30.19.
For official government weather report see part 1,
page 6.

SHIPPERS' ADVICES.

Special Forecast for Shipments Within Radius of 500 Miles.

Prepare shipments to reach destinations by Sunday night for temperatures as follows: North and
northweat. zero to 15 degrees; weat, 5 to 20 degrees;
south and east, 15 to 25 degrees.

EDITORIAL—PART 2, PAGE 4.

Why Banks Should Enter the New
System.
Sheridan at Gravelotte.
Breaking the Tablets.
Soft Living and Soft Thinking.
Dietary Heroes.

LOCAL.

"Wise insiders" found to have doubled their money selling school sites to
board of education.   Part 1, Page 1
Siegel Cooper & Co. directors to dou-
ble capital stock.   Part 1, Page 2
Dissolute women officially classified as
vagrants by court.   Part 1, Page 3
Weston to give plans for street car
subway tomorrow.   Part 1, Page 3
Jury completed for trial of first vote
fraud cases.   Part 1, Page 3
Ald. Pretzel seeks to prohibit agggreat-
ive dances.   Part 1, Page 3
Court forbids crippled boy to beg; a-
ther under $500 bond.   Part 1, Page 4
Municipal budget calls for $5,129,226
more than 1913.   Part 1, Page 7
Vocation school seen by Prof. Gault as
remedy for crime.   Part 1, Page 8
Society.   Part 5, Pages 2, 3, 7
Women's clubs.   Part 5, Page 3
Churches.   Part 5, Page 6
Suffrage.   Part 5, Page 7
Theaters.   Part 8, Pages 1, 2, 3
Music.   Part 8, Page 1

MOVEMENTS OF OCEAN STEAMSHIPS.

Arrived.	Port.
PRESIDENT LINCOLN..........	New York.
LORRAINE	New York.
AZOV	San Francisco.
MISSOURIAN	San Francisco.
Sailed.	Port.
PENNSYLVANIA	San Francisco.
CELTIC	Queenstown.
CARPATHIA	Gibraltar.
RUSSIA	Libau.
MADONNA	Angra.
ST. LOUIS	Southampton.
COLUMBIA	Glasgow.
BARBAROSSA	New York.
MINNEAPOLIS	New York.
CARMANIA	New York.
ADRIATIC	New York.
KURSK	New York.
GROSSER KURFUERST...........	New York.
NOORDAM	Rotterdam.
VADERLAND	Genoa.
CANOPIC	Genoa.
CARONIA	Liverpool.
HILONIAN	Seattle.

WIRELESS REPORTS.

	Due at New York
NIEUW-AMS...Out 710 miles.......Monday a. m.
Out 685 miles...Monday a. m...LAPLAND....
Monday a. m. VITRUVIA ....Out 713 miles...
HANOVER....Out 600 miles.......Monday a. m.
	Due at Philadelphia
BRESLAU.....Out 900 miles....Tuesday a. m.

DOMESTIC.

Attorney general, Missouri, denounces
Judge for rate decisions.   Part 1, Page 1
Dr. Hillis assigns Germany's suprem-
acy over France to women. Part 1, Page 7

FOREIGN.

Mexican rebels capture Ojinaga; federal garrison evacuates.   Part 1, Page 1
Union of South Africa near war from
labor troubles.   Part 1, Page 2

WASHINGTON.

New Haven road and government
agree on dissolution plan.   Part 1, Page 2
McReynolds gives his decision on
newspaper publicity law.   Part 1, Page 4
House probably will create special
committee on suffrage.   Part 1, Page 6

CALUMET.

Federal report bares conditions in
Calumet copper range.   Part 1, Page 5
Moyer leaves for Washington A. F. of
L. conference.   Part 1, Page 5

POLITICAL.

Row over Cook county Republican
control likely to spread.   Part 1, Page 6
Czarnecki tells women to register before signing petitions.   Part 1, Page 6
Senator Bristow of Kansas says he
will remain Republican.   Part 1, Page 6

TRADE AND INDUSTRY.

Real estate.   Part 1, Page 6
Commercial.   Part 2, Page 6
Financial.   Part 2, Page 7

The Adventures of
Kathlyn

BEAUTIFUL Kathlyn Hare speeds
from her luxurious home in California by land and sea to India. Too
late she learns she has been lured to
the wilds by a mysterious Hindu—the
villain who seeks to force her to be
his bride. She seeks for Kathlyn's father—now in India seeking more of the
animals he loves and that love him—
had saved the life of the king of Allaha, a province of India. For that the
king had made Hare and his heirs
eligible as successors to the throne.

Chapter 1, printed last Sunday in
"The Tribune," saw Kathlyn on her
way. In Chapter 2, appearing today,
she is brought to the throne she is destined unwillingly to ascend. Kathlyn's
life henceforth is a succession of
thrills, suspense, and mystery. Swiftly
she is swept from one terror to another. Through plot and intrigue she
scurries. She faces the ravening beasts
of the jungle. She emerges from one
ordeal triumphant, only to endure another. Fate and Love each time rout
Ambition and Revenge. But Ambition
and Revenge are hard to whip—so runs
the story.

There are twenty-six chapters—action in every line!

*Chapter 2, of this, Harold Mac-
Grath's Latest and Greatest
Novel, will be found on*

Page 3 of Part 7

*of Today's Issue of
The Sunday Tribune.*

MEXICAN REBEL CAPTURE OJINA

Many of Federal Garrison Desert and Cross River to the United States.

CLOSE OF LONG SI

Presidio, Tex., Jan. 10—The Mexic
els under Gen. Francisco Villa toni
tered Ojinaga, the federal garrison
retreated.

All of the federals who could do so
across the Rio Grande fords into
States territory. Among these wer
Salvador Mercado, who was Presiden
ta's chief military commander. He
the river and surrendered to Maj. Mc
of the United States army.

It was impossible for Maj. McNa
learn of what had become of the f
whether the bulk of them had taken
on this side or whether they scatt
points in Mexico. The country about O
is mostly desert, with little to sustain

Sends Over Government Reco

Before he had crossed the river Ge
cado sent a note to Maj. McNamee
Fifteenth United States cavalry as
the federals might send across the
some guns for which they had no ar
tion.

Maj. McNamee replied that any gu
would be seized and that the men b
them would be disarmed and forced t
Mercado sent over seven wagon
of government documents under the
of a wounded lieutenant, who also b
his personal effects. The wagons wer
into the United States army camp.

The entire United States border pat
ordered out to prevent a wholesale
federals to this side.

Means Control of North?

Villa has asserted that the capt
Ojinaga would place the rebels in con
the whole of northern Mexico. He
would decide whether the 4,000 Huer
diers, with their nine remaining ge
are to remain or be driven from the
of Mexico.

Villa was in personal command
rebels. He recently arrived at Ojinag
Chihuahua with large reinforcement
Today's battle proved to be one sided
ly because of the greater strength
rebels, but more because the federal
short on ammunition, they having be
able to replenish the supply which w
pleted by the six days of previous fi
around Ojinaga.

Hostilities Begun at Dawn

The advance on Ojinaga and the reo
of hostilities began just before sun
The rebels had more than 6,000 men c
in from the south and west.

Steadily creeping toward the federal
high on the plateau, the rebels, shrou
great clouds of dust, occupied positions
in four miles of the village before the
resistance. The outer federal ou
opened with a rifle volley and the
a few machine guns.

The rattling reply of the rebels wa
as to overwhelm the federals compl
They attempted to retreat in disorde
fifty of them were captured, while
others jumped into the river and sw
the American side.

At once the rebel routing of the f
outposts had its effect in the federal
son. Many of the outposts were withdi
the cattle were driven into the villag
women and children were hurriedly
patched across the river.

For many hours the battle continued
the rebels steadily advancing, until
finally entered the town.

Figure 3. Box on the front page of the *Sunday Tribune*, 11 January 1914.

which the film was playing also appeared in the daily "Amusements" sections. Before *Kathlyn,* items in this section were limited almost exclusively to legitimate theater and vaudeville shows. The only films to be listed in the "Amusements" section before *Kathlyn* were travel films that were seen as having an educational appeal.

The promotion of the serial was specifically designed to attract women. The first teaser advertisements for *Kathlyn* were placed on what was obviously considered, although not explicitly titled, the "women's" page of the *Tribune* at the time. This page featured columns that offered tips on health, fashion, household economy, and beauty. The content of these ads also targeted women: "Warning! Kathlyn will entice your husband from his fireside many an evening"; "You'll go without your dinner for a chance to see Kathlyn"; "Young Ladies: Watch your Sweethearts! Kathlyn is coming!"; "Don't flirt with Kathlyn"; and "Be careful! Kathlyn is dangerously beautiful" (see Figure 4). All of these ads used the appeal of vicarious adventure and curiosity

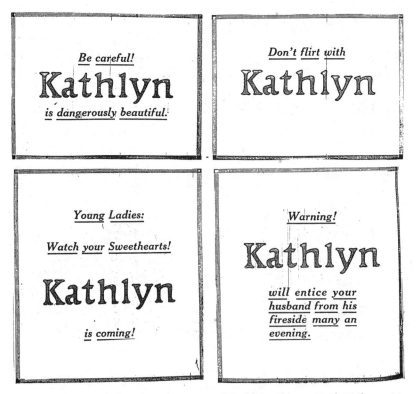

Figure 4. Teaser ads for *The Adventures of Kathlyn, Chicago Daily Tribune,* 11, 16, 18, and 20 December 1913.

to stimulate women to go out and see *Kathlyn*. They suggested that women move away from the home and miss their dinners to learn about Kathlyn. The ads addressed women directly, particularly those that warned of Kathlyn's charms, but they can also be seen to have an attraction for men. The thought of seeing a beautiful woman whom their wives are being warned about might have made men interested in seeing the films and more willing to take their wives to the moving picture theater in the evening. This initial appeal to attend the film in the evening also tied in with the "respectable" reputation being sought for the motion pictures, making filmgoing seem more like attending the legitimate theater.[47] Keeping the family together during leisure hours, and thus diminishing the hours that husbands spent in saloons (a form of leisure disapproved of both by many wives and by moral reformers), helped promote films as a "respectable" form of entertainment that supported middle-class values.

Promotion for the serial within the *Tribune* was not limited to advertisements. The day after the release of the first installment, the *Tribune* ran a story on page 3 with the headline "Filmed Novel a Movie Success." The article asserted, "The producers of *The Adventures of Kathlyn* have produced such a story in a way that without doubt marks a new era for the movies." Another story appearing on the third page of the *Tribune* on 17 January 1914, under the headline, "Crowds Besiege Kathlyn Shows," detailed how the police had to be called in to prevent chaos at screenings of the serial.[48] The placement of these stories so prominently within the newspaper is even more surprising when considered in relation to the articles about motion pictures that appeared in the *Tribune* just one week before the release of *Kathlyn*. The headlines of three stories that appeared on page 5 of the 22 December 1913 edition of the *Tribune* were "Inquisitive Mobs See 'Slave' Film," "Capital Forbids Film Show," and "Church Closes: Movies Cause." As these headlines indicate, the coverage of motion pictures in the *Tribune* before Kathlyn tended to focus on the negative aspects of the cinematic experience.

After *Kathlyn*, the *Tribune*'s coverage of motion pictures only increased. As Lloyd Wendt writes, "Patterson and King became convinced that newspapers were one of the compelling natural interests of the public, that newspapers should publish reports on the activities of the stars and writers in the new medium and that newspapers also should publish fiction daily."[49] On 5 February 1914, the *Tribune* began to publish movie "reviews" (actually synopses) under the heading "Today's Best Moving Picture Story."[50] By 11 February, the *Tribune* was occasionally offering reviews of more than one film. On 14 February

1914, the newspaper began publishing a directory of "High Class Moving Picture Theaters" that ran twice a week and listed the theaters (by neighborhood) and the films they were showing. This directory fit with Keeley's interest in providing service to the newspaper's readers and its advertisers. The *Tribune* suggested that this directory allowed people to plan their filmgoing from home (an idea with interesting ramifications for filmgoing practice). Motion picture theaters were also provided an organized outlet through which to inform people of their featured films. The success of this directory led the *Tribune* to expand its focus on motion pictures. A film section, first titled "Film and Screen" and changed after one week to "Right off the Reel," began on 1 March 1914. This section (which was rarely longer than one page) featured such columns as "Gossip of the Silent Players," "Notes of the Motion Dramas," and "In the Frame of Public Favor," which presented a large photo of an actor or actress and a brief biography.[51]

This increased coverage of motion pictures was undoubtedly related to the success of *The Adventures of Kathlyn*. According to Kalton Lahue, "Couples danced to a hesitation waltz named in her [Kathlyn's] honor, sipping Kathlyn cocktails between sets; the ladies wore Kathlyn style coiffures and hats while the gents carried a postcard pose of their favorite film star."[52] Another writer notes that more than fifty thousand copies of the Kathlyn postcard were sold in Chicago in a matter of days.[53] Although it is possible that this information is based on *Tribune* exaggeration, the perceived success of *Kathlyn* cannot be denied. The *Tribune* reported that *Kathlyn* "sent the circulation of The Sunday Tribune swiftly, upward."[54] One report estimated a 10 percent increase in circulation due to *Kathlyn*.[55] Wendt writes: "The success of the joint serialization was immediate and tremendous. *Chicago Tribune* Sunday circulation jumped almost 80,000, while the motion picture theaters showing *Kathlyn* were packed."[56] The newspaper also gained motion picture-related advertising, soon featuring advertisements from Universal and *Photoplay Magazine*.

The *Chicago Tribune* was not the only institution to notice the success of *Kathlyn*. Although Selig never made another serial, more than sixty were made between 1912 and 1920, many of which were coproductions by newspapers and film companies.[57] Examples from the spurt of coproduced serials that came out immediately following *Kathlyn* are *The Perils of Pauline* (Hearst-Eclectic, 1914), *Lucille Love* (*Chicago Herald*-Universal, 1914), *The Million Dollar Mystery* (*Chicago Tribune*-Thanhouser, 1914), and *The Exploits of Elaine* (Hearst-Pathé, 1915). Both newspapers and film studios attempted to profit from the public's embrace of the serial. In 1915, six of the seven newspapers in New York with circulations of more than 150,000 had serial tie-ins; in 1915 Universal and Pathé each released four serials, and six other studios had one serial each.[58] Although it seems that the filmed versions of these serials actually gained in popularity for a while (Pathé and Universal became especially known for their serials), certain newspapers did not profit from the experience as much as the *Tribune*. One explanation for this differential success is that some of the newspapers already had the filmgoing audience as readers, and therefore did not increase circulation as much as the *Tribune*.[59]

Kathlyn as Serial Queen

The above examination of the industrial factors that contributed to the creation of *The Adventures of Kathlyn* and provided the context for the serial indicates some of the ways that the *Tribune* and Selig negotiated their appeal to the new mass audience. An examination of the content of *Kathlyn* further indicates the ways in which the serial managed the tensions that emerged between the need to produce a form of entertainment that would interest people across gender and class lines. The decision on the part of Selig and the *Tribune* to coproduce what Ben Singer calls a serial queen melodrama was probably not an arbitrary decision. The content of these types of serials had an appeal for both newspapers and motion picture companies. Using the term *melodrama* with its traditional relationship to thrills, action, and adventure, Singer describes these films as representing women with "masculine" qualities, such as "physical strength and endurance, self-reliance, courage, social authority and freedom to explore novel experiences outside the domestic sphere."[60] In *The Adventures of Kathlyn,* the film's heroine sets off for India on her own to rescue her father, almost magically calms wild animals, and exhibits bravery in all sorts of dangerous situations. At the same time, however, these serials depicted women as victims being hurt by men.[61] This quality of danger to the women was used often to promote the films. The advertising copy for *Kathlyn* frequently mentioned the real-life risk to Kathlyn Williams. The copy for the ad on the day the first filmed installment opened enticed viewers to the theaters by telling them, "You will see her bound by fanatical natives on the top of a giant funeral pyre and watch the flames creeping over her helpless form. You will see her tied with thongs in a tiger trap as human bait for the blood thirsty beasts of the jungle. . . . Time after time, in scene after scene, this actress takes her life in her hands and walks grimly up to the very jaws of death."[62] Another ad urged people to "see this great actress risking her life in actual adventure with savage beasts in order to place this superb drama before you in all its thrilling realism."[63]

As Singer notes, a tension exists within these serial queen melodramas between the woman who is often physically abused and the woman who is bravely facing adventures outside the domestic sphere. He writes, "The genre thus couples an ideology of female power with an equally vivid exposition of female defenselessness and weakness."[64] Singer sees this tension as a working through of the anxieties brought about by women's suffrage and the "New Woman" who exists within the public sphere and has been represented in American culture since the late 1800s.[65] The dual positioning of women as independent and vulnerable also mirrored working-class women's position in the workforce, where they exercised their independence outside of the domestic space yet also became susceptible to the advances of their male coworkers.[66] Motion picture theaters were themselves a site of anxiety as a place where women were able to participate in public culture. It is not surprising, then, that films attempted (and perhaps still attempt) to negotiate the tension that their industry actually inspires. As Singer notes, women were most probably the primary target of the serials;[67] however, neither the film industry nor the newspapers wanted to alienate the male audience. Therefore, the independence of the "serial queens" was balanced by their presentation as spectacles and victims. Additionally, as Frank Nugent has observed, the depiction of strong women was supposedly appealing to men, who were offered "a relief from . . . rampant femininity."[68]

The *Tribune,* with its appeal to female readers, was also dealing with the anxieties provoked by the "New Woman" as it covered issues of suffrage without offending the paper's more traditional readers. In fact, judging from the newspaper text, it is not clear how much of a "relief" from the dominant stereotype of femininity *The Adventures of Kathlyn* would have been for either men or women. In relation to women's issues, this serial appears somewhat conservative. It is true that Kathlyn leaves the domestic sphere to face adventure with courage, and she is given some elements of power. She is associated with nature in an almost spiritual and forceful way. Rather than being associated with trees and flowers, she is connected to wild animals. In contrast to the popular depiction of women, Kathlyn also does not faint at the drop of a hat. In at least the first three episodes, Kathlyn faints only once—when she is shown an urn that is supposed to contain her father's ashes. This dedication to her father, which is primary throughout these episodes, shows Kathlyn as the dutiful daughter and probably made her more attractive (particularly to men). The focus on family also fit with the middle-class values that the serial was trying to incorporate. However, Kathlyn—like the working-class women of the time who exercised their desire for independence—is transgressive in her questioning of patriarchal institutions, mainly by her refusal to wed Umballah. Not only does she question the need for a woman to marry in order to rule a country, she also questions Allaha's law that requires her to marry. Despite all of these resistant qualities given to Kathlyn, her power is limited by her lack of control and her final reliance on men throughout the serial. Umballah tricks her into traveling to India, the only reason she goes is to help her father, and the members of the Allaha council (all male) work with Umballah to control her destiny. Kathlyn's bravery sets her up as an independent thinker, but she is still incapable of taking the action that will allow her to be her own savior. Kathlyn's strong-mindedness, no matter how noble, is usually seen to get her into dangers from which a man (a white man) must save her.

As the above discussion suggests, although *Kathlyn* was meant to appeal to women, with its images of strong and exciting heroines, the serial—at least the newspaper text—also attempted to limit the possibilities of women's independence and adventure outside of the home. It is doubtful, however, that making the woman dependent on the man in the last instance completely negated the impact of seeing a woman with physical and emotional strength. Additionally, the newspaper serial, at least, raised questions about the typical representation of women. Although Kathlyn was presented as an unusual woman, the serial also brought up issues surrounding the depiction of the "typical" woman. For example, at one point Kathlyn is described as bordering on hysterical, a stereotypical women's condition. The text states that hysteria "is sometimes but a step to Supreme courage."[69] This line works to appropriate a weakness ascribed to women and turn it into a strength. It is not certain how or if this kind of material was integrated into the filmed version, but the written text, at least, offered an alternative reading of the dominant depiction of women in popular culture.

Kathlyn Goes to India

The contradictions apparent in Kathlyn's positioning as a woman are also related to the class values that the serial was attempting to balance. Kathlyn was caught between the film heroine roles of the gamine and the virgin, the former embodying the adventurous independence that appealed to the working class and the latter representing the nineteenth-century middle-class values of purity and obedience.[70] The serial also balanced the cultural tropes of the middle and working classes in its treatment of the foreign setting and the resulting issues of ethnicity.[71]

Fitting with the melodramatic style of the serial, *Kathlyn* was set in India, which allowed for mysterious adventure. The setting of India also satisfied the traditionally middle-class interest in exotic travel.[72] Additionally, the inclusion of the foreign locale may have allowed middle-class viewers to see the serial as educational for the lower classes, much in the same way that amusement parks, with their romanticized representations of foreign lands, were seen to be educational for a class of people who would probably never have the opportunity to travel.[73] Within the text of *Kathlyn,* a great deal of time is spent describing India and generally establishing it as an exotic "other" place. The newspaper version of *Kathlyn* frequently used Indian words, such as "Memsahib" and "khitmatgar," giving a more authentic and educational tone to the piece. Articles about *Kathlyn* from the time of its release stated that certain panoramic shots were actually taken in India, people from India were employed on the set to ensure accuracy, and the serial was depicting Indian rituals never before filmed. *Motion Picture News* reported: "Many of the scenes showing the wonderful architecture and invested with the atmosphere of the Orient were taken in India. . . . It is claimed that this play for the first time shows many interesting, sacred rites performed in the lands of the Parsee."[74] Of course, it is possible that this information is the result of "exaggerated" Selig/*Tribune* promotion. However, there does seem to be an interest, even if it is false, in establishing *Kathlyn* as a sort of travelogue.

Although, as I have noted, the *Kathlyn* serial clearly established India as the "other," it also raised questions about the propriety of white rule over a foreign land. The issue of self-rule in India had recently entered the news with the growth of nationalism in the 1910s and some terrorist activity directed at the British in India. Of course, it was relatively easy for an American story to make judgments about the situation, creating a distance between America's benevolent "help" and Britain's imperialism. Describing Allaha to his daughters, Colonel Hare says, "Some day England will gobble it up; only waiting for a good excuse."[75] The issue of whether a white person should be ruling a foreign country at all is depicted as problematic within *Kathlyn.* Considering the prospect of becoming king of Allaha, Colonel Hare says, "As if a white man could rule over a brown one by the choice of the matter."[76] Kathlyn, who does not want to be queen of Allaha, echoes her father's sentiments: "It is impossible. . . . You are all mad, I am a white woman. I cannot rule over an alien race whose tongue I cannot speak, whose habits I know nothing of. It is impossible."[77] Even Umballah is given a recognition that race is an issue in the future leader of the country. He tells Colonel Hare, "Think you a white man shall sit upon this throne while I live?" For a moment, Umballah seems like a revolutionary working to free his country from white rule. But then he adds, "It is mine. I was his heir."[78] This line effectively turns Umballah back into a greedy villain rather than a freedom fighter.

Although it raises questions about the ethics of physical imperialism, the serial seems to support American methods of imperialism. As Rabinovitz writes: "By repetitively coding certain cultures and races as 'foreign, exoticized Other,' these displays promoted, through the pleasurable gaze, racial hierarchies to both its middle and working-class patrons. In addition, geographic regions that were preindustrial and populated by non-white races were depicted as legitimate objects for visual consumption."[79] Indian culture is made strange and different and is clearly established as a commodity to be purchased by the American viewers (quite explicitly in the serial's appeal to people to pay to read/view the serial in order to experience the "strange" land). At the same time, the depiction of the Indians as inferior objects certainly helped to reinforce immigrant audience members' identification with the serial's "American" characters.

The text of *Kathlyn* features many lines reflecting stereotypes about the "savage" Indian race, and film stills suggest that Orientalism was apparent within the film as well. Umballah is the villain who wants to "defile" the white blonde goddess. Umballah is also described as "ruthless and predatory after the manner of his kind"[80] (although here it is possible that the "kind" being referred to is his class, not his race). A final example of the racism within *Kathlyn* that I will offer is Kathlyn's reaction to Umballah's announcement that they are to be married. She begins:

"Marry you? O, no! Mate with you, a black?"
"Black?" he cried, as if a whiplash had struck him across the face.
"Yes, black of skin and black of heart." . . .
"So be it. There are other things besides marriage."
"Yes," she replied proudly; "there is death."[81]

The issue of which characters can speak and understand English and how they use this "power" is also important within *Kathlyn*. Umballah, who was raised out of his class and given a "white man's" education, can speak English, but he uses this knowledge to deceive Kathlyn and to try to gain power in order to suppress the people of Allaha. Others who speak English are seen to use this knowledge to serve white people. A married couple who both know English are appointed by Kathlyn to be her bodyguard and lady-in-waiting. Their use of their abilities to serve Kathlyn works to make them "good."

The downgrading of Indian culture does not completely counteract the seeds of cultural understanding that are also offered within the series. Gaps and contradictions emerge from the serial's attempt to appeal to men and women with varying class tastes. In the representation of both ethnicity and gender, the text attempts to balance different sides of issues to appeal to large audiences.

The content of *Kathlyn* as well as it promotion can be seen in relation to the intent of Selig Polyscope and the *Chicago Tribune*. Both the filmmakers and the newspaper executives were interested in increasing their audience/readership by attracting new groups of people. The large number of film/print coproductions among the more than sixty serials made between 1912 and 1920 illustrates that this means of increasing audience size interested not only Selig and the *Chicago Tribune* but media companies around the country. Encouragement on each company's part for its own "viewership" to test the other medium helped create a new "mass" audience for both the films and the newspapers. *The Adventures of Kathlyn* and many of the other serials of this period appealed to female, male, middle-class, lower-class, ethnic, and nonethnic patrons in an effort to create a more massive "mass" audience. At the same time, the formulation of this mass audience exposed its members to bits and pieces of different cultures. Peiss notes that in this new consumer culture, "the lines of cultural transmission travel in both directions."[82] The U.S. culture that was so long assumed to be formed within the top classes and passed down to the lower classes needed to be reformulated at this time. Through projects like *Kathlyn*, U.S. businesses—such as Selig Polyscope and the *Chicago Tribune*—selected and transformed different pieces of U.S. subcultures not only to attract but also to construct and shape the mass audience.

Notes

1. Rather than producing a number of self-contained episodes featuring recurring characters to constitute a series (such as the Edison Company and the *Ladies*

World Magazine's 1912 series *What Happened to Mary*), Selig Polyscope and the *Chicago Daily Tribune* created a story with "holdover" suspense endings (as displayed in the French *Fantomas* serial, which was being imported into the United States at this time).

2. Lauren Rabinovitz, "Temptations of Pleasure: Nickelodeons, Amusement Parks, and the Sights of Female Sexuality," *Camera Obscura* 23 (May 1990): 73.

3. Miriam Hansen, "Adventures of Goldilocks: Spectatorship, Consumerism and Public Life," *Camera Obscura* 22 (January 1990): 53.

4. For a more dramatic summary of *The Adventures of Kathlyn,* see Figure 1.

5. Located at Eastlake Park in Los Angeles, Selig's zoo was reported at the time to be the second-largest individually owned collection of wild animals in the world. "Selig Resources for 'Kathlyn' Series," *Motion Picture News,* 31 January 1914, 20. The acreage attributed to Selig's zoo varies from source to source, but the highest figure appeared in the *Motion Picture News* article just cited, which reported that Selig's lot consisted of forty acres of botanical gardens and different terrains on which Kathlyn's life could be put in danger. Bodeen estimates a more moderate size of twenty-two acres at the time. Dewitt Bodeen, "Kathlyn Williams," *Films in Review* (February 1984): 71. This zoo became a tourist attraction in 1915, and it is reported that when William Selig lost interest in motion pictures he turned his attention to his zoo. The similarities that can be seen between the father in the serial, Colonel Hare, who is supposedly a world-renowned wild animal collector, and "Colonel" Selig, also a collector of wild animals, are too obvious for anyone to believe that Selig was not somehow involved in the creation of the Kathlyn story.

6. The titles of the thirteen episodes are, in order, "The Unwelcome Throne," "The Two Ordeals," "In the Temple of the Lion," "The Royal Slave," "A Colonel in Chains," "Three Bags of Silver," "The Garden of Brides," "The Cruel Crown," "The Spellbound Multitude," "The Warrior Maid," "The Forged Parchment," "The King's Will," and "The Court of Death." Buck Rainey, *Those Fabulous Serial Heroines: Their Lives and Films* (Metuchen, N.J.: Scarecrow, 1990), 467.

7. Among other reasons, serials were popular within the motion picture industry for their consistent ability to draw people back to the movie theaters for each episode. Exhibitors took notice of the way in which serials often attracted returning viewers. Kalton C. Lahue, *Bound and Gagged: The Story of the Silent Serials* (South Brunswick, N.J.: A. S. Barnes, 1968), 24. In a meeting between the Edison Company and the Boston Branch of the General Film Company in October 1914, the distributors requested that the Edison Company produce a weekly two-reel serial. The General Film representatives suggested that exhibitors were anxious to show these films because they ensured a returning audience. L. W. McChesney, memo in Edison Papers: 1914 Motion Pictures, General, 19 October 1914.

8. Although the issues of the *Tribune* examined for this study were viewed on black-and-white microfilm, the serial did run in the "Color Section," indicating that the sketches may have been in color or that the film stills were tinted for publication.

9. "Selig Resources for 'Kathlyn' Series," 20. Despite this large number of newspapers carrying *Kathlyn,* one writer reports that Selig covered the entire country with only twenty-four prints of the filmed version of *Kathlyn* in order to save on costs. Kalton C. Lahue, *Ladies in Distress* (South Brunswick, N.J.: A. S. Barnes, 1971), 322. It is not likely that Selig could have provided for all the cities running the newspaper serial with only twenty-four film prints. If this report is accurate, this small number of prints leads to questions about *Kathlyn*'s distribution, such as whether all these cities were also showing the film (it is probable that they were, as that was the major hook of the serial) and how these serializations may have been staggered to allow this sort of film distribution.

10. This method of release also suggests that it was expected that people would be able to understand *Kathlyn* without first knowing the story, an important consideration

at a time when confusion sometimes prevented the understanding of movie plots. Eileen Bowser, *The Transformation of Cinema: 1907–1915* (Berkeley: University of California Press, 1990), 255.

11. MacGrath has been described as a storyteller who "can hold a reader's attention with a rapid succession of episodes depicting scenes and people of that wonderful land of no where." "Harold MacGrath," *National Cyclopedia of American Biography* 14 (1917): 480. His novels include the titles *Half a Rogue* (1906), *The Lure of the Mask* (1908), and *The Carpet from Baghdad* (1911).

12. Rainey, *Those Fabulous Serial Heroines*, 463.

13. Bodeen, "Kathlyn Williams," 67.

14. Rainey, *Those Fabulous Serial Heroines*, 459. Although some sources suggest that Williams loved animals, these are balanced if not exceeded by articles that discuss her fear of the animals with which she worked. Bodeen, "Kathlyn Williams," 68.

15. Rainey, *Those Fabulous Serial Heroines*, 461.

16. Ibid., 459.

17. James S. McQuade, "The Adventures of Kathlyn," *Moving Picture World*, 17 January 1914, 266 (reprinted in *Selected Film Criticism 1869–1911*, ed. Anthony Slide [Metuchen, N.J.: Scarecrow, 1982], 3).

18. Kathy Lee Peiss, *Cheap Amusements: Working Women and Leisure in Turn-of-the-Century New York* (Philadelphia: Temple University Press, 1986), 131.

19. Ben Singer, "Female Power in the Serial-Queen Melodrama: The Etiology of an Anomaly," *Camera Obscura* 22 (January 1990): 96.

20. Kenneth Macgowan, *Behind the Screen: The History and Technique of the Motion Picture* (New York: Delta, 1965), 186. Macgowan was the film critic for the *Philadelphia Evening Ledger*.

21. Bowser, *The Transformation of Cinema*, 121.

22. Merle Kaminsky, staff writer for Lerner Newspapers, untitled clipping from unknown newspaper, from Chicago Historical Society Films: Chicago, Movies, General, 14 May 1974.

23. John W. Tebbel, *An American Dynasty* (New York: Greenwood, 1968), 81.

24. Quoted in Lewis Jacobs, *The Rise of the American Film: A Critical History* (New York: Harcourt, 1939), 62.

25. Lloyd Wendt, *Chicago Tribune: The Rise of a Great American Newspaper* (Chicago: Rand McNally, 1979), 386.

26. James Keeley quoted in James Webster Linn, *James Keeley, Newspaper Man* (Indianapolis: Bobbs-Merrill, 1937), 167.

27. Tebbel, *An American Dynasty*, 89.

28. Hansen, "Adventures of Goldilocks," 52.

29. Linn, *James Keeley*, 178.

30. Keeley quoted in ibid., 18.

31. Peiss, *Cheap Amusements*, 65.

32. Ibid., 72.

33. Ibid., 65.

34. Joseph Medill Patterson, "The Nickelodeons: The Poor Man's Elementary Course in the Drama," *Saturday Evening Post*, 23 November 1907, 10. This article examines such topics as the makeup of the nickelodeon audience, technical aspects of film production and exhibition, and the types of stories being filmed and their rental costs. It also includes a breakdown of the expenses involved in running a nickelodeon. Frame enlargements from various motion pictures, including the filmed Sharkey-Jeffries fight, are used to illustrate elements of motion pictures. The caption under one frame reads, "A Typical Slapstick Comedy," and another frame is captioned "Notice the Excellent Pantomime."

35. Ibid., 38.

36. Ibid., 11.

37. Wendt, *Chicago Tribune,* 398.

38. Ibid.

39. Ibid.

40. Ibid., 386.

41. Tebbel, *An American Dynasty,* 92.

42. *Book of Facts: Data on Markets, Merchandising and Advertising* (Chicago: Tribune Company, 1927), 168.

43. Kaminsky, untitled clipping.

44. Macgowan, *Behind the Screen,* 188.

45. *The WGN* (Chicago: Tribune Company, 1922), 80.

46. *Book of Facts,* 39.

47. Later ads, however, would recommend that people attend *Kathlyn* either in the afternoon or in the evening.

48. "Filmed Novel a Movie Success," *Chicago Tribune,* 30 December 1913, 3; "Crowds Besiege Kathlyn Shows," *Chicago Tribune,* 17 January 1914, 3.

49. Wendt, *Chicago Tribune,* 393.

50. This leads to questions of whether the serial, with its twenty-four release prints, was actually financially successful for the film company.

51. In this section, the *Tribune* did show some favoritism toward *Kathlyn,* featuring Williams's picture in the "frame of public favor" in the first "Film and Screen" and frequently mentioning the film in its gossip columns.

52. Lahue, *Ladies in Distress,* 322. It is also interesting to note that Kathlyn was associated with the waltz and the cocktail—the outlets of dancing and drinking considered more respectable by the middle class. Peiss, *Cheap Amusements,* 96, 108.

53. Rainey, *Those Fabulous Serial Heroines,* 459.

54. *The WGN,* 80.

55. Rainey, *Those Fabulous Serial Heroines,* 459.

56. Wendt, *Chicago Tribune,* 393.

57. Singer, "Female Power," 91. Interestingly, despite the connection between Selig and the *Tribune,* a Selig film was not reviewed in that paper until 10 February 1914. Most of the films reviewed (if not all), at least initially, were films made by members of the Motion Picture Patents Company.

58. Ibid., 100; Raymond William Stedman, *The Serials: Suspense and Drama by Installment* (Oklahoma City: University of Oklahoma Press, 1977), 35.

59. Kaminsky, untitled clipping.

60. Singer, "Female Power," 91.

61. Ibid., 93.

62. Advertisement, *Chicago Daily Tribune,* 9 December 1913.

63. Advertisement, *Chicago Daily Tribune,* 2 January 1914, 8.

64. Singer, "Female Power," 117.

65. Ibid., 123.

66. Peiss, *Cheap Amusements,* 49.

67. Singer, "Female Power," 93.

68. Frank S. Nugent, "Glamour Girls: A Film Calvacade," *New York Times,* 25 June 1939.

69. Harold MacGrath, "The Adventures of Kathlyn," part 3, *Chicago Daily Tribune,* 18 January 1914, 3.

70. Elizabeth Ewen, "City Lights: Immigrant Women and the Rise of the Movies," *Signs* 5 (1980): 59–60.

71. The villains in movie serials were often marked as ethnic. Examples include *Patria* (1917), with Mexican and Japanese villains; *Yellow Peril* (1916), with Asian villains; and *The Perils of Pauline* (1914) and *The Diamond in the Sky* (1915), both of

which had Gypsy villains (Lahue, *Bound and Gagged,* 49). It is interesting to note, however, that the serials did not seem to have villains of European ethnicity, indicating an unwillingness on the part of filmmakers and newspapers to alienate the large European immigrant population.

72. Peiss, *Cheap Amusements,* 131.

73. Rabinovitz, "Temptations of Pleasure," 84.

74. "Selig Resources for 'Kathlyn' Series," 20.

75. Harold MacGrath, "The Adventures of Kathlyn," part 1, *Chicago Daily Tribune,* 4 January 1914, 3.

76. Ibid.

77. Harold MacGrath, "The Adventures of Kathlyn," part 2, *Chicago Daily Tribune,* 11 January 1914, 3.

78. Ibid.

79. Rabinovitz, "Temptations of Pleasure," 84–85.

80. MacGrath, "The Adventures of Kathlyn," part 3, 3.

81. MacGrath, "The Adventures of Kathlyn," part 2, 3.

82. Peiss, *Cheap Amusements,* 8.

3.
The Hollywood Flapper and the Culture of Media Consumption

Sara Ross

Building a Culture of Media Consumption: An Audience of Flappers and Their Mothers

The role played by films and related media in the construction of a consumer culture has long been a subject of interest to film historians. Feminist historians, in particular, have explored the interaction between the media industries and producers of commodities aimed at female consumers, such as fashion items, cosmetics, and domestic goods.[1] In order to play the role in the burgeoning consumer culture that has been so clearly documented by these historians, the film industry had to concern itself first with the details of creating, legitimating, and maintaining a culture of media consumption centered on its own products. As it would in later decades, the young film industry regarded other media industries as allies in the effort to posit the popular media as the arbiters of all other types of consumption. At the heart of the film industry's participation in the construction of a consumer culture were efforts to develop media consumers, not just film by film, but for the long term as well.

The early 1920s, the period in which the film industry secured its position as a mature industry, saw the development and refinement of many of the strategies that would place media consumption at the center of the growing consumer culture. As in the 1910s, members of the film industry were particularly interested in making filmgoing an acceptable habit for their female audience.[2] The importance of ensuring women's attendance at the theater was a message often repeated in the film trades. For example, Edward T. Dustin, manager of the Pathé Branch, St. Louis, asserted in a May 1920 *Moving Picture World* article that "women and children were the first real enthusiasts, and I believe they still are the backbone of the motion picture public. . . . Men will always follow where the family leads. . . . The women and children must never be lost sight of by those who lead the industry. Kill off that clientele and you will destroy the business."[3]

In addition, the industry was sensitive to a generational split in its patrons, and considered school- and college-age youths to be a distinct and important component of its audience. For example, a *Film Daily* review of the 1922 Universal release *The Married Flapper* praised it as "the sort of material that is particularly well liked by the younger element—the 'flapper' crowd."[4] A *Moving Picture World* article on the same film described how exploitation stunts aimed at flappers would also draw in young men, "to look the girls over."[5] Many theaters held "college nights" or created other strategies to appeal specifically to college-age patrons. For example, a theater manager in Columbus staged a fashion show to promote *April Folly,* featuring "girls" from Ohio State University, in order to draw college students and "local men" to his theater.[6]

Commentary in the trade papers indicated that those involved in producing, booking, and promoting films for young audiences needed to keep in mind the attitudes of both the older and younger generations. For example, manager John Frundt of the Clermont Theater in Chicago stated in a 1922 article in *Moving Picture World* that he made decisions about whether to book a film on the basis of whether "the mothers" might approve of the film for the younger generation. According to the article, "The Clermont seats about 600, and about one-sixth of its patronage consists of young folks."[7] "I have talked over photoplays with women and have learned to judge more from their stand-point," Frundt stated. "A slight thing will often bring their voluble condemnation. I recently decided not to book a popular picture now on the market, because of the heroine's insatiable desire for cigarettes."

Another example is found in Epes Winthrop Sargent's *Moving Picture World* column "Selling the Picture to the Public," from September 1922. Sargent criticized an exhibitor whose stunt for the film *They Like 'Em Rough* involved encouraging young men to pinch the arms or pull the hair of "the flappers," while saying "they like 'em rough." "'It got to be sort of a byword amongst the young jellies and flappers,' the exhibitor boasted, causing business to 'jump way up the two days we played the picture.'"[8] Sargent countered:

> Possibly the flappers liked this unique advertising stunt, but the trouble is that the publicity was not confined to the flappers. It is more than

probable that the parents of some of these youngsters objected to the manhandling these girls received and resented the license thus offered the young men to attempt familiarities that would not be countenanced under ordinary circumstances. . . . One such action can hurt business for months. It can undo all of the good impression for which level-headed exhibitors have been striving ever since the business of picture exhibition emerged from the era of the pitch dark house. It is the pictures and not the manager personally who will be blamed.[9]

Thus the article warns that exploitation aimed at attracting young people to the theater must be palatable to their parents as well if it cannot be "confined" to the younger audience.

In this period, the film industry thus sought to preserve its hard-won acceptance among the older generation, and in particular among its audience of adult women, and at the same time to attract their daughters' social crowd to the theater.[10] To do so, they would encourage a habit of media consumption among the young while making efforts to appease the perceived fears of the older generation as to the effects of this media consumption. The effort to balance these two goals is nowhere more apparent than in the construction of the flapper character in films and film promotion in the early 1920s.

The film industry began incorporating flapper characters in films at the end of the 1910s, and the character appeared in growing numbers in the 1920s. However, the filmic flapper was not an independent and original product of 1920s Hollywood. It drew its characteristics from representations of the flapper in other media, as well as from a variety of earlier young female types both within and outside of the medium of film. The literary antecedents of the filmic flapper were represented as avid consumers of popular media, making the flapper a site of discursive struggle over what it meant for young women to have access to the modern media.[11] The flapper character's controversial status as a media consumer presented both opportunities and dangers for the film industry. The potential opportunities for the use of the flapper character were further complicated by the fact that the term *flapper* was also frequently applied to a portion of the audience, and flapper characters were said to have a special appeal for these "flapper audiences."[12] Studying the strategies developed for representing this character can therefore reveal the mechanisms through which the film industry sought to balance the perceived needs and desires of its diverse audience while advancing its own goals of building and sustaining the habit of media consumption.

In this essay, I first consider the context within which the flapper came to be represented in Hollywood films as an avid consumer of popular culture, using examples of the film flapper's literary antecedents. I then take the adaptation of the 1923 novel *Flaming Youth* into a 1924 First National film of the same name as a case study of how the film industry used the sensational aspects of the flapper character to promote media consumption by its younger patrons while at the same time attempting to protect itself from censure by older patrons and citizens groups. In the case of *Flaming Youth,* cooperation between the film and publishing industries was used both to reward ongoing media consumption and to create varying levels of knowledge that might help to "confine" certain meanings to those audience members who chose to pursue them.

Perhaps more than any other character in film, the flapper was defined through her use of consumer goods, particularly clothing and cosmetics. Throughout the 1920s, this characteristic was exploited through such familiar and straightforward strategies as product tieups and product placement. Identified as the flapper was with a variety of props and accoutrements, the character was an ideal focal point for the promotion of the myriad goods of the "cosmetic age." For example, the press book for First National's 1924 film *The Perfect Flapper* includes tieups with twelve fashion and beauty products, and asserts that "when one thinks of the flapper the accompanying idea is clothes-clothes-clothes. That's ninety percent of the flapper—clothes, fashion."[13] The advertising copy for each tied-up product made further assertions about the flapper's need for consumer goods. The press book proclaims: "No flapper can be perfect without Wonderstoen"; "Every perfect flapper essentially wears Vanity Fair"; and "Djer-Kiss and the Flapper are synonymous."[14]

At the eye of this storm of consumer goods, positioned in such a way as to mediate their use, is the film itself. The press book for *The Perfect Flapper* attempts to place media consumption at the center of all other types of consumption by claiming an all-important position of knowledge as to the correct way to use the products that are advertised. It does so through the film's star, Colleen Moore, who is labeled "America's Perfect Flapper." Exhibitors are advised to encourage young women to "compete" with Moore for the title of perfect flapper by entering the "Perfect Flapper Contest." To enter, the town's "flappers" are to be advised first to study the behavior and appearance of Moore in the film and its lobby stills. Each must then buy a "Colleen Moore Perfect Flapper Frock" and have her picture taken by a cooperating photographer in a "characteristic Colleen Moore pose."

The girl who most closely resembled Moore in each town would be eligible to win a prize.

In a similar example, in August 1922 the film *The Married Flapper* was tied in with flapper parades and reviews held in two parks in Kansas City, in which "local flappers" competed for prizes. According to *Moving Picture World*, "Taking advantage of the park's advertising, the Universal publicity representative ran letters over the signature of Marie Prevost, star in 'The Married Flapper,' advising the girls to go and see her in the picture, get pointers and then enter the contest."[15] In addition to prizes and recognition in local contests, the winning flapper, by her successful emulation of Prevost, could win a trip to Universal City and a screen test. Such flapper contests were repeated by a number of exhibitors in the early 1920s, and *Moving Picture World* advised exhibitors, "You are losing money if you do not work this stunt and play it clear across the boards and back again."[16]

These exploitation stunts and contests assumed both a high degree of familiarity with media representations of the flapper and a willingness to emulate them on the part of the "local flappers." Although it is not possible to track the behavior of the local flappers, such assumptions about this audience did have a basis in an established practice of presenting ongoing media consumption and emulation as a rewarding activity for young women. The finer points of this practice can best be understood through case studies such as the one that follows. However, in order to understand clearly the place of the flapper character in this pattern of encouraging media consumption, it is useful first to consider the background of this type.

Literary Antecedents: The Flapper as Media Consumer

The flapper made her first significant American print appearances in the mid-1910s. In that period, the flapper joined the similar character of the modern debutante as a new kind of young female character among the larger panoply of female types that populated American popular culture.[17] Once the term *flapper* was introduced, the social construction of its meaning relied on complex interactions among different popular media as well as the self-representations of young women. Although the latter are hard to trace, representations of the flapper in the popular media are more accessible.

Although the etymology of the term *flapper* can be traced back further still, H. L. Mencken appears to have introduced the term into American mass media in 1915 with his *Smart Set* essay "The Flapper."[18] In that essay, Mencken claimed that although Germany and France had words equivalent to England's "the Flapper," there was no American word for what he then dubbed the "American Flapper." The physical details of the flapper's appearance might change somewhat over the years, but one aspect of her nature as introduced by Mencken would be featured in virtually all portrayals of the character. Mencken's flapper is characterized by the dichotomy between her innocence and her knowledge. This seemingly contradictory state of affairs is made possible by her passionate and indiscriminate consumption of the modern media. As Janet Staiger has observed about Mencken's essay, "The New Woman has become the woman she is by reading newspapers, magazines, plays, novels, and nonfictional tomes. She goes to the opera. She also, apparently, occasionally sees movies."[19]

Thus the flapper's knowledge has not come from experience, according to Mencken, but from exposure to the media, especially popular novels and motion pictures. Mencken treats the flapper's embrace of the information found in these media as humorously excessive, but nevertheless charming:

> For example, she has a clear and detailed understanding of all the tricks of white slavers. . . . She is on the lookout for them in matinee lobbies and railroad stations. . . . She has a keen eye for hypodermic needles, chloroform masks, closed carriages. She has seen all these sinister machines of the devil in operation on the screen. She has read about them in the great works of Elizabeth Robins, Clifford G. Roe and Reginald Wright Kauffman. She has followed the war upon them in the newspapers.[20]

Several other features of Mencken's description of the flapper's media consumption are worth noting. First, much of the knowledge gained by Mencken's flapper relates to sexual topics. Although virginal, she has become blasé when it comes to shocking sexual revelations in the media. "She saw 'Damaged Goods,'" Mencken writes, "without batting an eye, and went away wondering what the row over it was all about. The police of her city having prohibited 'Mrs. Warren's Profession,' she read it one rainy Sunday afternoon, and found it a mass of platitudes."[21] At the heart of the flapper's contradictions, then, is the fact that she has been exposed to the sexiest material that modern culture has to offer, and yet is neither shocked nor "spoiled" by it. Mencken also suggests that the flapper has gained access to these materials despite efforts by her elders to prevent her from doing so.

Following Mencken's essay, a number of other essays and stories about flappers and/or flapperlike characters appeared in the *Smart Set*.

A central characteristic of the flapper continued to be her media-gained knowledge, a characteristic that was typically rendered as humorously excessive and indiscriminate. For example, in an August 1915 short story, "The Girl Who Read Bestsellers," Albert Payson Terhune details the problems that arise when, Hilda, a typical "girl of the period," puts too much faith in the verisimilitude of the popular novels that she has read. When her suitor's car breaks down on a lonely road, Hilda foolishly races off into the woods, believing that the well-meaning young man intends to seduce her.[22]

Thyra Samter Winslow's December 1915 short story, "Little Emma," tells a similar tale of a young woman's naive belief in the scenarios of popular fiction. The story concerns the well-read Emma Hooper, who leaves her small-town Iowa home for Chicago with the intention of catching a millionaire sugar daddy. "On the train, she figured it all out," Winslow writes. "Country girls were always important in a large city. She knew that. Didn't she read about them in the 15-cent magazines every day?"[23] After a series of failures, Emma receives aid from an experienced gold digger in becoming a more sophisticated consumer of both fashion and the media. She drops her gaudy clothes for a simpler, more elegant style and gives up musical comedies and vaudeville in favor of the drama. The result is that she catches her millionaire. In these stories, the young women in question have gone too far in basing their ideas about sexual relationships on the wrong sorts of popular media. They are therefore in need of guidance to bring their media consumption to the requisite level of sophistication.

The treatment of young women as avid and imitative consumers of popular media in the *Smart Set* is similar to discussions of the modern debutante that appeared in *Vanity Fair,* another of what George H. Douglas has labeled the "smart magazines" of the 1910s.[24] *Vanity Fair* took a slightly different approach to the deb, however, with essays that combined a larger dose of admiration with their humor. Going one step beyond the humorous portrayals of indiscriminate faith in the media offered in the *Smart Set, Vanity Fair* often explicitly presented itself as the solution for young women in need of a guide to sophisticated media consumption. For example, *Vanity Fair* editor Frank Crowinshield discussed the benefit to debutantes of reading *Vanity Fair* in a number of his "In Vanity Fair" essays in 1915 and 1916. Crowinshield placed an emphasis on providing knowledge to women in his first editorial for the magazine, in 1914, and several of his essays in the following years contained humorous self-congratulations on *Vanity Fair*'s role in young women's education.[25] They described sophisticated young debutantes and then revealed that they owed all of their sophistication, and therefore their allure, to *Vanity Fair*.

Crowinshield wrote one such essay, in January 1915, in the form of a letter from one man of society to another. The author exclaims on the way that the debutantes have taken over the fashionable world of New York:

> The other night I sat at dinner next to one of the most promising of the pack. My dear boy, I was taken off my feet. She knew everything. Alert, full of an intelligent interest in books, drama, music, golf, art, fashion, humor, dogs, sports, opera, motors, dances, sculpture, essays, restaurants, shops, and Heaven only knows what. . . . I put it down, naturally enough, to wide reading. It couldn't all come from experience; their little bodies wouldn't hold so much. Some day I am going to find out just what it is they do to learn it all.

Later in the essay, the author reveals the source of his companion's precocious knowledge:

> In the course of the evening, I must have met thirty debutantes. And, here is the oddest thing, I asked them what they read and they all assured me that they never read anything but Vanity Fair, a paper which has only been going for two winters. It appears that it is solely due to Vanity Fair—and the rage for it here—that the debutantes have ceased being simpering little idiots and have developed into able and intelligent human beings.[26]

A similar essay, from the December 1915 *Vanity Fair*, describes "three wise virgins" who embody the appeal of the "modern maiden" of 1915. They bear a close resemblance to Mencken's flapper in their contradictory character traits: "So young, so wise . . . so silly, so comprehending. So tremblingly poised upon the threshold of life and yet so versed in all its tragedies and mystery." The essay enumerates the fifteen aspects of fashionable knowledge that these young women possess, concluding with "#15. And finally they know where they have acquired all of this knowledge. And they know too that if they want to continue outwitting their sister-women . . . they have simply *got* to read Vanity Fair."[27]

The representation of the alluring debutantes in these essays as *Vanity Fair* readers thus serves as a not-so-subtle encouragement of this behavior in others. One might question whether, with their sometimes condescending tone, the essays are designed to appeal to the kind of young women they portray or to presumably more sophisticated readers who are laughing at them. Unlike the essays in the *Smart Set,* which seem to comment on the flapper from the outside only, the articles in *Vanity Fair* suggest both possibilities. Although this is a question too large to be answered completely here, the indications are that *Vanity Fair* was addressing both types of readers. Although these essays are tongue-in-cheek, this does not obviate their strategy to outline the knowledge that is desirable for a young woman aspiring to fashionability and to promote *Vanity Fair* as the source of this knowledge. The catalogs of topics mastered by the young women in several of these articles ("opera, shopping, motors"), not surprisingly, bear a striking similarity to *Vanity Fair*'s table of contents. The editorial aspects of the magazine also strongly suggest that it is attempting to appeal to the presumed desires of its readers to be stylish as well as sophisticated and ironic. For example, between February and June 1915, the magazine gave detailed descriptions of Irene Castle's latest hairstyles in several articles, only to mock the "females" that "ape Irene" in another.[28]

In addition, the address of advertising in the magazine seems to favor those readers who might wish to emulate the sophisticated debutantes and flappers to which it devotes so much editorial space. Advertisements tend not only toward gowns, hats, and perfumes, but specifically toward products aimed at younger women, including items for trousseaux and information for "the bride-elect."[29] Some advertisements take on a tone similar to that employed in descriptions of the flapper and/or debutante in the essays discussed. For example, an ad for Gouraud's Oriental Cream begins, "To the Summer Girl. Amid all your sports—dancing and continual round of pleasures you should remember one thing first—last and always—protect your dainty delicate complexion."[30] The products advertised in *Vanity Fair* thus benefit from association with the sophistication and allure that the essays explicitly promise to readers of the magazine.

Thus the *Vanity Fair* articles that insist that in order to avoid being "simpering little idiots," young women must subscribe to the magazine can be read to be at least partly intended as a straightforward pitch. The early development of the flapper character in the context of the ironic editorial style of the "smart magazines" thus contributed not only to the representation of the flapper as a media consumer, but also to the typical strategies of representation of the type. The sarcasm with which young women are discussed in *Vanity Fair* is a stylistic signature of the smart magazines, and also provides the potential for the stories to be read in multiple ways, perhaps even by the same reader. If the flapper's supposed immersion in the popular media was a source of amusement, in these essays it was also the source of her surprising allure, and therefore her power.

Stories of the flapper and other variations of the modern girl rapidly moved beyond the smart magazines into mainstream periodicals. The characterization of the young woman who gains her worldview from the media was present here as well, although it was adapted to fit the editorial style and perceived readership of each given text. An especially early, and interesting, example is found in a series of essays in the *Ladies' Home Journal* that treated girls' exposure to the media with a great deal of suspicion. If the smart magazines related the flapper's media consumption to questions of her level of cultural sophistication, the *Ladies' Home Journal* was more interested in its moral effects. From October 1915 to March 1916, the *Ladies' Home Journal* published a six-part series titled "Her Diary: The Day-to-Day Story of a Modern Girl."[31] The "diary" traces the youthful romances of a young woman named Betty, who describes herself as "dreadfully flapperish." The series shares the *Vanity Fair* strategy of appropriating the voice of the flapper to make its points about her.

Like those of her sisters in the smart magazines, Betty's initial attitudes are all informed by her consumption of novels, theater, periodicals, and motion pictures. She reads "yellow magazines" looking for scandals, and states, "Mother wouldn't let me go to those Brieux plays, but of course I heard all about them and I've been to see stacks of other plays that were about as bad, only she didn't happen to know what they were, of course."[32] She forms the intention of avoiding marriage based on novels she has read, saying that she wants to "keep up the excitement" like "Cleopatra—and Récamier—and Ninon de Lenclos—only dad took the book away from me before I found out how she finished up."[33] She also imitates her favorites from popular culture, practicing an "Irene Castle–Isadora Duncan combination polka" before her mirror, and making eyes at her beaux in imitation of Irene Castle's facial expressions. Despite their halfhearted attempts to intervene, Betty's parents, and her mother in particular, are portrayed as having allowed her too much access to popular culture.

In large part because of her unrealistic and media-influenced attitudes, Betty is initially in danger of several moral lapses, including drinking, petting, and marrying for money. For example, at one point Betty is allowed to see a play that she says "would pump life into a wooden indian," and that is directly responsible for putting her into a sexually compromising situation. "When the curtain went down tonight," she says, "I could have been crazy about anybody—and Jimmy was right there."[34] During their subsequent unchaperoned taxi ride home, Jimmy attempts to kiss Betty.

The *Ladies' Home Journal* appears either to have had some negative response to the first installment or at least to have anticipated it. An editorial in the November 1915 issue states, "Some have said of the first part of 'Her Diary': 'Why do you portray this girl? She is not worth publishing.'" The editorial goes on to urge: "Let us wait until she progresses a little in the madness of her chase for the froth. Let us suspend judgment, and after another installment or two you may see something that will not only interest you but will depict this type of girl as she really is in a great many instances. . . . Let us wait and see what account she will give of herself."[35] Not surprisingly, Betty's behavior "improves" in later installments. Her media-generated ideas begin to fall away as she interacts with men and gains more knowledge of "real life." Instead of "fun, fun, fun!" and "thrills," she begins to feel an irresistible desire for babies and a home. Finally, despite the latitude allowed by her well-meaning mother and the influence of her social-climbing aunt, Betty marries the poor man she loves in the final installment.

As with the examples from the smart magazines, the *Ladies' Home Journal* adapted the type of the media-loving flapper to its own editorial needs, addressing the perceived concerns of its readers about the effects of the modern media on girls. Adopting the flapper's voice, it created a morality play in which a girl's inherent goodness and natural desire for family life overcome the influence of her exposure to too much of the wrong kind of contemporary culture. The series also worked in a caution about the wrongheadedness of mothers who allow their daughters too much latitude in making choices about what they consume.

These are only a few early examples from a body of flapper-related fiction and nonfiction that ballooned at the end of the 1910s and the beginning of the 1920s. They serve to show, however, that the strategy of representing the flapper as an avid media consumer could be adapted to match the perceived attitudes of different audiences toward those media. The mixture of irony and admiration for the flapper in articles in the smart magazines could create a dual address to sophisticated young men and women, encouraging the "right" kind of media consumption, while cautionary tales in periodicals like the *Ladies' Home Journal* addressed the perceived concerns of older women about the materials to which their daughters were exposed. The film industry, in turn, would make its own use of the established patterns of representing the flapper as a media consumer and would exploit the type's potential for creating a dual address to the audience.

The flapper character began to make appearances in films as early as the late teens, and in 1920, the first feature film with a flapper protagonist, Selznick Pictures' Olive Thomas vehicle *The Flapper,* was produced. The film made use of many of the established conventions for representing the character. Like her literary predecessors, Thomas's flapper is characterized by her faith in the knowledge she has gained from the media.[36] The next few years found the film industry experimenting with different ways of adapting the character to its own needs, using both the titillating potential of the flapper's unconventional behavior and the potential for moralizing exhibited in the example from the *Ladies' Home Journal.*[37] The representation of both fictional flappers and the "flapper" audience as avid media consumers proved to be a neat match with the film industry's promotional strategies, which attempted to place media consumption at the heart of the larger consumer culture.

The flapper contests discussed earlier in this essay represent an example of the film industry's explicit attempts to position members of their "flapper" audience as media consumers, after the pattern of fictional flappers, by directly rewarding careful study and successful emulation of the behavior and appearance of the flappers represented within their texts. At a deeper level, however, the industry cultivated strategies that rewarded an ongoing media habit among its audience of young women. This could be done, in part, by forging ties with other media and creating a complementarity of their consumption. Associated First National's 1923 *Flaming Youth,* starring Colleen Moore, provides an example. *Flaming Youth* was adapted from the highly successful and controversial best-selling novel of the same title, published by Boni & Liveright and serialized in the *Metropolitan Magazine.*[38] In adapting the novel for film, First National made use of not only the novel's content, but also the history of its promotion and reception, creating an interplay between the two texts.

Adaptation and the Interplay of Texts:
The Production Context for *Flaming Youth,* the Novel

Flaming Youth, the novel, was released on 25 January 1923. It chronicles the escapades of the Fentriss girls, three flapper daughters of an upper-class family. The novel differs from the examples discussed above in the degree of its flapper characters' unconventionality, and it is readily apparent why it provoked controversy. In the course of the story, the girls drink, pet, and engage in premarital and extramarital sex. One of the girls has an abortion following a marital rape. The novel develops the protagonist, Pat, in particular, as a thoroughly modern heroine, who makes "Her Diary's" Betty appear utterly Victorian by comparison. Pat "necks" and drinks at an early age, has sex with the man she loves before their marriage, and proposes an experimental marriage with him. However, despite the differences between *Flaming Youth's* Pat and the *Ladies' Home Journal's* Betty, *Flaming Youth* does have several narrative strategies for portraying the flapper in common with "Her Diary." Like Betty, Pat is meant to be an appealing heroine. She hides an "innocent" nature behind her unconventional behavior, and she ultimately relinquishes her modern ideas in favor of conventional marriage, introducing a moral lesson to the end of her story. In addition, like "Her Diary," the novel provides a position of moral superiority from which the behavior of the flappers can be observed, in the form of the character of Dr. Osterhaut.

Dr. Osterhaut, a friend of the Fentriss family, is charged by the girls' dying mother to look after them, and he provides periodic commentary on the activities of the girls. For example, in a letter describing Pat, he writes that she is "keen on" the "latest books of the day," and "any book spoken of under the breath." "She considers *Town Topics* an important chronicle," he states, "and *Vanity Fair* a symposium of pure intellect." Furthermore, he complains, "she would doubtless identify Lister as one who achieved fame by inventing a mouth wash. . . . But to be found ignorant of the most recent trend of the movies or the names of their heroes, or not to know the latest gag of some unspeakable vulgarian of the revues—that would overwhelm her with shame."[39] Thus, as with the earlier examples, the attitudes and choices of the novel's young characters are shown to be influenced by their exposure to the media. In addition, an outside voice provides ironic commentary on the flapper's interest in the popular media.

Publicity about the novel, as well as its formal strategies, emphasizes that Dr. Osterhaut functions as a discursive stand-in for the author, and therefore as an outside observer of the flappers' behavior. For example, in the foreword to the novel, the author states:

> Men understand women only as women choose to have them, with one exception, the family physician. He knows. He sees through the body to the soul. But he may not tell what he sees. Professional honour binds him. Only through the unaccustomed medium of fiction and out of the vatic incense-cloud of pseudonymity may he speak the

truth. Being a physician, I must conceal my identity, and, not less securely, the identity of those whom I picture.[40]

The doctor thus frames the novel's shocking events with the authority, and mildly suggested condemnation, of a medical professional, although the writer of *Flaming Youth* was in fact the author Samuel Hopkins Adams, writing under the pseudonym of Warner Fabian.

The combination of an ultimately sympathetic portrayal of Pat's behavior, within the framing fiction of a family doctor who writes a condemning exposé of the flapper, can be seen as a specific strategy to exploit the most sensational aspects of flapper behavior while shielding the novel from condemnation as much as possible. Like the examples from *Vanity Fair*, this strategy positions the text so that it can easily be read in different ways by different readers. It provides potential reading positions of both identification with the girl's rebellious behavior and moral superiority for those who focus on the doctor's attitude in their reading of the novel.

This strategy of providing different possible reading positions with relation to the novel's controversial content was also present in the promotion of *Flaming Youth* by its publisher. B&L was a new and maverick publishing house, and its policies were dominated by co-founder Horace Liveright. Liveright actively sought out and published unconventional and cutting-edge material, from controversial works of nonfiction by authors such as Freud and Trotsky to the modernist literature of James Joyce and T. S. Eliot, to racy best-sellers such as Gertrude Atherton's *Black Oxen* and Fabian's (Adams's) *Flaming Youth*. The latter two novels both capitalized on the sensational potential of the flapper character.[41]

The association of the flapper character with a complex mixture of sensationalism, modernity, social commentary, and highbrow "literature" was a good fit with B&L's distribution strategies. High on the list was the potential for sensation connected with discussions of the flapper character. The main ingredients that all B&L titles seemed to share were the quality of sensationalism and the ability to provoke controversy. These ingredients had to be carefully balanced for the works to provoke interest without being too heavily censored. Censorship was a constant threat for B&L's titles, whether due to the explicit sexual content of best-sellers and works of psychology or due to the political content of work like Trotsky's.[42] Controversy was not merely a problem faced by B&L, however; it was a built-in element of the publisher's promotional strategy.

B&L capitalized on the notoriety that came from attempts to censor its books by incorporating controversy into its marketing plans—for example, by including the condemnations of censors in its ads.[43] Although selling books or other printed matter on the basis of controversy was not a new tactic, Liveright made an art of such tactics. In the promotional campaign for *Flaming Youth,* B&L ran numerous advertisements in *Publishers Weekly* along the lines of the following ad from 10 February 1923. The ad gives a list of the shocking attributes laid at the door of modern women by *Flaming Youth*:

> Flaming Youth intimately portrays the woman of today—restless, seductive, greedy, discontented, craving sensation, unrestrained, more than a little selfish, intelligent, uneducated, sybaritic, following blind instincts, slack of mind, trim of body, neurotic, vigorous, a worshipper of tinsel gods at perfumed altars.
>
> Everyone is asking, WHO IS WARNER FABIAN who thus indicts woman? . . . We repeat, WHO IS WARNER FABIAN, that has startled the book world by writing another best seller?[44]

This campaign posed the author of the book as the center of mystery and controversy. The strategy therefore provided a sense of the risqué nature of the book while retaining a focus on the author as a salable commodity that was typical of the publishing industry. In addition, this strategy allowed the ad text to bring up the sensational content of the book under the guise of presenting the author's indictment of modern women. The creation of the author character, Warner Fabian, and the effort to pose him as the center of controversy, due to this "indictment," can be seen as an attempt to divert controversy from a more likely focal point, namely, the shocking content of the book.

Thus the Warner Fabian character discussed in publicity for the book, like Dr. Osterhaut in the novel, places the content within an authoritative frame, an effect that is more pronounced in the advertising text. This promotional strategy might serve to create a thin veneer over the sensational nature of the novel while still alluding to it obliquely. The strategy may not have provided much in the way of practical protection against censorship, as the book was brought into court in several communities. However, it did give a rhetorical justification for the book's sensational content, which may have contributed to its general acceptance.

Boni & Liveright was also on the cutting edge of other new trends in promotion and exploitation within the publishing industry. Among its exploitation strategies, B&L expanded on the traditional arena of advertising in periodicals, using tactics that were described as "vulgar" by other publishing houses, including a heavier concentration of ads and a more overt, emphatic rhetorical style in its ad text.[45] B&L also moved its ads out of traditional venues, putting up giant billboards in urban locations.[46] In addition, B&L became the first publishing house to hire a specialist in the new field of public relations in 1920, when it retained the services of Edward Bernays, described as the "founding father" of public relations.[47] Bernays helped the firm develop such strategies as making book releases into media "events" and getting movie stars to comment on its titles. B&L subsequently generated publicity not only about its titles, but about the house as a whole, and about Liveright himself.

B&L was also actively involved in the trend toward greater cooperation with the film industry, hiring Manuel Komroff, a former critic for *Film Daily,* as head of the production department, instituting tie-ins with stars and gaining prominent product placement of B&L's books in films and film publicity.[48] For example, in the film version of *Flaming Youth,* Colleen Moore, as Pat, is seen reading a prominently displayed copy of the B&L title *Black Oxen* in one scene. Clara Bow's flapper character in *Black Oxen* is in turn shown reading *Flaming Youth,* and later clutches it defiantly to her chest as she comes under attack from her staid grandmother. At this overt level, then, the representation of the flapper as a consumer of sensational media could be translated into mutual product placement between novels and their film adaptations.

However, the interaction of the novel and film versions of *Flaming Youth* went beyond product placement and a presold title. Although many of the more sensational aspects of the novel were removed in the film version, including the abortion subplot, this did not mean that they would necessarily disappear from the consciousness of the audience. The reputation of the sensational best-seller would have been known to a large part of the film's audience. As one review stated, "With this title and the word-of-mouth discussion that has developed around a racy book of this type, you certainly can figure on plenty of business with this."[49] The audience's knowledge might also be supplemented by familiarity with the broader reputation of B&L.

Furthermore, strategies used for *Flaming Youth,* at the levels of both film content and style and marketing, encouraged some audience members to call upon associations with the racier novel. The film and its surrounding promotion thus provided reading positions that could reward viewers who were familiar with the novel, or with other texts that portrayed the activities of the flapper set, by playing on associations that were not present in the film text alone. First National therefore positioned the film as part of a larger media culture that rewarded ongoing consumption on the part of segments of the audience. Others might remain happily unaware of some of the film's racier associations, or a least unable to point their fingers at any specific problem with the film. Although promotion for the film did not openly solicit emulation of the media, as did some of the films mentioned above, the strategies used to present *Flaming Youth* demonstrate the subtle but persistent encouragement of media consumption that was an integral part of the film industry's construction of the flapper character.

"It Is Not as Bad as the Book, but People Think It Will Be": *Flaming Youth*, Sensation Seekers, and the "Shocking Angle"

Like the novel, the film version of *Flaming Youth* was a great financial success, finding its way onto three out of six distributors' lists of the "10 Best Box Office Titles of 1923," as reported in *Film Daily Yearbook*.[50] The film put the story through the familiar process of condensation necessary when a novel is made into a feature film, restricting the focus primarily to Pat and cutting out the darker subplots.[51] The most startling transgressions are eliminated from explicit representation in the story. However, Pat is still described in the studio's synopsis as "notorious in her set because of her promiscuity," and she refuses Scott's first offer of marriage on the grounds that it "will spoil romance." The synopsis also demonstrates the producers' desire to retain the full implications of Pat's near relationship with a bohemian musician, Leo, stating, "He asks all that love implies without marriage."[52] In addition, despite avoiding explicit representation of some the novel's more daring subplots, the film version implicitly invokes them in ways that would be legible to those audience members who were familiar with the novel or other flapper-related texts.

As in the earlier portrayals of the flapper described above, Pat's rebellious behavior in the film version of *Flaming Youth* includes consumption of risqué popular texts, such as B&L's *Black Oxen*. The *Wid's Weekly* review noted that the film "registered a very good ad for another First National picture, 'Black Oxen,' when Colleen was shown virtually 'eating it up.'"[53] Audience members familiar with the daring reputation of both texts could thus gain the added pleasure of being "in the know" during this scene, a pleasure that might be further enhanced if they noticed the reciprocating scenes of Bow reading the novel *Flaming Youth* in the film *Black Oxen*.[54]

Another scene that calls on associations with the racier novel is the "skinny-dipping" scene. The novel's version of the scene, in which one of the flapper sisters swims naked with a group of men and women, and runs into her dismayed suitor while still in the buff, was the most notorious of its many shocking incidents, and led to many imitations in later flapper stories. Although the explicit details of the episode are absent from the film version, this scene is given great stylistic emphasis as an extravagant number. The picture title that opens the scene shows figures in silhouette jumping into a pool. For audience members who were aware of the scene in the novel, the title might serve as something of a tease. The title proclaims the scene "The dedication of Mr. and Mrs. T. Jameson James' new swimming pool" and, in a smaller font, states, "Motto for the evening: Water, water everywhere, but not a drop (of it) to drink."

Although the title lets the audience know that the skinny-dipping scene is coming, the coed swimming party does not immediately follow its representation in the picture title. Instead, earlier events from the lavish, drunken pool party are portrayed. The revelry escalates until, at the end of the scene, a young man says, "I vote to light up the swimming pool and take a plunge—any way we like!" At this point, Colleen Moore's Pat asks her companion to take her home, so that her character is not present for the actual skinny-dipping. The following highly stylized scene, like the picture title, is shown in silhouette and from a distance, as the partyers are dimly seen casting aside clothes and leaping or throwing each other into the pool, all the while dancing wildly. Due to the style of shooting, it would be quite possible that a viewer unfamiliar with the content of the novel might not realize the full implications of coed nudity in the scene. These scenes therefore offered the possibility of a slightly different reading position for those viewers who familiarized themselves with other flapper texts, including the novel *Flaming Youth*.

This strategy of encouraging different reading positions operates to a much more obvious degree at the level of the promotion of the film by individual exhibitors. Strategies for the exploitation of the film, in some cases, were more explicit in encouraging viewers to call on a wider set of associations, including the "bad" reputation of the novel, whereas in other cases these associations were played down. It is therefore at the level of exhibition that the full flexibility of strategies for the film can be best understood.

As Richard Koszarski has pointed out, during this period, "exhibitors considered themselves showmen, not film programmers." They relied on the feature as only part of the total "attraction."[55] Exhibitors added to the film layers of their own material, including not only music and stage shows, but also publicity in the forms of advertising, tieups, and ballyhoo. These other elements contributed to the total package of *Flaming Youth* as it was presented to the public. In promoting *Flaming Youth,* exhibitors might capitalize on the reputation of the novel and cooperate with booksellers to encourage and reward viewers who were seeking a thrill and were "in the know" with regard to current pop culture texts. At the same time, because the content of the film was not as "bad" as the book, they were somewhat shielded from the criticism of censors and citizens' groups.

The signature image used to promote *Flaming Youth* was a variation on the famous skinny-dipping incident, translated as a nude, silhouetted female figure taking the plunge. Exhibitors made their own decisions as to how, or even whether, to use this racy image. Some exploited the image for all it was worth. For example, the manager of the Metropolitan Theater in Atlanta put up a 17-by-35-foot sign with the nude silhouette, in black against a red and yellow ground, and reported long queues due to the fact that "a lot of people thought it was a scene from the play."[56] The Majestic Theater in Lacrosse, Wisconsin, opted against using the nude figure altogether. Nevertheless, the theater attempted in its own way to create links between the film and flapper culture. It used a truck bearing figures from the film holding balloons, "supposed to be the last word at jazz parties."[57] Other exhibitors keyed their use of publicity to specific audiences. For example, the Olympia Theater in Boston flew a banner for the film over two college football games in the week before it opened.[58]

Other exploitation strategies called more explicitly for audiences to create associations through knowledge of the book. As reported in *Moving Picture World,* the Strand Theater in Milwaukee placed a large book against the box-office rail, with the advice "not to open the book and read page 305 unless a shock was desired." *Moving Picture World* continued, "Of course there was no page 305 in the display and the curious had to hurry off to some book store and get a copy of the story and having gone to all that trouble, most of them were firmly sold on the idea of seeing the play on the screen as well." On page 305 of the initial edition of the novel, Pat tells Dr. Osterhaut that she has had sex with her suitor, and she is not sorry about it. The *Moving Picture World* article advised that exhibitors should consider carefully whether this "'shocking' angle" was best for their houses, but added that it would be sure to sell tickets. Furthermore, it stated, it would "put you in good with the book handlers, and that is a desirable end that will last past this picture, since you will desire other hook-ups."[59]

An exploitation manager in Orlando, Florida, further described the role of audience awareness of the reputation of the novel in bringing in the best business of the season for the film. He stated that "Flaming Youth is a wonderful box office attraction if advertised truthfully. It is not as bad as the book, but people think it will be, so advertise it that way and they will come and the picture is good enough to send them away satisfied."[60] *Moving Picture World* added, "In other words, the sensation seekers will think that the statement that the story has been modified is camouflage and will come, but the manager has his fingers crossed and they can't kick." Far from disappointing the audience, the story reported that the theater "got all the money they could hold, and manager H. B. Vincent did not have a kick."[61] These examples show the elaborate nature of the strategies employed by various exhibitors to tailor their exploitation campaigns to create a suggestive atmosphere for the film that rewarded the efforts of "sensation seekers" to see through the camouflage and make associations between the film and the racier novel.

"A Warning to Flappers": *Flaming Youth* and the Moral Lesson

Exhibitors might seek to appeal to sensation seekers in their campaigns for *Flaming Youth,* but they also had to concern themselves with the potential for local censorship or negative reactions from the community. Whereas film industry sources were cautious about identifying who the sensation seekers they referred to might be, other groups expressed no doubts that the film was intended to appeal to young people. For example, an Associated Press article picked up by the New Brunswick, New Jersey, *Home News* reported: "Showing of the motion picture, 'Flaming Youth,' starring Colleen Moore, at a local theatre has provoked a storm of protest. Members of the Women's Club here were given a private showing of the film last night prior to its public exhibition today and declared that 'it is not a fit picture for young people to see.'" The article further reports that "Mayor Spencer Baldwin also attended the private showing last night at the request of the women but said he could see nothing wrong. 'It is just what goes on in every day life,' he said. He refused to heed the women's request that permission to show the picture be refused."[62] Censors in Seattle reportedly did not share Mayor Baldwin's opinion. A *New York Telegraph* article reported that, on a warrant signed by George Bouckaert, chairman of the Seattle Board of Theatre Censors, Seattle theater manager Leroy V.

Johnson was arrested on a charge of "exhibiting a motion picture of objectionable nature" for showing the film.[63]

In the face of this kind of objection to the film, exhibitors tried various strategies to smooth the path for their showings of *Flaming Youth*. Given this context of community responses, many of these efforts appear to have been designed not so much to sell tickets directly as to assuage the fears of members of the community about allowing their daughters, in particular, to attend the film. For example, the Latchis Theater in Keene, Vermont, took an approach that relied on a strategy similar to the novel's use of the family doctor as a voice of authority and condemnation. It ran an ad stating that city officials found the film to be of moral benefit and included in the text of the ad a doctor's "Warning to Flappers."[64]

Another exhibitor published ads that contained reassurances that the film had a good moral lesson, but still included hints that it had some titillating incidents. *Moving Picture World* reported that the Isis Theater in Houston, Texas, ran advance screenings of the film for censors and citizens' groups. It then incorporated the comments of the censors into advertisements for the film, just as B&L often did in its book campaigns. Reportedly, "the censors saw nothing objectionable in the picture, since they looked for the lesson, but the head of a local society said it was naughty-naughty, since he saw only the incidents. The theater paralleled the opinions in the newspaper advertising and left it to the public."[65] Thus the public could be made aware that the film had some titillating "incidents" while at the same time receiving reassurance of the morality of its "lesson."

Exhibitors thus walked a precarious line when they booked a film such as *Flaming Youth*. Although the film version of such a novel by necessity eliminated the most shocking incidents, a successful exhibition strategy could satisfy young sensation seekers, their parents, and the censors by attempting to provide different levels of meaning for different audiences. The sensation seekers could be encouraged to draw upon the context of their ongoing media consumption to extrapolate upon what was on the screen and the marquee, and thus be rewarded with the feeling of being "in the know." At the same time, if parents and censors were not as aware of such associations, they might be appeased by the absence of extreme incidents and by the moral lesson that the film provided in the end.

The details of the promotional campaign for *Flaming Youth* demonstrate the complexity of the efforts made by various agents of the film industry when incorporating the flapper character into film industry practices. The association of the character with avid media consumption meant that portrayals of flappers opened up myriad opportunities for encouraging media consumption on the part of film audiences. However, for the film industry to succeed in its long-term plans to build a culture of media consumption among its younger viewers, it had to consider the fears of the older generation about the impact that participation in such a culture would have on their children, particularly their daughters. The flapper character served as a focal point of negotiations over the meaning of young women's consumption of films and other media.

The challenge before the film industry was to portray media consumption as an activity in which it was both desirable and acceptable for young women to engage. Although *Flaming Youth* may not have met these goals perfectly, the film's box-office success ensured that its strategies for representing the flapper and for encouraging media consumption would have an impact on the many flapper films that came after. The film industry's central role in developing the consumer culture of later decades was founded upon the success of such strategies.

Notes

1. See, for example, Charlotte Cornelia Herzog and Jane Marie Gaines, "Puffed Sleeves before Tea-Time: Joan Crawford, Adrian and Women Audiences," *Wide Angle* 6, no. 2 (1985): 24–33; Hilary Radner, *Shopping Around: Feminine Culture and the Pursuit of Pleasure* (London: Routledge, 1995); Jane Gaines and Charlotte Herzog, eds., *Fabrications: Costume and the Female Body* (London: Routledge, 1990); and Jane Gaines and Michael Renov, eds., "Female Representation and Consumer Culture" (special issue), *Quarterly Review of Film and Video* 11, no. 1 (1989). Lynn Spigel and Denise Mann, in "Women and Consumer Culture: A Selective Bibliography," *Quarterly Review of Film and Video,* 11, no. 1 (1989), provide numerous further citations on this general topic.

2. Shelley Stamp Lindsey discusses the industry's interest in attracting and keeping female patrons in the 1910s in "The Women in the Audience: Addressing Female Movie Patrons in the Transitional Era" (paper presented at the annual meeting of the Society for Cinema Studies, Dallas, March 1996). See also Shelley Stamp Lindsey, "Screening Spaces: Women and Motion Pictures in America, 1908–1917" (Ph.D. diss., New York University, 1993).

3. "The First Big Theater Show and Some Lessons to Be Learned from It," *Moving Picture World,* 1 May 1920, 710.

4. *Film Daily* review of *The Married Flapper,* as cited in *Moving Picture World,* 14 October 1922, 595.

5. "'A Married Flapper' Plenty of Publicity," *Moving Picture World,* 1 September 1922, 45.

6. "Still Another New Angle to Popular Fashion Show," *Moving Picture World,* 24 April 1924, 570.

7. Mary Kelly, "Around Chicago Picture Theatres: Clermont Has Clean Policy; Bookings Please the Mothers," *Moving Picture World,* 17 April 1922, 427.

8. Quoted in Epes Winthrop Sargent, "Selling the Picture to the Public: Sometimes

a Stunt That Sells Seats Will Eventually React against the House," *Moving Picture World,* 30 September 1922, 381.

9. Ibid. A further example can be found in an article in which Charleston Theater manager F. M. Francis complained about the inclusion of the word *jazz* in film titles such as *Children of Jazz* and *Jazzmania.* Such titles, he stated, lead to embarrassment when mothers call up to ask about the show before allowing their children to attend. "More about Jazzy Titles, This Time from an Exhibitor," *Moving Picture World,* 10 March 1923, 152.

10. A further discussion of the film industry's negotiation of the perceived tastes of younger and older female viewers will appear in my forthcoming dissertation, "The Hollywood Flapper, 1920–1932" (University of Wisconsin–Madison).

11. The characterization of flappers as passionate and indiscriminate consumers of the media is of course itself a new variation on the long-existing strategy of representing young women as humorously media obsessed. See, for example, Catherine Morland, the gothic-novel-loving heroine of Jane Austen's *Northanger Abbey* (1818). Literary types too numerous to mention must therefore be seen to be among the flapper's antecedents. More proximate antecedents can be found among the film versions of such young female types as the baby vamp, the bohemian, the feminist, the madcap, and the butterfly. For further discussion of both literary and filmic antecedents of the flapper, see ibid.

12. Examples in which the flapper on film and the flapper in the audience were conflated in industry rhetoric can be noted in the examples drawn from the films *The Married Flapper, The Perfect Flapper,* and *Flaming Youth* presented later in this essay. Another example is provided by an ad in *Moving Picture World,* 16 September 1922, for *Wildness of Youth,* a 1922 film from 20th Century, which proclaimed, "The Great American Flapper can now see herself! . . . Read the title and take a guess how many young people will dare to stay away!" (160).

13. "National Tie-Up Section," *Exhibitor's Trade Review* (Associated First National Pictures), 24 May 1924, in the collection of the Margaret Herrick Library, Academy of Motion Picture Arts and Sciences, Los Angeles.

14. Ibid.

15. "'A Married Flapper' Plenty of Publicity," 45.

16. "Flapper Contest Is Expanded in Prizes," *Moving Picture World,* 30 September 1922. The article describes how "Paramounteers" used the stunt at several Paramount theaters in Colorado.

17. For discussion of the proliferation of female types between 1876 and 1918, see Martha Banta, *Imaging American Women: Idea and Ideals in Cultural History* (New York: Columbia University Press, 1987).

18. H. L. Mencken, "The Flapper," *Smart Set,* February 1915.

19. Janet Staiger, *Bad Women: Regulating Sexuality in Early American Cinema* (Minneapolis: University of Minnesota Press, 1995), 3.

20. Mencken, "The Flapper," 1.

21. Ibid., 2.

22. Albert Payson Terhune, "The Girl Who Read Bestsellers," *Smart Set,* August 1915.

23. Thyra Samter Winslow, "Little Emma," *Smart Set,* December 1915, 36.

24. Douglas includes the *Smart Set, Vanity Fair, New Yorker, Life,* and *Esquire* in this category of magazines that "struck a neat balance between the older highbrow magazines such as *Harper's Monthly* and *Atlantic,* on the one hand, and the mass-circulation giants on the other." George H. Douglas, *The Smart Magazines* (Hamden, Conn.: Archon, 1991), 11.

25. In his first "In Vanity Fair" column, in March 1914, Crowinshield declared: "For women, we intend to do something in a noble and missionary spirit, something which, so far as we can observe, has never before been done for them by an American

magazine. We mean to make frequent appeal to their intellects. We dare to believe that they are, in their best moments, creatures of some cerebral activity . . . and we hereby announce ourselves as determined and bigoted feminists." Frank Crowinshield, "In Vanity Fair," *Vanity Fair,* March 1914, 24.

26. Frank Crowinshield, "A Word about Debutantes," *Vanity Fair,* January 1915, 15.

27. "The Fable of the Three Wise Virgins," *Vanity Fair,* December 1915, 33.

28. "Mrs. Vernon Castle, and Her New White Wig," *Vanity Fair,* March 1915, 22; "Told in the Boudoir," *Vanity Fair,* February 1915, 74; "To the Vernon Castles," *Vanity Fair,* June 1915, 52.

29. See, for example, advertisements for Anna B. McCullough Gowns and Blouses and La Boheme Toilet Water, *Vanity Fair,* March 1916, 126; Morehead and Jardine and Co. Hats, *Vanity Fair,* March 1915, 82; and Haas Brothers Distinctive Dress Fabrics, *Vanity Fair,* February 1915, 74. See also advertisements for McGibbon and Co. Linens for Trousseaux, *Vanity Fair,* April 1915, 86; and Dean's Wedding Suggestions for the Bride-Elect, *Vanity Fair,* March 1915, 82, and April 1915, 86.

30. Advertisement for Gouraud's Oriental Cream, *Vanity Fair,* July 1915, 83.

31. "Her Diary: The Day-to-Day Story of a Modern Girl. Number I: The Hour of Her Debut," *Ladies' Home Journal,* October 1915; "Number II: The Hour of Thrills," *Ladies' Home Journal,* November 1915; "Number III: The Hour of Dreams," *Ladies' Home Journal,* December 1915; "Number IV: The Hour of Doubt," *Ladies' Home Journal,* January 1916; "Number V: The Hour of Decision," *Ladies' Home Journal,* February 1916; "Number VI: The Hour Divine," *Ladies' Home Journal,* March 1916.

32. "Her Diary. Number I," 16. This excerpt raises the problem of the proliferation of "bad" popular culture beyond the monitoring ability of parents.

33. Ibid.

34. "Her Diary. Number III," 18.

35. Editorial, *Ladies' Home Journal,* November 1915, 9.

36. For example, finding herself alone in a big city, Thomas's character, Genevieve King, drops her handkerchief. The intertitle supplies the information: "She had read of a girl meeting a prince by doing this." Genevieve is surprised when, instead of a prince, she meets a wolf.

37. For further discussion of the film industry's development of the flapper during these years, see Ross, "The Hollywood Flapper."

38. *Flaming Youth* had sold in excess of one hundred thousand copies by the first anniversary of its release, according to Boni & Liveright (B&L) advertising, and had gone through sixteen editions. Advertisement for *Flaming Youth, New York Times Book Review,* 2 March 1924, 20. The novel appeared on the best-seller list in *Publishers Weekly* for several months in 1923.

39. Warner Fabian, *Flaming Youth* (New York: Boni & Liveright, 1923), 128.

40. Warner Fabian, "A Word from the Writer to the Reader," in *Flaming Youth.*

41. Although *Black Oxen*'s sensational central issue is the "rejuvenation" of its heroine, it also introduces a flapper character as her foil.

42. For further discussion of B&L's policies, see Tom Dardis, *Firebrand: The Life of Horace Liveright* (New York: Random House, 1995).

43. See, for example, Dardis's discussion of B&L's handling of the work of Trotsky in ibid., chap. 3.

44. Boni & Liveright advertisement for *Flaming Youth, Publisher's Weekly,* 10 February 1923, 378–79.

45. See Dardis, *Firebrand,* 94. In a typical example, a B&L ad in the 10 February 1924 *New York Times Book Review* carried the headline "Must Books!" with eleven large exclamation points.

46. See, for example, the discussion of the campaign for Emil Ludwig's surprise best-seller, *Napoleon,* in Dardis, *Firebrand,* 150.

47. Ibid., 119–22.

48. Ibid., 137.

49. Review of *Flaming Youth*, source unknown, in Colleen Moore Scrapbook 2, Margaret Herrick Library, Academy of Motion Picture Arts and Sciences, Los Angeles.

50. "10 Best Box Office Titles of 1923," *Film Daily Yearbook* (New York: Film Daily, 1923), 499.

51. I have located only a fragmentary print of the film, on which I base my descriptions of the film's style. Other comments on the film's content are based on the First National synopsis submitted for copyright purposes to the Library of Congress and on reviews of the film, as noted.

52. Synopsis, *Flaming Youth*, First National Pictures, 1924, Library of Congress.

53. Review of *Flaming Youth*, Colleen Moore Scrapbook 2.

54. Images of Moore and Bow reading *Black Oxen* and *Flaming Youth*, respectively, were also the subjects of numerous publicity stills for the films.

55. Richard Koszarski, *An Evening's Entertainment: The Age of the Silent Feature Picture, 1915–1928* (New York: Charles Scribner's Sons, 1990), 9.

56. "Colleen Moore Was Atlanta Ballyhoo," *Moving Picture World,* 5 January 1924, 47.

57. "Painted Players Given Balloons," *Moving Picture World,* 9 January 1924, 481.

58. "Flaming Youth Was Oversold in Boston," *Moving Picture World,* 12 January 1924, 126.

59. "A Curiosity Angle Sold Flaming Youth," *Moving Picture World,* 12 January 1924, 128.

60. Quoted in "Made Season Record with Flaming Youth," *Moving Picture World,* 5 January 1924, 49.

61. Ibid.

62. "Hackensack Women Oppose Film, but Mayor Permits It." *Home News* (New Brunswick, N.J.), 17 January 1924, in Colleen Moore Scrapbook 3, Margaret Herrick Library, Academy of Motion Picture Arts and Sciences, Los Angeles.

63. "Seattle Censors File in 'Flaming Youth Act,'" *New York Telegraph*, 2 March 1924, in Colleen Moore Scrapbook 3, Margaret Herrick Library, Academy of Motion Picture Arts and Sciences, Los Angeles.

64. "Clubs Attempt to Stop Big Feature by Advance Showing to the Officials," *Moving Picture World,* 15 March 1924.

65. "Opposed to Censor; He Sold the Play," *Moving Picture World,* 15 March 1924, 208.

4.

Hollywood in the 1920s: Youth Must Be Served

Cynthia Felando

"Youth is in the saddle and must be sold first."[1] Starting in the early 1920s, this edict was issued with such frequency that eventually it became a taken-for-granted part of the popular wisdom. Indeed, during the 1920s, youth was visible in American popular culture as never before, as both a commodity to be sold and a demographic market to be sold to. American industries eagerly took steps to recognize and to construct a distinct youth market, and the popular media did the same. As one shrewd observer noted: "Manufacturers definitely cater to youth. . . . they not only design what they know will appeal to young men and women but they also make these articles well within their financial reach."[2] But perhaps no industry was more committed to developing a youth market than Hollywood. *Photoplay* suggested the scope of the preoccupation: "There's a new spirit abroad in Hollywood and youth is its slogan."[3]

Although young people had been a part of the audience from the earliest days of the cinema, it was not until the early 1920s that Hollywood explicitly acknowledged and addressed them. In this essay, I examine the role the movie industry played in this far-reaching transformation of American culture by providing a historical analysis of the emergence of Hollywood's hugely successful cultivation of "youth" as a key consumer category.[4] In addition, I explore the role that Hollywood played in constructing the first American youth culture and the process whereby young people shifted their primary identification from family and elders to other youths. An assortment of primary documents from the 1920s, including trade papers, fanzines, and other popular magazines, offers striking evidence about the origins of Hollywood's axiom that to "serve" the sizable youth market, it was necessary to "picture" youth. I preface this discussion with an explanation of the term *youth* and a review of the fascination with the subject in popular culture, so as to help sketch a discursive milieu that will illustrate how the most prominent themes associated with 1920s youth culture were uniquely inflected in Hollywood's own discourses.

The American film industry's address to immigrant audiences, working-class audiences, and female audiences during the silent period has been well documented by film historians, although, for the most part, the sizable youth audience during this era has been overlooked.[5] Since the mid-1980s, film scholars generally have identified the 1950s as the time when Hollywood undertook its earliest attempts to identify and address a youth audience strategically; however, there is impressive evidence that the film industry had mapped this territory decades earlier. Perhaps the most influential film history to address the relationship between Hollywood and youth is Thomas Doherty's *Teenagers and Teenpics: The Juvenilization of American Movies in the 1950s,* which, in addition to a remarkably trenchant discussion of teen movies and the industry's attention to "teenagers," offers some widely accepted although ultimately untenable claims. Doherty argues, for example, that "prior to 1956, there was no industrywide consensus on the vital importance of the teenage market, much less an earnest assault on it," because "not until the 1950s did it become unmistakably clear that the movies were *disproportionately* a juvenile medium."[6] To support his thesis that Hollywood first undertook a "courtship of the teenage audience" in the 1950s, Doherty quotes from Edgar Dale's *Children's Attendance at Motion Pictures,* one of the conservative, reform-oriented Payne Fund Studies reports, which claimed that "the effect of motion pictures is, therefore, universal."[7] According to Doherty, Dale's conclusion was intended to mean that the "movies affect the young *in equal measure* to other groups."[8] Thus Doherty concludes that prior to the 1950s the film industry conceived of its audience as heterogeneous and multigenerational, as a vague "public," and, furthermore, that movies were specifically designed to be a "universal entertainment"—for the whole family.[9] However, to rely upon an "effects"-oriented social science source to support claims about Hollywood's institutional goals in the 1920s is questionable. In other words, the Payne Fund researchers' endeavor to determine the differential *effects* of movies upon spectators is conflated with the thesis that the industry's intended *address* was to an undifferentiated audience. However, it should be noted that Doherty's focus is upon "teenagers" specifically, whereas in the 1920s, *youth* was a slightly more general term that included high school– and college-aged people. As Doherty notes, the term *teenager* emerged after the 1920s and was meant to refer to those in their "-teen" years. Yet the argument that Hollywood for the first time in the 1950s was keen to address a preadult audience remains problematic. Film scholar Jon Lewis has offered a rather similar argument: "The astonishing emergence of youth culture after the Second World War . . . prompted an immediate response from the burgeoning postwar consumer-leisure industry. Just as sociologists and cultural historians began talking about the phenomenon of youth culture, the advertising . . . and movie industries took aim at this new target market."[10]

The notion that the 1950s constituted the crucial period in terms of Hollywood's efforts to identify and address a youth market can be revised through a demonstration that it was in the early 1920s that the film industry first started to speak about the profitability of appealing to youth in the audience by depicting youth onscreen. As *Photoplay* observed in 1927, "The motion picture industry deals essentially in commodities and its greatest commodity today is youth."[11]

The Emergence of "Youth"

As early as the 1890s, both popular and scientific commentary used the term *youth* to designate a discrete period of life between "childhood" and "adulthood." In contrast, during the nineteenth century, *childhood, youth,* and *young people* were interchangeable terms that referred to people up to eighteen or twenty-one years old.[12] Furthermore, definitions of youth were gendered: whereas men up to forty-five years old could be described as young, for women youth was said to end with marriage or by the early twenties.[13] After the turn of the century, however, although *youth* was a well-worn and elastic term, it had acquired significant new connotations. By the late 1910s and early 1920s, commentary about the "younger generation" had reached a near-fever pitch, and young people were relentlessly scrutinized by a broad range of emergent professionals, from social scientists and social workers to motion picture producers and exhibitors.[14]

As British cultural scholar Mica Nava has demonstrated, definitions of youth are "neither constant nor coherent" in any given historical period, but instead are characterized by shifting and sometimes contradictory opinions. Thus there is no agreement among social institutions about which age group definitively constitutes "youth," and young people are contradictorily described as the mainstay of industries such as music and fashion and, alternately, as in need of supervision and control—a characterization that is germane to an understanding of the relationship between youth and Hollywood during the

1920s.[15] Nevertheless, in general terms, by the 1920s youth was understood as a period of life marked by biological events at its beginning
and by social events at its end, for both males and females. As one observer argued: "The period of youth . . . extends roughly from the beginning of adolescence to the onset of maturity when the individual
settles down to business and home responsibilities."[16] Prior to the
1910s and 1920s, the young people who were defined as socially problematic and who were most closely monitored in popular and scientific
discourses were those from outside the white middle class; they included
poor and adolescent immigrants, "juvenile delinquents," and young female prostitutes who were described primarily in terms of criminality
or a failure to assimilate. By the 1920s, however, the focus had shifted
to white, middle-class youth, and the notion of youth as a delinquent
class was largely displaced by the notion of youth as a consumer class.

With regard to the U.S. economy in general during the 1920s, what
historian Frederick Lewis Allen has termed "Coolidge prosperity" lasted
for seven years, between 1922 and 1929, during which there was a
frenzy of consumption.[17] Notably, this period of prosperity closely paralleled the cultural preoccupation with the subject of youth. At the
time, social scientists tended to agree that, compared to previous generations, contemporary youth had more money to spend, more things to
buy, and a greater desire to buy, although researchers neglected to col-
lect quantitative data about the specific amounts and sources of money
youth had at their disposal. In *Middletown*, the classic sociological
analysis of life in the mid-1920s, Lynd and Lynd reported that a significant new source of generational tension in families was economic, as so
many of young people's new social activities—from school to leisure
pursuits—required money. Whether they earned it outside the home or
in the form of an allowance, the authors contended that youth "of all
classes carry money earlier and carry more of it than did their parents
when they were young."[18] Similarly, the 1933 President's Research
Committee on Social Trends spoke to the issue of money and youth,
arguing that during the 1920s the family had become "less of a consumption unit than ever before," because its "spending money" was
routinely distributed among several members of the family. Not surprisingly, merchants throughout the United States confirmed that children were "buying more things . . . unassisted by their parents."[19]

A review of the popular media from the 1920s reveals that countless American industries eagerly sought to attract the attention of these
youthful consumers. Following social scientists who claimed that
youth was a highly suggestible stage of life, many industries targeted

and helped to construct a brand-new youth market. Several magazines were inaugurated during the late 1910s and early 1920s that were intended for a youth audience, usually college and university students, including *College Humor, College Comics,* and *New Student.* Also, popular magazines and advertisers that addressed a general audience developed strategies apparently meant to give them "youth appeal." In terms of visual style, for example, the illustrations of the decade's most popular cartoonist, John Held Jr., which parodied modern youth and were favored by them, appeared in a variety of magazines, including *Life, Look, Cosmopolitan, Judge, Harper's Bazaar,* and *Motion Picture Classic.*[20] Likewise, advertisers took special care to target youth. An Ivory soap ad published in the August 1927 issue of *Photoplay* praised youth with a bold headline, "How Youth 'de-bunked' clothes—and living," and with copy that credited them with taking "the artificiality out of American taste" (Figure 1).[21] Even ads for local churches embraced modern youth, or at least used them as a marketing hook. A group of Kansas City businessmen, for example, placed a "jazzy" newspaper ad that was peppered with slang terms intended to entice "flaming youth" to go to church; it promised "thrills galore in Christian life."[22]

During the early twentieth century, a youth peer culture took shape as middle-class young people began to spend more and more time with each other at school and during leisure activities. A key factor was the marked rise in enrollments at high schools, colleges, and universities in the 1910s and 1920s; in addition, secondary and postsecondary schools were reconfigured as students were increasingly organized by age into specific "grades."[23] Consequently, the young person's primary identification with his or her family was displaced, in part, by generational identifications that became available both locally and nationally— through school, mass media, and consumer culture—and an unprecedented generational consciousness took shape both among and about youth. According to social historian Paula Fass, youth peer groups helped to promote a distinctive consumer ethic through their emphases on physical appearance, social activities, and constant conformity to popular new styles. Youth fads, in particular, were a key component in this process because they epitomized the rapid pace of modernity and consumerism. By 1925, considerable commentary insisted that the lures of consumption reflected a "powerful trend" that affected all youth.[24]

One of the key lures was the movies. As social historians have shown, in the early twentieth century the newly available commercial amusements—especially the movies—were a significant factor in the

How Youth "de-bunked" clothes- and living

YOUTH demanded simple clothes instead of these fussy, elaborate styles of the 1900's. Clothes more expressive of youth's own slim, natural grace—clothes easier to wear in the thousand-and-one activities of modern women!

Youth wanted entertaining simplified, too. Informal suppers and tea-dances—for stately mid-Victorian dinners and cotillions!

And haven't you noticed how our modern young women have taken simplicity for the keynote in furnishing their homes? Youth has taken the artificiality out of American taste. Today down to the smallest details of appointment, the simplest taste is the best.

Even in choosing toilet soap

Where thirty years ago, on bathroom toilet stands you found gaudy-colored soap in florid wrappers, today you see the well-bred simplicity of Ivory. Ivory is a favored soap in Boston's quietly beautiful Back Bay, on Chicago's select North Shore, in the distinguished homes that line North Washington Square, New York City.

These thoroughly modern women of cultivated taste like Ivory's delicate, unpretentious whiteness. This is just another proof of Ivory's refinement, of course. It means absolute purity in the oils that go into Ivory's blending. Ivory knows no artificial "make-up."

Lather that is royally lavish

They enjoy Ivory's gentleness, too, the soft indulgence of its lather. And the smooth freshness of skin that results when the royally lavish suds have been rinsed away. They like the courtesy with which Ivory floats—so that they can always keep it within reach!

And being really sophisticated, these women are not misled by Ivory's modest price. It is Ivory's own good taste that is responsible. Its lack of tinsel, bright colors, strong perfumes! They know that if they paid a dollar a cake, they could buy no finer soap.

If you have never tried Ivory won't you let us contribute to the acquaintance? Until September first we shall be very glad to send you—free—three cakes of the dainty new member of the Ivory family, Guest Ivory. Simply send your request with your name and address to Procter & Gamble, Dept. 450-H, Cincinnati, Ohio.

IVORY SOAP
The best taste is the simplest taste

Figure 1. Ivory soap advertisement published in the August 1927 issue of *Photoplay*.

development of a distinct youth culture. Indeed, the motion picture theater became an important new public space for young people, who favored it as a social activity beyond the purview of their parents, and "the movies" became a favorite destination for friends and couples.[25]

Although innumerable U.S. industries in the 1920s strategically

designed their appeals to youth, the appeals sometimes proved problematic as they were met by fierce critics who chastised them for
brazenly commodifying youth. The conservative magazine *Woman's
Home Companion,* for example, complained about the members of the
"older generation" who exploited youth by producing "floods of
cheap and careless discussion, [and] commercializing youth in jest and
tale and news story."[26] Yet such complaints were largely ineffective
against the claims of the growing ranks of critics who championed the
links between youth and consumerism. For example, during the 1920s,
advertising specialists emerged, along with a few primitive demographic
analyses, that claimed to provide scientific profiles of consumers. And
there was no shortage of expert advice about how to inculcate youth
with a crucial capitalist credo, that the "American citizen's first importance to [this] country is no longer that of citizen but that of consumer."[27] Such experts concluded that this lesson was acquired quite
readily, because young people were "extremely suggestible and easily
led."[28] Similarly, as Goode and Powel argued in a 1927 marketing
analysis titled *What about Advertising?* above all else the task before
American businesses was to recognize that "youth must be served"
because they were responsible for the majority of purchases in the
United States.[29]

In terms of the popular critical terrain that advertisers and industries negotiated when they addressed the youth market, it is especially
noteworthy that both conservative and radical commentary tended to
define youth in sexual and moral terms. Youth were said to be governed by a "new morality" that violated traditional expectations about
service to family and the "nobler instincts" in favor of pleasure seeking
and gender mixing. Accordingly, youth were dubbed "flaming,"
"wild," and "jazz mad." Also, the activities said to be preferred by
youth took on sexual connotations, including dancing, drinking, dating, and "dizzying recreation, late parties, speedy automobiles"[30]—
and, of course, these were the very activities that were most prominent
in media portrayals of youth.

Overwhelmingly, when critics spoke in specific terms about youth
in the 1920s, they were gendered. That is, typically the "problem of
modern youth" was defined more specifically as a problem with young
women.[31] Further, rhetorical slippages between the terms for youth and
gender were quite common. For example, a *Literary Digest* article
whose title promised it would deliver a "case against the younger generation" alleged: "There can be no doubt but that *young people* do look
upon life in general with a greatly revolutionized view. The pride of the

girl of today is in the fact that she is ignorant of nothing."[32] Interestingly, however, the critics who issued dire warnings that modern young women would bring "a harvest of social demoralization" were countered by writers who offered reassurances that it was young women who would guarantee the survival of society, because they were both practical and honest: "The girl of to-day has certain new virtues of 'frankness, sincerity, seriousness of purpose,' lives on 'a higher level of morality,' and is on the whole 'more clean-minded and clean-lived' than her predecessors."[33] This marked ambivalence about the morality of youth also typified Hollywood's discourses.

The "Age Factor" in Hollywood

In 1920, a feature article in *Photoplay* deliberated about whether movie exhibitors should cater to younger or to older patrons. Its conservative Christian author, Margaret Sangster, favored the older audience and offered evidence from a theater owner who said that movies were most vital to "people with gray hair" because such audience members had a more intense emotional and intellectual rapport with films than did younger viewers. The theater owner further reported that older viewers had proven to be more loyal customers: "They follow the picture [with] whole-souled interest. . . . They respond more quickly than the young people to a good story. . . . They can be relied upon as the steady patrons of any well kept theater." Sangster offered a moral rationale for favoring older viewers with the contention that movies provided unobjectionable amusement to old-fashioned spectators who disapproved of other modern leisure activities as too risqué, especially the theater, dancing, and nightclubs.[34] However, within just a few years, the argument espoused by this conservative author about the unique rapport between the movies and older viewers was not only rare in Hollywood's discourses, its premises were applied to the youth audience specifically and eventually were cited as evidence of the movies' pernicious influence.

In the early 1920s, Hollywood began to make a new and explicit distinction between the "youth audience" and the "family trade" and to promulgate the notion that a youth market should be cultivated in order to expand the movie audience in general.[35] The industry described the economic rationale for addressing youth in terms of both long- and short-range goals—as a means by which to gain immediate profits as well as to establish enduring loyalty to Hollywood. Throughout the decade, Hollywood solicited youth with a vengeance and asserted that young people made up the largest and most important segment of the movie audience. So, like countless other institutions in the United States, the film industry increasingly defined the motion picture audience demographically, and youth was described as the most profitable segment. Hollywood sought to address young consumers not only through film content but also through promotional campaigns that featured modern, contemporary youth. In addition to revealing the origins of Hollywood's institutionalized practices related to the address to youth, such efforts indicate the industry's earliest expectations about what constituted effective appeals and its ideological assumptions about the tastes and desires of American youth.

The terms and themes that Hollywood deployed in its early discourses about youth are present in a fascinating little advertising manual from 1922 titled *The Age Factor in Selling and Advertising: A Study in a New Phase of Advertising*, which was produced by the publisher of *Photoplay*. Claiming to provide "pioneering" marketing strategies for conquering the new frontier of American youth, it offered quantitative data to validate its claims "scientifically." The manual is noteworthy for the means by which it frames its argument and especially for its circumspect treatment of the themes that often troubled popular observers about modern youth, especially about youth, pleasure, and morality. I will discuss *The Age Factor* in some detail here because it also provides a productive example of the emergent Hollywood discourses that explicitly articulated the interrelated notions that youth constituted a consumer majority, a highly impressionable and influential group, and that to represent youth was the most effective method for selling to youth.

Despite its publisher, *The Age Factor* did not address members of the film industry; rather, it was directed toward American manufacturers, retailers, and advertisers in the wearing apparel, home furnishings, and musical instrument industries. Although it was likely intended to persuade readers to buy advertising space in *Photoplay*, the manual indicated that the research it reported was undertaken to respond to businessmen who had "expressed a desire for the facts" regarding the emergence of the "Younger Generation" as a "business element." The primary argument was far-reaching indeed: that the "freshly awakened interests of Youth in every field represent an influence that may no longer be ignored."[36] In the context of the relatively new scientific discourses and their popular variants that characterized youth as a unique social category and developmental period, *The Age Factor* offered tips for "catching the attention of youthful customers." Purportedly based on questionnaire data solicited from an assortment of advertisers and retailers, the manual represents an early manifestation of the "new psychology of selling," whereby the goal was to fulfill consumers' desires rather than to convince them that they should buy. As advertising psychologist Henry C. Link explained, the new approach focused on studying "people's wants and buying habits . . . as the best clue to what they *will* buy, in contrast with the older emphasis on overcoming their sales resistance to articles which we think they *should* buy."[37]

The Age Factor said that people between the ages of eighteen and thirty were the largest proportion of the consumer market and, perhaps more important, that they wielded plenty of spending money—a potential "gold mine of profits."[38] A seductive vision was conjured for profit-seeking readers: "Youth comes tripping down the avenue throwing money left and right in a veritable orgy of spending." Further, the manual argued that youth were crucial to American businesses, not only in terms of their immediate purchasing power but also in terms of their power to influence other consumers:

> The ages of the prospective customers of merchandise today are far more important than have hitherto been generally considered and . . . men and women between the ages of eighteen and thirty either form the majority of buyers for products sold in this country or are able to dominate the market by their indirect influence.[39]

As evidence, the manual provided myriad anecdotal accounts from retailers and advertising executives who claimed they owed their high profits to a recognition that youth represented both a numerical majority and a model of consumerism for youth and adults. Indeed, according to these businessmen, young people allegedly "set the styles" that others eagerly followed, and youth could be counted on to persuade reluctant parents to buy: "A quick pressure on youth is often the best way to get the bigger, slower parent going."[40] Along with anecdotal evidence, *The Age Factor* provided a daunting and often repetitive array of statistics and graphs culled from the questionnaire data to persuade readers that young people were responsible for the majority of purchases of clothing, home furnishings, and musical instruments.

Like the popular media's appraisals of youth, the general argument of *The Age Factor* was not gender specific, however, the overwhelming bulk of the "scientific" data and theoretical premises referred only to young women. References to young male consumers were very few and tended to be buried. In particular, the manual urged readers to focus on the young female consumer exclusively because she was especially vulnerable to new appeals: "Her mind is opened . . . every new impression

```
Store  The Boston Store                    City Prov. R.I.

Department   Ready to Wear

Name of person interviewed   Mr. E. E. Flint


1.  What percentage of all purchases are made by the following
    age-groups:

         a. Under 18 (flapper type)    15

         b. 18-30 yrs    40

         c. 30-45 yrs    30

         d. 45 yrs and over   15

                         100%


2.  What per cent of all purchases are "double" purchases.
    That is, the daughter and the mother, or a young girl
    and an older woman.   75

         a. When the mother and daughter come together and
            the purchase is for the daughter, does the daughter
            invariably make the decision for herself?  Yes

         b. When the mother is buying for herself, does she
            like the advice of a younger person as to style,
            etc.?                              Yes


3.  What is the average age at which a girl begins to buy
    for herself?
                                        14


4.  General remarks on the younger element in buying.

Price matters very little to the younger girl.  She will often
come in with her mother, pick out a dress which the mother
feels is more than she can pay but nearly always the dress the
girl picks out will be the one finally taken regardless of the
price.     The young buyer is very much inclined to be rattle-
headed and buy whatever strikes her fancy regardless of value.
These girls are however, usually good judges of style and
goods which they purchase must be absolutely up to the minute
or they will have nothing to do with them.

Mr. Flint thinks that the numbers of the young buyers are
increasing rapidly and that they will continue to do so for
some time.
```

A typical report form used in the Barton, Durstine & Osborn investigation.
The definiteness of the questions asked greatly aided the investigators in compiling
an exact and authentic report.

Figure 2. Questionnaire from *The Age Factor in Selling and Advertising: A Study in a New Phase of Advertising*, 1922.

writes itself indelibly upon it," and her "desire often outruns prudence."[41] Although *The Age Factor* persistently affirmed its scientific validity, the questionnaire its researchers administered to obtain the primary data was hardly "objective"—it asked about female consumers only. That is, questions were strategically worded to cue specific responses. The following is representative: "When the mother and daughter come together and the purchase is for the daughter, does the daughter invariably make the decision for herself?" (see Figure 2). Similarly, the manual's illustrations and sample advertisements depicted young women far more than they did young men. One surrealistic illustration in particular is revealing: it depicts a male scientist peering through a microscope in his endeavor to study consumers—but his subject is elusive, as a young woman is shown standing just beyond his field of vision and the reach of his groping hand (Figure 3). The contradiction between the manual's premises and the evidence deployed to support them

Figure 3. Illustration from *The Age Factor.* A male scientist attempts to study consumers, with a young woman just beyond his grasp.

is noteworthy; in other words, although gender was rhetorically de-emphasized, visually and quantitatively it was young females who were clearly the primary concern. Like the text, the manual's illustrations evoke film historian Charles Eckert's canny description of the "one girl" who underpinned the merchandising revolution of the 1920s and 1930s, as evidenced by the ads: "Out there, working as a clerk in a store and living in an apartment with a friend, was one girl—single, nineteen years old, Anglo-Saxon, somewhat favoring Janet Gaynor."[42] And, like the ads to which Eckert refers, *The Age Factor*'s illustrations depicted stylish yet wholesome young women whose rapt attention to the consumer goods paraded before them, from automobiles to clothing to home furnishing, was foregrounded. The difference between Eckert's girl and *The Age Factor*'s was that in some cases the young women in the latter were in the company of their elders. As the manual's text explained, the young female consumer was an easy sell who was motivated more by style than price or durability and who had a knack for convincing her elders to buy—on her terms. By depicting young women with their elders, the manual cleverly circumvented concerns about granting young women the new power of purchasing and implied that their spending was morally justified. Indeed, the manual endorsed a new philosophy: the family that buys together stays together.

After providing considerable data about the significance of the youth market and its preferences, *The Age Factor* turned to the realm of psychology to lend further credibility to its claims. The impressively titled "Psychology of Youth" chapter argued that, compared to adults, young people were psychologically the most "plastic" and "impressionable" consumers. Quoting psychologist William James, the manual claimed that the important habits that shape one's "life-long character" are established between the ages of eighteen and thirty, so it behooved businesses to create strong impressions during this psychological window of opportunity, "before the mind is 'set,'" in order to "make a convert, or a customer."[43] The implication was that businesses would reap both immediate and long-term rewards—as the buying habits formed in youth would last a lifetime.

In terms of general advertising strategies, *The Age Factor* advocated representing youth above all else. The idea was to enhance the processes of identification by helping youth "to project itself" into the situations and settings seen in the ads. Readers were instructed that the secret to selling to youth was to "dramatize youth's interests"—especially sports, parties, music, dancing, and romance. However, these were precisely the activities considered most problematic by conservative critics, who invariably read them in sexual terms. As Fass has noted, what 1920s social critics considered most threatening was that youth lacked moral standards and controls and instead were motivated entirely by sexual desires and pleasure seeking. As a result, images of out-of-control youth filled the popular press, and such behavior was equated with sexual license.[44] Perhaps to preempt such negative presuppositions, *The Age Factor* opened auspiciously with a quotation from conservative filmmaker D. W. Griffith, at the time Hollywood's most respected authority on the subject of filmmaking and youth:

> The sensitive, dominating, responsive and vital element in every group of people is the young—those between the ages of eighteen and twenty-five. They constitute the largest number in every crowd. The crowd follows the young. . . .
>
> I study young people. . . .
>
> If there is any secret about the source of my ideas, and knowing what will appeal to the largest number of people, it will be found there.[45]

Despite the manual's fan magazine publisher, it made few references to the movie industry, so Griffith's opening quotation was a striking rhetorical move that seems intended to legitimate the subject matter and that further implied that Hollywood was a privileged institutional authority on the subject of youth as consumers. The first illustration was a full-page photograph, facing Griffith's quotation, that closely resembled the visual style and subject matter the director employed in his feature films to portray virtuous youth (Figure 4). Specifically, it was a soft-focus, low-contrast image depicting two young women looking hopefully into the distance as though into the future; the florid caption suggested the distinction of this crucial period of life: "Youth the Aspiring. Youth and its limitless ambition. . . . It reaches for the stars. Youth is hungry, insatiable for life with its rich experiences and sensations. For Youth, life in all its fullness lies AHEAD."[46] Yet, despite this modern pronouncement, the illustration did not depict *modern* femininity—these young women were dressed in long, loosely draped gowns, they had pinned-up, unbobbed hair, and their poses were demure and statuesque, in sharp contrast to the increasingly prominent depictions of slim, short-skirted, and dynamically posed flappers that already had started to appear in popular culture.

In addition to Griffith's ostensible endorsement of *The Age Factor*, the remainder of the manual's illustrations carefully contained any potentially worrisome sexual connotations. Most often, they portrayed

Youth the Aspiring

Youth and its limitless ambition. . . . It reaches for the stars. Youth is hungry, insatiable for life with its rich experiences and sensations. For Youth, life in all its fullness lies AHEAD.

Figure 4. "Youth the Aspiring," from *The Age Factor in Selling and Advertising: A Study in a New Phase of Advertising*, 1922.

contemporary yet virtuous-looking young people innocently enjoying modern pursuits with parents or same-sex friends, including shopping for and enjoying their new purchases. Less frequently, the illustrations depicted newlywed couples as they purchased their way to domestic heterosexual bliss, thus offering reassurances that youthful consumption supported rather than threatened the survival of the American family. So, despite its risky subject matter, *The Age Factor* framed its modern appeal in terms of traditional sexuality and morality and suggested that youth's flaming impulses could be economically sublimated—into healthy consumerism. Further, in addition to characterizing the act of spending money as pleasurable, the manual suggested that 1920s youth were *entitled* to some fun in order to heal historical wounds: "Shouldn't they enjoy themselves—these sons and daughters of an age that has known all too many sorrows?"[47]

In terms of the oft-noted link between the movies and youth, *The Age Factor* confirmed the connection by arguing that the movies were a fruitful source of trends that appealed to youth's "imitative instinct." Quoting retailers, it claimed the younger generation was showing "more interest and judgment" in household products than earlier generations because the movies showed beautiful things that "[gave] them ideas."[48] The manual suggested that movies functioned as, to borrow Eckert's term, "living display windows," and urged readers to study the movies to stay in touch with the new items and styles that might strike the purchasing fancy of youth.[49]

Out with the Old

In the 1920s, Hollywood started producing films with contemporary themes that were expected to appeal to youth audiences, and the newer films partially eclipsed those with more traditional themes and stars, such as Mary Pickford, Lillian Gish, and Douglas Fairbanks. The industry nurtured a new generation of stars with modern young images, such as Colleen Moore, Clara Bow, Joan Crawford, Gary Cooper, and Buddy Rogers. Indeed, one of Hollywood's most adamant assertions at the time was that young people in the audience wanted to see young performers onscreen. *Photoplay* put it simply: "The fans are young and the new stars are young."[50] In particular, Hollywood's depictions of modern youth were most prominent in two wildly successful and often overlapping movie categories: collegiate and flapper movies.

The collegiate fad that swept the United States in the 1920s underscored the importance of students as both consumers and trendsetters. Hollywood capitalized on the trend by featuring collegians onscreen in features and shorts, and by designing promotional campaigns that targeted young moviegoers specifically.[51] Exhibitors' trade journals, for example, offered a selection of promotional "stunts" meant to attract the "student patronage" from local high schools and colleges by appealing to the students' school spirit. Such strategies included decorating theater lobbies with school banners, offering half-price "student tickets," and staging contests between rival high schools and colleges.[52] Promotional campaigns for flapper movies typically combined "youth appeal" with "sex appeal." Print ads for 1923's *Flaming Youth,* the film that launched the flapper film cycle, employed youth's slang terms to promise that the movie would feature "neckers, petters, white kisses, red kisses, pleasure-mad daughters," even though such language scandalized conservative critics and usually promised far more than the films delivered.[53] Other schemes for promoting youth movies and stars included celebrity appearances at well-publicized school events. In November 1926, for example, Paramount sent Clara Bow to a well-attended University of California, Berkeley–Stanford football game in order to promote her upcoming flapper movie *It.*[54] Not surprisingly, given the emphasis on attracting the youth market, national surveys indicated that by the 1920s, political, business, and artistic personages had been replaced by movie stars as the favorite role models of American youth, who were enthusiastically adopting the styles sported by their favorite stars.[55]

Hollywood's commentary acknowledged that producing movies and promotions for the youth audience was risky, given the efforts of noisy reformers and censors who denounced the films as salacious. The studios offered economic justification by repeating that a majority of the "new audience" was young and "demanded" contemporary film content—even if it meant offending the sensibilities of the older generation. As film historian Benjamin Hampton observed: "A new generation of moviegoers, not in sympathy with the way of life of its elders, was demanding pictures in harmony with the life it was leading or, at least, hoped soon to lead."[56] Paramount chief Adolph Zukor said that, in the early 1920s, Hollywood enthusiastically met that demand by designing movies that featured sophisticated youth and modern themes:

> The postwar revolution of manners and morals had set in. . . . The younger generation evidently was hellbent on emancipation. Their elders watched this revolution aghast. The film industry was caught in the middle. Our prime aim . . . is always to keep abreast of audience taste and ahead if possible. And the moviegoers were mainly young people. . . . Consequently film subject matter was changing to fit the times.[57]

Along with Hollywood's portrayals of youth onscreen, youth was a significant behind-the-scenes commodity. A preponderance of young directors worked in Hollywood, many of whom specialized in youth films, including Frank Tuttle, Malcolm St. Clair, and Wesley Ruggles.[58] According to Sidney Kent, head of Famous Players–Lasky's sales and distribution, in the early 1920s the most important factor involved in "taking the bunk out" of motion pictures (i.e., ensuring high profits) was generational: "I have watched a steady advance in personnel. Every time the wheel turns, a few old film men are tossed off." And with them, he implied, went their less popular ideas.[59] The fan press similarly touted the youth of Hollywood's workers, claiming that "the youth movement . . . pertains not only to actors but to executives, writers, directors, technicians, salesmen."[60] The claim is supported by data, brought to light by film historian Lary May, that indicate more than two-thirds of film actors and actresses of that era were less than thirty-five years old, three-fourths of actresses were less than twenty-five years old, and the majority of screenwriters were between twenty-five and thirty-five years old.[61]

Youth Go the Movies

Although "hard" data about the actual rates of attendance for youth are relatively sparse, especially compared to the information gathered after World War II, there is striking evidence that young people were a large proportion of the cinema audience during the 1920s. The Payne Fund studies, for example, sought to answer the question, "How often do youth attend?" Interestingly, the researchers readily admitted that one of their goals was to discredit the Motion Picture Producers and Distributors of America's claim that alleged that youngsters made up only 5.2 percent of the audience and to undermine a separate claim, by William Hays, that youngsters accounted for only 8 percent of the audience.[62] In contrast, the Payne Fund studies reported that children and "youth" were 37 percent of the audience, although young people were only 31 percent of the total U.S. population. More specifically, the researchers claimed that children less than fourteen years old accounted for about 15 percent of the audience, whereas young people between fourteen and twenty years old, "the ages of youth or adolescence," accounted for nearly one-fourth of the motion picture audience.[63] Lynd and Lynd made a similar claim: that young people "bulked large" in the movie theater; however, they examined the attendance of high school–aged youngsters and ignored that of younger children.[64] *Middletown*'s survey data indicated that among boys and girls in the three upper years of high school, more than 60 percent had been to the movies at least once in the preceding week, and they had attended mostly with friends rather than parents or guardians. The

Payne Fund studies objected in particular to the tendency for young people to attend movies with friends or young siblings rather than with their elders, deeming it a "peculiarity of youthful movie-going." Specifically, the researchers reported, "At as early an age as thirteen upwards of seventy per cent of the girls go to the movies either with brothers and sisters, 'someone else,' or with their own friends; and more than sixty-two per cent of all boys are similarly companioned."[65] In the legendary summary report, *Our Movie Made Children*, Henry James Forman offered a strangely suggestive conclusion about youth's proclivity for the movies: "'A movie a week' is with us as a national slogan, almost a physical trait absorbed by the children with their mother's milk."[66] Contemporary film historian Terry Ramsaye agreed that youth was a significant part of the cinema audience, and he emphasized their sheer economic power: "This amazing power of the screen is a reflection and proof of the new dominance of youth. . . . the buying of merchandise in this new after-the-war world is dictated by youth . . . which predominates in the audiences of the screen theaters, where youth gets its dreams and romance and desires served in fancy."[67]

The fact that social scientists were more concerned about the moviegoing habits of adolescents than about those of younger children could be related to the widely expressed concern about the "declining dominance of the home and early sophistication of the young," as youth came under the influence of other young people and of commercial institutions in particular.[68] The highly regarded youth critic George Coe captured the sentiment with his observation that "the youth is 'in' on few things with his elders. . . . His human contacts are chiefly with other youth."[69] Indeed, to many contemporary observers, the high proportion of young people in the cinema audience was alarming proof of youth's increasing autonomy and of the rejection of nineteenth-century values concerning the supremacy of the family. Conservative reformers, for example, alleged that, for youth, the movies exceeded the influence of parents and other traditional community authorities, such as the church, and so should be subject to government regulation.[70]

Hollywood Symbolizes Itself as Youthful

During the 1920s, contemporary observers often noted the national obsession with "Americanism" and the decreasing tendency to elevate Europe as the sole arbiter and source of "culture." Often, popular commentary praised America's youth and vigor, and favorably contrasted it with Europe—then considered antiquated and, following the war, impoverished.[71] But for Hollywood and other popular culture industries, youth rather than America was the definitive symbol of modernity. Alternately, popular critics characterized Hollywood as a key symbol of America's youth and strength. The symbolic link between youth and Hollywood was quite prominent throughout the 1920s and had a variety of configurations. For example, the film industry's promotional discourses emphasized its youthfulness to account for both its successes and its shortcomings. That is, Hollywood's moral transgressions—both on- and offscreen—were attributed to the industry's relative youth and inexperience compared to other popular media. Soon after he was appointed head of the Motion Picture Producers and Distributors of America, to serve as Hollywood's guardian of morality following widely publicized scandals, William Hays declared that he had evaluated the film industry and concluded that there was "nothing wrong with the moving pictures—except youth."[72] He thereby suggested that Hollywood's troubles were temporary and forgivable. Similarly, in trade, fan, and other popular magazines, the industry's successes—specifically its responsiveness to audience "demands" and assembly-line efficiency— were attributed to its youth and willingness to change with the times, or to what *Photoplay* called a "quickened, more intelligent spirit."[73]

Whether praised or condemned, youth was the foremost symbol of modernity in American popular culture during the 1920s. Hollywood exploited the symbolism by working to project a modern identity, repudiating its past obsessions, and declaring itself young. The fan and trade press clearly distinguished the film industry of the 1920s from its independent predecessors of the 1910s by asserting that Hollywood was modern and youthful, thus, in part, replacing the critical preoccupation with differentiating the motion pictures from the "legitimate" theater.[74] A tongue-in-cheek *Photoplay* feature in 1928 gently mocked the earlier era with photographs of movie stars from the late 1910s and a title that joked they were from prehistoric times: "B.C.—Meaning Before Close-Ups" (Figure 5).[75] Indeed, the fan magazine was frequently enthusiastic about the growing generation gap between Hollywood and its independent elders (Figure 6):

New stars. New names. New faces. New ideas. . . .

The youth movement is not restricted to any one lot in Hollywood. . . . it is dominating the whole screen world. . . . *Passé* personalities have given way. Youth, cry the studios and the fans. . . .

Youth! It's the new battle cry of filmdom. . . .

Figure 5. "B.C." spread from *Photoplay*, 1928.

Figure 6. "Youth" spread from *Photoplay*, 1927.

. . . This year . . . marks the complete overthrow of the older generation, the complete mastery of the new.

. . . Youth calls to youth and the hand that cranks the camera
rules the world.[76]

Photoplay's reference to "passé personalities" was a thinly veiled allusion to the still-beloved but less-profitable stars, such as Pickford, Gish,
and Fairbanks, whose stars had risen in the 1910s. As the 1920s progressed, the magazine made fewer and fewer references to Gish and
Pickford, and the articles that did speak about them described them as
hopelessly out of step with modern rhythms. In Pickford's case, several
articles in 1928 publicized her failed attempts to save her flagging career by modernizing her image, most notably by cutting her famous
curls.[77] On other occasions, the fan press was more ambivalent about
the first generation of stars, so commentary about them fluctuated,
sometimes in the same articles, between reverence and insult. The film
historian William Everson effectively captures the shift: "The early
twenties saw the gradual disappearance of those stars solidly locked
into the innocent, almost [Victorian] simplicities of the pre-1920's—or
if not their disappearance, their reduction in importance."[78] Despite
Hollywood's claims that its efforts, in terms of film content and promotion, were made merely to conform to the changing tastes of modern
youth, certainly the industry both solicited and helped to construct the
changes in taste. In addition, like the many and varied ways that Hollywood worked to construct a space for youth consumers, it helped to
make youth a desirable commodity in popular culture in general. At
least part of its success in this regard was related to the industry's efforts
to symbolize itself as youthful.

Following its remarkable success in the 1920s, Hollywood has
steadfastly maintained its faith in the notions that youth is the majority
of its market, that young people are easy marks with money to spend,
that youth identify with each other more than with their elders, and
that those who picture youth persuade youth—to buy.

Notes

1. *The Age Factor in Selling and Advertising: A Study in a New Phase of Advertising*
(Chicago: Photoplay Magazine, 1922), 14.

2. Elizabeth Hurlock, *The Psychology of Dress: An Analysis of Fashion and Its
Motives* (Salem, N.H.: Ayer, 1929), 174, 178.

3. Ruth Waterbury, "Youth," *Photoplay*, November 1927, 46–47, 134–35.

4. I use the term *youth* in this essay to refer to young people in late "adolescence" and early "adulthood," roughly between the ages of sixteen and the early twenties.

5. See, for example, Judith Mayne, "Immigrants and Spectators," *Wide Angle 5*, no. 2 (1983): 32–41; Elizabeth Ewen, "City Lights: Immigrant Women and the Rise of the Movies," *Signs 5*, no. 3, supplement (1980): 45–65; Miriam Hansen, "Pleasure, Ambivalence, Identification: Valentino and Female Spectatorship," *Cinema Journal 25*, no. 4 (1986): 6–32; Gaylyn Studlar, "The Perils of Pleasure? Fan Magazine Discourse as Women's Commodified Culture in the 1920s," *Wide Angle 13* (1990): 1, 6–33.

6. Thomas Doherty, *Teenagers and Teenpics: The Juvenilization of American Movies in the 1950s* (Boston: Unwin Hyman, 1988), 14, 71.

7. Edgar Dale, *Children's Attendance at Motion Pictures* (New York: Macmillan, 1935), 73; quoted in ibid., 14.

8. Doherty, *Teenagers and Teenpics*, 14.

9. Ibid., 1–2.

10. Jon Lewis, *The Road to Romance and Ruin: Teen Films and Youth Culture* (New York: Routledge, 1992), 3.

11. Waterbury, "Youth," 47.

12. Joseph F. Kett, *Rites of Passage: Adolescence in America, 1790 to the Present* (New York: Basic Books, 1977), 11. However, as Kett notes, legal, religious, and military institutions during the nineteenth century made somewhat more precise distinctions between childhood and youth.

13. For example, a 1914 novel described a male character as, "young at forty-five, and yet already gray." Owen Johnson, *The Salamander* (Indianapolis: Bobbs-Merrill, 1914), 127.

14. Goodwin Watson's examination of the *Readers' Guide to Periodical Literature* entries for "youth" between 1918 and 1930 found the highest number of entries in 1922 and 1926; further, in 1926 there were twenty times as many articles about youth indexed as there had been in 1918 (Kett, *Rites of Passage*, 310). My own analysis of the *Readers' Guide* indicates that, in terms of the column space devoted to the general subject "youth" during the 1920s, the peak period was 1925 to 1928, when three full columns were published. Also, the volumes for 1922 to 1924 and for 1929 to 1932 each had one and a half columns, whereas the volume covering 1919 to 1921 had less than one column.

15. Mica Nava, "Youth Service Provision, Social Order and the Question of Girls," in *Gender and Generation,* ed. Angela McRobbie and Mica Nava (London: Macmillan, 1984), 1–2.

16. Hurlock, *The Psychology of Dress,* 174. Another writer explicitly associated the period of youth with school, by specifying people of "both sexes who are in the adolescent period, particularly those of secondary school and college age." George A. Coe, *What Ails Our Youth?* (New York: Charles Scribner's Sons, 1925), 1.

17. During this period, corporate economic growth was about 300 percent, industrial production almost doubled, and workers' wages increased, although far less than the rate of corporate increases. William E. Leuchtenburg, *The Perils of Prosperity: 1914–1932* (Chicago: University of Chicago Press, 1958), 178, 193–94. Frederick Lewis Allen uses the term "Coolidge prosperity" as a chapter title in his classic work *Only Yesterday: An Informal History of the Nineteen-Twenties* (New York: Blue Ribbon, 1931), 159.

18. Robert S. Lynd and Helen Merrell Lynd, *Middletown: A Study in American Culture* (New York: Harcourt, Brace, 1929), 141. The "Middletown" the researchers studied was Muncie, Indiana.

19. President's Research Committee on Social Trends, *Recent Social Trends in the United States: Report of the President's Research Committee on Social Trends,* vol. 2 (New York: McGraw-Hill, 1933), 866.

20. Shelley Armitage, *John Held, Jr: Illustrator of the Jazz Age* (Syracuse, N.Y.: Syracuse University Press, 1987), 20.

21. Advertisement, *Photoplay,* August 1927, 28.

22. "A Jazz Appeal to 'Flaming Youth,'" *Literary Digest,* 24 April 1926, 32.

23. Between 1900 and 1930, college and university enrollments increased by 300 percent, and high school enrollments increased by 650 percent, with the greatest increases occurring during the 1920s. Paula Fass, *The Damned and the Beautiful: American Youth in the 1920s* (New York: Oxford University Press, 1977), 124; see also Gilman Ostrander, *American Civilization in the First Machine Age: 1890–1940* (New York: Harper & Row, 1970), 256.

Fass offers a compelling thesis about the demographic trends that prompted the growing attention to youth, including the decline in family size among middle-class Americans and the increase in the proportion of people fifteen to twenty-four years old compared to those in higher age groups (123–24).

24. Fass, *The Damned and the Beautiful,* 119–67, 228–30. Fass traces the origins of the first modern middle-class youth peer culture specifically to the codes and trends followed by students on college and university campuses, which were often depicted in the popular media and then widely imitated by other American youth.

25. For discussion of the significance of movies to young people and the emergence of "dating," see Beth L. Bailey, *From Front Porch to Back Seat: A History of Courtship in America* (Baltimore: Johns Hopkins University Press, 1988), 18; John D'Emilio and Estelle B. Freedman, *Intimate Matters: A History of Sexuality in America* (New York: Harper & Row, 1988), 197.

26. Aurelia Henry Reinhardt, "The Problem of the Modern Girl," *Woman's Home Companion,* March 1928, 24.

27. Quoted in Lynd and Lynd, *Middletown,* 88.

28. Hurlock, *The Psychology of Dress,* 183.

29. Kenneth M. Goode and Harford Powel Jr., *What about Advertising?* (1927); reprinted in *The Plastic Age (1917–1930),* ed. Robert Sklar (New York: George Braziller, 1970), 87–97.

30. June E. Downey, "Is Modern Youth Going to the Devil?" *Sunset Magazine,* March 1926, 34.

31. For example, although the *Literary Digest* ostensibly sought to answer the question posed in the title of its feature article "Is the Younger Generation in Peril?" the opening paragraph specified that young women were its exclusive focus. *Literary Digest,* 14 May 1921, 9–12, 58–73. Likewise, despite its title, *Sunset's* "The Jazz Age: Some Expressions of Opinion from the Young People Themselves" offered only the opinions of "college girls"; D. E. Phillips, *Sunset Magazine,* March 1926, 35ff. For an interesting— and rare—reversal of this tendency, see Willard Thorp, "This Flapper Age," *Forum* 68 (August 1922): 639–43, which discussed young men only. Also, for discussion of the disproportionate attention given in popular discourse to the sexuality and morality of young women, see Fass, *The Damned and the Beautiful,* 23.

32. "Case against the Younger Generation," *Literary Digest,* 17 June 1922, 42, emphasis added.

33. "Is the Younger Generation in Peril?" 61.

34. Margaret E. Sangster, "Middle Age and the Movies," *Photoplay,* August 1920, 63.

35. During 1920 and 1921, *Weekly Variety* published numerous references to poor box-office figures and to the diminishing dependability of the "family trade."

36. *The Age Factor,* 9, 10.

37. Henry C. Link, *The New Psychology of Selling and Advertising* (New York: Macmillan, 1932), xiii.

38. *The Age Factor,* 43.

39. Ibid., 10.

40. Ibid., 40.

41. Ibid., 21, 43.

42. Charles Eckert, "The Carole Lombard in Macy's Window," in *Fabrications: Costume and the Female Body,* ed. Jane Gaines and Charlotte Herzog (London: Routledge, 1990), 109.

43. *The Age Factor,* 42, 21.

44. Fass, *The Damned and the Beautiful,* 20–21.

45. *The Age Factor,* 9.

46. Ibid., 8.

47. Ibid., 370.

48. Ibid., 32.

49. Eckert, "The Carole Lombard," 103.

50. Waterbury, "Youth," 134.

51. These films include *The Plastic Age* (1925), *The Freshman* (1925), *The Campus Flirt* (1926), *The Fair Co-Ed* (1927), and *So This Is College* (1929).

52. "Practical Showmanship Ideas," in *Film Daily Year Book of Motion Pictures* (New York: Film and Television Daily, 1928), 706.

53. For an analysis of the historical importance of *Flaming Youth,* see Cynthia Felando, "Searching for the Fountain of Youth: Popular American Cinema in the 1920s" (Ph.D. diss., University of California, Los Angeles, 1996).

54. David Stenn, *Clara Bow: Runnin' Wild* (New York: Doubleday, 1988), 108.

55. Fred I. Greenstein, "New Light on Changing American Values: A Forgotten Body of Survey Data," *Social Forces* 42 (1964): 441–50.

56. Benjamin B. Hampton, *A History of the Movies* (New York: Covici, Friede, 1931), 214. For a similar claim, see Lewis Jacobs, *The Rise of the American Film: A Critical History* (New York: Harcourt, Brace, 1939), 406.

57. Adolph Zukor, with Dale Kramer, *The Public Is Never Wrong* (New York: G. P. Putnam's Sons, 1953), 202.

58. Frank Tuttle's youth-themed films include *Love 'Em and Leave 'Em* (1926), *Kid Boots* (1926), and *Varsity* (1928); Malcolm St. Clair's include *Are Parents People?* (1925), *A Social Celebrity* (1926), and *Gentlemen Prefer Blondes* (1928); and Wesley Ruggles's include *The Plastic Age* (1925), *Silk Stockings* (1927), and *Are These Our Children?* (1931).

59. Sidney Kent, quoted in Frederick James Smith, "Taking the Bunk Out of Pictures," *Photoplay,* July 1926, 81.

60. Waterbury, "Youth," 46.

61. Lary May, *Screening Out the Past: The Birth of Mass Culture and the Motion Picture Industry* (New York: Oxford University Press, 1980), 188, 256.

62. Dale, *Children's Attendance,* 65; Henry James Forman, *Our Movie Made Children* (New York: Macmillan, 1933), 17.

63. Dale, *Children's Attendance,* 1–2, 54.

64. Specifically, the researchers claimed that 70 percent of high school boys and 61 percent of high school girls had been to the movies at least once during a weeklong period. Lynd and Lynd, *Middletown,* 263–65.

65. Forman, *Our Movie Made Children,* 24.

66. Ibid., 16.

67. Terry Ramsaye, "What the Pictures Do to Us," *Photoplay,* April 1927, 135.

68. Lynd and Lynd, *Middletown,* 140.

69. George Coe, *What Ails Our Youth?* (New York: Charles Scribner's Sons, 1925), 9. Also, in his autobiography, Motion Picture Producers and Distributors of America chief Will Hays recalled a survey conducted among high school principals, noting that in response to a question that asked "whether the school, the church, or the

home 'had the greatest influence in molding the character of our young people today,' 70 per cent scratched off all three and wrote in, 'The movies.'" Will H. Hays, *The Memoirs of Will H. Hays* (Garden City, N.Y.: Doubleday, 1955), 396.

70. In addition to the Payne Fund studies, see the following for other examples of conservative condemnations of the relationship between youth and the movies: Paxson Ellis Oberholtzer, *The Morals of the Movies* (Philadelphia: Penn, 1922); William Short, *A Generation of Moving Pictures* (New York: National Committee for Study of Social Values in Motion Pictures, 1928).

71. Ostrander, *American Civilization*, 228.

72. William Hays, quoted in Richard deCordova, *Picture Personalities: The Emergence of the Star System in America* (Urbana: University of Illinois Press, 1990), 134.

73. Waterbury, "Youth," 135.

74. As deCordova has suggested, "It seems that the cinema, once it began to develop and promote its own stars was much more intent on basing it on a cult of youth than the theater had been" (*Picture Personalities,* 52). For an account of the origins of the term *legitimate theater* as a defense against the "upstart movie industry," see William K. Everson, *The American Silent Film* (New York: Oxford University Press, 1978), 152.

75. Interestingly, the feature's subtitle implied that the initials "B.C." might also be read as "Before Clara (Bow)": "Some photographs from the old family album taken a decade ago, in the days when 'It' was only a pronoun and bobbed hair merely a rumor"; "B.C.—Meaning Before Close-Ups," *Photoplay,* August 1928, 76–77.

76. Waterbury, "Youth," 46–47, 134–35.

77. See, for example, Adela Rogers St. Johns, "Why Mary Pickford Bobbed Her Hair," *Photoplay,* September 1928, 33ff; Louise Brooks, "Gish and Garbo," in *Lulu in Hollywood* (New York: Alfred A. Knopf, 1983), 85–92.

78. Everson, *The American Silent Film,* 196.

5.
Hollywood Exoticism:
Cosmetics and Color in the 1930s

Sarah Berry

> Thirty years ago, no lady ever made up. . . . And now, from the green-
> ish or umber sheen of her eyelids to the flame or saffron of her lips
> and nails, the lady of to-day is a subtle and marvelous creation based
> on the entity that is—Herself.
>
> "Vogue's Eye View of the Mode," 1934[1]

Since the early days of the star system, Hollywood femininity has been
closely tied in with the marketing of cosmetics, and one of the most important stylistic vehicles for this relationship was the glamour of exoticism. The stereotypes of exotic ethnicity deployed in Hollywood films
were both repeated and modified within cosmetics advertising of the
1930s, and numerous female stars endorsed makeup brands. It has been
argued that the use of exoticism in cosmetics advertising has historically
"displaced" discourses of race and gender via a "language of 'color' and
'type.'"[2] This can be seen as a suppression of racial difference, but commercial discourses have also worked to normalize difference by treating
it euphemistically. For example, in the early 1930s Max Factor began
designing cosmetics to correspond with a range of complexion, hair, and
eye colors, and this "personalized" color-matching system (which was
widely adopted by other brands) avoided issues of race by describing
differences in skin tone as aesthetic categories or "complexion types."

Cosmetics advertising of the 1930s certainly utilized stereotypes
(popular makeup products used "Tropical," "Chinese," and "Gypsy"
colors), but it was significant, nevertheless, because it described beauty
in terms of multiple points on a spectrum, rather than a single, mono-
chromatic ideal. The paleness that many women, both "white" and of
color, had struggled for years to create with bleach creams, arsenic and

lead powder, veils, and parasols was significantly modified by Hollywood's familiarization of the sensual, painted face. This relativization of beauty norms also resulted from the expansion of a commercial beauty culture that relied economically on the promotion of new looks, new faces, and new colors. The thirties' exotic makeup lines can thus be seen as an early form of commodified multiculturalism aimed at maximizing cosmetics sales. By mid-decade, most cosmetics manufacturers had stopped advertising traditional, lily-white facial powder altogether.

By the end of the decade, the cinematic projection of sexuality onto nonwhite women, typically characterized as dangerous "vampires" or tragic native girls, had also been modified. Sensuous and dusky, dark-haired sirens like Dolores Del Rio, Dorothy Lamour, Hedy Lamarr, and Rita Hayworth had replaced pale platinum blondes as icons of glamour. It is difficult to interpret such changes in fashion iconography, but what is clear is that the 1930s saw a relative increase in the range of beauty types on the American screen and in advertising, suggesting that the dominance of white, monoracial beauty was significantly challenged by previously marginalized female identities.

From their first appearance at the turn of the century, Hollywood's ethnic stereotypes were predicated on the notion that there exists a category of nonethnic "whiteness." Even in the late 1930s, when Mendelian genetic theory had disproved the concept of "pure" races with evidence of the human gene pool differentiated only by temporary geographic isolation, Hollywood perpetuated myths of racial purity and the dangers of "mixed blood." Films and publicity materials continued to refer to racial purity even as genetic theory was becoming popularized in the form of pro-assimilation arguments, which gradually displaced hereditarian and eugenicist racism in mainstream ideology.[3] At the same time, however, Hollywood's constructions of race were visualized in the form of clearly artificial "ethnic simulacra," the cosmetic basis of which was often described by publicity in terms of the wonders of Hollywood makeup illusionism.

These "simulacra" are the material of what Ella Shohat calls Hollywood's "spectacle of difference"—its creation of ethnicity as a consumable pleasure.[4] One of the primary products of this spectacle, the image of exotic beauty, was indispensable to the recuperation of cosmetics. The frequent use of exotic female stars as endorsers of women's beauty products thus appears to be at odds with nativist norms of beauty, just as women's obsession with Valentino's, Novarro's, and Boyer's passionate sexuality was seen as a rejection of culturally approved but boring WASP masculinity.[5] One way to explore the controversial popularity of "ethnic" beauty is to look closely at the discourses around it, such as the way that racial difference was used in marketing and the range of readings that such strategies made available.

The artificiality of Hollywood's ethnic categories was visible not only in discourses about cosmetics, but also in publicity about non-white stars and films that represented hybrid racial identities. Notes from the Production Code Administration's censorship of *Imitation of Life* (1934), for example, are symptomatic in their unease about Peola, the film's mulatta character (played by Fredi Washington). Washington's image onscreen clearly undermined the myth of racial "purity," but the Hays Office responded by referring to the character of Peola as "the negro girl appearing as white." The film disturbed the PCA because it undermined the visual inscription of race-as-color, as well as implicitly referring to the history of miscegenation. The Hays Office insisted that the invisibility of Peola's race was "extremely dangerous" to "the industry as a whole," and stipulated that the film script attribute her lightness to an albino-like aberration within "a line of definitely negro strain."[6] The difficulty of inscribing racist essentialism in terms of skin color also emerges in *Photoplay*'s description of Nina Mae McKinney, star of *Hallelujah!* (1929), which begins, "Nina isn't black, she's coppery" and concludes with the comment, "She may be black, but she's got a blonde soul."[7] The visual culture of Hollywood glamour and consumerism made it increasingly difficult to assign fixed positions to glamorized racial stereotypes.

Ella Shohat and Robert Stam have pointed out how the "racial politics of casting" in Hollywood effectively "submerged" the multiculturalism that is at the center of American national identity, replacing it with a visually coded racial hierarchy.[8] But the constant publicizing of Hollywood's cosmetic illusionism, along with marketing discourses obsessed with the "makeover," undermined the racial essentialism that required stereotypes to be taken as signs with real-world referents. Hollywood's exoticism of the 1930s was a product of centuries of Eurocentric representations and decades of racist production practices. But these films also popularized a form of exoticism-as-masquerade, within an increasingly diverse market for both Hollywood films and associated goods like cosmetics, subjecting their images to an idiosyncratic process of consumer appropriation.

The Makeover and the Max Factor

Modern cosmetics have been promoted in terms of a fairly recent concept of "democratic" beauty, based on the proposition that with good grooming and makeup, every woman can be beautiful in her own unique way. This concept of beauty as universally attainable is predicated on a new sense of the body's malleability and constructedness, and, like the notion that one's personality can be endlessly modified through fashion, it supports the requirements of a consumer economy. Within the Judeo-Christian tradition, however, concepts of physical beauty have been even more controversial than debates over the legitimacy of fashion. Beauty as a social value continues to be highly problematic from a range of perspectives, including contemporary feminist ones. But the condemnation of physical beauty has historically been linked to attempts to control women's sexuality. Until the nineteenth century, many books on beauty were, in fact, written by church officials or professional moralists and reflected a long-standing European model of "split femininity" symbolized by the Madonna and the whore.[9] The rise of commercial beauty culture was predicated on a softening of this moral critique, allowing for significant changes in the representation of femininity.

The eighteenth century saw a growing consumer market for practical advice on techniques of cosmetic self-improvement. As the nineteenth century progressed, the value of beauty for both men and women within a growing capitalist and service economy became clear, resulting in a gradual recognition of beauty as a legitimate form of social capital. Women's cosmetic self-maintenance came to be seen as one of the requirements of feminine social value, rather than an unethical preoccupation with personal vanity. This led to a plethora of beauty guides that originated and circulated in England, France, and the United States. Their authors included "society beauties," professional writers on fashion and etiquette, and purveyors of scientific beauty treatments. The nineteenth century produced a fairly limited range of cosmetic aids, however, particularly by comparison with the wide range of cosmetics that had been used by members of the social elite in the seventeenth and eighteenth centuries. Nineteenth-century bourgeois women limited their use of beauty products to items such as refined soap, lotions and astringents for softening the skin, hair oils and tints, and facial powder. In 1866, poisonous white facial powders made from lead or arsenic salts were finally replaced by an oxide of zinc, which was cheap and became available to working-class women.[10]

Christian anxieties about physical beauty and cosmetic self-adornment remained powerful, however, until the popularity of cheaper cosmetics after World War I began to mitigate the social stigma of makeup.[11] In the transitional prewar period, bourgeois women's interest in cosmetics was made morally acceptable by the quasi-spiritual philosophies of "beauty culturists." These were primarily female entrepreneurs who, like Elizabeth Arden and Helena Rubenstein, had some knowledge of dermatology but even more marketing skill. They made cosmetics morally acceptable by promoting a philosophy of "natural beauty" to be achieved through good health, expensive massage, and "scientific" skin treatments. Their approach combined Christian moralizing about the need for inner perfection with the pleasures of salon pampering; as one advertisement asked, "Is your complexion clear? Does it express the clearness of your life? Are there discolorations or blemishes in the skin—which symbolize imperfections within?"[12]

But this mind-body philosophy also implied that individuals who were less than beautiful could be assumed to have *inner* "imperfections," a link between physical appearance and moral interiority that had been popularized by the nineteenth-century pseudoscience of phrenology. In addition, philosophies of "natural beauty" set their standards according to Northern European ideals, implying that racial difference could be read as aesthetic and moral imperfection. Such theories represented a nativist bias in the United States that became increasingly virulent in response to new patterns of immigration and resulted in the eugenics movement. Eugenics brought together Christian notions that the body is a mirror of the soul, a Darwinist emphasis on heredity, and a pseudoscientific notion of racial purity. It aimed to purify the "white" race by restricting immigration and miscegenation, and by preventing "deviant" bodies from reproducing.[13]

Following World War I, however, nativist claims to physical and aesthetic superiority became increasingly incompatible with the demands of the new consumer economy. Given the requirements of hereditarian beauty—a WASP pedigree, lots of fresh air, and virtuous thoughts—most American women would have been doomed to an inferior visage. But consumer marketing professionals needed all women to look in the mirror and see potential beauty so that new products could be positioned as a means of self-improvement. The cosmetics industry had also begun to shift from a "class" to a mass market in the nineteenth century, when white-collar women were confronted with the value placed on their personal appearance in the commercial service sector.[14] This market of working- and middle-class women gradually became far more significant to the cosmetics industry than its traditional market of elite female consumers.

The growing presence of women in service sector work and the entertainment industry throughout the nineteenth century meant that female beauty became increasingly visible as a form of social capital. New women's magazines and self-help literature facilitated the rise of a commercial beauty culture that increasingly looked to actresses to legitimize new modes of self-adornment.[15] Throughout the nineteenth century, cosmetics manufacturers had solicited letters of endorsement from reigning theatrical divas to be printed in publications aimed at bourgeois women.[16] In the early twentieth century, however, endorsements by cinema stars began to outnumber those from "legitimate" stage actresses, as popular appeals to a mass market for beauty products displaced reliance on elite consumers.

Helena Rubenstein opened a salon in London in 1908 and by 1916 had begun a chain that included salons in several major U.S. cities. Mainstream American women were still reluctant to adopt her eye shadow, however, and Rubenstein turned to Hollywood for promotional help by designing the Orientalist eye makeup for Theda Bara in *A Fool There Was* (1915).[17] With their heavy, seductive eyes and "vampire lips," Hollywood silent-film stars such as Bara, Nita Naldi, Pola Negri, and Alla Nazimova successfully challenged American norms of childlike beauty epitomized by Dorothy and Lillian Gish and Mary Pickford. Their success can be seen in the popularity of Clara Bow's huge eyes and "bee-stung lips," which were incorporated into the innocent but assertive sexuality of late-twenties flappers such as Colleen Moore and Joan Crawford.[18] By 1934, the style pedagogy of Hollywood was metaphorized in a film featuring Thelma Todd as a model who demonstrates the miracle of cosmetics in the window of a beauty emporium, while a simultaneous "close-up" image of her face is projected alongside her in the shop window, attracting a crowd of onlookers (in *Hips, Hips, Hooray*).

Makeup played a significant technical role in the production of the Hollywood screen image. The use of heavy makeup on film actors was initially necessary to conceal the skin's red corpuscles, which were visible on orthochromatic film; the makeup also hid imperfections exaggerated by the camera and provided a more consistent image for continuity purposes. By the early 1930s, panchromatic film stock allowed the use of a thinner greasepaint, and studio makeup artists began producing a carefully shaded and contoured face for the Hollywood screen—a look that was further stylized by studio lighting and photographic retouching.[19] In order to maintain the image he had created of Marlene Dietrich, Josef von Sternberg supervised all her studio portraiture: to make Dietrich's nose appear more aquiline, von Sternberg once

painted a thin silver line from the bridge to the tip of the nose and focused a small spotlight on it, with effective results.[20]

The stars' faces were individualized with a range of signature features: the shape of the mouth and eyebrows, the color and form of the
hair, and the amount and style of eye makeup worn. Stars usually
maintained consistent makeup styles from film to film, except when
playing "character" roles, although they adapted to and modified
broader fashions in makeup. Joan Crawford's mouth, for example,
was painted inside her natural lip line throughout the 1920s, to make
her mouth appear smaller and rounder. In 1932, however, her lips were
fully painted, and the following year the films *Letty Lynton* and *Rain*
displayed an even fuller, somewhat overpainted mouth. As one article
noted, "The lipstick extended beyond the corner and the mouth was
greatly exaggerated in both thickness and length." In spite of the controversy this caused, Crawford's trendsetting established what came to
be seen as the "natural"-shaped mouth.[21]

The logic of an expanding consumer market for cosmetics helps to
account for steady increases in the variety of products available from
the early twentieth century onward. In 1931, an article in *Harper's
Magazine* commented:

> A quarter of a century ago perfume, rice powder, and "anti-chap" for
> the hands constituted the entire paraphernalia of a woman's boudoir
> table. Now that table looks like a miniature chemist shop. No detail
> of appearance which can safely be entrusted to artifice is ever left to
> nature. . . . As a result feminine beauty, once the Creator's business, is
> now Big Business's.[22]

The article reported that over two billion dollars were spent each year
on beauty products, and that forty thousand beauty shops were scattered across the United States. The marketing strategies that fueled this
growth were based on a few key concepts, most of which had also been
applied to fashion marketing. These included the cultivation of a personal style chosen from a range of "types," the idea that this style
could be changed at will, that an openness to change was necessary for
finding or perfecting one's style, and that Hollywood stars represented
idealized types for emulation and also demonstrated the effectiveness
of cosmetic self-transformation.

Profiles of female stars in Hollywood fan magazines inevitably include a photograph of the star when she had just arrived in Hollywood. Much is made of the quaintness of her appearance in contrast to
the astounding beauty she has cultivated since, which is credited to

both her drive for self-improvement and the skill of studio makeup artists and designers.[23] In the 1933 article "These Stars Changed Their Faces—and So Can You!" this process is described in terms of facial features that have been "remodeled" by particular stars:

> Though styles may change in dresses and hats, most of us cart about the same old face . . . year in and year out. And sometimes we'd be glad to exchange the old looks for some new ones. But how can it be done? The movie stars are showing you! . . . In the new films, there are many "new faces," which have been remodeled over familiar frames. And something tells us that these new eyebrows, lips and hairlines are going to be as avidly copied by Miss America as the Hollywood clothes styles have been.[24]

Beauty advice columns of the early 1930s focused increasingly on the use of cosmetics, as indicated by the article "What Any Girl Can Do with Make-Up." The columnist describes a young woman who went from "demure" to sophisticated, thanks to "a new coiffure, a different line in clothes, and most important of all, a new make-up scheme." The column concludes by suggesting, "Why don't you try a few changes . . . we girls of 1930 have waked up to make-up!"[25] A Max Factor advertisement in the same issue repeats this narrative in the form of a testimonial by Bessie Love (an MGM star) titled "I Saw a Miracle of Beauty Happen in Hollywood":

> She was just like a dozen other girls, but Max Factor, Hollywood's Make-Up Wizard, by the flattering touch of make-up, transformed her into a ravishing beauty. . . . Revealing the secret of how every girl may obtain New Beauty and New Personality.[26]

The degree of artifice employed by Hollywood makeup artists was actually played up in beauty articles, and the very artificiality of the made-over face was celebrated as evidence of the democratization of beauty:

> There is a corrective formula for everything that is wrong with the feminine face. . . . The miracle men know what that is. They put it to work. And they transform those who are average . . . into individuals whose attraction and charm circle the globe.[27]

The concept of the "makeover" is regularly promoted in Hollywood fan magazines, although the first use I found of the term itself was in January 1939: in a beauty column, several female stars describe their New Year's fashion and beauty resolutions, which articulate concisely the cosmetics marketing strategies noted earlier. Anne Shirley, for example, "feels that only by experimenting can a person discover what's most becoming to her," and Joan Blondell states categorically, "The whole secret of beauty is change. . . . A girl who neglects changing her personality gets stale mentally as well as physically. So I'm going to vary my hair style, my type of make-up, nail-polish, perfume." In this article, constant self-transformation is also described as a source of pleasure, rather than just a means to an end. The makeover epitomizes consumer marketing, because it is a process that is simultaneously goal oriented and its own reward—it offers the pleasure of potentiality: "If you get bored with yourself at times, let your resolution be to do something about it. Experiment with new make-ups, change your hairstyle and make yourself over into a new person."[28] Advertising for beauty products, however, still emphasized the positive results of their use—such as romance or a job—and cinematic makeover sequences often had even more dramatic consequences.

Along with self-transformation and change, the promotion of color was a successful cosmetics-marketing concept. Just as product stylists in the 1920s stimulated the market for household products by designing them in vibrant colors, cosmetics began to be produced in an ever wider range of tones by the end of the twenties. For cosmetics, the fashion "type" became linked to hair and eye color rather than personality, encouraging women to try a variety of makeup hues to see which ones matched their own coloring. In 1928, Max Factor changed the name of his cosmetics line from Society Make-Up to Color Harmony Make-Up, on the advice of his marketing agency, Sales Builders, Inc. Their research showed that women usually bought cosmetics items in different brands; if the need to buy "harmonized" products was stressed, however, women would buy every article in the same brand. The result was the Max Factor "Color Harmony Prescription Make-Up Chart," which indicated the complementary shades of powder, rouge, and lipstick to be used according to complexion, hair, and eye color. This "harmonizing" concept was part of a widespread technique of marketing women's fashion separates and accessories as complementary "ensembles." Richard Hudnut cosmetics used it successfully in an "eye-matched makeup" line, which offered a variety of cosmetics chosen according to eye color, and advertising for Lady Esther cosmetics cautioned, "The wrong shade of powder can turn the right man away! . . . so I urge you to try all my shades."[29]

One of the most significant aspects of the use of color to promote the growth of cosmetics was the introduction of new facial powders and rouges that were meant to accommodate a wider range of skin tones. In previous centuries, women had bleached, enameled, and powdered their faces with a range of frequently toxic substances. A gradual change took place, however, as outdoor activities like bicycling and tennis became popular among upper-class women and working-class women moved from farm to factory labor. Suntanned skin became associated with bourgeois leisure, while pallor represented long hours worked in sunless factories. In addition, beach resorts like the Riviera became meccas for social elites in the 1920s, resulting in a vogue for suntan as a visible sign of upper-class travel. As a writer for *Advertising and Selling* mused:

> What inherent urge causes people to paint upon their faces the visible marks of their political or social levels? . . . The outdoor complexion has now met with consumer recognition . . . prompted by the desire to imitate leisure—that leisure which may go to Florida, Bermuda or California and bask in the sun.[30]

Cosmetics manufacturers took notice of the new acceptability of non-white skin and began to produce darker powders as well as artificial bronzing lotions. By 1929, Jean Patou and Coco Chanel had introduced suntan products, and Helena Rubenstein was selling Valaze Gypsy Tan Foundation. Other cosmetics manufacturers were blending powders to be "creamy" rather than white, and producing "ochre," "dark rachel," and "suntan" shades. Joan Crawford was credited with spreading the trend among Hollywood flappers—in addition to tanning her face, Crawford browned her body and went stockingless, a style that was popular "for sleeveless, backless frocks." Predictably, hosiery soon became available in darker colors as well.[31]

The end of the suntan fad was predicted periodically in early-thirties magazines, and Joan Crawford was reportedly told by MGM to stop tanning because she looked "like a lineal descendent of Sheba" and "contrast[ed] strangely with the pale Nordics in her films."[32] Instead, it became the norm for women to tan in the summer, or even year-round if they lived in a warm climate. Golden Peacock Bleach Cream and other facial bleaches, which were advertised regularly in women's magazines until the late twenties, appeared only rarely after the early 1930s, although skin lighteners were still marketed to the African American community.[33] But as the racist quips about Crawford's suntan attest, the end of idealized pallor did not mean the end of the color line in American culture. What it accompanied, however, was a period of intensified commercial and cinematic representation of non-Anglo ethnicity in the form of an appropriable exoticism. But the implication of such marketing was that nonwhite beauty cultures had an increasing influence on the mainstream. The cosmetics industry's maximization of its market through exoticism, in other words, resulted in a diversification of aesthetic ideals rather than the promotion of exclusively nativist, "white" beauty.

Figure 1. Joan Crawford in a publicity photograph for MGM, circa 1933.

Hollywood Exoticism and Beauty Culture

An expanded range of color tones had been introduced into mainstream cosmetics by the late 1930s, but the discourses surrounding this change had a complex history, both in Hollywood and in the marketing of cosmetics. Silent-screen "vamps" and the love goddesses who succeeded them were products of Hollywood's participation in a long tradition of projecting sexual licentiousness and exoticism onto colonized subjects. In the United States, European obsessions with the East were augmented by political and economic designs on Latin America and the South Pacific, giving rise to additional ethnic stereotypes and erotic "others" associated with those cultures. From its beginning, cinema had played a significant role in the popularization of imperialist fantasies and ethnic stereotypes, and the Hollywood studios found that the sexual exoticism associated with these themes was consistently popular.

Hollywood offered a range of nonwhite characterizations throughout the thirties, from the "Latin Lover" roles of Ramon Novarro and Charles Boyer to the Latin, Asian, and South Seas beauties played by stars like Dolores Del Rio, Lupe Velez, Dorothy Lamour, and Hedy Lamarr. The European stars Greta Garbo, Marlene Dietrich, and Lil Dagover were also Orientalized in many films and described as embodying a "pale exoticism." The casting of Euramerican actors in ethnic roles was commonplace in Hollywood, and the process of transforming them via elaborate character-makeup techniques was often discussed and illustrated in magazines.[34] Most non-Anglo Hollywood performers, however, had their names Anglicized to eliminate any reference to their cultural background. Others were chosen to represent foreignness, and rarely allowed to do anything else. On occasions when a star constructed as ethnic played a white role, it was noteworthy. When the Mexican actress Dolores Del Rio was cast as a French-Canadian lead in *Evangeline* (1929), *Photoplay* noted that, "After winning a place on the screen because of her sparkling Spanish beauty and the fire of her performances, [she] now steps into a role that might have been reserved for Lillian Gish. It's a tribute to her versatility."[35]

More frequently, non-Anglo actors played a wide range of exotic roles; Lupe Velez was cast as a Chinese woman in *East Is West* (1930), a Native American in *The Squaw Man* (1931), and a Russian in *Resurrection* (1931). There was interchangeability among all ethnic roles, but movement from ethnic typecasting to white roles was rare. One of the most notorious cases of casting discrimination in the 1930s took place when MGM asked Anna May Wong to audition for the role of the maid, Lotus, in their 1937 production of *The Good Earth*. The Los Angeles–born Wong had performed successfully on the stage in London and Europe and was the most popular Chinese American performer in Hollywood. In spite of Wong's status the leading role in *The Good Earth* was given to Austrian actress Luise Rainer. Disgusted, Wong refused to play Lotus, questioning why MGM was asking her to play "the only unsympathetic role" in the film while non–Chinese Americans played the main characters.[36]

In the United States, these characterizations were screened in the context of a nativist backlash against immigration aimed at both Asians and the "new immigrants"—Jews, Italians, and Eastern Europeans who arrived in the late nineteenth century. Unlike their Anglo, German, and Nordic predecessors, the "new immigrants" were perceived as being unfit to assimilate into a nativist-defined American identity, which was in danger of being "mongrelized" by their presence. In 1907, the U.S. Congress established an Immigration Commission to look into the impact of the new immigrants on the country; two years later, its report led Congress to exclude and deport specific categories of immigrants. According to David Palumbo-Liu, "From 1921 to 1925, nearly thirty thousand people were deported," and over the next five years that number doubled; the Tydings-McDuffie Act of 1934 effectively restricted all Asian immigration.[37] Hollywood's exotic ethnicity of the 1930s thus arose in the context of social anxiety about race, but it also represented an ongoing attraction to and fascination with idealized forms of ethnicity.

Hollywood ethnicity in the 1930s also had hierarchical distinctions, with Castillian Spanish "blood" as the most idealized and assimilable form of nonwhiteness possible. Like the Mediterranean-influenced French and Italians, the Spanish were seen as both exotic and European. Dolores Del Rio was repeatedly described as having an "aristocratic" family in order to distinguish her from mixed-race Mexicans, and the studios' disregard for Spanish-speaking countries' linguistic differences led them to dub films into Castillian Spanish even when they were set in Mexico, Cuba, or Argentina. Actresses described as Spanish appear to have outnumbered any other ethnic category in the late 1920s and early 1930s; in addition to Del Rio and Velez, the performers Raquel Torres, Conchita Montenegro, Arminda, Rosita Moreno, Movita Castaneda, Maria Casajuana, and Margo all appeared, for a while at least, on screen and in the pages of fan magazines. The sex appeal of the "Latin type" is clear from an article noting that Casajuana was discovered when Fox, "on the lookout for sultry types, staged a beauty contest in

Figure 2. Anna May Wong in a publicity photograph for *Limehouse Blues,*
Paramount, 1934.

Spain."[38] Like the "Spanish blood" that redeems Valentino's character
in *The Sheik* (1921), Spanishness was often Hollywood's ethnically acceptable alibi for hot-blooded sexuality. It was also used as a racial default setting for performers who played a range of ethnic roles; a magazine profile of Margo, whose biggest Hollywood role was as a Russian in
the Orientalist fantasy *Lost Horizon* (1937), notes: "Margo's exoticism
is not an affectation. It is an inheritance bequeathed by her Castillian
ancestors."[39]

Nativist ideology had often stressed the role of women in maintaining "racial purity": in 1922, feminist Charlotte Perkins Gilman
supported the eugenics movement by calling on women to utilize
"their racial authority" in order to "cleanse the human race of its
worst inheritance by a discriminating refusal of unfit fathers." The
same year, the Cable Act declared that any female citizen who married
an immigrant who was unable to naturalize would automatically lose
her own citizenship. As Palumbo-Liu notes, the only other act for
which one's citizenship could be revoked was treason; a woman's conception of a child with an "alien" man was thus seen as the equivalent
of treason.[40] Miscegenation was identified as "race suicide" and was
included in the Motion Picture Producers and Distributors of America
(MPPDA) list of representational prohibitions when Will Hays became

president in 1922, removing the possibility that any Hollywood film narrative could include a nontragic cross-racial romance.[41] But the use of exotic female stars as endorsers of beauty products, like the popularity of "Latin" male stars, directly contradicted such hereditarian racism and its nativist beauty norms.[42] By promoting stars who represented a sophisticated ethnicity designed to be mass-marketed internationally, Hollywood utilized "the spectacle of difference" in ways that allowed for antiessentialist readings.

Hollywood's émigré performers were a crucial part of the film studios' attempts to maximize international distribution, and numerous production decisions about casting, dialogue, and representational issues were also made in relation to the requirements of nondomestic markets.[43] The consideration of different national codes of censorship was a particularly relevant factor, as was the popularity of specific stars overseas. In 1933, *Variety* took stock of the value of Hollywood stars in foreign markets:

> There are some picture stars in the U.S., very popular here, who are even more popular abroad. . . . The foreign stars in the U.S., of course, like Marlene Dietrich, Maurice Chevalier, and Lillian Harvey can be figured on to garner at least as large a harvest outside the American boundaries as within them. Not true of Greta Garbo or Ronald Colman, however, because of the amazing strength both have at home.[44]

The importance of stars as global commodities was highlighted when the studios, attempting to maintain their foreign markets following the transition to sound, tried making multiple foreign-language versions of selected films; in most cases, a completely different cast was used—without the English-speaking star. But when the original star happened to be bilingual (as were Dietrich, Garbo, and Novarro), a foreign-language film could be produced with equal star value, doubling profits.[45] This desire for international appeal accounts for much of Hollywood's consistent poaching of foreign talent. Arguing in support of Hollywood's use of non-American labor in 1937, an attorney for the MPPDA told a congressional committee on immigration and naturalization that "some of the world-wide character and appeal of American motion pictures must be credited to the employment of foreign actors."[46]

Hollywood's use of stars representing "foreignness" can therefore be seen as an attempt to target three distinct audiences: (1) Anglo-American viewers who liked exoticism, even if only in terms of racist stereotypes; (2) an immigrant-American audience interested in multi-

Figure 3. Greta Garbo in a publicity photograph for *Mata Hari*, MGM, 1931.

cultural characters; and (3) nondomestic viewers with varying linguistic and cultural preferences. The desire to create a global product thus put the studios somewhat at odds with the racist xenophobia of 1930s America. Such a conflict between audiences was also evident in the studios' battles with the Christian right over what mainstream moral standards were, resulting in stricter Production Code enforcement after 1934. Hollywood's glamorization of racial difference and simultaneous pandering to racist stereotypes can thus be attributed, in part, to marketing conflicts and the desire to create non-Anglo characters that were acceptable both at home and abroad.

The Technicolor Face: "Jungle Madness for Cultured Lips"

Twentieth-century cosmetics advertising vividly documents the importance of Hollywood exoticism to the construction of a new kind of beauty achievable through a more colorful use of makeup—a discourse linked to Hollywood's gradually increasing use of Technicolor from the mid-1930s onward. Early Technicolor sequences had been used in black-and-white films of the 1920s to highlight spectacular scenes such as fashion shows or elaborately decorated sets, while color simultaneously appeared in consumer product design and advertising graphics. In 1932, however, the Technicolor company developed a three-strip process that, although expensive, was used for big-budget costume and adventure films. Big-budget productions became increasingly popular by mid-decade, on the theory that, as David Selznick argued, money could be made during the Depression only by producing either a lot of cheap films or a few expensive ones.[47]

The new Technicolor process was first tested in a Disney cartoon, *Flowers and Trees* (1932), then in a two-reel short called *La Cucaracha* (1934), and finally in the feature *Becky Sharp* (1935). Three-strip films initially tended, like earlier two-strip sequences, to be in spectacular rather than realist genres because of anxieties that viewers would find the color jarringly stylized when paired with a realist mise-en-scène. Color was thus used in musicals or backstage entertainment/fashion films like *The Dancing Pirate* (1936), *A Star Is Born* (1937), *Vogues of 1938* (1937), and *The Goldwyn Follies* (1938); in Westerns such as *Dodge City* (1939), *Drums along the Mohawk* (1939), and *Jesse James* (1939); or in fantasy/costume dramas such as *The Garden of Allah* (1936), *Ramona* (1936), *The Adventures of Robin Hood* (1938), *Gone with the Wind* (1939), and *The Wizard of Oz* (1939). Selznick International Pictures also produced a successful Technicolor comedy, *Nothing Sacred*, in 1937.

The question of whether Technicolor would be accepted by viewers as compatible with Hollywood's realist conventions focused, in particular, on the importance of the face as a privileged signifier. In 1920, a producer warned that Technicolor threatened to overwhelm the screen with visual information, which conflicted with established goals of focusing attention on performers' faces and eyes through lighting and cinematography: "The human being is the center of the drama, not flowers, gardens, and dresses. The face is the center of the human being. And the eyes are the center of the face."[48] Another critic complained of early Technicolor that "when the figures retreat to any distance, it is difficult to distinguish their expression."[49] Anxiety that facial features could not be photographed in color with the same attention-riveting results that had been achieved in black and white became central to the Technicolor firm's research. As David Bordwell has indicated, "The firm was at pains to compromise between developing a 'lifelike' rendition of the visible spectrum and developing a treatment of the human face that would accord with classical requisites of beauty and narrative centrality."[50]

One way in which the chaos of the Technicolor palette was adapted to Hollywood norms of facial representation and beauty was through the use of performers whose style could be "naturally" associated with bright colors. Female stars who were "the Technicolor type" had "vivid" features and personalities, which often meant that they were exotically ethnic. When *Motion Picture* ran a profile of the actress Steffi Duna titled "Steffi Is a Perfect Type for Color," Natalie Kalmus, Technicolor's production adviser, was asked why Duna had been chosen for the first three-strip films (*La Cucaracha* and *The Dancing Pirate*). She listed Duna's qualifications: "A colorful complexion; a contrasting shade of hair; natural rhythm (color accents a woman's gracefulness you know); a personality vivid enough to counter-balance the most brilliant kind of setting; and she's the type that can wear picturesque clothes." Along with having "natural rhythm," Duna was described as exotic: "Steffi of Hungary . . . and all the bright romance of it sings in her blood. In Budapest, you see, children are weaned on the gypsy music. . . . Steffi could dance to it before she could talk."[51]

The description of ethnicity in terms like *vivid, colorful,* and *picturesque* was also commonplace in the promotion of such stars as Dolores Del Rio (the "Sparkling Spanish beauty") Tala Birell ("She's as exotic as a red camellia"), and Anna May Wong ("She brings to the screen . . . the mysterious colors of her ivory-skinned race").[52] But the advent of Technicolor produced even more emphasis on the relationship between color and exotic beauty, with Hollywood stars playing a central role in the promotion and naturalization of "colorful" femininity.

Along with Duna, a new style of tropical exoticism appeared in the mid-thirties that contrasted sharply with Garbo's "pale exoticism."[53] It had been visible in the 1920s deluge of South Seas island films, which usually featured romance between a white hero and a native woman, because the Production Code Administration considered such couples relatively nonthreatening and ruled by 1937 that romance between "white" characters and the "Polynesians and allied races" did not constitute miscegenation.[54] The island girl made a dramatic reappearance in the early thirties, just in time for a major fashion vogue in tropicalism. Balinese batik appeared in beachwear, along with the "Goona-Goona bathing suit" and a general "Javanese influence." By 1935, an advertisement for brassieres declared, "Women of the Isle of Bali have always had the most beautiful breasts in the world," and a Tahitian-style bathing suit advertisement noted: "It all started in the Riviera. Smart women . . . adopted the daring costumes and colors of primitive islanders." *Vogue* concluded that "it's smart, this year, to look like a Balinese maiden when you have the figure for it," and also advised:

> If you are wearing a swathed Oriental evening frock . . . your make-up should be as glamorous as possible—deep, mysterious eye shadows, with perhaps a touch of gold or silver. This is the moment to use mascara on your lashes, and even indulge in kohl, and to make yourself, in general, as exotic as you possibly can.[55]

The following year, Dorothy Lamour made her sarong debut in *The Jungle Princess* (1936) and became synonymous with the tropical look in subsequent films such as *The Hurricane* (1937), *Her Jungle Love* (1938), and *Tropic Holiday* (1938). By 1938, Lamour's long, dark hair, sultry brown eyes, and prominent red mouth were being emulated widely, as an advertisement for lipstick in "a wicked new shade" indicates: "Jungle madness for cultured lips . . . the sublime madness of a moon-kissed jungle night . . . the most exotic color ever put into a lipstick."[56] Also available was "tropic beauty for your fingertips," with nail polish in shades including "Congo," "Cabaña," and "Spice."[57]

The Lamour "type" was seen as a boon to the cosmetics industry as well as to Technicolor, because her dark hair and skin tone could accommodate a wide range of cosmetics. The perfect expression of this type appeared in 1938, however, when Hedy Lamarr caused a sensation with her appearance in *Algiers*. Whereas Lamour was called "untamed and torrid," Lamarr was a "red-lipped, tawny-eyed, black-haired girl" whose "lush, exciting beauty" combined sensuousness with an aloof glamour.[58] The Max Factor company was central to the promotion of sultry new stars like Lamarr, Ann Sheridan, and Rita Cansino (soon to be Hayworth), using them to endorse the new, multicolored approach to cosmetics. One Max Factor advertisement, featuring a photograph of Lamarr, stated: "Beauty's secret attraction is color . . . for it is color that has an exciting emotional appeal." Soon older stars followed the new "brunette trend"; Joan Bennett switched from blonde to raven hair and even duplicated Lamarr's long bob with a center part, her distinctive downward-curving eyebrows, and wide red lips. Bennett noted that with her new coloring, she could tan her face, wear stronger shades of makeup, and use heavier, "more Oriental" perfumes.[59]

Max Factor had been commissioned to devise an improved makeup foundation for use with Technicolor, one that could be layered in different shades without being too thick or reflective. The result was Pan-Cake makeup, which made its official debut in Walter Wanger's *Vogues*

Figure 4. Rita Hayworth in an advertising photograph for Max Factor, circa 1938.

of 1938. According to reviews of the film, the goal of Technicolor realism had been reached with a "natural" rendering of facial tones and features. One critic devoted most of his review to a discussion of the new makeup, and another wrote that the actresses "were so lifelike . . . it seemed like they would step down from the screen into the audience at any minute."[60] Once Technicolor and cosmetics manufacturers had established both the beauty advantages of color and the naturalism of the new representational palette, it remained for Pan-Cake makeup techniques to be promoted to consumers. Referred to as "shaded" or "corrective" makeup, it was said to give Dietrich "that lovely exotic high-cheekboned look" and to disguise numerous structural imperfections in other stars' faces. Contoured makeup could, in effect, give anyone high cheekbones, a "new nose" or "larger eyes." Most important of all, the process required the use of more than one foundation color—potentially doubling sales of facial powder. To make cheekbones stand out, one could powder them with a light shade and apply a darker "shadow" underneath. If, like Dietrich, one applied the shadow in a triangle shape, the results would be "positively Oriental."[61]

Technicolor makeup techniques were thus said to increase the transformative qualities of makeup as well as the range of complexions and colors located within the new norms of natural-looking beauty. A *Photoplay* beauty column of 1938 was devoted to a discussion of the "Technicolor . . . school of beauty"; in addition to exoticism, the Technicolor face was said to represent the full range of different complexion and coloring types among women. Using *The Goldwyn Follies* as an example, the writer suggested that there are at least thirteen different "variations of coloring" represented by women in the film, offering female viewers the opportunity to find their own "color harmony" among the many facial shades available. In addition, she pointed out that film stars now wear "different make-ups for different color gowns, so that the whole ensemble is a perfect blending of color." The column was essentially an advertorial for the Max Factor company's "personalized color palette" system, even incorporating the company's slogan of "color harmony" into the text. But it also demonstrates the way that the growth of the cosmetics industry was predicated on women's use of an ever greater range of products and colors on their faces.[62]

Hollywood exoticism was thus central to discourses that fueled the renaissance in cosmetics, as were Technicolor and the desire for export-market appeal. The high point of Hollywood's vivid exoticism was reached in the 1940s, with the Technicolor figure of Carmen Miranda. "Good neighbor" films like *The Gang's All Here* (1943) presented not only the archetype of the Hollywood Latina (with huge eyelashes, red lips, and a multicolored "tutti-frutti hat") but also a pro-Latin American sensibility designed to foster Pan-American solidarity against the Axis powers. Miranda's first Hollywood film, *Down Argentine Way* (1940), features a musical number in which the blonde-haired Betty Grable emulates Miranda's look, wearing vivid makeup, an ornamented turban, costume jewelry, and a ruffled, off-the-shoulder gown. Gable represents the consumerist assimilation being promoted by such films, in which Latin American style is domesticated through music and comedy. Soon, numerous American women would also emulate Miranda by wrapping their hair in colorful floral scarves for factory work and using bright red lipstick and costume jewelry to make their rationed outfits more exotic.

Orientalist Fashion and Exotic Masquerade

European Orientalist fantasy was integral to the marketing of cosmetics and self-adornment from the eighteenth century onward. As Kathy Peiss has noted: "Advertisers created narratives about beauty culture through the ages, bypassing the Greco-Roman tradition in favor of Egypt and Persia. Cleopatra was virtually a cult figure, displayed in advertising to all segments of the market."[63] In the early nineteenth century, English and French Orientalist salon painting had popularized myths of Islamic beauty, centered on fantasies of the harem. In Ingres's painting *Bain Turq* (The Turkish Bath, 1862) a group of women lie entwined in each other's arms, adding a frisson of lesbianism that was not uncommon to the genre. Reina Lewis has argued that the myth of the harem is typical of Orientalist discourses, with the desire to breach the harem walls symbolizing the drive to colonize and possess Eastern lands. However, Orientalist paintings frequently depicted the most desirable harem women as light-skinned. A common alibi for this was their identification as Circassian women, a Turkish ethnic minority said to be light-skinned and more beautiful than any other women on earth. Lewis concludes:

> The pale harem women oscillate between being like and not like European women, i.e. as both the permitted and the forbidden object. Part of the frisson of the white odalisque comes from the projection of the white wife (the licit object) into what amounts to a brothel situation (an illicit site): she is pitied but desired as the fantasy combination of Europe's splitting of female sexuality.[64]

Orientalist beauty can thus be seen as a fantasy of feminine beauty unfettered by Christian taboos against female sexuality. Notwithstanding Lewis's reading of their potential meaning for male viewers, such images may also have resonated with European and American women's interests in the possibilities beyond Victorian norms of female sexuality and self-presentation. The cult status of Cleopatra within twentieth-century beauty discourses, for example, suggests that the power associated with Eastern sensuality had a strong appeal among women as well as men. Beauty salons were often described as sites of collective female pleasure that emulated the harem's luxurious baths, massages, and all-female exercise rituals. Throughout the late nineteenth and early twentieth centuries, Orientalist beauty was offered to Western women as a means of transgressing the strictures of split femininity: by temporarily adopting signs of exotic sensuality through makeup and clothing, Western women could present themselves as a combination of (white) virtue and (nonwhite) sexuality.[65]

The projection of female desire onto a fantasy of Eastern and Southern eroticism was particularly visible in Orientalist women's fiction, most notoriously in the 1919 novel *The Sheik* (written by Englishwoman E. M. Hull), which was filmed in 1921 with Rudolph Valentino, turning him into an icon of female desire for non-WASP sensuality. Similarly, in Robert Hichens's 1904 novel *The Garden of Allah,* the English heroine, Domini, travels to North Africa, "aching" to experience "elemental forces" and be "free from the pettiness of civilized life."[66] Domini has a passionate love affair with a Russian man, although he leaves her in the end and returns to the monastery from which he has fled. The book was a huge success in the United States; it was filmed in Hollywood three times (1916, 1927, 1936) and staged twice as a theatrical spectacle, in 1907 and 1912, complete with sandstorms and live animals. According to William Leach's history of American consumerism, "the Garden of Allah" became a shorthand term for Orientalist luxury in a range of contexts, from numerous "Allah" fashion shows to the lavish Sunset Boulevard estate of Hollywood star Alla Nazimova, which she named the Garden of Allah.[67]

The eighteenth century saw the first wave of widespread fashion Orientalism in clothing, with the use of embroidered Chinese silk and Indian cotton as well as the styling of gowns "*à la turque*" and the wearing of Arab burnooses. The mid-nineteenth century saw a huge renaissance of Orientalist fashion with the "opening" of Japan and its influence on the visual arts.[68] Throughout the late nineteenth and early twentieth centuries, the rich threw *Arabian Nights* parties and dressed up like rajahs and harem dancers, or decorated their homes with the ornate carpets, cushions, and curtains associated with Islamic luxury.[69] Orientalist style could also express rebellion or bohemianism, as it had for Victorian female dress reformers when they wore loose "Turkish" or "Syrian" trousers under their tunics. French designer Paul Poiret became the undisputed master of Orientalist fashion in the 1910s: his vision combined modernist formal simplicity with decorative pastiches of Islamic and Asian motifs. In 1911, Poiret gave a "Thousand and Second Night" party to celebrate his new "Oriental" look; he appeared costumed as a sultan, and his wife, Denise Poiret, played the "favorite of the harem" in a gold cage with several female attendants.[70]

Orientalist fashion, in both couture design and ready-to-wear markets, had an upsurge in popularity in the mid- to late 1930s. In *Mata Hari* (1931), Greta Garbo appears in gold lamé from head to toe, with tight gold leggings and boots worn under a long jacket and turban. In one scene, Garbo wears a more revealing gold lamé costume while performing a slow, writhing dance around a large deity sculpture, demonstrating her "pale exoticism," if not her dancing talent. The promotion of cosmetics as a form of self-transformation was also linked in a number of films to Orientalist associations with luxury and female sexuality. Lacquer red was an important Orientalist color, according to a 1936 advertisement for Helena Rubenstein's Chinese Red lipstick and rouge:

> Flaming flowers, lush vivid fruits, the bright plumage of an exotic bird. . . . Chinese Red is high, clear, brilliantly attuned to this season of intense color. It is vivid, young—with lots of red for flattery and just a hint of gold to give you a touch of the exotic. To pallid skin it lends a lovely glow. To dusky skin it adds a vibrant accent. It lifts every skin to new heights of enchantment.[71]

The phrase "Chinese Red" thus evokes a number of key cosmetic and marketing concepts: natural vividness, exoticism, and youth, as well as adaptability to a range of skin tones. The same year, Elizabeth Arden introduced a summer line of "Chinese and Copper" makeup; the Chinese foundation is in an "amber tone that makes you look like a Manchu princess" and is to be worn with "Dark Nasturtium" lipstick and rouge, black eye pencil, and blue-green "Eye Sha-do."[72]

Along with the opulence of the Manchu princess, the Orientalism of the mid- to late thirties also signified stylistic modernity. As in the art direction of *Lost Horizon,* which combined Chinese and modernist design, Chinese-inspired fashion appears, in several films, to indicate a character's aesthetic sophistication.[73] *The Painted Veil* (1934) stars Greta Garbo as Katrin, a German woman who moves to China, whose elegant Chinese-style outfits contrast dramatically with the old-fashioned ruffled dresses and wide-brimmed hats of other expatriate European women. Katrin embraces the Orient, as demonstrated in a scene in which she walks dreamily through a chaotic street festival and enters a temple containing gigantic statues of Buddha and Confucius. In this scene, she wears a white turban and floor-length white coat; their elegant streamlining and Orientalist details make her look both modern and mystically elegant.

Orientalism had been a defining aspect of the 1930s silhouette since 1931, when the Exposition Coloniale in Paris exposed designers to wide-shouldered dancing costumes from Bali and Thailand, which Schiaparelli immediately incorporated into the shoulder-padded silhouette she had used in suits the year before.[74] The peak of Orientalist fashion diffusion, however, was in the mid-thirties, when the ever-adventurous Schiaparelli was pictured in the August issue of *Vogue* having "gone native" in Tunisia to learn "the mysteries of Oriental sewing, draping, and veil twisting," just as her travels to India had inspired the presence of several saris in her line the previous year.[75] Hollywood followed, and occasionally introduced, such Orientalist trends because of the continued popularity of exotic narratives. From the mid-thirties onward, studio designers created numerous costumes with turbans, sari-wrapped bodices, and "Persian draping."

By the late 1930s, these styles had become decisively mainstream. *Photoplay* exclaimed in 1939, "All smart women are going Oriental for fall," listing required accessories such as a "Maharaja's turban," several "heavy ropes of golden beads," "earrings that jingle like Hindu dancing girls'," and "a wide silver bracelet fit for a Maharanee."[76] The "let's dress up" tone of this description, like *Vogue*'s article on Schiaparelli's adventures in Tunisia, highlights the importance of fashion throughout the thirties as a vehicle for fantasy. Accessories and cosmetics were the least expensive means of subtle self-dramatization and masquerade; simply by drawing one's eyebrows up slightly at the ends, instead of down, and wearing Chinese colors like red and black, one could assume an air of adventure and sophisticated chic.[77] Frank Capra's film *The Bitter Tea of General Yen* (1933) incorporated this trend into its Orientalist captivity narrative, with a "makeover" sequence that offers a transgressive appeal second only to the film's interracial romance.

In *The Bitter Tea of General Yen,* the heroine's desire for the exotic is initially cloaked by her intention to pursue missionary work in Shanghai. Megan Davis (Barbara Stanwyck), a plainly dressed member of an old New England family, instead becomes trapped in the midst of civil war fighting and is knocked out; she is then rescued by the elegant, French-speaking warlord General Yen (Nils Asther). Megan wakes surrounded by the opulent luxury of Yen's summer palace, but also to the sound of prisoners of war being shot outside her window; this contrast between aesthetic refinement and moral barbarism is repeated throughout the film as a characterization of Chinese culture. After three days of refusing to dine with Yen, Megan sits on her balcony watching young lovers on the riverbank outside her room and falls into a dream. In this surreal vignette, an evil-looking caricature of General Yen enters her room and reaches out with long, clawlike fingers while she screams. Suddenly another man, wearing a dapper suit, white hat, and mask, bursts in through the window and rescues Megan by destroying the evil Asian. They embrace, and she removes the mask from his face, happily discovering that he, too, is General Yen. They gaze into each other's eyes, Megan lies back on the bed, and they kiss.

Megan's conflicted desire for Yen is paralleled by her fascination for his courtesan Mah-Li (Toshia Mori), who always appears elaborately made-up and dressed. Mah-Li convinces Megan to join her at dinner with Yen, offering to help her dress. In a montage sequence with multiple dissolves, Megan is bathed, perfumed, and dressed in silken lingerie by Mah-Li and her servants, and a range of ornate Chinese gowns are displayed before her. She chooses the most elaborate one, with huge, glowing silver sequins, loose, embroidered sleeves, and a sequined fringe below the knee. The gown contrasts dramatically with the plainness of Megan's own dress. Mah-Li then has her carved vanity table carried in, commenting that Megan is "in need of powder and paint." Megan appears intrigued by Mah-Li's display of cosmetics and, picking up a powder puff, she muses, "Yes, perhaps I am." Following another dissolve Megan is seen transformed, wearing the glittering dress with long, ornamental earrings, her hair coifed, face powdered, eyes shadowed, and lips painted the same dark red as Mah-Li's. For the first time in the film, Megan is shown looking like a glamorous movie star, and her satisfaction with this image is immediately followed by a flashback to her fantasy of kissing General Yen. As the image disappears, Megan looks unhappily at her beautiful reflection, scoops cream onto her fingers and begins removing the makeup. She is next seen coming to dinner with her face bare, hair primly tied back, wearing the disheveled dress she arrived in.

This makeover sequence clearly associates Megan's pleasure at being groomed and gowned by Mah-Li with her illicit desire for General Yen, but while her desire for Yen remains taboo, her makeover offers viewers the satisfaction of seeing Stanwyck's star glamour restored in a particularly opulent style. The makeover is repeated at the end of the

Figure 5. Nils Asther and Barbara Stanwyck in a publicity photograph for *The Bitter Tea of General Yen*, Columbia, 1933.

film, when Yen declares his love for Megan. She begins to cry and runs to her room; in her confusion, she sees the vanity table and begins to transform herself again. Still in tears, Megan is shown in close-up, putting on Mah-Li's makeup in a sequence intercut with Yen's preparation of poisoned tea for himself, having lost his political power and failed to gain Megan's love. As he is about to drink the tea, Megan enters his darkened room wearing the sequined gown. The scene is shot with heavy lens diffusion, making the gown's large sequins burst into luminous circles of light as she moves through the shadows. As Yen strokes her hair, Megan begins to cry again, and he drinks the poison. Megan's desire for Yen is figured as a *Madame Butterfly*-like tragedy that requires the death of Yen so that he can await Megan in heaven, where, as he suggests, there is no racial difference. Megan's emulation of Mah-Li, on the other hand, creates the film's most visually dramatic moments and represents, within the film's racist narrative, an acceptable resolution of her desire for the exotic through fantasy and self-adornment.

Orientalist fashion and cosmetics tended to aestheticize particular forms of cultural and racial difference so that they could be visually appropriated. These stylized forms of cultural referencing helped to promote the expansion of a commercial beauty industry from one that idealized normative "white" features to one that thrived on exoticism as a form of commodified multiculturalism. Orientalist and primitive femininity had long functioned as a Western fantasy of a nonsplit female sexuality, and the association of cosmetics with exoticism gradually helped overshadow the stigma of the "vamp" attached to women's use of cosmetics. Clearly, the ethnic stereotypes that circulated onscreen and in cosmetics marketing were mystifications of cultural difference and the politics that structured them; they also perpetuated a sexualization of nonwhiteness that could be oppressively deployed. At the same time, the popularization of sultry, dark-hued feminine glamour and the marketing of cosmetics in terms of a spectrum of colored features helped to displace nativist beauty norms to which non-Anglo American women had long been seen as inferior. This relativization of norms, upon which cycles of stylistic change and product development depended, exposed exotic beauty types as signs of imaginary ethnicity. To some extent, Hollywood's exploitation of the "spectacle of difference" worked against the mimetic inscription of ethnicity that linked exterior appearance to essentialist racial categories. It also suggests that, in spite of the exclusionary immigration policies of the 1930s, international markets and domestic product diversification led to the erosion of nineteenth-century nativist beauty norms, changing the face of popular culture to a significant extent.

Notes

1. "Vogue's Eye View of the Mode," *Vogue*, 1 June 1934, 41.

2. Kathy Peiss, "Making Faces: The Cosmetics Industry and the Cultural Construction of Gender, 1890–1930," *Genders* 7 (spring 1990): 164.

3. David Palumbo-Liu, "The Bitter Tea of Frank Capra," *positions* 3, no. 3 (1995): 782.

4. Ella Shohat, "Gender and Culture of Empire: Toward a Feminist Ethnography of the Cinema," *Quarterly Review of Film and Video* 13, nos. 1–3 (1991): 68.

5. See Gaylyn Studlar, *This Mad Masquerade: Stardom and Masculinity in the Jazz Age* (New York: Columbia University Press, 1996).

6. Feature film entry for *Imitation of Life,* in *The AFI Catalog of Motion Pictures Produced in the U.S.: Feature Films, 1931–1940,* exec. ed. Patricia King Hanson, assoc. ed. Alan Gevinson (Berkeley: University of California Press, 1993), 1013; Susan Courtney, "(De)Coding Hollywood's Fantasy of Miscegenation" (paper presented at the annual meeting of the Society for Cinema Studies, Dallas, March 1996).

7. McKinney's mother is also described as a woman "of light skin, who might have Spanish blood." Herbert Howe, "A Jungle Lorelei," *Photoplay,* June 1929, 118–19.

8. Ella Shohat and Robert Stam, *Unthinking Eurocentrism: Multiculturalism and the Media* (London: Routledge, 1994), 189, 224, 220.

9. Arthur Marwick, *Beauty in History: Society, Politics, and Personal Appearance c. 1500 to the Present* (London: Thames & Hudson, 1988), 70.

10. Gilbert Vail, *A History of Cosmetics in America* (New York: Toilet Goods Association, 1947), 77–78, 87, 98–99; Kate de Castelbajac, *The Face of the Century: 100 Years of Makeup and Style* (New York: Rizzoli, 1995), 12.

11. De Castelbajac, *The Face of the Century,* 46.

12. Peiss, "Making Faces," 147; Lois Banner, *American Beauty: A Social History through Two Centuries of the American Idea, Ideal, and Image of the Beautiful Woman* (New York: Alfred A. Knopf, 1983), 214.

13. Mark H. Haller, *Eugenics: Hereditarian Attitudes in American Thought* (New Brunswick, N.J.: Rutgers University Press, 1963), 153.

14. Marwick, *Beauty in History,* 245; Banner, *American Beauty,* 207, 217.

15. Fenja Gunn, *The Artificial Face: A History of Cosmetics* (London: Newton Abbot, 1973), 128, 139; Lillian Russell, "Beauty as a Factor in Success on the Stage," *Woman Beautiful,* April 1910, 39.

16. Vail, *A History of Cosmetics,* 102.

17. Helena Rubenstein, *My Life for Beauty* (London: Bodley, Head, 1964), 58–59.

18. Fred E. Basten, with Robert Salvatore and Paul A. Kaufman, *Max Factor's Hollywood: Glamour, Movies, Make-Up* (Santa Monica, Calif.: General, 1995), 34, 90.

19. Alicia Annas, "The Photogenic Formula: Hairstyles and Makeup in Historical Films," in *Hollywood and History: Costume Design in Film,* ed. Edward Maider (London/Los Angeles: Thames & Hudson/Los Angeles County Museum of Art, 1987), 55–56.

20. De Castelbajac, *The Face of the Century,* 75.

21. Ruth Biery, "The New 'Shady Dames' of the Screen," *Photoplay,* August 1932, 28. In letters to the editor, fans reportedly "liked 'Letty Lynton' but wished Joan wouldn't use so much eye and mouth make-up." "The Audience Talks Back," *Photoplay,* August 1932, 6–7.

22. Jeanette Eaton, "The Cosmetic Urge," *Harper's Magazine,* February 1931, 323.

23. See Carolyn van Wyck, "Photoplay's Own Beauty Shop," *Photoplay,* April 1932, 55.

24. Dorothy Manners, "These Stars Changed Their Faces—and So Can You!" *Motion Picture,* June 1933, 32–33.

25. Carolyn van Wyck, "Friendly Advice on Girls' Problems: What Any Girl Can Do with Make-Up," *Photoplay*, August 1930, 18, 116.

26. Advertisement, *Photoplay*, August 1930, 101.

27. Adele Whitely Fletcher, "Miracle Men at Work to Make You Lovelier," *Photoplay*, July 1939, 26.

28. Carolyn van Wyck, "Photoplay's Own Beauty Shop," *Photoplay*, January 1939, 66.

29. Basten, *Max Factor's Hollywood*, 80; Roland Marchand, *Advertising the American Dream: Making Way for Modernity, 1920–1940* (Berkeley: University of California Press, 1985), 132–40; advertisement, *Photoplay*, September 1939, 77.

30. Marie du Bois, "What Is Sun-Tan Doing to Cosmetics?" *Advertising and Selling*, 12 June 1929, 19.

31. De Castelbajac, *The Face of the Century*, 44; advertisement, *Photoplay*, June 1929, 76; advertisement, *Photoplay*, August 1929, 105.

32. Dorothy Spensley, "The Most Copied Girl in the World," *Motion Picture*, May 1937, 30–31.

33. Peiss, "Making Faces," 160.

34. In her early career, Myrna Loy's heavy-lidded eyes and round face inspired producers to cast her in a series of "native" roles, including Chinese, Malay, Hindu, Egyptian, and French-African women. By 1936, however, a *Photoplay* caption noted that whereas "she used to play slant-eyed Oriental seductress roles, today she is the ideal screen wife." *Photoplay*, August 1936, 42.

35. Photograph caption, *Photoplay*, July 1929, 22.

36. Edward Sakamoto, "Anna May Wong and the Dragon-Lady Syndrome," *Los Angeles Times*, 12 July 1987.

37. Palumbo-Liu, "The Bitter Tea," 761.

38. "New Pictures," *Photoplay*, May 1929, 21.

39. Denise Caine, "Beauty Is Kin Deep!" *Motion Picture*, September 1937, 51.

40. Charlotte Perkins Gilman quoted in Studlar, *This Mad Masquerade*, 163; Palumbo-Liu, "The Bitter Tea," 761.

41. Thomas Cripps, *Slow Fade to Black: The Negro in American Film, 1900–1942* (New York: Oxford University Press, 1977), 94.

42. Studlar, *This Mad Masquerade*, 163.

43. Ruth Vasey, "Foreign Parts: Hollywood's Global Distribution and the Representation of Ethnicity," *American Quarterly* 44, no. 4 (1992): 625.

44. "U.S.' Overseas Panickers," *Variety*, 26 September 1933, 3.

45. Kristin Thompson, *Exporting Entertainment: America in the World Film Market 1907–34* (London: BFI, 1985), 162.

46. Vasey, "Foreign Parts," 625.

47. David Selznick is said to have run Selznick International Pictures on this premise. Thomas Schatz, *The Genius of the System: Hollywood Filmmaking in the Studio Era* (New York: Pantheon, 1988), 178.

48. Quoted in David Bordwell, Janet Staiger, and Kristin Thompson, *The Classical Hollywood Cinema: Film Style and Mode of Production to 1960* (New York: Columbia University Press, 1985), 355.

49. Quoted in Fred E. Basten, *Glorious Technicolor* (New York: A. S. Barnes, 1980), 27.

50. Bordwell et al., *The Classical Hollywood Cinema*, 356.

51. Virginia T. Lane, "Steffi Is a Perfect Type for Color," *Motion Picture*, August 1936, 43.

52. Photograph caption, *Photoplay*, June 1929, 22; "Two New Exotics," *Photoplay*, May 1932, 74; photograph caption, *Motion Picture*, April 1924, 21.

53. Madame Sylvia, "Garbo's Glamor . . . Mystery or Misery?" *Photoplay*, December 1936, 56–57.

54. Vasey, "Foreign Parts," 629.

55. Advertisement, *Vogue*, 1 December 1932, 3; advertisement, *Vogue*, 1 January 1933, 28; advertisement, *Vogue*, 1 December 1934, 117; advertisement, *Vogue*, 1 January 1935, 79; "Native Charm," *Vogue*, 1 January 1935, 29; "The Javanese Influence," *Vogue*, 1 June 1935, 44.

56. Advertisement, *Photoplay*, December 1935, 110.

57. Advertisement, *Photoplay*, October 1938, 90.

58. Ruth Waterbury, "Close Ups and Long Shots," *Photoplay*, June 1938, 13; Sara Hamilton, "Hedy Wine," *Photoplay*, October 1938, 21.

59. Advertisement, *Photoplay*, October 1938, 21; Basten, *Max Factor's Hollywood*, 139, 163; advertisement, *Photoplay*, September 1938, 77; Carolyn van Wyck, "Photoplay's Beauty Shop," *Photoplay*, November 1939, 10–11; Barbara Hayes, "Hedy Lamarr vs. Joan Bennett," *Photoplay*, November 1939, 18–19.

60. Quoted in Basten, *Max Factor's Hollywood*, 147.

61. Jan Fisher, "If You Want to Be a Glamorous Beauty," *Photoplay*, November 1937, 5; Carolyn van Wyck, "Photoplay's Beauty Shop," *Photoplay*, March 1938, 8.

62. The marketing strategy of encouraging women to buy different lipsticks to match their dresses began in 1931. See Carolyn van Wyck, "Friendly Advice on Girls' Problems: New Make-Up Theory," *Photoplay*, September 1931, 16; Carolyn van Wyck, "Photoplay's Beauty Shop," *Photoplay*, January 1938, 60.

63. Peiss, "Making Faces," 159. See also Vail, *A History of Cosmetics*, 74–78.

64. Reina Lewis, *Gendering Orientalism: Race, Femininity, and Representation* (New York: Routledge, 1996), 172.

65. Ibid., 113.

66. William Leach, *Land of Desire: Merchants, Power, and the Rise of a New American Culture* (New York: Vintage, 1993), 109.

67. Ibid., 110.

68. Richard Martin and Harold Koda, *Orientalism: Visions of the East in Western Dress* (New York: Metropolitan Museum of Art, 1994), 15, 35, 53, 73.

69. Leach, *Land of Desire*, 105.

70. Peter Wollen, *Raiding the Icebox: Reflections on Twentieth Century Culture* (London: Verso, 1993), 2.

71. Advertisement, *Vogue*, 1 April 1936, 109.

72. Advertisement, *Vogue*, 1 July 1936, 82.

73. "China Influences the Young Modern," *Photoplay*, August 1936, 64–65.

74. Jane Mulvagh, *Vogue History of 20th Century Fashion* (London: Viking Penguin, 1988), 112.

75. "Schiaparelli among the Berbers," *Vogue*, 15 August 1936, 44–45.

76. Frances Hughes, "Crystal Gazing into Fall's Fashion Futures," *Photoplay*, August 1939, 65.

77. Photograph and caption, *Photoplay*, July 1935, 71.

6.
From Apocalypse to Appliances: Postwar Anxiety and Modern Convenience in Forbidden Planet

Rick Worland and David Slayden

Writing about postwar horror and science fiction cinema, David J. Skal trenchantly observes that "the new American prosperity of the early 1950s was won atop the largest bone pile in human history."[1] When we compound Skal's chilling image with the omnipresent threat of nuclear apocalypse hanging over America's gleaming new cars and orderly suburbs, we arrive at *the* compelling paradox of post–World War II culture—the intimate association of unprecedented affluence and anxiety. *Forbidden Planet* (Fred McLeod Wilcox, MGM, 1956), one of the best-remembered movies of the decade's science fiction boom, encodes many historically intriguing icons, images, and social themes of America in the Atomic Age. Despite its continuing popularity, the film is rarely taken seriously. Often dismissed as a juvenile if stylish comic book, or ritually plumbed for its pop Freudianized recasting of *The Tempest*, *Forbidden Planet* is in fact a key popular text illuminating the contradictory dynamics of Cold War America. Here, the famous "Monster from the Id" assumes secondary importance as the film's genre-based mediations of America's emerging suburban landscape, consumer culture of abundance, and atomic anxiety form the crucial background for the obvious Oedipal struggle between Professor Morbius (Walter Pidgeon) and Commander J.J. Adams (Leslie Nielsen) for the love of Altaira (Anne Francis).

In this analysis, Robby the Robot, the enduring emblem and true "star" of the movie, emerges as the pivotal character, an insistent symbol of the bountiful postwar economy. A high-tech marvel himself, Robby performs as an all-purpose servant/worker/homemaker and simultaneously as an inexhaustible manufacturing plant for both heavy-industrial equipment and consumer goods. Steel, electronics, opulent housing, liquor, jewelry, and stylish clothing—none is beyond Robby's productive capacity. In the film's vision of Morbius's private "island" on planet Altair IV, largely constructed by Robby, *Forbidden Planet* presents instantly recognizable artifacts extrapolated from glossy period advertising for suburban homes, appliances, autos, and other consumer comforts. Small wonder Robby the Robot quickly became a widely circulated icon representative of the 1950s as a whole.

In Professor Morbius's motherless household, the homemaker role seems to be split between Altaira and Robby in a reconfiguration of the dichotomous Victorian feminine roles of angel of the hearth and whore of the street, only in this case the worldly version is Robby as a quasi-industrial fount of consumer goods that deliver the latest in modern convenience. Seen in this light, to a contemporary audience Morbius's futuristic dwelling and a model home in the latest suburb are directly comparable. And so are the roles expected of the woman who would run such a household, being responsible for and meeting the demands of postwar domestic bliss. She would have given up her more worldly (and masculine) "Rosie the Riveter" role for that of managing the domestic economy of the suburban home. In Altaira, she would identify expectations that would so feminize her as to make her nonthreatening to the G.I. adjusting to the economic and social changes in peacetime American life (an adjustment widely discussed in terms of emasculation and enervation, a weakening of the "frontier" character that had made the United States a world leader). In Robby, she would see the transformation of her energies as a vital member in the wartime workforce to a solver of domestic problems through expertise in consumption—consumption linked to the latest in modern convenience made possible by technology.

When, in 1956, William H. Whyte Jr. proclaimed that, "as a normal part of life, thrift is now un-American,"[2] he prefigured the more publicized remarks of Vice President Richard Nixon three years later at the opening of the American National Exhibition in Moscow on 24 July 1959. In what came to be called the Kitchen Debate with Soviet Premier Nikita Khrushchev, Nixon equated consumption with freedom in a speech calculated to validate the free enterprise system, and went on to reference the purchasing power of the average American worker as evidence of a classless society in the United States: "Let us start with some of the things in this exhibit. You will see a house, a car, a television set—each the newest and most modern of the type we produce. But can only the rich in the United States afford such things? If this were the case, we would have to include in our definition of rich the millions of America's wage earners."[3] The postwar boom had indeed placed America's wage earners in a position to buy. Nixon pointed out what they were buying; but that he should do so in support of his argument with Khrushchev about the superiority of capitalism over communism suggests the extent to which these items had become symbolically weighted, that they were connected to and supported a way of life that was somehow uniquely American. In the everyday battles of the Cold War, buying "a house, a car, a television set" had become acts of patriotism, and consumerism had itself become both a means of assimilation into American society and a sign of the upward mobility that was possible. Manipulating the newly popular iconography of science fiction, *Forbidden Planet* charts the peaks and valleys of upward mobility through its multivalent symbols of robot, Id Monster, and flying saucer. The spaceship will finally depart Altair IV carrying an idealized postwar couple as well as figurative encapsulations of the many benefits of the surging American economy touted by Vice President Nixon.

Forbidden Planet: The Movie

Forbidden Planet begins with Commander J.J. Adams, skipper of space cruiser C-57D, dispatched to Altair IV in search of the *Belleraphon* expedition, which has been missing for twenty years. Professor Morbius, the original party's only survivor, warns Adams's ship away on approach. Robby the Robot, Morbius's automaton servant, meets the ship and takes Adams and his officers to the home of the professor and his daughter, Altaira. For years, Morbius has studied the fantastic technology of the Krell, the extinct alien race that once inhabited the planet. He insists Adams depart at once or risk destruction by the mysterious "planetary force" that wiped out the *Belleraphon* group. As Adams predictably falls for the nubile "Alta," who has never seen any man except her father, his ship is attacked by a fearsome invisible monster.

To learn more about the attacks, Doc Ostrow (Warren Stevens) hastily employs the Krell's "brain-boosting machine" but is overwhelmed by the strain. Before he dies, Doc tells Adams that the Krell were engaged in a radical scientific project to transform themselves into beings of pure mental energy when the technologically unleashed power of their base emotions manifested ravening "monsters from the Id" that destroyed them. Adams deduces that the creature attacking his crew is actually a materialization of Professor Morbius's own primitive passions. When Alta declares her love for the commander and prepares to depart with him, the Id Monster emerges and stalks the couple through the Krell laboratories. Realizing his terrible mistake, Morbius confronts and renounces the monster—a self-realization tantamount to self-annihilation, which nevertheless spares the life of his daughter— and then rigs a Krell furnace to explode the entire planet lest its secrets fall into the hands of human beings not yet wise enough to receive them. Later, safely aboard the spaceship, Adams and Alta observe the incineration of distant Altair IV.

Along with such predecessors as the Flash Gordon movie serials of the 1930s, *Forbidden Planet* falls into the science fiction subgenre sometimes derisively called space opera. Such tales are typically juvenile action-adventure fantasies wearing futuristic trappings, often involving warfare between Earthmen and various semibarbaric alien villains along with half-dressed damsels who require repeated rescue by square-jawed heroes. An ambitious, effects-laden film released by MGM, recently the jewel of the Hollywood studio system, *Forbidden Planet* inflates a typical pulp romance plot with resplendent production values and counterbalances science fiction's traditionally dubious reputation with a gloss of high-culture references calculated to increase its thematic cachet. The film's reframing of the plot of *The Tempest* (an inspiration for the screenwriters but largely an interpretive red herring) is finally less important than its subtle construction of Adams and Alta as a futuristic Adam and Eve.[4] In her encounter with J.J. Adams, Alta's dawning awareness of "forbidden" sexual knowledge leads to her expulsion from an edenic garden where wild beasts are her docile pets. The growling face of Alta's once-pet tiger (nature), which turns suddenly vicious after her first kiss, recurs later in the snarling face of the Id Monster (natural libido unnaturally accelerated by superscience), suggesting a basic similarity. Given the terrors of the place they have left and the bright future apparently awaiting the couple aboard the spaceship now piloted by the marvelous Robby, Alta is less expelled than rescued by Adams from a false paradise. Pointed cultural allusions and futuristic setting aside, however, the film's fictional world is really 1950s America, its icons and assumptions immediately recognizable to postwar audiences.

"Would Sixty Gallons Be Sufficient?"

During the 1950s, the bulk of consumer spending went for automobiles, television sets, and household furnishings and appliances. In the four years following World War II, Americans bought 21.4 million cars, 20 million refrigerators, 5.5 million stoves, 11.6 million televisions; they also moved into over 1 million new housing units annually, thus establishing a long-running trend that Nixon detailed for Khrushchev: "Thirty-one million families own their own homes and the land on which they are built. America's 44 million families own a total of 56 million cars, 50 million television sets and 143 million radio sets."[5] Nixon's case for American superiority was argued largely in terms of the range of technologies available for consumption, and these technologies, for the most part, were designed for the home and family. When he described a model home, Nixon emphasized that it was furnished with modern appliances that "make easier the life of our housewives." The model home was situated in the suburbs, of course. As Elaine Tyler May points out in her summary of the Kitchen Debate, "Nixon's knockout punch in his verbal bout with the Soviet Premier was his articulation of the American postwar domestic dream: successful breadwinners supporting attractive homemakers in affluent suburban homes."[6]

The postwar period witnessed an explosion of consumer goods; more goods became available to more people than ever before. Whether symptom or cause, this development signals a major cultural shift in values from permanence to transitoriness, with an emphasis placed on novelty and change. When Khrushchev criticized U.S.-produced housing as lasting no more than twenty years, Nixon turned this criticism into a virtue, countering that the American system was developed to take advantage of new technology. The country was forward-looking, and this faith in the future could be found in its everyday objects, which were themselves designed to convey ideas of progress and modernity. The American industrial designer Henry Dreyfuss wrote in 1955 that the impetus for the changes in design of modern kitchens had been brought about "by two things which had nothing to do with cooking a meal or taking a bath—the automobile and the airplane. Actually, the auto and the plane have become symbols of the nation's scientific imagination and a vital part of its psychology, establishing trends and influencing people in everything they buy."[7]

If indeed the airplane and the automobile could influence the design of kitchen appliances and plumbing fixtures, the sudden appearance of the science fiction movie genre in 1950 and its subsequent quick rise to commercial viability for the first time in Hollywood history seems less remarkable. Moreover, contra Susan Sontag's famous thesis, the immediate embrace of science fiction by youth audiences especially was not then solely attributable to nuclear fear, although this does form a crucial part of the historical and cultural matrix, and indeed is more pertinent to *Forbidden Planet* than usually noticed. Yet it is important to remember that the wondrous Robby the Robot is also a by-product of the Krell's advanced science. Morbius tells Adams that after his first experiment with the aliens' "brain-boosting machine," he lay unconscious for two days. When he awoke, the first thing he tinkered together with his newly elevated intelligence was Robby. The professor repeatedly downplays the significance of his discoveries, dismissing them as minor dabbling beside the vast scientific achievements of the godlike aliens he finally calls "my beloved Krell." Yet it is Robby the Robot that clearly captures the imagination of J.J. Adams and subsequently that of more than one generation of film viewers. As a character, Robby's fussy demeanor and dry humor enliven an otherwise low-key drama. Indeed, this mechanical prop, performed by two different actors, his voice supplied by a third, is even given a separate tongue-in-cheek credit line, "And Introducing Robby the Robot," a special card usually reserved for ingenues.

Robby is in fact a consumer society fantasy, a device that can synthesize any material one desires with instantaneous, automated efficiency in between slavish personal attendance of his master. Virtually a perpetual-motion machine, Robby is said to be self-maintaining and autonomous, the same capacity Morbius ascribes to the immense relics of Krell technology: "I have reason to believe that sixteen years ago, a minor alteration was performed throughout the entire eight thousand cubic miles of its own fabric," he says, guiding Adams and Ostrow through the titanic alien complexes. With characteristic utilitarian bluntness, the commander asks simply, "What's it all for?" Despite his hauteur, Morbius clearly does not know, and quickly changes the subject. Whereas Morbius can only guess at the know-how behind a hypothetical event, Robby brings fantastic Krell science down to a human-sized scale of finely tuned, apprehensible utility.

As an engine of production, Robby is apparently as inexhaustible as the colossal machinery that brought him to life. Among his accomplishments, the robot built Morbius's luxuriously appointed house of the future; he does all the housework and cooking; designs, runs up, and accessorizes Alta's new dress; synthesizes sixty gallons of booze for the spaceship's cook (Earl Holliman); manufactures heavy steel shielding and electronic instruments for Adams's crew; serves as chauffeur in a futuristic automobile trimmed with fins à la Harley Earl's extravagant postwar Cadillacs; and is last seen piloting the commander's spaceship. And what's more, as Professor Morbius demonstrates in a famous scene, inviolable programming makes Robby incapable of harming human beings. When Morbius orders his servant to shoot the astronaut with his own ray-gun to demonstrate, Robby's transparent head sizzles and buzzes with self-destructive short circuits instead. The technology and science Robby embodies are wholly benign and domesticated.

Robby's remarkable capabilities are presented as carefully controlled and elegantly modulated to serve human needs, from the challenging to the mundane. In one scene staged across the width of the roomy CinemaScope frame, the bulky Robot beautifies Morbius's living quarters by arranging a bouquet of flowers—as if he has just read the latest article on interior decorating in *Better Homes and Gardens*—while behind him, Alta's pet monkey tries to steal fruit from a bowl on the table. Still arranging flowers, and without even turning to observe directly, Robby shoos away the thief with a gentle electric zap shot from the back of his head. The film's congruence with the Eisenhower era was confirmed earlier when Adams and his officers witnessed a demonstration of Robby's domestic prowess as food producer as well as cook, waiter, maid, and (using the "household disintegrater beam") garbage disposal, prompting the surprised commander to proclaim the robot "a housewife's dream!"

Common discussion of the film's overt Freudian allegory seldom associates issues of gender and sexuality with Robby. Asked whether he is male or female, the robot responds, "In my case, sir, that question has no meaning whatsoever." (Robby's voice was dubbed by a male actor, and the robot is addressed in the film as "he.") However, Hollywood's Production Code Administration, even in the period of its rapidly waning authority, fretted over explaining Robby's hypothetical gender. Characteristically vigilant to the script's treatment of the scene in which Adams observes Alta swimming nude, the censors also pointedly cautioned MGM on the portrayal of Robby's gender: "Please avoid a full-length shot of Robby when Doc questions it, whether it is male or female"[8] (and MGM did). The PCA clearly worried about inviting any unsavory inspection of the robot's chassis to see if it carried—or lacked—any special attachments. Robby is genderless at best, emasculated at worst.

In any event, as a physical threat—either sexual or violent—his equipment is harmlessly irrelevant. He is a controlled, because self-controlling, force; as Morbius demonstrates, it is not in Robby's nature to harm his masters. As the film demonstrates, the master's primitive urges are what should be feared. Here, technology is portrayed as essentially neutral. Yet if Robby is indeed a "housewife's dream," he may be said to be so primarily in the sense that he has replaced the traditional housewife altogether. Alta lost her mother in the Id Monster's first rampage, yet when Robby solicitously advises the spacemen to fasten their seat belts as he prepares to drive them to meet Morbius, Doc Ostrow comments that the machine "looks after us like a mother." But "mother" is only one of the many possible combined domestic and commercial roles the automaton plays.

It Came from Alamogordo

Susan Sontag's influential 1965 essay "The Imagination of Disaster" is the locus classicus for the now familiar reading of the Cold War subtext of postwar science fiction movies. Sontag sees the American military's cinematic clashes with alien invaders or irradiated freaks as expressing a widespread but sublimated fear of nuclear holocaust.[9] The best-known examples, most initially identified by Sontag, include *The Thing* (1951), *The Day the Earth Stood Still* (1951), *War of the Worlds* (1953), *Them!* (1954), *This Island Earth* (1955), and Japan's *Godzilla* (1954). However, discussions of the undercurrent of nuclear dread in fifties science fiction rarely include *Forbidden Planet*. Sontag's survey of two dozen genre films produced from 1950 to 1964 does not mention the title at all, though, interestingly, she alludes to Shakespeare's Prospero as "one of the oldest images of the scientist."[10] The particular accomplishment of *Forbidden Planet* is not to raise yet again the specter of nuclear apocalypse, but the antidote the film simultaneously posits: the paradise of modern consumer convenience provided and embodied by Robby the Robot.

In his survey of postwar cinema, *Seeing Is Believing*, Peter Biskind disputes Sontag's reading of 1950s science fiction, arguing that the genre's cultural representation of technology was not simply a displaced metaphor for nuclear terror or creeping communist subversion; indeed, Biskind contends that American science and industry are more often portrayed positively in a variety of postwar films and genres. For many politicians and intellectuals of the time, American productive capacity was both a material reflection of the superiority of our socioeconomic institutions (as Nixon had argued) and a theoretical necessity underpinning the age of "consensus politics" that would ultimately allow the United States to prevail in the Cold War while achieving a prosperous and harmonious society at home.[11] The idea—indeed, the idealization—of technology and its tangible results in heavy-industrial production and plentiful consumer goods was, according to Biskind, generally embraced and celebrated by the period's dominant pluralist ideology. Rather than expressing fear of "technology" per se, Biskind sees postwar cinema exhibiting foremost a profound distrust of utopian promises ideologically outside "the vital center."

Still, while the ubiquity of the new and improved in postwar society provided signs of inevitable progress, it also signaled a wholesale change in social relations, obscuring existing class lines and confusing social identity. Hope for the future was typically accompanied by anxiety over one's place in it. And anxiety over what shape the future would take was often expressed in terms of technological resistance or hesitation. Popular media played a significant role in selling technology to the consumer, repeatedly instructing the public on how to consume the technologies and why. If magazines, television, radio, and film provided reassurances, they also offer a record of the anxieties that collected around a culture shaped increasingly by the "scientific imagination."

Underneath the wonders of modern convenience presented in *Forbidden Planet* is the question of what horror or catastrophe wiped out the *Belleraphon* crew, not to mention an entire civilization. More subtly than its genre contemporaries, *Forbidden Planet* indeed links the extinction of this entire species to nuclear holocaust. During the tour of the long-deserted but still-functioning Krell laboratories, Professor Morbius casually remarks that a single alien furnace emits the energy of "ninety-two-hundred thermonuclear reactors." Visually, the sequence emphasizes the vast dimensions of the alien complexes with high-angle, optical composite shots that reduce the Earthmen to ants lost in canyons of flashing light and throbbing arrays of industrial power. Effectively exploiting the new CinemaScope process, *Forbidden Planet* contains relatively few close-ups; most of the film plays in long shots and medium shots to showcase its expensive production design— ornate sets, matte paintings, props, and visual effects. To borrow Paul Schrader's famous insight about film noir, *Forbidden Planet* is a movie in which settings visually dominate the characters.[12] Human figures reduced to insignificance by the awesome scale of foreboding technological power provide a popular metaphor for confronting the Bomb no less compelling than the radioactive mutants and bug-eyed marauders more commonly associated with 1950s science fiction.

Like the Krell labs themselves, the central fear of the postwar period lies just below the surface of what is essentially a children's movie, dread unleashed by the recent memory of Hiroshima and Nagasaki and sustained by the publicity surrounding nuclear testing. Consider, for example, the "Doomsday Clock" on the cover of every issue of the *Bulletin of the Atomic Scientists*. When the clock first appeared in 1947, it was set at seven minutes to midnight. With the arrival of hydrogen bombs in 1952, the editors moved the hand forward to two minutes to midnight. As Spencer Weart argues in *Nuclear Fear,* the symbolism suggested by this maneuver is obvious: "Nuclear midnight meant the end of time."[13] The imminence of nuclear holocaust juxtaposed the thrill of atomic empowerment with the terror of annihilation. In the early 1950s, people appeared to be apathetic about nuclear weapons, but psychological testing conducted decades later revealed that such behavior was in fact a displacement of deep-seated psychological terror, suggesting that the earlier response was one of denial.[14]

At least one possibility is that this denial was framed and encouraged by a combined effort of mercantile interests and the mechanisms of publicity that both stimulated and chronicled economic growth in the postwar period. Within the film itself, while the Id Monster stalks Morbius from the depths of his own unconscious mind, in the contemporary social context, the hydrogen bomb is the ferocious doppelgänger shadowing Robby, the friendly techno-nanny and industrial horn of plenty. As Robby himself is an offshoot of Krell science, the film repeatedly indicates that the culture of consumer abundance and the threat of apocalyptic destruction stem from the same source. Weart writes:

> A 1946 survey concluded that few citizens thought of any constructive uses when atomic energy was discussed; "to the general public atomic energy means the atomic bomb." . . . As of 1953, the drive toward a civilian nuclear industry was confined to some nuclear scientists, their followers in journalism and government, and a small minority of industrialists. But those groups could be persuasive, fired as they were not by dry facts but by a vision of saving the world and leading it to an atomic utopia.[15]

He further notes: "A secret report . . . in November 1955 boasted that the ['Atoms for Peace'] campaign 'detracted popular attention away from the image of a United States bent on nuclear holocaust,' diverting the public eye to 'technological progress and international cooperation.'"[16]

This new acceptance of the atom would be achieved by domesticating nuclear energy, turning the possible devastation of the existing world into the technological marvels of a future world through the various created connotations of *modern* in the postwar period and its linkage with *convenience* in popular discourse. The prevalence and uses of *convenience* as a sort of talisman of progress are important in their focus on individual indulgence, repeatedly suggesting a liberation from a burdensome past into a bright and newly proscribed future, a "new frontier." This future utopia, made possible by consumer technologies, is in fact a reworking of the subtle and enduring myth of the golden age. The modern age scenario of the postwar period combined the cult of progress with a progressive agenda aided and abetted by technology—particularly the car and television mass marketed as aids for self- and societal transformation. The multiple discourses concerning machines and culture in the postwar period divide simply into two opposing camps or patterns of belief: those who saw technology (and therefore the future) as positive and something to be embraced with optimism and those who, recalling the devastation of the atomic bombings, saw technology as problematic at best and the future world it could create as something to be feared as much as anticipated.

One of the essential missions of publicity at this time was to deflect worry over nuclear war and redirect the energy of this fear into excitement about the possibilities technology presented for the future. That this was done largely through consumer goods is immensely interesting: the maneuver is literal and symbolic at the same time because it domesticates the wonders of the Atomic Age, moving attention from destruction of the world to the conveniences of the home. Robby, we should remember after all, is the ultimate appliance. And note simply that he has a name; in the timeworn practice of utilities advertising, he has been warmed up or humanized. Television commercials extended the reach of advertising into people's homes, as did the abundant lifestyles portrayed on the screen. TV situation comedies in the postwar years, especially those aimed at ethnic or working-class audiences, eased the transition from a Depression-bred psychology of scarcity to an acceptance of spending. The dramas of daily life on these programs, as Elaine Tyler May notes, often revolved around "the purchase of consumer goods for the home. Characters in these programs urged each other to buy on installment—'to live above one's means was the American Way,' and to spend rather than save."[17] Living above one's means could also be seen as a source of anxiety during this time, but financial insolvency pales in comparison to the awareness of living in a world with the potential to be vaporized at any moment. So consumerism can be seen as being motivated personally by a faith in the future, as well as providing reassurances that there would be a future.

The Kitchen Debate resituated the Cold War as a conflict over the commodity gap rather than the missile gap. Nixon said:

> To us, diversity, the right to choose, . . . is the most important thing. We don't have one decision made at the top by one government official. . . . We have many different manufacturers and many different

> kinds of washing machines so that housewives have a choice. . . .
> Would it not be better to compete in the relative merits of washing
> machines than in the strength of rockets?[18]

This focus on convenience (as the key element to a modern way of life
especially) provided a means of refocusing postwar uneasiness from a
military and international perspective to a localized concern situated in
the home. Yet the inadvertent results of this maneuver may sometimes
seem jarring, even desperate. Jack G. Shaheen and Richard Taylor,
writing in the anthology *Nuclear War Films,* point to a jaw-dropping
1954 newspaper ad. On the day of a highly publicized hydrogen bomb
test, an advertisement claimed: "The bomb's brilliant gleam reminds
me of the brilliant gleam Beacon Wax gives to floors. It's a scientific
marvel."[19]

Combining Sontag's and Biskind's analyses, we may recognize that
the elitist Professor Morbius and the frightening power of the Krell indeed exemplify the results of unchecked "extremism" and dangerous
utopian dreaming that many postwar intellectuals saw as characteristic
of totalitarian fascism and communism; we have suggested that the
rampaging Id Monster represents *Forbidden Planet*'s particular figura-
tion of nuclear holocaust. However, the nearly unfathomable Krell
technology is of a wholly different order than that represented by
Robby, who exists only to synthesize and dispense limitless goods and
services on demand. Once Robby and Altaira are wrested away from
the mad scientist and put under Commander Adams's sanely moderate,
democratic control, the resulting sci-fi vision of American society
formed aboard *the spaceship* at the conclusion defines the film's authentic utopia—one whose views and values converge with dominant
trends of the Eisenhower decade.

Liftoff for Levittown

The flying saucer represented as the safe new home at the finale of
Forbidden Planet provides another example of transferal and domesti-
cation of a popular postwar icon. The term *flying saucer* entered
American vernacular after a rash of now infamous sightings of alleged
extraterrestrial vehicles in 1947; Hollywood picked up and virtually
standardized both the term and the prop design from the outset of the
1950s science fiction boom. Aliens arrived aboard flying saucers in the
Republic serial *Flying Disc Man from Mars* (1951), as well as in *The
Thing, The Day the Earth Stood Still, Invaders from Mars* (1953),
This Island Earth, Earth vs. the Flying Saucers (1956), the notorious

Plan 9 from Outer Space (1959), where they seem to be made of pie tins, and many others. The Cold War undercurrent of this obsession is clearly revealed in a little-known B picture simply called *The Flying Saucer* (1950), in which American agents investigate UFO reports in Alaska and discover the unscrupulous assistant of a brilliant scientist who is attempting to sell his chief's advanced experimental craft to Soviet spies.[20] No Martians, pods, or "intellectual carrots" here; it's the Russians, pure and simple.

The flying saucer quickly became an immediately understood sign of technological superiority identified with threats of invasion and planetary annihilation. *Forbidden Planet,* however, manipulates these established connotations in fascinating ways. There are in fact two "flying saucers" in the film. Morbius's house of tomorrow is identifiably a ranch-style home, with its mix of indoors and outdoors and the casualness of its arrangements, yet its basic structural design reiterates the domed, curvilinear shape of Commander Adams's spaceship. The *domus morbius,* built over the entrance to the Krell labs, mediates between the magical potential/overwhelming threat of the vanished aliens and the useful, efficient spacecraft that Adams commands. The subtle association of Morbius's home with the flying saucers that typically transported ghastly aliens to Earth in fifties sci-fi underscores the professor's role as the true threat in the film. Yet it is important to grasp that in the C-57D, a typical saucer construction is viewed positively for perhaps the only time in this crucial decade of genre history. (The movie begins and ends with shots of the space cruiser in flight.) The double meaning of flying saucer in *Forbidden Planet* (Morbius's Krell-house/Adams's spaceship) parallels the potent duality of the Id Monster/Robby the Robot. To the extent the negative terms of each pair serve the jeremiad function of many science fiction tales, the traditional American faith in science and technology as progressive forces may be chastened, although hardly abandoned entirely.

The film's final words, spoken by J.J. Adams, reassure Alta that her father's name will not be forgotten and that his death, and that of the Krell, will serve to teach us that "we are, after all, not God." These quasi-religious reassurances come aboard the safety of the spaceship as the film affirms the traditional heterosexual, monogamous pairing of Adams and Alta—Mr. and Mrs. Suburban America. (An actual shipboard wedding scene was filmed, but was cut from the release version.) With Robby now at the controls, the unmistakably all-American crew of C-57D—familiar types plucked off the bombers and subs of fifties war movies—carries away the one tangible benefit of Krell science in manageable, "user-friendly" form. The robot's enthusiastic final line, "Aye, aye, Skipper!" makes clear that this boundless technological marvel who can only help, never harm, humans is now firmly under proper control. A truly space-age vision of 1950s America is posited as the genuine utopian alternative to the destructive extremism of Morbius and the Krell. The future indeed looks as bright as the brilliant gleam of Beacon Wax.

And yet, just outside the window of the spaceship—a large rectangular aperture not unlike the touted "picture window" of postwar suburban homes—Alta and Commander Adams can easily observe the fiery end of Altair IV. This final sequence completes the thematic and visual mingling of affluence and anxiety throughout *Forbidden Planet*. The film's fairly obvious struggle to harness sexual energy recedes in comparison to the far more foreboding and vital task of constraining the overwhelming destructive capacity of nuclear energy and ways to redirect and reinvest that fear—a struggle scarcely concluded despite the movie's superficially cheery ending.

Conclusion: Outer Space as Domestic Space

Forbidden Planet's transformation of the flying saucer into the postwar suburban home can now be seen as one of the first of many such cultural domestications of outer space for American consumers in this period, a conception that became increasingly prevalent with the launch of the Soviet *Sputnik* satellite in the year after the movie's release and the start of the "space race." Walt Disney may have begun the trend in 1955, when Disneyland opened and prominently featured the futuristic Tomorrowland; alongside the park's rocket trip to Mars ride after 1957 was the Monsanto corporation's "Home of the Future," a dwelling that would have seemed familiar to Professor Morbius and Robby.[21] (Disney animators had in fact created the glimpses of the snarling Id Monster's transparent outline when it briefly materialized as a pulsating electrical horror.) In 1960, the Los Angeles architect John Lautner built the Malin residence, also known as the Chemosphere House, in the hills above the rapidly sprawling suburbs of the San Fernando Valley. Appropriately overlooking Universal Studios, the rounded octagonal structure with slanted-glass windows ringing its circumference was intended as an innovative solution to a steep hill site conventionally deemed unbuildable.[22] Lautner perched the domicile on a single slim pillar; complete with skylight dome on top, the Chemosphere House appears to most observers to resemble the familiar flying saucer of fifties sci-fi.[23]

The 1962 Seattle World's Fair, also known as the Century 21 Exposition, billed itself as "America's Space Age World's Fair." Its futuristic theme involved an experiment in city planning that aimed to revitalize Seattle's downtown well beyond the time of the exhibition itself.[24] Like the Chemosphere House, Century 21's most famous icon, the Space Needle, projects a flying saucer design up onto a high pillar to convey an impression of flight. The same year the Seattle exhibition opened, TV viewers met George Jetson, head of a recognizably postwar suburban family of the supposedly distant future who, along with their robotic maid, dwelled in cloud cities reminiscent of Lautner's curvilinear designs. *The Jetsons* was the first of several TV programs of the early sixties that were, in the words of critic Lynn Spigel, "premised on an uncanny mixture of suburbia and space travel."[25] Perhaps the most famous of these was *Lost in Space,* featuring the space-faring Robinson clan (archetypically suburban despite their silvery flight suits) whose *Jupiter II* spaceship looks as if Lautner's Chemosphere House had simply lifted off from its mooring pillar and headed for the stars.[26] But *Forbidden Planet,* having little do with Shakespeare and much to say about postwar American culture, had first charted this course from Altair IV to Levittown and back.

An incisive commentary on the shape of a mass-mediated future was the exhibit staged by the Independent Group at Whitechapel Art Gallery, London, on 8 August 1956. "This Is Tomorrow," as Brian Wallis notes, drew heavily from "the repertoire of popular culture: billboard size robots, optical illusions, Marilyn Monroe, advertisements, a rock 'n' roll jukebox, a giant beer bottle, and a cineramic wall of film posters." Wallis goes on to make the point that "the funhouse installation challenged the exclusivity of the dominant ways of regarding art, and opened an avenue for a more democratic analysis of art and cultural criticism."[27] Robby the Robot was a central feature of "This Is Tomorrow." A fourteen-foot-high cutout model taken from a poster for the movie depicted Robby cradling the unconscious and extremely curvaceous body of Altaira, an image that did not appear in the film. Beyond noting that this group of British artists was deliberately flaunting their "Americanisation" to oppose (what they saw as) the sterile modernism advocated by art critics such as Herbert Read, there is an additional and adjacent point to be made when we consider where the images selected came from and the ideas that governed their selection. Of the variety of possible tomorrows imagined, the artists creating this installation chose to see a future shaped by science and technology, advertising, and movies, an early embrace of the "Americanisation" that is now seen as the shaping force of global culture. It is the plausible matrix of these images at this time—and their popular utility and reception—that informs *Forbidden Planet*.

"The robot," wrote the Independent Group's Lawrence Alloway in 1956, "can symbolise bland acceptance of machines or fears of a violent sexual nature. Common to both extremes is the retention of the human image. At a time when many artists are looking for iconographies with which to express 'the times' with a high degree of accessibility, the popular arts have it."[28] Why did these images drawn from American commercial culture—particularly the King Kong–like pose of Robby the Robot carrying Anne Francis—resonate for those asking and suggesting answers to the question "What will tomorrow bring?" And why was this question asked repeatedly within the contexts of culture and technology? Of master and slave? Of salvation or annihilation? The answer can be found largely in *Forbidden Planet*'s encapsulation of the uneasy, mass-market peace between man and machine. In the apocalyptic shadow cast by the threat of thermonuclear holocaust, could the technological modern conveniences offered by consumerism provide a significant and believable means of salvation? Enter Robby.

At the time of *Forbidden Planet*'s release, American society was experiencing a significant transformation in identity driven by an unprecedented prosperity that, reiterating Skal's pronouncement, "was won atop the largest bone pile in human history." Concern with the human makers of the various technologies populating the postwar period becomes a fundamental question in the mix of American anxiety and affluence, as evidenced in *Forbidden Planet*—where such a concern could be said to be the film's central theme. The unusual juxtapositions found in mass media—the Bomb and Beacon Wax, Robby and the deadly Id Monster, the explosion of Altair IV viewed by Alta and Commander Adams from the picture window of their spaceship—are in fact typical instances of these contiguous relationships in the postwar period. *Forbidden Planet* resonated for the members of Britain's Independent Group as well as the American public because it further suggested the rise of a new order, a democratization of culture or an "aesthetics of plenty": the aristocratic Morbius's domain giving way to the pragmatism of Commander Adams's plebeian vision is comparable to the rising power of the masses in postwar America.[29] The film supports the idea of this rise (and convergence) with the cross-class pairing of Adams and Altaira; Morbius's futuristic ranch house, replete with the latest in modern conveniences, is very much the country-home ideal depicted in advertisements, magazines, and TV shows of the time. A significant part of *Forbidden Planet*'s popularity can be said, then, to have stemmed from its ability to organize and address the potent anxieties of postwar America and suggest the panacea of consumption for easing these fears. The film's continued value and interest as a text resides in its linking of modern convenience (made possible by the advances of science) and modern dread (can humans wisely use the power unleashed by the advances of science?), a linking that still resonates in a postmodern, premillennial context where consumption and culture repeatedly overlap and redefine each other.

Notes

1. David J. Skal, *The Monster Show: A Cultural History of Horror* (New York: Penguin, 1994), 229.

2. William H. Whyte Jr., "Budgetism: Opiate of the Middle Class," *Fortune,* May 1956, 133.

3. Richard Nixon quoted in Elaine Tyler May, *Homeward Bound: American Families in the Cold War Era* (New York: Basic Books, 1988), 163.

4. For detailed discussion of the production of *Forbidden Planet,* including interviews with many key production personnel and much otherwise unavailable material, see the special double issue of *Cinefantastique* 8, nos. 2–3 (1979).

5. Nixon quoted in May, *Homeward Bound,* 163.

6. Ibid., 18.

7. Henry Dreyfuss quoted in Adrian Forty, *Objects of Desire: Design and Society from Wedgwood to IBM* (New York: Pantheon, 1986), 199.

8. Joseph I. Breen to Dore Schary, 8 May 1955; Breen to Schary, 24 February 1955; "Forbidden Planet," MPAA/Production Code Administration files, Margaret Herrick Library, Beverly Hills, Calif.

9. Susan Sontag, "The Imagination of Disaster," in *Against Interpretation and Other Essays* (New York: Delta, 1966), 209–25.

10. Ibid., 217.

11. Peter Biskind, *Seeing Is Believing: How Hollywood Taught Us to Stop Worrying and Love the Fifties* (New York: Pantheon, 1983), 102–36. As Biskind says of *Forbidden Planet* specifically: "Robby the Robot was a servant and tool, not a master nor enemy. . . . He was the latest thing in labor-saving devices, a Waring Blender, Mixmaster, and Electrolux vacuum cleaner all rolled up into one" (106).

12. *Variety*'s critic responded to the movie in this way as well: "With all the technical gadgetry on display and carrying the entertainment load, the players are more or less puppets with no great acting demands made." *Variety,* 12 March 1956, clipping in "Forbidden Planet," MPAA/Production Code Administration files, Margaret Herrick Library, Beverly Hills, Calif.

13. Spencer R. Weart, *Nuclear Fear: A History of Images* (Cambridge: Harvard University Press, 1988), 217.

14. For another discussion of this complex historical issue, see Paul Boyer, *By the Bomb's Early Light: American Thought and Culture at the Dawn of the Atomic Age* (New York: Pantheon, 1985). Interestingly, although American reviewers never made the connection, upon the 1959 rerelease of *Forbidden Planet* in Australia, local censors ordered the elimination of "all shots of alleged nuclear monster." "MPAA Report received

from local censor board in the territory named," "Forbidden Planet," MPAA/Production Code Administration files, Margaret Herrick Library, Beverly Hills, Calif.

15. Weart, *Nuclear Fear,* 162.

16. Ibid., 163.

17. May, *Homeward Bound,* 172.

18. Nixon quoted in ibid., 17.

19. Quoted in Jack G. Shaheen and Richard Taylor, "The Beginning or the End," in *Nuclear War Films,* ed. Jack G. Shaheen (Carbondale: Southern Illinois University Press, 1978), 6.

20. See Phil Hardy, ed., *The Overlook Film Encyclopedia: Science Fiction* (Woodstock, N.Y.: Overlook, 1991), 125–26.

21. "The Monsanto home was the International Style humanized, scaled down for human consumption, curved into friendly shapes, and rescued from severity by a showroom's worth of push-button phones, lighting panels, pole lamps . . . and an Atoms for Living Kitchen [i.e., a microwave oven] by Kelvinator." Karal Ann Marling, "Imagineering the Disney Theme Parks," in *Designing Disney's Theme Parks: The Architecture of Reassurance,* ed. Karal Ann Marling (Montreal: Canadian Centre for Architecture, 1997), 144–46.

22. Frank Escher, ed., *John Lautner, Architect* (New York: Princeton Architectural Press, 1998), 113.

23. See, for example, a photo feature on the Chemosphere House in the *New York Times*: "Perched atop a thirty foot column . . . this 'flying saucer' house is futuristic in its exterior, design, and construction materials. . . . The interior is a blending of rich textures with simple modern furnishings." "People Who Live in Flying Saucers Key Decor to the Landscape," *New York Times,* 29 April 1961, L14.

24. For an excellent discussion of Century 21, see John M. Findlay, *Magic Lands: Western Cityscapes and American Culture after 1940* (Berkeley: University of California Press, 1992), esp. 214–64.

25. Lynn Spigel, "From Domestic Space to Outer Space: The 1960s Fantastic Family Sit-Coms," in *Close Encounters: Film, Feminism, and Science Fiction,* ed. Constance Penley, Elisabeth Lyon, Lynn Spigel, and Janet Bergstrom (Minneapolis: University of Minnesota Press, 1990), 204–5.

26. This cult TV series has more direct connections to *Forbidden Planet.* Bob Kinoshita, one of the principal designers of Robby, rendered the Robinsons' faithful robot with the famously waving mechanical claws and flat-bubbled head. In one of several movie and TV appearances after leaving Altair IV, Robby even "guest starred" as an evil automaton in "War of the Robots," a 1965 *Lost in Space* episode.

27. Brian Wallis, "Tomorrow and Tomorrow and Tomorrow: The Independent Group and Popular Culture," in *Modern Dreams: The Rise and Fall and Rise of Pop* (New York: Institute for Contemporary Art/Clocktower Gallery, 1988), 9.

28. Lawrence Alloway quoted in Eugenie Tsai, "The Sci-Fi Connection: The Independent Group, J. G. Ballard, and Robert Smithson," in *Modern Dreams: The Rise and Fall and Rise of Pop,* 71.

29. For more on the Independent Group, see David Robbins, ed., *The Independent Group: Postwar Britain and the Aesthetics of Plenty* (Cambridge: MIT Press, 1990).

PART II

CONSUMING CREATORS

7.
"Chi-Chi Cinderella": Audrey Hepburn as Couture Countermodel
Gaylyn Studlar

That's more than a dress—that's an Audrey Hepburn movie.
Jerry Maguire (Tom Cruise), in *Jerry Maguire* (1996)

Although the "mammary madness" of the 1950s represented by stars such as Marilyn Monroe, Jayne Mansfield, and Jane Russell has been much discussed, Hollywood's promotion of another, contrasting model of film femininity in the postwar period has been little remarked upon.[1] This "countermodel" to a voluptuous, hypersexualized, and distinctly American femininity is found in the star image of Audrey Hepburn, where it offers interesting implications for studying the complex negotiations of gender construction in relation to mass culture. My goal in this essay, then, is to show how Hepburn's representation in specific film texts of the 1950s and, more generally, as a star discourse figured also in publicity articles, film advertising, and other extratextual materials is enmeshed in a diverse array of cultural meanings centered on the notion of fashion—and more specifically, of Paris high fashion—as a privileged signifier of a utopian consumer culture linked to an idealized (if ideologically problematic) feminine identity.

Director Stanley Donen has remarked, "Audrey was always more about fashion than movies or acting."[2] Jackie Stacey has suggested that glamorous female stars of the 1940s and 1950s almost inevitably functioned as "fashion models" for women spectators who watched actresses' star vehicles and associated their own attainment of ideal femininity with the consumption of clothes.[3] Nevertheless, it is obvious too that certain female stars were privileged more than others as fashion commodities constructed to solicit the attention of their female audience's "shopper's eye" and serve as role models for a femininity inseparable from fashion. To understand Audrey Hepburn as such a fashion commodity as well as a star commodity, we must start with a consideration of the state of haute couture at the end of World War II.

In February 1947, Christian Dior unveiled a collection that heralded the return of the French fashion industry in the world market. The impact of this collection was unprecedented. The "New Look"—as *Harper's Bazaar* editor in chief Carmel Snow dubbed it, constituted a revolution that would influence women's fashions for the next full decade.[4] If the success of the collection was soon strikingly clear, so was Dior's purpose. That, he stated, was nothing less than to supplant the era of "women soldiers built like boxers" with "women-flowers [with] soft shoulders, flowering busts, fine waists like liana and wide skirts like corolla."[5] Dior explained the quick acceptance of the New Look on both sides of the Atlantic: "Women longed to look like women again," he said, because there had been a "universal change of feeling."[6]

Dior's New Look established the aesthetic norms of haute couture into the mid-1950s while it heralded an enthusiastic revival of Paris as the center of the fashion industry. In the 1960s, its influence as a phenomenon went into precipitous decline as lady clients and their fortunes died out. At the same time, ready-to-wear and a multiplicity of international design influences, often derived from youth-oriented "street clothes," rose to prominence. This all occurred within a radically changing social atmosphere. Designer Cristóbal Balenciaga noted in explanation of why he closed his fashion house in 1968: "The life which supported couture is finished."[7]

Yet, in the late 1940s and 1950s, the glorious anachronism of haute couture, led by Dior's New Look, reestablished Paris's traditional domination of U.S. as well as European fashion trends. American manufacturers and retailers longed to exploit once again the status of superiority enjoyed by Parisian designers. What the war cruelly withheld from American women desiring Continental chic they were eager now to provide. French fashion houses were keenly aware of their postwar dependence upon U.S. business practice and American consumers who could afford French luxury goods. By the mid-1950s it was estimated that 70 percent of haute couture clients were Americans. For those who could not go to France for fittings, enthusiastic retailers such as I. Magnin brought Parisian design to upper-class clientele at one-half the cost of Paris models, and an absence of meaningful fashion piracy laws in the United States made it possible to accommodate aspiring middle-class women with more affordable French-influenced wardrobe choices.[8]

Difference, of course, was sold as a key appeal in the New Look's design innovation. Plenitude replaced wartime austerity, exhibitionism replaced functionality. More to the point, long replaced short, billowing yardage replaced sparse wartime allotments, and diaphanous fabrics replaced sturdy materials promising patriotic longevity. The New Look short-circuited the evolutionary process of fashion as emergent designers such as Hubert de Givenchy emphasized "youthful" ideas and took mannish styles like the shirtwaist and gave them new, romantic life with delicate fabrics and impractical ornate detailing.[9] Throughout the 1950s, collections from Dior, Givenchy, Balenciaga, and other Paris fashion houses provided the continuous innovation expected of fashion but still sustained the spirit of Dior's postwar return to an elegant hyperfeminine fashion ideal inspired by the belle epoque.

Hepburn and the Show Window of Hollywood

Hollywood became a key "show window" for selling the New Look and its image of femininity. As Maureen Turim has noted, Paris's high-fashion New Look was soon translated into homegrown Hollywood costume design. The "sweetheart line" co-opted the New Look's full skirt, pinched waist, and dropped neckline (or, for nighttime, the strapless bodice). Its name reflected its bodice shape as well as its association with youthful femininity. The sweetheart line became the basic dress design used to symbolize visually the transformation of the immature bobby-soxer into a marriageable woman in films such as *A Date with Judy* (1948) and *Father of the Bride* (1950).[10] Specific cinematic versions of the sweetheart line, such as Edith Head's glamorous flower-swathed version of the dress for Elizabeth Taylor in *A Place in the Sun* (1951) were popularized by affordable imitations in the U.S. ready-to-wear market.

But it was not until 1953, when Audrey Hepburn asked to add the Parisian dresses of Givenchy to her wardrobe for Billy Wilder's *Sabrina* (1954), that French high-fashion fully broke into postwar Hollywood as costume design.[11] Edith Head was credited with costume supervision and received an Oscar for the film for costume design, but the most memorable and imitated designs were Givenchy's: a slim sophisticated town suit, a black satin cocktail dress, and a magnificent strapless white ball gown with black and gray embroidery and black ruffle. The couturier was relatively unknown in the United States when Hepburn asked him to provide designs for *Sabrina,* but that situation would soon change. The opening of *Sabrina* in Paris was timed to Givenchy's spring-summer 1955 collection; in the United States, Sabrina look-alike contests promoted both the film and the Givenchy look. The designer's success was assured: "*Sabrina* brought me more new clients then I could handle," he later remarked.[12]

Sabrina also marked the beginning of the public definition of Hepburn, in which Givenchy fashions function as an important, recognizable component of her identity as a star personality. Hepburn and Givenchy would be inseparably linked, both onscreen and off. He would design her "costumes" for *Funny Face* (1957), *Love in the Afternoon* (1957), *Breakfast at Tiffany's* (1961), *Charade* (1963), *Paris When It Sizzles* (1964), and *How to Steal a Million* (1966). It came to be reported that she turned down films that would not permit her to use him as either her costume designer or consultant.[13] In addition, Givenchy would become the designer of choice for Hepburn's personal wardrobe for almost twenty years.[14] That fact was personal but not private: the star would become the subject of fashion news and featured on numerous occasions in Givenchy dresses, suits, ball gowns, and hats in elite fashion magazines such as *Vogue* (American) and *Harper's Bazaar*. Hepburn commented on her inseparability from high fashion: "In a certain way one can say that Hubert de Givenchy has 'created' me over the years."[15]

Even in this, Hepburn's association with Givenchy conformed to the established standards for an upper-class woman's relationship to her couturier. In American fashion magazines in the 1950s, anonymous models displayed new fashions, but special multipage layouts presenting haute couture were often reserved for women of the upper class. They were identified by their family connections as statesmen's wives, debutante daughters of the old rich, and even members of royalty. Hepburn joined the ranks of these social elite as a role model when, after her appearance in *Sabrina* in 1954, she appeared in *Vogue*: this arbiter of American fashion declared her to have "established a new standard of beauty and every other face now approximates the 'Hepburn look.'"[16] The "Hepburn look" was now a commodity subject to being reproduced. Throughout 1955, numerous models resembling Hepburn could be seen in fashion features and advertisements in *Vogue* displaying dark, cropped hair, thick eyebrows, swanlike necks, wide-eyed youthfulness, and thin bodies.[17]

The new standard of feminine beauty as narrow and underdeveloped was not instigated by Givenchy or Hepburn, but Hepburn epitomized this type in the movies, where it was a decided contrast to the shapely, buxom norm for female stars. Givenchy proclaimed Hepburn to have "the proportions of the ideal woman" at 32-20-35, five feet, seven inches tall and 110 pounds.[18] Postwar high fashion made the physical ideal of the French mannequin—long, slender neck, slim-waisted body, and long legs—the increasingly desired physical type for fashionable clothes. In New Look fashions, inner dress construction (or padded bras and girdles) could provide the necessary body shaping that would leave the long, graceful neck and thin arms intact. There was a discernible trend in the fifties toward suits and skirts that were less fulsome (especially in the fall and winter collections), with less emphasis on the bosom and more on a straight signature silhouette: Dior introduced the sheath in 1953 and the A-line in 1955; Givenchy, the chemise in 1956. These mid-1950s figure-revealing New Look developments "demanded" a slim body. The true test of the appropriate body type for high fashion became the pencil-slim suits, such as the one Hepburn wears in *Sabrina*. By 1957, the *New York Times* remarked that Dior himself was growing fatter and fatter, but "his mannequins get thinner and thinner, straighter and straighter, flatter and flatter."[19] Satirizing this phenomenon, in Hepburn's *Funny Face* the fictional editor of *Quality* fashion magazine declares, "Who cares if the New Look has no bust!" In real life, it was said that many American men did care—very much. Suffering from "Dior phobia," they vociferously protested the appearance of the flat look in their wives and girlfriends who followed fashion.[20]

The beginning of the Givenchy/Hepburn collaboration was aided by the fact that *Sabrina* was one of the biggest box-office draws of 1954. A frothy light comedy, it is a Cinderella story in which the title character, a chauffeur's daughter (Hepburn), is sent to Paris for cooking lessons. Her father hopes that this move will help her get over her teenage crush on David (William Holden), the playboy son of the Larrabees, the wealthy Long Island family that employs him. Months later, Sabrina prepares to return home. She writes her father: "If you should have any difficulty recognizing your daughter, I shall be the most sophisticated woman at the Glencove Station." On her return, she is much changed in appearance—and attitude, for she is ready to capture the heart of dallying David, even though she knows he is to be married to a woman whose wealthy father owns the sugar plantations that workaholic brother Linus Larrabee (Humphrey Bogart) must acquire for a multimillion-dollar business venture.

Fashion plays a central role in transforming Sabrina from a sexually frustrated adolescent with a ponytail "like a horse" into an immaculately groomed, chic woman who can jump across class lines into the arms of a fabulously wealthy suitor. *Woman's Home Companion* described *Sabrina* as a movie in which the main character "learns how a girl dresses and talks to attract a man."[21] The *Hollywood Reporter* review recognized the fashion-centered feminine appeal of the film: "This is the best woman's picture since *Three Coins in the Fountain*. It is too bad that the storytelling wardrobe . . . has not been shot in color."[22]

Although Billy Wilder was not known as a director of "woman's pictures," the film's emphasis on its female protagonist often takes a form that, paradoxically, resembles a fashion show aimed at a distinctly female audience even though men are marked as those who primarily look at Hepburn within the film. Throughout *Sabrina*, Hepburn's poses and the manner in which she is photographed suggest the conventions of high-fashion photography. When she appears at the Glencove train station in a pencil-slim Givenchy town suit, she adopts the chic pose and accoutrements (a rhinestone-collared poodle) that female audiences would immediately recognize from the pages of *Vogue* or *Harper's Bazaar* as well as from newspaper fashion and consumer product advertisements. This was because high fashion was big business in the 1950s, and its influence saturated the imagery employed for a wide range of consumer marketing. Women shaped like couture mannequins, posed like them, and wearing clothes indebted to Paris fashion were used to sell a vast array of consumer products, from automobiles to lipstick. During these years, in the words of one scholar, "fashion was everywhere."[23]

The fashion show approach to presenting Hepburn is most memorably demonstrated in the party scene that marks Sabrina's move from "over the garage" into polite society. On the veranda of the Larrabee mansion, David looks for Sabrina as he dances with his fiancée, Elizabeth (Martha Hyer). He suddenly stops. A full shot that reverses the field of vision shows Sabrina sweeping up in a fast walk to the edge of the balustrade that defines the dance floor. Her movement suggests a model making an entrance on a fashion show runway. There are cuts to medium shots and close-up reaction shots of men looking in open-mouthed awe of her. Then we are offered a close-up of her face as she sways to the music. A cut back to David reveals him attempting to get rid of his fiancée. Sabrina is then shown in medium shot surrounded by men as David calls her name and reaches out to take her hand. After they dance, she waits for David at the indoor tennis court. An overhead long shot shows her dancing by herself, sweeping her dress's train around her as she moves to the band's rendition of "Isn't It Romantic."

The star of this scene is Hepburn *in* Givenchy's evening dress. Jane Gaines has argued that costume was necessary in classical Hollywood film to create a pleasurable female spectacle, but had to remain subservient to the dramatic content of the story and controlled so that it would not "divert the viewer's attention from the story itself."[24] Film critic Molly Haskell, writing of her teenage response to Hepburn, provides an interesting clue to this scene. She says: "Having no special clothes memory, I'm surprised at how vividly I recall design and detail of this dress."[25] However, such a memory is not surprising at all if we recognize that at this moment the film allows costume to overtake the normal central role of narrative. As a consequence, *Sabrina*'s violation of Hollywood norms may also account for the complaint voiced in one review of the film, which noted, "Her actual invasion of the dancing party on her return [from] Europe is basically a bad and incredible portion of the picture."[26]

The Larrabee party scene may be "bad and incredible" from one perspective, but Haskell's vivid memories of Sabrina's ball gown support the conclusions drawn by Jackie Stacey from her interviews of British women who were avid consumers of American films of the 1940s and 1950s. She suggests that these women actually enjoyed disruptions of classical narrative that permitted the foregrounding of fashion and star styles (clothing as well as hairstyles and makeup).[27] No wonder that Hepburn star vehicles, especially those reliant on contemporary fashion, would, at some level, all turn into fashion shows meant to appeal to women spectators interested in haute couture. Hepburn is fetishistically displayed for the male characters, as in the Larrabee party scene, but at the same time this scene and others, such as Sabrina's encounter with David at the Glencove train station, provide the film's female audience members ample time and a generous view so that they may study costume details and admire the heroine's enviable ability to use fashion as a traditional feminine path to social improvement and, of course, romantic happiness.

Fantasies of a More Fashionable Femininity

As Richard Dyer has noted, "Wearing Haute couture bespeaks luxury, wealth, refinement and, less obviously, power."[28] Givenchy's costumes/fashions sell Hepburn as an image of femininity that consistently enjoys these associations. *Sabrina* suggests that fashion designs in and of themselves may be important appeals to women viewers, but worn by specific stars in fantasy-evoking situations of the high life, they could form an even more potent appeal to spectators.

Sabrina offers the narrativization of a female consumer fantasy of fashion's transformative possibilities. Sabrina breathlessly responds to

Mrs. Larrabee's revelation that she did not recognize her: "Have I changed, have I really changed?" In *Sabrina*, Hepburn is transformed from an invisible and miserable adolescent into the ideal ingenue, combining high spirits with refinement and beauty. Publicity on the actress anticipated the paradoxical duality of personality (adolescent but womanly, high-spirited but refined) as an essential aspect of her persona that her films would emphasize. An early *Life* photo feature on the star declared Hepburn to be "both waif and woman of the world . . . disarmingly friendly and strangely aloof . . . all queen . . . and all commoner."[29] Although Hepburn's persona (onscreen and off) retains qualities of the adolescent after she is transformed into a fashion plate, haute couture becomes naturalized as a fundamental articulation of a truer, happier femininity that emerges only when it is allowed the expressive medium of fashion.

Female audiences who were familiar with high-fashion magazines and news items on society's elite would immediately recognize that *Sabrina* visually presents its transformed heroine not just as the equal, but as the superior to her female rivals in terms of high-society standards of fashion and manners. David's fiancée is a shapely blonde clothed in a tulle black strapless sweetheart-design dress. Her appearance is coded as lacking the restraint appropriate for an unmarried society woman. Her blonde hair looks dyed; she is gloveless, and wears more jewelry (pearl choker necklace and diamond bracelet) than would be proper for a young woman of "breeding."[30] Ironically, she appears déclassé and decidedly nouveau riche compared to Sabrina, whose appearance demonstrates that taste cannot be bought: she has a better-developed fashion sense than her financial betters. While retaining her adolescent playfulness, Hepburn's character is sexualized within limits that are largely defined by her elegant haute couture dress and graceful, model-like physicality. Givenchy's designs establish Sabrina as womanly and sexually available, but haute couture of the 1950s would also have connoted sexual discretion and social refinement. These qualities were associated with the aristocratic debutantes and wealthy young married women (such as Mrs. John F. Kennedy) who graced the pages of high-fashion magazines in the 1950s.

"This is where she belongs," says the Larrabees' cook of Sabrina's debut in high society. Although fashion provides the means by which Hepburn is elevated in class, the film is careful to establish that this glamorous transformation, with its promise of social mobility, does not cut off Sabrina's emotional connection to her original class, to the people who comprise her "family." High-fashion clothes may express wealth and sexual sophistication, but the plotlines of Hepburn's films and her characters' behavior qualify both of these attributes. Sabrina must remain as good as she is beautiful. As she dances with David, she sweetly smiles and waves to a group of servants who stand behind a hedge to watch her triumph. Later, the butler is so thrilled by her romantic success with David that he thrusts a drink tray at a guest to serve as he scurries away to tell the other servants, "You should see Sabrina, the prettiest girl, the prettiest dress, the best dancer—the belle of the ball!"

The Cinderella theme of the girl of modest means becoming a chic, desirable woman through clothes is an element of the Hepburn persona sustained through many of her films. Hepburn's commodification as an elegant, Continental-flavored ingenue continued to be asserted through her couture clothes, upper-class accent, refined manners, and balletic carriage even if the plots of *Sabrina, Funny Face, Breakfast at Tiffany's,* and *Charade* did not allow her to be wealthy. Following fashion logic if not narrative logic, her characters often end up in Paris, as in *Funny Face,* where Hepburn plays antifashion bookseller Jo, who was described by *Look* magazine as a "bedraggled book worm."[31] Jo denounces the fashion photography crew that invades the Greenwich Village bookstore where she works. They want to use it as a backdrop for fashion photos, but she says the bookstore's owner "doesn't approve of fashion magazines. It's chi-chi and an unrealistic approach to self-impression as well as economics." Her loose tweed jumper, sensible shoes, and shapeless hairstyle suggest that she shares his opinion, as do her comments that she thinks fashion photography consists of "men taking idiotic pictures of idiotic women." However, the fashion photographer, Dick Avery (Fred Astaire), tenderly kisses her, and when she is alone, a high-fashion hat left behind from the magazine shoot becomes the vehicle for a musical reverie that signals she is not beyond being won over by fashion as well as romance.

Like *Sabrina, Funny Face* insists on a transformation that affirms not only the heroine's acceptance of but her *love* for the new fashionable self that emerges. Jo succumbs to *Quality* magazine's desire to turn her into "the world's most glamorous mannequin." At first, she only wants to use the magazine's promised trip to Paris to meet her intellectual idol, but her initial runway appearance in a Givenchy evening gown is, like the Larrabee party in *Sabrina,* a film-stopping moment. She is applauded by all the fashion business experts but also by maids and janitors, who put the beautification-is-a-woman's-obligation-to-herself seal of approval on Jo's transformation into a "bird of paradise." By the end of the film, Jo proclaims her love for fashion (all Givenchy, of course), modeling, Paris, and the architect of her makeover, Avery.

Haute Couture as a Young Idea/l

Perhaps more than any other Continental-flavored female star in the 1950s, including American-born Grace Kelly, Hepburn's youthful screen persona took the edge off of haute couture's long-standing association with serious, mature beauty and paved the way for a youthful feminine market for high fashion. In 1952, *Vogue* acknowledged this market of potential consumers through the debut of its "Young Idea" feature, aimed at readers seventeen to twenty-five years old. In the postwar scene, the broader emerging youth market was regarded as a distinct target for the romantic prettiness and delicacy of detail associated with the New Look, especially as practiced by Givenchy.[32] Hepburn became an important marketing strategy for Givenchy, especially in his appeal to a more youthful clientele traditionally epitomized by the society debutante. But, ironically, Paris design of the 1950s, while paying lip service to youthful styling, produced designs that rarely possessed those qualities that reliably could be agreed upon to represent the ease and freedom of youth.[33]

Perhaps that is why, as we shall see, there are some apparent contradictions in how Hepburn's films were marketed to and received by younger female viewers. On the one hand, Hepburn's films did provide some sense of youthful freedom by setting off the traditional couture elegance and refinement of the star's costumes with her youthful physicality and voice, as well as her characters' playful behavior. For example, in *Sabrina* Hepburn appears in the archetypal "little black dress" signaling Continental chic for Sabrina's dinner date with Linus Larrabee in Manhattan. Her Givenchy-designed black satin cocktail dress is beautifully accessorized by a small sequined hat and black gloves. Yet it is in this elegant outfit that she proceeds to spin around madly in Linus's executive chair until she is so dizzy that she collapses across his office conference table. Such moments illustrate how Hepburn's persona brought high fashion down to earth and made it emotionally accessible to young, middle-class women.[34] However, in spite of Hepburn's youthful aura, the haute couture of the 1950s emphasizes the alignment of high fashion with class norms that would not disintegrate in fashion photography and magazines until the 1960s and 1970s.

Although her haute couture attire sustains the ideals of New Look femininity, it is significant that Hepburn's appearance is tinged by boyishness and the suggestion of youthful physical immaturity.

One British critic icily observed in response to *Sabrina,* "Surely the vogue for asexuality can go no further than this weird hybrid with butchered hair."[35] Molly Haskell has also remarked—albeit more positively—on Hepburn's androgynous qualities. Haskell believes the star's onscreen representation of the "adolescent freedom" of a pubescentlike flat female body evoked strong feelings of identification with young female audiences who longed to be free (again) of "those secondary sex characteristics designed explicitly to imprison them in the role of woman and mother."[36] To Haskell, Hepburn's appeal to adolescent girls resided partially in her ability to imply "the resolution of painful conflicts."[37]

If this is so, then Hepburn's relationship to her youthful female audience supports Jackie Stacey's claim that film stars "representing cultural ideals of feminine beauty and charm played a key role in the processes of identity formation";[38] they offered a model of the transition to adult femininity that told young female spectators that the transformation from child to woman was dependent on self-improvement defined largely as the cultivation of a fashionability linked to consumerism. Nora Sayre, reminiscing also about the 1950s, suggests the powerful element of conformity in the Hepburn image: "Many adolescent girls of the fifties were almost tyrannized by the image of Audrey Hepburn: Hers was the manner by which ours was measured, and we were expected to identify with her, or to use her as a model."[39] Ironically the height of conformity, Hepburn's haute couture persona softens the oppressive blow of maturation into feminine conformity by asserting fashion's romanticized status as an art form created almost exclusively in the twentieth century for the individual—and collective—enjoyment of women.

Thus Hepburn's films could be read by her audiences as a parallel reality, where fashion was presented not as costume design of purely fictional origin and dimensions, but as having a built-in real-world status as designs appropriate for women viewers/consumers to buy, copy, or creatively adapt. Female spectators were encouraged by Hepburn's films, extratextual promotion, and publicity, to identify with the star as an ideal who represented a utopian fantasy of consumption. Stacey suggests that such a spectator fantasy did not necessarily depend on the actual purchase of clothing, but could be played out through gazing and fantasizing about "an ideal feminine self-image through imaginary consumption": "The desire to clothe your favorite star, to predict her taste and style" becomes part of the spectator's sharing of an "imagined intimacy with the Hollywood ideal."[40] However, Stacey's research also suggests that women spectators frequently copied movie fashions through adapting what they already owned, playing make-believe, or purchasing "styles which give them a feeling of connection with their ideal."[41]

The possibility of pursuing these avenues seems to be borne out by at least one aspect of the promotion of *Breakfast at Tiffany's*. *Photoplay* offered an article titled "How Does a Girl Become a Woman?" in which Hepburn's Givenchy dresses for the film were compared to similar clothing and jewelry that promise "chic without the Givenchy price."[42] *Funny Face* advertising copy promised, "All the Paris fashions of tomorrow in the picture that sets a new style in film musicals!" But, in contrast to this, the press book for *Funny Face* discusses a national magazine promotion and tie-in exhibitors' campaign based not on Givenchy's "Paris fashion," but on the designs of Edith Head that appear in the "Think Pink" sequence early in the film:

> In its March issue, *Seventeen Magazine* is devoting 12 pages to the fashion theme, "Think Pink," with tie-in copy explaining its origin in "Funny Face" and giving full picture credits. Leading department stores across the country are participating in this fashion promotion, which features fashions by 27 national manufacturers. Participating stores will back the promotion with fashion shows, window and departmental displays, tie-in ads, radio and television spots, and promotion and publicity based on the "Think Pink" fashions.[43]

The "Think Pink" musical sequence in *Funny Face* demands to be read as a satire on a then current fashion trend, but in the film's exhibition practice, this very same trend is interpreted as having "feminine appeal [that] is so great that it's the basis of a national magazine promotion." Edith Head appeared on Art Linkletter's CBS television program *House Party* to stage "a pink fashion show," and exhibitors were told to exploit *Funny Face*'s "bearing on the new fashions" by arranging local tie-ins with "department stores and shops that cater to women's fashions and beauty aids."[44] The only Givenchy design that appeared in the advertising campaign for the film was a wedding dress. In fact, the costumes from Hepburn's films that feminist film critics remember as important to them as adolescents infatuated with Hepburn's star appeal are as frequently those "antifashion" outfits that clothe Hepburn in her adolescent, pre-fashion-model mode as they are the haute couture of Givenchy that completes the characters' fashionable transformations.

Within this context, Elizabeth Wilson finds the dominance of haute couture in Hepburn's films "surprising" and recollects the impact that Hepburn's noncouture costumes had on teenagers. She reads against the grain of *Funny Face* to see Hepburn as the "beginning of youth protest against cultural conservatism."[45] She remembers Hepburn being "celebrated as a girl in black drainpipe trousers and a Left Bank sweater."[46] These elements constitute the costume (designed by Edith Head) that Hepburn wears in her spontaneous "jazz" dance in a Left Bank nightclub. Black pants and sweater were also more typical of the kinds of clothes Hepburn donned for early photo features in magazines such as *Life*.

Wilson's memories of the source of the star's fashion appeal and her undervaluing of haute couture's presence in Hepburn's films may be a testament to the power of female desire in relation to female film stars. Her memories may also have their origin in the mixed signals that were sometimes sent by Hepburn's film publicity. Most advertisements for *Funny Face* featured a dominating image of Hepburn in black sweater, pants, and loafers; she reaches for the sky as her face registers a blissed-out expression of soulfulness. Some advertisements acknowledged the musical score by George and Ira Gershwin, but others asserted, "When Audrey rocks—you'll roll!" Some advertisements went so far as to change the Hepburn "flat look" to meet the dominant star standard of buxom beauty.

The appeal to youth in the ad campaign for *Funny Face* suggests the studio's recognition that haute couture may not have been of much interest to a large number of young people. Similarly, ambivalence was expressed in the ad campaign for a later Hepburn vehicle, *How to Steal a Million*. The association of Hepburn with Givenchy was so strong by 1966 that the trailer for *How to Steal a Million* declared one attraction of the film to be "magnificent wardrobe by Givenchy." Like *Sabrina*, this film offers show-stopping moments for Hepburn to display his designs, which alternate between looking dowdy and appearing to be virtual tongue-in-cheek parodies of high-fashion excess. In the exploitation plan, Givenchy designs were used in a tie-in with McCall's patterns and were featured in the July 1966 issue of *McCall's* magazine.

Nevertheless, the film's ad campaign suggests that high chic was not a useful tool in selling Hepburn's image to a younger audience. All the ads featured her in clothes that do not appear in the film. These advertising-only costumes had a decidedly "mod" look, complete with fishnet stockings. Hepburn's hairdo was completely altered to conform more to popular mod standards, and she assumed an awkward (legs crossed while standing, one arm up) exhibitionistic pose typical of 1960s sexualized high-fashion photography.[47] This bifurcation of Hepburn's fashion commodification with *Funny Face* and *How to Steal a Million* suggests the attempt to sell her (and her films) to a broad female audience that was recognized as having potentially different fashion fantasies, some rooted in the current "youth cult" and others attuned to the appeal of haute couture.

Buying Your Designer Personality

If fashionable clothes were defined in the 1950s as crucial to a woman's ability to attain her ideal self, in the case of Hepburn this consumer-centered phenomenon extended to the star herself. She spoke her undying gratitude for Givenchy's ability to give her true identity: "His are the only clothes in which I am myself," she was reported as saying in 1956. "He is far more than a couturier, he is a creator of personality."[48] In a later tribute to her favorite designer, she said, "I depend on Givenchy in the same way American women depend on their psychiatrists."[49] Hepburn's relationship to Givenchy was not constructed publicly as a crass commercial endorsement designed to profit the star, but a class- and sex-stereotyped venture based on mutual appreciation and platonic friendship. He was marked as the genius. She was his muse. In 1955, he hired a look-alike mannequin ("Jackie") to inspire him in her absence—and, also, perhaps, to remind his customers of his most famous celebrity client.[50] He named fabrics for Hepburn, dedicated collections to her, and created a perfume for her that he then graciously permitted other women to buy: advertisements for L'Interdit in *Vogue* in 1964 featured a wistful close-up of Hepburn's face and reminded potential consumers of the product's exclusive origins: "Once she was the only woman in the world allowed to wear this perfume."

Unlike professional models (and movie stars onscreen), the aristocratic women featured in fashion magazines wore clothes that, it was implied, they were not just modeling but owned. Hepburn's appearance in couture followed this convention and also defined her relationship to Givenchy in terms apart from those normally associated with Hollywood designers and female stars. For example, in November 1964, Hepburn graced the cover of *Vogue* and was featured in a sumptuous ten-page layout in which she modeled "her favourites from the new Givenchy collection." The accompanying text said that the featured evening gowns from the collection were ones that she might wear to the various major city openings (New York, Chicago, Los Angeles) of her newest film, *My Fair Lady*.[51] The fashions were followed by an article by Cleveland Amory titled "The Phenomenon of *My Fair Lady*" and an advertising section in which models displayed fashions from Bonwit Teller and other major stores. This section was headlined, "My Fair Lady: The Off-Screen Fashion Life" and was introduced by a cameo photograph of Hepburn in the Cecil Beaton–designed Ascot dress from *My Fair Lady*. This introduction of the "*My Fair Lady* influence" of "purely contemporary prettiness . . . headlong charm . . . heartbreaking allure," was followed by models who were photographed so as to appear to be in the foreground of various scenes of the film. The copy emphasized the film tie-in with tag lines such as "Overture to a new Fair Lady in fashion" and "On the street where you live: the new romantics in costume form."[52] This was an obvious promotion of Hepburn's latest film vehicle through the exploitation of her association with high fashion and its department store offspring. It assumed her appeal to a potential audience of women with both an interest in fashion and the monetary ability to buy it in its more expensive manifestations. The status of Hepburn as fashionable and even fashion setting (through the dominance of haute couture) was defined as a centerpiece to fantasy scenarios incorporating fashion as part of a romantic adventure that could incorporate elements of *My Fair Lady*.

Audrey Hepburn grew older, but her characters and her cumulative screen persona barely did. For many years, her characters continued to be delineated as young, marriageable women (usually without a profession). Although there were notable exceptions (such as *The Nun's Story,* 1959), in her films throughout the 1950s and especially into the 1960s, she usually played younger than her actual age in roles that called for her character's sexual awakening. Even as late as *How to Steal a Million,* Hepburn (at thirty-six) plays a character who lives with her "papa" and reacts to a kiss from Peter O'Toole with the wide-eyed confusion of an adolescent stirred by a first kiss. Reviews made an issue of her age. One noted: "On occasion William Wyler shoots her through gauze turning her even more into a brunette Doris Day."[53] Another, in a gentler spirit, observed, "Though not as young as she used to be, Miss Hepburn has lost none of her fey charm as a comedienne."[54] Another review of *How to Steal a Million* suggested the repetitive nature of her characterizations: "Audrey Hepburn is at it again, dressed to the nines by Givenchy, bejeweled by Cartier, terribly chic . . . [she] responds with her usual selection of charms, looking girlishly amazed, standing slightly knock-kneed, walking with a tiny tiptoe teeter."[55] By this time, the Givenchy-Hepburn connection, while still finding sympathetic publicity in *Vogue,*[56] was worthy of a cinematic

in-joke. Preparing for the caper, Hepburn must don the unflattering attire of a charwoman. "That's fine. That does it," her companion in lar-
ceny, Simon Dermott (Peter O'Toole), says. "Does what?" she asks.
He: "Well, for one thing, it gives Givenchy a night off."

Stanley Donen would soon give Givenchy more than a night off.
The director insisted that Hepburn use ready-to-wear for her costumes
in his seriocomic analysis of a failing marriage, *Two for the Road*
(1967). For the first time in film, Hepburn donned ready-to-wear lines,
albeit by top "mod" London and Paris designers such as Mary Quant
and Paco Rabanne. The star's break from Givenchy's haute couture
made news as part of the film's radical departure from Hepburn's established screen persona. Falling off the couture pedestal, her character
would simultaneously fall off the moral pedestal long associated with
Hepburn's nice-girl heroines. The role of jet-setting Joanna Wallace was
much more daring than the public had come to expect of Hepburn. In
Two for the Road her character commits adultery, swears, and appears
nearly nude.

Hepburn would continue her association with Givenchy and appear consistently on "best dressed" lists, but her career trailed off simultaneous to the waning influence of Paris haute couture. She would
return to the screen on occasion, as in Peter Bogdanovich's *They All
Laughed* (1981), and appear middle-aged and chic, but her fashion influence was a thing of the past. That is not to say that her androgynous,
gamin image of undernourished femininity was completely passé. At
least for a time, Hepburn would be replaced by a celebrity fashion
model also androgynous and gamin, although possessed, too, of significantly different characteristics: the Cockney fashion model Twiggy embodied a rebellious break with refinement, class consciousness, and
Paris luxury fashion that Hepburn could never achieve.

The Key to Happy Endings

An analysis of Audrey Hepburn's image and its illustration of a convergence of stardom and fashion tells us a great deal about the cultural
field of post–World War II America, its representation of femininity for
a mass audience, and the specific textual and extratextual means used
to address the perceived needs of women in this era. I have attempted
to suggest the dimensions of meaning offered by Audrey Hepburn's
"adolescent" body and elfin charm cloaked in upper-class haute couture. The shaping of her screen persona suggests how the ubiquitous
1950s fashion culture for women, based on haute couture ideals, presented itself as enabling rather than constraining a coherent feminine

identity, coherent although based on the primacy of a transformative capacity that must overcome cultural problematics inscribed in film—and fashion—in terms of class, gender, sexuality, and age.

Nevertheless, differences among recollected responses to Hepburn's bifurcated image suggest the variety of possible "resistant" readings of the star as haute couture icon as well as a rejection, perhaps, of the film industry's presentation of her as the epitome of antielitist youthfulness at the same time it offered her as the exemplar of well-financed fashionability. In this, there is the hint that adolescent female viewers, in particular, may have resisted identification with Hepburn's onscreen transformation into proper femininity through Paris high-fashion commodification. Other viewers, however, may have accepted the film's textual and extratextual strategies of commodifying the star as utopic, a viable consumer-centered model for achieving ideal feminine identity as well as the key to enjoying cinematic happy endings.

Elizabeth Wilson has suggested that fashion attempts to resolve at the imaginary level those social contradictions that cannot be resolved otherwise.[57] Hepburn's star persona manages to merge a number of apparent oppositions: she is playful but elegant, thoroughly American but faintly and aristocratically European, elite but democratic, androgynous but hyperfeminine. More specifically, Hepburn's inscription of filmic fashionability succeeds in solving the contradictions inherent in the transformation of the playful adolescent of androgynous body and immature sexuality into the securely heterosexual, "grown" woman comfortable with conventional femininity. In this way, Audrey Hepburn's stardom appears to have negotiated successfully the problem of woman's sexual difference through a fantasy of feminine hybridity, class hybridity, and fashion hybridity. Through such means, her star persona accommodated the desire for a restoration of the "natural" prewar gender norms but also anticipated the winds of feminine change that would soon blow the petals of the New Look's "flower women" away.

Notes

1. For a discussion of 1950s comedy in relation to voluptuous female stars, see Ed Sikov, *Laughing Hysterically: American Screen Comedy of the 1950s* (New York: Columbia University Press, 1995). *Photoplay* declared Hepburn to be "flatchested, slimhipped and altogether un-Marilyn Monroeish." See Radie Harris, "Audrey Hepburn—The Girl, the Gamin and the Star," *Photoplay*, March 1955, 100. See also Earl Wilson, "Is Hollywood Shifting Its Accent on Sex?" *Silver Screen*, July 1954, 40.

2. Stanley Donen quoted in Ian Woodward, *Audrey Hepburn* (New York: St.

Martin's, 1984), 183. Dwight MacDonald negatively reviewed Hepburn in the late 1950s, noting: "She is not an actress, she is a model, with her stiff meager body and her blank face full of good bone structure. She has the model's narcissism, not the actress' introversion." Quoted in Barry Paris, *Audrey Hepburn* (New York: G. P. Putnam's Sons, 1996), 162.

3. Jackie Stacey, *Star Gazing: Hollywood Cinema and Female Spectatorship* (London: Routledge, 1994), 196–97.

4. Snow was said to have declared: "It's quite a revolution, dear Christian, your dresses have such a new look." Quoted in Katell le Bourhis, "The Elegant Fifties: When Fashion Was Still a Dictate," in *New Look to Now: French Haute Couture 1947–1987,* ed. Stephen de Pietri and Melissa Leventon (New York: Rizzoli, 1989), 14.

5. Christian Dior, *Christian Dior and I* (New York: E. P. Dutton, 1957), 35.

6. Christian Dior, *Talking about Fashion* (New York: G. P. Putnam's Sons, 1954), 23. Contrary to Dior's declaration of "universal" acceptance, there were some protests, especially in the United States, against the longer skirts hiding women's legs and the inappropriateness of the "wasp" waist for hale and hearty American women.

7. Cristóbal Balenciaga quoted in Sandra Barwick, *A Century of Style* (London: George Allen & Unwin, 1984), 165.

8. For a discussion of how postwar couture was sold in the United States through the custom salon, see Melissa Leventon, "Shopping for Style: Couture in America," in *New Look to Now: French Haute Couture 1947–1987,* ed. Stephen de Pietri and Melissa Leventon (New York: Rizzoli, 1989), 23–27.

9. Givenchy's success with American women was predicted in "De Givenchy, a New Name in Paris," *Life,* 3 March 1952, 61–64.

10. Maureen Turim, "Designing Women: The Emergence of the New Sweetheart Line," in *Fabrications: Costume and the Female Body,* ed. Jane Gaines and Charlotte Herzog (New York: Routledge, 1990), 215–19.

11. Marlene Dietrich went straight to Dior for her New Look wardrobe for the British made *No Highway in the Sky* (1951) and *Stage Fright* (1950), but these were produced in Britain. Hepburn's recounting of how Givenchy's work came to be used for *Sabrina* appears in a 1962 *Cine-Revue* interview in which she states: "For *Sabrina,* Billy Wilder agreed to let me add a few Parisian costumes to the ones created by Edith Head. The dresses put forward by Hubert de Givenchy were divine. I felt as though I had been born to wear them. My dearest wish . . . was that Billy would allow me to keep them." Hubert de Givenchy and Musée de la mode et du costume, *Givenchy: Forty Years of Creation* (Paris: Paris-Musée, 1991), 116.

12. Hubert de Givenchy quoted in Warren Harris, *Audrey Hepburn* (New York: Simon & Schuster, 1994), 129.

13. Paris, *Audrey Hepburn,* 123.

14. Barry Paris reports that Hepburn finally strayed from Givenchy because the cost of buying from his collection became too much for her when she was not working and that, living in Italy as the wife of psychiatrist Andrea Dotti, she felt she had some obligation to use Italian designers. See ibid., 255–56.

15. Audrey Hepburn, "The Costumes Make the Actors: A Personal View," in *Fashion in Film,* rev. ed., ed. Regine Engelmeier and Peter W. Engelmeier (Munich: Prestel, 1997), 10.

16. Cecil Beaton quoted in Nicholas Drake, ed., *The Fifties in VOGUE* (New York: Henry Holt, 1987), 76.

17. See, for example, a model used for "Black, White: Brightest Young Colours in Town," *Vogue,* 1 April 1955, 155; and an advertisement for a Junior Sophisticate dress in *Vogue,* 15 May 1955, 13.

18. Givenchy and Musée de la mode et du costume, *Givenchy,* 117.

19. Françoise Giroud, "Backstage at Paris' Fashion Drama," *New York Times Magazine,* 27 January 1957, 24.

20. See Valorie Steele, *Paris Fashion: A Cultural History* (New York: Oxford University Press, 1988), 276; Richard Donovan, "That Friend of Your Wife's Named Dior," *Collier's,* 10 June 1955, 34–39.

21. Philip T. Hartung, "Companion Family-Approved Movies: *Sabrina,*" *Women's Home Companion,* September 1954, 10.

22. Jack Moffitt, "*Sabrina,*" *Hollywood Reporter,* September 1954, n.p., in *Sabrina* clipping file, Academy of Motion Picture Arts and Sciences, Margaret Herrick Library (hereafter cited as AMPAS).

23. Jennifer Craik, *The Face of Fashion: Cultural Studies in Fashion* (London: Routledge, 1994), 105.

24. Jane Gaines, "Introduction: Fabricating the Female Body," in *Fabrications: Costume and the Female Body,* ed. Jane Gaines and Charlotte Herzog (New York: Routledge, 1990), 19.

25. Molly Haskell, "Our Fair Lady Audrey Hepburn," *Film Comment* 27, no. 2 (1991): 10.

26. Review of *Sabrina, Los Angeles Times,* 23 September 1954, n.p., in *Sabrina* clipping file, AMPAS.

27. Stacey, *Star Gazing,* 181, 192–95.

28. Richard Dyer, "Social Values of Entertainment and Show Business" (Ph.D. diss., Birmingham University, Center for Contemporary Cultural Studies, 1972), 339.

29. Mark Shaw, "Audrey Hepburn, Many-Sided Charmer," *Life,* 7 December 1953, 128.

30. On the fashion rules that the chic American woman needed to follow in the 1950s, see le Bourhis, "The Elegant Fifties," 16–19.

31. "Chi-Chi Cinderella," *Look,* 14 May 1957, 116.

32. "Young Idea," *Vogue,* 1 September 1954, 111.

33. For example, one fashion article emphasized the "youthful freshness" of Italian fashion and even used a Hepburn look-alike as a model, but the suits featured hardly seemed "casual" and "easy-moving" as the text suggested. See "Italian Collections, Their New Young Look," *Vogue,* 15 March 1955, 84–87.

34. Publicity also helped in this. Givenchy's wedding gown for *Funny Face* was featured in some advertisements for the film. Although not in a magazine venue aimed at young women, Hepburn was featured gleefully trying on a hat "in the exclusive shop of couturier Hubert de Givenchy" in Ed Feingersh, "A Star in Motion," *Popular Photography,* April 1957, 78.

35. Clayton Cole, "*Sabrina,*" *Films and Filming,* November 1954, 20.

36. Molly Haskell, *From Reverence to Rape: The Treatment of Women in the Movies* (New York: Holt, Rinehart & Winston, 1973), 268. Similar explanations have been given to account for Twiggy's popularity as a model for young women of the 1960s. See Craik, *The Face of Fashion,* 84.

37. Haskell, "Our Fair Lady," 10.

38. Stacey, *Star Gazing,* 197.

39. Nora Sayre, *Running Time: Films of the Cold War* (New York: Dial, 1982), 133–34. Sayre goes on to remark, "Hepburn blended cuteness and elegance with a sham innocence that almost insulted human nature. . . . no one over fifteen could have remained so sheltered as her screen personae—not even in the Fifties" (134).

40. Stacey, *Star Gazing,* 198.

41. Ibid., 205, 200–201. The baby boomers' connection to Hepburn still finds a consumer mode of expression through everything from Hepburn calendars (1999) to a Hepburn collectible doll (1998) outfitted in the little black dress from *Breakfast at Tiffany's.*

42. "How Does a Girl Become a Woman?" *Photoplay,* May 1955, 68–69.

43. *Funny Face* press book, 25, AMPAS. *Vogue* anticipated the film's "Think Pink" musical number with a similarly conceived although decidedly nonsatirical fashion feature in 1955. See "Vine Rose," *Vogue,* 15 November 1955, 128–33. For a discussion of First Lady Mamie Eisenhower's predilection for pink and the "decisive moment" in 1955 "when the rest of America went pink, too," see Karal Ann Marling, "Mamie Eisenhower's New Look," in *As Seen on TV: The Visual Culture of Everyday Life in the 1950s* (Cambridge: Harvard University Press, 1994), 8–49.

44. *Funny Face* press book, 25, 26, AMPAS.

45. Elizabeth Wilson, "Audrey Hepburn: Fashion, Film and the 50s," in *Women and Film: A Sight and Sound Reader,* ed. Pam Cook and Philip Dodd (Philadelphia: Temple University Press, 1993), 40, 36–38.

46. Ibid., 40.

47. *How to Steal a Million* press book, AMPAS.

48. Givenchy and Musée de la mode et du costume, *Givenchy,* 111.

49. Quoted in "Audrey Hepburn at 40," *McCall's,* July 1969, as quoted in Steele, *Paris Fashion,* 255.

50. Givenchy and Musée de la mode et du costume, *Givenchy,* 127. "Jackie" appeared in a Givenchy advertisement for a sweater ensemble in *Vogue,* 1 March 1955: "Expect More Than the Traditional . . . When Givenchy Creates the Sweatered Look in Orlon" (32). It could be argued that Hepburn was not necessarily Givenchy's most famous client (the Duchess of Windsor and Grace Kelly were also customers), but she was definitely the most influential fashion leader among his clients. Jackie Kennedy wore his designs on a visit to Versailles in 1961. See "Givenchy," *Look,* 21 November 1961, 110–13.

51. Fashion layout, *Vogue,* 1 November 1964, 142–51.

52. *Vogue,* 15 October 1964, 29–49.

53. "*How to Steal a Million,*" *Los Angeles Magazine,* October 1966, n.p., in *How to Steal a Million* clipping file, AMPAS.

54. Philip K. Sheuer, "Audrey Charms in 'Steal a Million,'" *Los Angeles Times,* 14 July 1966, n.p., in *How to Steal a Million* clipping file, AMPAS.

55. "Counterfeit Comedy," *Newsweek,* 25 July 1966, n.p., in *How to Steal a Million* clipping file, AMPAS.

56. Violette Leduc, "Steal-Scening with Hepburn & O'Toole," *Vogue,* 1 April 1966, 172–73.

57. See Elizabeth Wilson, *Adorned in Dreams: Fashion and Modernity* (London: Virago, 1985), 222.

8.
Sharon Stone in a Gap Turtleneck
Rebecca L. Epstein

To be indiscriminate, haphazardly thrown together, trapped in the current "hip" uniform is the affliction of a modern Hollywood in search of its style.

Patty Fox, *Star Style: Hollywood Legends as Fashion Icons*, 1995[1]

In 1978, Charles Eckert's "The Carole Lombard in Macy's Window" revealed the birth of the interaction among Hollywood, merchandising, and American women's consumer practices. With an especially keen eye toward correlating clothing manufacturing with studios' cinematic and promotional productions, Eckert saw film audiences in the first half of this century, and women in particular, as psychologically manipulated into consumerism through the fantasies of film. The showcasing of products in films and "star endorsement" selling techniques, according to Eckert, both cultivated and exploited an emotional materialism based on a dream world of Hollywood narratives and American consumerist ideology and identity.[2]

Given major transformations of the Hollywood studio system, the fashion industry, and American consumer culture since the 1940s, how do we assess the relationship between film audiences and successful actresses relative to popular fashion in the late 1990s? Integral to the history of the public consumption of celebrity-associated products has been the merchandising of female film star "looks"; Joan Crawford's square-shouldered suits and Marilyn Monroe's hourglass glitter matched in fashion popularity Audrey Hepburn's streamlined feminine elegance and Diane Keaton's masculine and millinery frump. But I believe that recent decades have reversed the roles of the Hollywood film actress (as clothing style arbiter) and the female movie spectator (as

179

clothing style consumer). Although certain costumes within films may still inspire female fashions (such as the fad embrace of leg warmers and ripped sweatshirts following the release of *Flashdance* in 1983), Keaton, in fact, with her "Annie Hall" look, appears to have been the last in a line of Hollywood actresses whose eponymous on- and off-screen style filtered down into the mass marketplace. (Indeed, a 1996 issue of *W*, a high-gloss, high-fashion magazine, indicated this stall in Hollywood stars' ability to influence dress styles when, in an article on the impact of Hollywood film on popular fashion, the most current example was that of Keaton.) So why, given a history of connections between the American film and fashion industries, is an actress most famous for her clothing in the 1970s considered the last star who, "with a combination of personal style and great design," could "send an audience straight from the cinema to the store"?[3]

This essay examines what I believe is the decreasing location of movie audiences as *consumers* of celebrity fashion and their increasing place as *critics* of celebrities' fashion "taste." This change, I argue, repositions the popular actress from a dictator of fashion trends to a consumer of the public's "wears." Ultimately, the most acute evidence of this thesis lies in popular critiques of celebrity fashions: from best- and worst-dressed lists to the fashion reporting in supermarket tabloids to the copious celebrity costume coverage at film-industry-related awards shows. Here, female film stars are the target of my investigation due to the persistent commodification of fashion as a feminine interest and the ideological embeddedness in American Culture of women, more than men, as objects of display. And because I seek an understanding of a present moment in American culture through a range of phenomena, this chapter begins with a historical overview followed by a contemporary analysis. In this way I aim to reveal an evolving continuum of intersections of the film and fashion industries through their most visible link: the fashionable Hollywood female star.

Dressing the Scene: Film Fashion Icons from Swanson to Keaton

The relationship of American film to fashion vis-à-vis consumerism goes back to Hollywood's silent era. Cecil B. DeMille, director of films renowned for their material excesses (including the first filmed shopping spree) also introduced audiences to Gloria Swanson, his "clothes horse" diva, whose luxurious costumes brought the conspicuous consumption of fashion into filmgoers' view. Known for her elongating, draped column dress styles to give the illusion of height to her four foot, eleven inch frame, Swanson's glamour on screen playing society woman roles translated to her offscreen persona. Indeed, her stardom was in part both created and strengthened by public knowledge of the actress's own unique and abundant wardrobe.[4] Swanson's and other silent stars' visual appeal was only forwarded by the period's fan magazines, which, as Mary Ann Doane has noted, "linked female obsession with stars, glamour, gossip and fashion."[5] More pointedly, the film frame in this period became, according to Doane, a "Bazinian window to the world" in which objects were fetishized and femininity becomes entwined with conspicuous consumption and decoration.[6] In 1932, Mae West then stepped into Swanson's showcase and became one of the next major film fashion idols with the release of *Night after Night*. Already a success on the stage, West's formidable full figure and wry, ribald performance style greatly contrasted with the delicacy of Swanson's body and character type, yet she too gained much renown for displaying herself in opulent dress; her (ultimately controversial) sex appeal sparkled eminently from her signature beaded, form-fitting gowns.[7]

Both Swanson and West styled themselves, codifying their public images through their personal wardrobe tastes. However, with the bloom of the studio system in the 1930s and the flowering in kind of sound and studio wardrobe departments, the female film star relative to her fashion image underwent its first major shift. Now, instead of actresses supplying their own costumes as they had often during the silent era, studios began "fashioning" their stars, dressing them to suit the cinematic spectacles of what became the "Golden Age" of Hollywood.[8] Professional costume designers now outfitted actresses to project glamour and feminine material indulgence while, across the lot, in-house publicity machines actively promoted potential shining stars. Although the majority of Hollywood film actresses during this period swam in an imposed sartorial sea of satin and organza, a few did emerge to proffer distinctive "looks" on- and offscreen. Most notably: reclusive Greta Garbo became known for her figure-concealing high necklines and face-shielding hats; sexually mysterious Marlene Dietrich found fame with her gam-glorifying skirts as well as her masculine shirt-pant ensembles; and Joan Crawford brought square-shouldered styles to the fashion front with the help of Gilbert Adrian, MGM's chief costume designer, who "materialized" Crawford's typically arch characters and persona through sharp, shaped suits.[9] Crawford's fashion fame began before she established a trademark look, however; as Charlotte Herzog and Jane Gaines have noted, the white organdy dress that Adrian designed for the actress to wear in *Letty Lynton* (1932) became the first prominent example of a film costume permeating the marketplace; the dress, with arm ruffles anticipating shoulder pads, is alleged to have launched the sale of five hundred thousand copies throughout the United States.[10]

Adrian's costuming of Crawford glorified her naturally broad upper body, and his stylings simultaneously "suited" the period's (primarily) female movie audiences. Enduring cloth restrictions and conforming to new labor demands, women found their wartime fashions taking on more masculine shapes and mobilizing cuts. Indeed, the confluence of cultural and economic forces shaping the relationship of film costume and popular fashion trends during Hollywood's Golden Age is the story, as Eckert has asserted, of studio marketing techniques exploiting consumer and social practices through the cultural embrace of film. Most notably, "cinema shops" in department stores, the increasing employment of film stars in advertisements for personal products, and the continued glamorization of stars and their lives through fan magazines and gossip in national presses kept Hollywood actresses and their apparel in full view, tempting consumers to emulate stars' manufactured style. Prefeature newsreels showing the latest high-fashion dress designs in Europe (particularly Paris) also cultivated movie audiences' equation of the filmed with the fashionable image. Popular film was increasingly "prefiguring" audiences' taste, becoming a mode of dress display and educating clothing consumers. Similarly, as Herzog has shown, department store fashion shows in films became a narrative device that also transported values of style from movie scenes into home closets, linking the glamour of Paris, for example, to the local department store.[11] And yet when it came to anticipating, if not in fact proselytizing, the next clothing trend, the standard lag time from a film's production to its release required costume designers to "plan" for changes in fashion a year in advance. Costumers, as a result of this industrial factor, followed but also fostered such changes by just slightly altering clothing shapes for films so that they did not look "dated" or simply overly familiar in a year's time.[12]

Indeed, new film-related fashion trends were, by definition, always respectable to a mass audience and rarely emerged out of the blue. For example, Crawford's and Dietrich's successful masculine deportment in the 1930s, a time, paradoxically, of primarily hyperfeminized females on film, eased the way for the trousered and "feminist forward" image of actress Katharine Hepburn in the 1940s.[13] Hepburn, like her stylish predecessors, illustrated once again that the effectiveness of a signature look lay in the invisible border between person and persona. Hepburn, the actress, seemed to audiences to "play herself" onscreen, expressing her own gender politics in many of her roles. And, in the thirties and forties, as many white, middle-class women broke from their exclusively domestic roles because of either personal ideology or economic necessity, they found in the looks of Dietrich, Crawford, and Hepburn a way to negotiate through dress their fantasies of social respectability and material comfort along with their quests for self-determination, professional power, and sexual agency.

With the end of the war came new phases on the film, fashion, and culture fronts. In particular, 1947 marked the beginning of the decline of the studio system enabled by corporate divestiture and the infiltration of television into the mass sphere, Christian Dior's attempt at revitalizing the Parisian fashion trade through his wasp-waist "New Look" for women, and the movement in the United States toward suburbanization. Combined, these factors set the looks of film stars who fashioned the 1950s. Doris Day, for instance, and her wholesome, milky-white complexion and girl-next-door characters sprang to life on the screen with the help of a full skirt and fully enhanced (but also *fully covered*) bosom inspired by Dior's choice silhouette. Indeed, Dior's own inspiration for his New Look was the resurrection of the lost "aspects of femininity" in women's fashion, which he achieved through an indulgent use of fabric to accentuate and celebrate female hips and breasts.[14] Although Dior was a Frenchman, his designs translated well to Americans who knew that if the construction of the clothes themselves could not effect the desired "inverted Y" (and later, "X") shape, they could find "support" in an array of "foundation garments" that were now being manufactured and promoted to assist women's fashionable and cultural "restructuring." Of course, as Francine Du Plessix Gray has observed, the New Look was not "new" at all: the 1950s celebration of women's sexuality through a restricted figure to effect a childbearing shape "turned back the clock" in women's fashion and social emancipation to la belle epoque of female subservience to men's wealth and status.[15] Nevertheless, this "mammary madness" era produced blonde bombshells such as Jayne Mansfield, Kim Novak, and Tippi Hedren who exploited the feminine sexuality that Dior's designs only began to suggest. With these stars, the full skirts quickly narrowed to a body hugging, immobilizing slimness. Marilyn Monroe became one of the most famous fashion icons of this period, turning the crisp edges of Dior's stylings into soft, luscious curves. Monroe's famously accentuated cleavage and derriere, combined with her sex-kitten portrayals onscreen and in public, shaped a specific, signature "look" in and of the 1950s.[16]

In the early 1960s, however, new fashion icons began challenging the reign of studio imperialism over star fashion successes. The burgeoning youth culture proved an especially formidable fashion force, changing the face of popular taste through the fine and performing arts. In addition, celebrity discourse became laden with greater complexity and irony. Twiggy, a stick-thin teenage English model, and Jackie Kennedy, America's first lady, were only two women in this "style-obsessed era" who claimed status as fashion icons without Hollywood's help.[17] And yet, with actress Audrey Hepburn, Hollywood contributed to the climate as well, offering up what became one of its most enduring images of female fashionability. Hepburn began achieving recognition as a film actress in the 1950s, but her costuming, which combined gamine, tomboy charm with understated elegance, created a "look" that carried into the following decade and "figured" even more in the future. Elizabeth Wilson has noted that Hepburn, due to her working relationship with Paris couture designer Hubert de Givenchy, assisted the bringing of haute couture to the masses. To be sure, the combination of mobility, simplicity, and respectable pedigree that Givenchy's minimalist clothes, in addition to Hepburn's sprightly roles, afforded the actress was integral to her look's successful embrace and replication by the public.[18]

Following Hepburn, the field of new and enduring film fashion plates remained barren for more than ten years, until Diane Keaton appeared in 1977 as Annie Hall in the film of the same name. Keaton came, however, after an important occurrence in cinema-inspired style when, in 1967, Theadora Van Runkle's costume designs for *Bonnie and Clyde* caused an explosion of 1930s retro styles in women's popular fashion.[19] Faye Dunaway received praise as the fabulously fashioned "Bonnie" in long, flared "midi" skirts (which noticeably contrasted with the contemporaneous miniskirt craze), but it is crtical to note that in each of her follow-up roles, the actress wore differently styled habiliments that failed to set any major fashion trends. Dunaway in *Bonnie and Clyde,* then, marked an important shift from actress-based to character-based influences on popular female fashion. Whereas previous film-inspired fashions tended to conflate the actress's personal style with her many characters' dress, now famously copied "looks" were being generated by an isolated character; in this case, the public's wardrobe emulation was of "Bonnie," not Faye. So when Keaton's renowned "Annie Hall look" of loose-fitting menswear and brow-skimming hats skyrocketed in 1970s fashion consciousness, although in part reminiscent of the Golden Age–styled successes as well as the feminist strides of slacks-wearing Dietrich and both Hepburns, Keaton's look *was not* the product and marketing tool of a film studio. In addition, it *was* named for her character. And this despite the public's knowledge that Keaton's was a primarily autobiographical performance in a role opposite the film's author and her former paramour, Woody Allen.[20] Because Keaton (who over time has deviated little from her desexualized layering for either on- or offscreen appearances) is the last film actress to effect an enduring signature look, how do we assess this move from actress-based to character-based fashion trends? Moreover, what is the role of the film star as possible fashion icon in the 1990s, and how does her audience receive and define her attempts, if any, at her own "look"?

The Changing Room: The 1960s and Celebrity Style Chaos
Discussed in innumerable texts, the 1960s were an uproarious time in American popular culture. Sociopolitical upheavals throughout the decade rapidly affected and overturned the status quo in many Americans' lives, including their approach to fashion. As Valerie Carnes has noted, 1960 marked the beginning of the reign of new fashion icons who embodied a "pop iconology of youth, kinkiness and fun."[21] In the interest of "sheer surface shimmer," fashion and other popular presses and entertainment media showcased "real girls, Swingers, Gamines, Ingenues, Kooks, Chicerinos, Littlegirls, JetSetters, SurferChicks, Hippie Girls, Beautiful Creatures, Free Souls . . . all impeccably packaged, pretty, kinky, kooky, and young."[22] Up to this time, fashion style choice typically signified the wearer's socioeconomic class. Now, however, popular dress also widely codified diverse "lifestyles" and indicated the wearer's sociopolitical values. A generation of young designers from England who benefited from their country's postwar push of secondary education included former art students such as Mary Quant, who turned fashion into a symbol of an internationally rebellious youth culture.[23] Significantly, Quant's own critical success with her geometrical and girlish designs at lower than couture prices also reflected the attention of the international world of fashion as it moved away from the wealthy and elite consumer and toward the middle-income fashion follower. Carnes continues:

> No longer were trends dictated by the Parisian salons, to move from the couture downward to knock-off mass houses and thus into the streets. Now, unlike the situation in 1947 when the New Look was thrust upon a reluctant mass market, fashion did not originate on Seventh Avenue or in Right Bank Parisian salons. Rather, the new

iconology of fashion started in Greenwich Village, on Carnaby Street, in the discotheques and bistros of Paris and St. Tropez, and worked its way up with dizzying speed into designers' workrooms, store windows, and at last into the pages of *Elle, Bazaar,* and *Vogue.* No longer did mass fashion "knock off" or copy, the couture; now the couture was in the curiously ironic position of knocking off mass fashion.[24]

In both Europe and the United States, the 1960s ushered in widespread critiques of and retaliations from dominant culture. As part of a concurrent trend of questioning the grandiosity and pomposity of American celebrities and materialist icons, American pop artist Andy Warhol appropriated and subverted the Hollywood film industry's self-bloating processes by creating his own "underground" film "Factory" and its stars. He also painted to challenge the meaning of, and method behind, famous images, as celebrities, but also common household products, became "trademarks" of his canvases. Ultimately, Warhol's work complemented the increasing attention to exoticism and the search for one's "true self" through fashion, as well as the adoption of modern materials and fabric prints to aid clothing's more artistic presentation in fashion photography, film, and popular music. In this environment, professional fashion models, too, were becoming style setters, inserted into popular culture through the magazine trade and the work of "reality-based" photographers such as William Klein, who took fashion shoots out of the studio and into the urban scene. Red-haired model Suzy Parker had gained national prominence and envy in the 1950s, but the media and artistic hyperexposure of models such as Twiggy, Jean Shrimpton, and Cheryl Tiegs increased both the visibility and the respectability of fashion models as dress personalities.[25]

By 1969, the decade's changed social sensibilities had been fully incorporated into the fashion trade. With mass clothing production at new heights and "radical chic" altering dress styles of the American public, designers such as American Calvin Klein were turning "street fashions," mostly dominated by denim into a best-selling craze. In 1973, the Levi-Strauss Company even received a citation calling its blue jeans the single most important contribution to worldwide fashion.[26] Haute couture was responding to this "bottom-up" trend (if you will) by succumbing to a largely pret-a-porter industry; Pierre Cardin, Courrèges, Gucci, Pucci, and Hermes were some of the designers in the United States and abroad creating ready-to-wear, more practical styles for active, if moneyed, women. In addition, many American couturiers were realizing how to compete with the Parisian trade—as celebrities of their own creation(s). "Big personality" designers such as Bill Blass and Oscar de la Renta now actively effected their own name fame, ingratiating themselves and their designs with wealthy clients before inundating mass-marketing and merchandising outlets with apparel bearing their "designer" logos and signatures.[27] Middle-class women who once followed fashion through film stars were now looking for "looks" from a downscaling fashion industry, "branding" themselves with clothing from self-promoting designers hoping to tap a large middle-income demographic.

Carnes states, "For the young and the would be young of the decade, fashion (by the late 60s) was a theater in the streets, an instant lifestyle and often an instant politics and ideology (Left = Hip; Right = Straight)."[28] And so it was in this climate of challenged political and social conformity—and with allegiances exposed through manner of dress—that the leveling of "high" with "low" style began. As a result, film actresses were decreasingly able or even desiring to hold court as fashion templates, their modesty illustrating a changed view of celebrity style supremacy. In a 1970 interview, Edith Head, once chief costume designer for Paramount Studios and by this time a winner of seven Academy Awards for her work, perceived a major difference between young female stars of the late sixties and early seventies and their forebears. Most notable was the younger women's failure to affect "trademark" fashion or unique, personal style. Unlike Mae West or Joan Crawford, who "established something which was a definite person," contemporary actresses (such as Jane Fonda, Ali MacGraw, and Katharine Ross) were no longer "clotheshorses, they don't depend on the glamour image." According to Head, the signature star look was giving way to the paradoxically conformist nonconformism of "doing one's own thing as part of the Now scene." Head characterized these women as distancing themselves from the privileges of personal designers and glamorous Hollywood personas, which contrasted with the "plain modern pictures" studios were churning out and the countercultural age of which these women were a part. Theirs was an "anti star image, anti glamour, anti the whole fantasy of early Hollywood." Head bemoaned "the new look, an image of now," in an era of budget cutting and reorganized studios in which "wardrobe people will go out and buy a dress or suit instead of having it tailor made. It is another generation of thinking . . . and I hate it." Asked if these young stars were at all influencing the public's fashion sense or style, Head answered emphatically, "No. They like to be amusing . . . and do whatever is the current fad."[29]

What Do You Think? Popular Critiques of Celebrity Fashion

Head's comments indicate that by the late 1960s, actresses were giving up their roles as style arbiters, tempering their "elite" status as stars due to industrial and cultural concerns. Meanwhile, journalists also were actively biting at Hollywood fashion pretension. Significantly, the 1960s marked the beginnings of tabloid newspapers such as the *National Enquirer* and the *Star*; part idol makers, part idol breakers, theirs was a "new kind of celebrity reporting" originating in Eugenia Sheppard's gossip column in the *New York Herald Tribune* and "perfected," in fact, by the writers of the fashion trade magazine *Women's Wear Daily*. As Banner notes, this journalism combined "insouciance with a willingness to shock" and was increasingly iconoclastic in its exposure of the good, the bad, and the ugly of public personalities in a consumer culture. Included in the reporting was attention to celebrities' dress:

> Fashion now emerged as a significant variable in celebrity reporting. Not only were the personal doings of designers deemed newsworthy, but a designer attribution was also given to dresses worn to parties and other social events. The attribution functioned as a validation for women's taste, but it also served as an advertisement for the importance of consumerism in their lives.[30]

Most illustrative of this burgeoning criticism of stars' styles, in 1960 Richard Blackwell, a moderately successful American couturier, began writing an annual, nationally syndicated column listing the best- and worst-dressed women of Hollywood. Fully expecting "'The List' to last a season at the very most," Blackwell's exposure of screen stars' refined but also tacky taste found an amazed but amused audience, whom Blackwell believed to be "people relieved that someone had the nerve to say out loud what, in truth, they had been thinking for years."[31]

Blackwell's column was, in fact, the latest entry in a history of celebrity fashion critiques. The practice extends back to the nineteenth century, when European theater critics catering to the elite would comment on both the performances and the performers' costumes. By the 1920s, published fashion critiques took on a different form when a group of Parisian designers started a "best-dressed list" for which they polled only each other to decide the "most elegant" among their clients, most of whom were royalty, society women, and women working in the fashion industry. This annual list was published internationally in newspapers. (The *New York Times*, in an effort to defuse charges of elitism, assured its readers that the women on the list "must do more than invest the sum of $50,000 with the Paris dressmaking trade. She must have brains, poise and vivacity.")[32] The list was adopted by American couturiers in 1940 after the war temporarily halted the Paris industry, followed by fashion publicist Eleanore Lambert, who created a list based on ballots cast by a range of celebrities, fashion editors, and designers. Regardless of the judges, however, the list tended to include the same women each year, and in 1959 it was finally retired due to its predictability and tedium. *Women's Wear Daily,* revamped in 1960 from a trade paper to a "gossipy, opinionated, often vicious but always readable source of [fashion] information," carved the next niche for rating celebrity style. The newly arrogant publication, under the direction of publishing scion John Fairchild, had become, in fact, "a kind of society gossip sheet" especially renowned for employing superlative categories to adulate rich people considered to be "in" (the "Impeccables," the "Goddesses," the "Cat Pack").[33]

That same year, when Blackwell began offering his opinions and self-proclaimed expertise in a nationally syndicated newspaper column by adding a "worst-dressed" component to a "best-dressed" list, however, he effectively changed the look of looking at "looks." In fact, Blackwell's "best" list has held decreasing interest for followers as the author has become famous for his annual gibes at the public figures he believes should "know" how to dress well. "The List has always stressed celebrities," Blackwell asserts, "because these people have no excuse."[34] Assuming that moneyed people have access to "the best of everything," Blackwell uses his worst-dressed list to argue that if his subjects do not know the trappings of "good taste," they should heed the advice of someone who does. For Blackwell, that authority is himself—and, by implication, his column's readers.

Blackwell's first celebrity fashion critiques, written to "comment on current trends, poke fun at pomposity, ridicule arrogance, and point the finger at the ones who deserve it most," came when film audiences were beginning to feel the effects of the Hollywood studio system's being restructured in the wake of television and a changing leisure landscape.[35] The elimination of in-house costumers and the bulk of Golden Age star-making apparatuses seemed as never before to turn the success of a star over to his or her audience. Indeed, the recognition that both celebrity journalism and audience preferences could "make" a star more than studio publicity departments may have also led audiences to sense their entitlement to "make over" the stars in the audiences' own desired images. With Hollywood in search of a new identity, a major generational and social rebellion at hand, and the "domestication" of film stars as many began appearing in television programs and made-for-TV movies, actresses were no longer in a position to dictate the day's popular fashions.

So, as television came to stem the film industry in the 1950s and early 1960s, and with women's time, in particular, allotted to activities around the home, there came a relationship between viewers and their small-screen stars that was different from that between viewers and big-screen stars. As Senator John F. Kennedy proved during his presidential campaign, television magnetism was a powerful popularity tool. Viewers had certain expectations of the faces that seemingly entered their homes, and this included a more quotidian approach to dress. In 1996, Nancy Friday revealed how this trend only intensified over the years, explaining (in a *TV Guide* issue that also listed the best- and worst-dressed characters from the 1995–96 season) that audiences consistently seek and develop a certain level of comfort with television performers, as if they are personal acquaintances present in the flesh. And, regarding trendsetting dress styles, viewers, Friday claimed, are circumspect. "A lot of pre-shop shopping takes place with the tube on," she noted, hinting at the tenuous influence of television actors and actresses on popular fashion.[36] Of course, the impact of most of these television performers on fashion trends is also contained by the major commercial networks' tilt toward social conservatism and the "mid-cult" demographic to which they most actively cater. Moreover, the audience embrace of television performers' appearance, just as it evolved with film stars, is directed toward the characters, not the actors; when Jennifer Aniston, playing the part of "Rachel" on the highly watched mid-1990s NBC sitcom *Friends,* launched a revolution in soft coiffures, her hairstyle was requested in salons and referred to across the country as the "Rachel," not the "Jennifer."

Film studio costume designers' roles as image makers also began to fade as television grew in appeal and acceptance. No longer the leading entertainment industry, film studios folded their expensive wardrobe departments and producers began hiring freelance costumers. Today, these "stylists" work in television studios as well, and they are acknowledged in popular magazines and awards ceremonies as the Svengalis of both film and television stars, despite their regular reliance on off-the-rack, store-bought clothing. Ultimately, the public recognition of stylists' skills, coupled with the accessible, mass-market items they employ, results in an absence of actresses conveying a uniquely personal, let alone personal*ized,* style.

In 1970, Head hoped the Hollywood star image through dress that she had helped to cultivate during her years as a costume designer was not "dead forever." As of the late nineties, female starlike fashion is in fact evident—but in a different form and figure than Head ever fully experienced. And arguably, it is at awards shows and in other public appearances—and no longer in the films themselves—that the Hollywood actress, relative to her "fashion-ability" now finds her strictest scrutiny. Head, commenting on her role as a dress adviser to stars, characterized the exposure of the person rather than the persona at such events, stating, "Don't forget [the Academy Awards] is the one time a year a star presents herself to the public as herself, not as a film character."[37]

Perhaps the industrial movement away from movies revelling in glamorous contemporary clothing display (with the exception of the "historical costume drama") has only enhanced the public's awareness and opinion of how stars should dress for public, ceremonial appearances. A popular shift in favor of simple, unadorned shifts, for instance, came to light in a 1996 broadcast of *Joan Rivers' Summer Movie Fashion Review* on the E! cable network, one of the many modern commentaries on celebrity fashions following Blackwell's lead.[38] Sitting with young American designer Cynthia Rowley, whose sheath-like designs are reminiscent of Givenchy's for Audrey Hepburn, and "fashion expert" Leon Hall, Rivers and her guests purred and hissed at clips of stars dressed for the red carpet catwalks of movie premieres. Women in solid-colored, sleeveless shift dresses and minimal accessories received the most praise. More interesting discussion came late in the show, however, when, sensing the significance of her (self-proclaimed) status as a critic of film stars' taste, Rivers asked her jury, referring to days gone by, when a stunning screen costume worked in tandem with signature style, "Will we ever see someone like a Joan Crawford?" Rivers received her response from Rowley, who, like Head years earlier, said, "No." Costume design for women's modern film roles, particularly in apocalyptic action films, is based on "tank tops and rags," Rowley declared, and revealing bodies more than celebrating clothes. Hall agreed, adding, "Clothes in films today are to cover the asses of the masses," composed primarily of off-the-rack items. Rowley's remark also indicates that with exercise refined to a science in late-nineties culture, the star's physical body has become the object for mass display and emulation as once were the costumes that adorned it. The personal costume designer has given way to the personal trainer, the creator of costumes that suggested the body replaced by a sculptor of the real thing.

Help Me with This, Will You? The Star-Designer Relationship

Rivers's query was, however, propelled as much by current trends in narrative cinema and celebrity scrutiny as by the ongoing history of the star/designer relationship. Indeed, the question as to whether we will ever have another style setter "like a Joan Crawford" is provoked by changes in the film, fashion, and entertainment industries, as well as celebrity exposure. After all, how many of today's films' fans know the names of *any* of the *many* stylists who dress their favorite stars? In great contrast to earlier periods in film costume history, when Adrian and Head, along with studio-era costumers Travis Banton, Orry-Kelly, Walter Plunkett, and Irene Sharaff were renowned for their talents of the eye as well as needle and thread, more recent audiences are likely to know a costume's name only when a noted fashion designer crosses industries, bringing patterns and pinking shears to designing dress for film. Such designers' moments have included Giorgio Armani for *American Gigolo* (1980) and *Sabrina* (1995) and Jean-Paul Gaultier for *The Cook, the Thief, His Wife & Her Lover* (1989), *City of Lost Children* (1995), and *The Fifth Element* (1997).

The integration of couture with popular cinema was, in fact, attempted in 1931 when Gloria Swanson brought Coco Chanel to Hollywood to infuse films with Chanel's classic cuts. But the difference in designing for film (film costume must be of a color, pattern, and shape that "read" well, and several versions must exist to suit different camera angles), coupled with Swanson's temper, sent Chanel back a year later to Paris, where her talents were more readily welcomed and displayed. The couture gap was not bridged again until Givenchy began designing for Audrey Hepburn—the two names becoming inseparable. The recent employment of couture designers as costume designers, however, has failed to revitalize glamour on the screen. This may be due in part to the public recognition of fashion designers as celebrities and, in turn, the de-exoticizing of design styles prior to their reaching the big screen. A 1995 attempt to "bring back" Hollywood glamour in film demonstrated the significance of fashion's overfamiliarity. For a remake of *Sabrina* (1954), originally starring Audrey Hepburn in costumes by Edith Head and Givenchy, Julia Ormond, an actress with a few disparate roles behind her, played the lead role in dresses by the widely known Armani. Without a predetermined sense on the part of the audience of Ormond and Armani as an image-making team, the two had separate impacts on the film, the vivacity of the costumes distinct from the performance of the actress. Both Ormond and Armani had been successful in their respective but increasingly intercompetitive industries, but their combination in this effort proved disorienting and overly contrived. In fact, with all the hype surrounding the remake's ambitions, a feared result occurred: irrespective of the film's other deficiencies, all the attention to and expectations of the costumes led the clothes to over-shadow, or "wear," the character. As Gaines has asserted, "[Golden Age] star designing effects the synthesis between character and actress." But here, such a synthesis failed to take place; Armani's eagerly antici-pated costumes bore no relation to Ormond's prior fashion image (such as it was), nor did they harmonize her with her character.[39]

Rather than costuming actresses for their craft, in the 1990s design-ers have formed relationships with stars relative to stars' public—rather than screen—appearances. Nowhere is this more apparent than at the Academy Awards ("The Oscars of Fashion," wrote one journalist),[40] where the details of which actress is wearing what designer give a nod to both the star and the name on the label she wears. And with each new awards show on the circuit comes more discussion of celebrities' fashions—and a heightened risk of their donning duplicate gowns.[41] Significantly, this "embarrassing" result of clothing design massification and designer worship has led to a simultaneous swing back to custom costume days: with designers and stars crowding the same spotlight, many seek press distinction by working in "exclusive" relationships.

Indeed, the ability to effect a unique but aesthetically embraceable image in both camps has never been so sought after and yet so difficult to obtain. Armani, in addition to bringing "high" design back to film in the 1980s with *American Gigolo,* is also significantly credited as one of the first designers to court numerous stars to wear his designs at awards shows.[42] Many have since followed his lead, seeing the unpar-alleled promotional opportunity that lies therein. And yet overproduc-tion has led designers more recently to consider "tailoring" their out-put to fewer bodies—and actresses, in their own ever-competitive and exclusive field, are happy to oblige them. Trying to re-create "the whole Hepburn/Givenchy thing," stars and designers are desperate to stand apart from mass merchandise and familiar "looks," searching for the artists who will best complement the shaping of their desired images.[43] But the "Hepburn/Givenchy thing" succeeded in part be-cause of its brilliant turning of elite fashion into the popular; now au-diences are not only more knowledgeable about designer apparel, they can access its cheap, mass-market copies. (Some late-nineties dress manufacturers copy Oscar-night gowns so quickly, the dresses are in stores in time for prom season.) Moreover, the increased migration of actresses to high-fashion modeling, accompanied by accelerating media attention to "supermodels," provides the most apt explication of the vanished star-designer relationship. Models, after all, are by vocation mannequins, dressed differently for each professional or public appearance and molded by stylists to sell the latest clothing and products. Their job is to wear innumerable aesthetic "looks." Not unlike today's models are today's actresses, appearing in different designers' wares onscreen and with each public appearance. In other words, "someone like a Joan Crawford" has given way to someone like supermodel Cindy Crawford—no relation.

Madonna's New Clothes: The Reinvention Revolution

This "give a look, take a look" approach in current celebrity dressing may have initially derived from the stars of the sixties' stripping away of the elite star image identity. Then came the rise of model culture, escorted in by the celebration and massification of both fashion designers' names and their merchandise. The discussion of this contemporary matrix would be incomplete, however, without acknowledgment of the role of Madonna, a pop singer, film actress, and perpetual fashion trendsetter in the last decades of the twentieth century. Madonna captured the world's attention in the 1980s as a pop singer of considerable fashion sass: from her ratty hair and fishnets, which her "wannabe" teenage female fans adopted, to her Monroe-esque "material" glamour girl to a severe, fatless figure "voguing" in Gaultier, Madonna introduced popular culture to the art of "reinvention" through clothing, attitude, and physical form. A queen of music videos broadcast on nationally received cable channels MTV and VH1, Madonna exploited "model-like" look variegation, a young and consuming demographic's servitude to television, and her own contradictory (often proclaimed "postmodern") feminist front. Additionally, her gradual physical makeover from fleshy "virgin" to lean machine dialogued with the peddling of "celebrity fitness" in the eighties; rather than influencing clothing trends, many actresses appeared before the public in physical fitness and body-sculpture home videos, in this way selling a signature "bodily" (not clothing) look. Madonna's success as an actress may never match her achievements as a musical performer, but her singing and fashion-affecting career took off after her role in her first feature film, *Desperately Seeking Susan* (1985). In the film, Madonna portrayed the same type of brash girl with a bold fashion sense as the one who danced and sang in her own, increasingly popular, music videos. Indeed, *Desperately Seeking Susan,* the tale of a woman (Rosanna Arquette) searching for happiness by affecting a new identity inspired by

"Susan" (Madonna), was a "makeover movie" for a makeover genera-tion.[44] The braggadocio of the big-business, big-spending Reagan era and its impact on fashion included a return to Crawford's big-shouldered shape in "power dressing" and the "desperation" to change social and economic status and, ultimately, "harden" one's appearance. The desired "look" of the 1980s, for both men and women, conveyed a machinistic autonomy with the excesses and extremes of financial success.[45] Madonna's (and Susan's) image of confidence, consumerism, and copious accessories suited the era well.

Although Madonna's efforts to keep fashion pundits anticipating her next favorite fashion style may have been a calculated attempt to "stay alive" in an increasingly fickle and transient popular consumer cul-ture, her effect on celebrity style is without doubt. Her much-remarked-upon postmodern look-of-many-looks engaged both mass consumerism and the commercial theory of product obsolescence: a new image meant new "stuff." Moreover, her assertive control over her career, coupled with a mainstream musical sound, also helped Madonna handily walk the line of the good-girl/bad-woman divide essential to her stardom.[46]

Perhaps Madonna's initial ragtag/boy-toy look found easy entry into the pop culture marketplace because the pop/rock music industry was then bearing witness to an array of heavily costumed and made-up male and female performers, such as Boy George, Prince, Cyndi Lauper, and Dee Snyder (of the pop-metal band aptly named Twisted Sister). But Madonna's own independence and keen business acumen unques-tionably afforded her continued success through her constant alteration and division of look and image. And, as a result, she has profoundly in-fluenced modern Hollywood stars' looks. Madonna is the story behind Valerie Steele's remark in an article on celebrity "makeover madness" in the cosmetics-oriented fashion magazine *Allure*: "There used to be more of a sense in America that there should be a correspondence be-tween the inner true you and your outer appearance." Now, instead of keeping a set look because changing it would deceptively divert atten-tion from the celebrity's "real" self, the "stylistic chaos" of frequent makeovers is accepted as "playful," as well as "the rage."[47]

Having grown through pubescentlike rebellious phases of out-landish outfits, by 1996 Madonna was honing a "respectable" image as a serious mother and dedicated film actress, showing the extremes of re-spectable celebrity dressing by appearing in public in either exercise wear or haute couture. She also illuminated changes in Hollywood's fashion mettle through her role in *Evita* (1996), a film adaptation of a Broadway musical based on the life of Argentina's charismatic former first lady, Eva Perón. Playing a woman known for her love of fine fashion and great fame, Madonna again played a self-similar role. She also assisted costume designer Penny Rose in the choice of the more than sixty 1940s-inspired outfits she wears in the film, many purchased in secondhand stores (like those she combed as "Susan").

Anticipating a run on similar styles in department stores, Touchstone Pictures (a division of Walt Disney Studios) put its merchandising machismo into overdrive, readying "Evita Boutiques" to open in Bloomingdale's department stores across the nation. Dubbed "power glamour," the Evita look included a commodity tie-in with Estee Lauder cosmetics. And although, as was appropriate for reasons previously discussed, her costuming was *not* being heralded as the "Madonna look," the expectation was that Madonna's extrafilmic celebrity—as a fashion icon and popular entertainer—would bring the merchandisers of *Evita*-related goods great profits. "While 40s revivals [in fashion as launched by the fashion industry] have failed recently, we're hoping this one will work because of Madonna," one executive ambitiously offered, adding that he hoped "[the Evita look] would supplant the Annie Hall and the Jackie O looks."[48]

With the target demographic for the *Evita* items (dresses, accessories, cosmetics) a youth market generationally distant from Hollywood's glamour days, the merchandise was priced "exclusively," perhaps to heighten its allure. Ultimately, however, the high prices dissuaded the intended consumers. In fact, with the Evita look, the Eckertian model of studio merchandising of women's products failed miserably, as the campaign, competing with too many fashion forces and Madonna's own mainstreaming, fell flat within weeks of the movie's release.[49] Madonna did, however, win a Golden Globe for her performance and, a few weeks after giving birth to her first child, accepted the award in couture. She wore a Dolce & Gabbana gown that not only barely contained her nursing bosom but was also a far cry from the apparel she was expected to sell in stores. And yet it is important to note that, around the time of *Evita*'s opening, the supermarket tabloid *Star*, which carries its own celebrity fashion review pages and the celebrity-maligning column "Would You Be Caught Dead in This Outfit?" carried a center spread on how to obtain the Evita look inexpensively. The article, by virtue of its content and site of publication, circumvented the plan for "power glamour," immediately "down-marketing" the prefabricated fashion. It also precisely "character"ized the female masses' socially negotiated and economically empowered connection with celebrity styling in the late 1990s.[50]

The Madonna/Evita circumstance indicates how Hollywood's fashionability has come to arrive largely extrafilmically, from actresses' lives offscreen more than on, and from star-studded public appearances that are subject to the approval of those in the "real world" who view them. Middle-class culture and fashion had melded previously in Hollywood, when the Depression era, for instance, witnessed the appropriation of couture's perennial "little black dress" for a working-class character.[51] In fact, this item's restraint and simplicity in design still receive great favor with the viewing public in the late nineties, and perhaps also explains the indelible chic of Audrey Hepburn.[52] Whether the outgrowth of American culture's Puritanical underpinnings or visual symbols of "good taste," Edgar Morin explained in 1960 how moderation would bring a film star fashion praise. There is a paradox, Morin asserted, in how beloved stars dress to convey simplicity and extravagance simultaneously, and "this exquisite modesty is necessary to bring a star to her apotheosis: When her fans tear her clothes."[53] In the nineties, however, the apotheosis is when her fans *wear* her clothes—provided, as I will now show, they don't already own them.

Au Courant: Sharon Stone in a Gap Turtleneck

In 1996, Sharon Stone, an "A list" Hollywood actress who came to fame through what she was wearing (or, perhaps more to point, the underwear she was not wearing) in *Basic Instinct* (1992), waltzed down Oscar's red carpet in a black ensemble. Upon being asked, Stone announced to the world that her apparel for the evening, despite her having her choice among several designer gowns, was thrown together at the last minute from items she already had in her closet. Her jacket was Armani, her skirt "old," and her black mock turtleneck, she said with a smile, was from the midpriced international chain store the Gap.

Stone's self-proclaimed love of high fashion and her recognition as an "A-list" movie star have kept her on the public catwalk since her notorious appearance in *Basic Instinct*. Indeed, Stone has not only appeared in product advertisements, like many of her celebrity cohorts, but she has also appeared on runways as a model in top designers' haute couture shows.[54] Stone, although typically brazen and firm with the press, is adulated and admired by the tabloids' fashion journalists, arguably the most difficult media makers to please. She is, in fact, consistently praised in tabloid fashion spreads—her Gap turtleneck appearance was one of her many moments of scandal-sheet splendor.

Combining the simple elegance of Audrey Hepburn and the assertive attitude of Mae West and Madonna, Stone's aesthetic and personal style have translated well to the mass movie and merchandise marketplace. Using fashion to her advantage, Stone has negotiated the tensions of late-nineties Hollywood female stardom: irrespective of her movies and the roles she plays in them, she remains in public discourse simultaneously glamorous, precious, attractive, practical, and tough. That she is celebrated for her taste in clothing, adoring couture but still daring to wear an item so completely geographically, economically, and aesthetically accessible (and Gap scrambled to fill stores with the past-season item following her wearing of it), bears testimony to the skewed paradigm of the contemporary fashionable female film star. Stone is popular not necessarily because of her acting ability, but because she is as much a model for a fashionable film star as she is a film star fashion model. As a result, W unabashedly pronounced her "Sharon Stone: Fashion Icon," her sometimes diminished presence on the silver screen balanced by her increased appearance in couture apparel on both designers' and public show runways. Not since Madonna has an actress from the late twentieth century achieved such consistent attention to her dress, her wardrobe profoundly capturing and endearing her to her audience.[55]

Stone, like her contemporary screen sisters, dons numerous designers' fashions. One designer she has particularly favored over the past few years, however, is Vera Wang. Wang, an Asian American designer, worked behind the scenes for Vogue for eighteen years before opening a shop to sell her own dress designs. Interestingly, Wang's public recognition prior to that her film celebrity clientele provided was through her bridal gowns and, most famously, her costumes for figure skater Nancy Kerrigan, the 1994 Olympic Silver Medalist. All eyes were on Kerrigan, and, naturally, what she wore, when she competed while recovering from an assault in which her U.S. Olympics teammate Tonya Harding had been implicated. So it was through an internationally televised ice show, a sport of spectacle for mass, primarily female, audiences and defined in the United States by middle-income participants, that Wang found herself catapulted into the conversation of mainstreamed high fashion. Suiting Morin's composite, Wang's dresses are beloved for their lack of ostentation despite luxurious fabrics and figure-refined forms, and actresses show up at functions in Wang designs both custom and non.[56] After the sixties' and seventies' bottom-up "radical chic" and eighties' top-down "excessory chic," the look of the nineties is "simple chic," and Wang's clothes "fit" perfectly.[57] Wang has been so popular with the public that she was named "1996 Designer of the Year" on E! network's *Joan Rivers' Fashion Review*. She was also the "Oscar fashion correspondent" in 1997 for the syndicated television celebrity news show *Entertainment Tonight*.

It's a Wrap: How to "Look" Now

During the 1950s, Edith Head was one of several "experts" on fashion who dispensed everyday dressing advice to average American women. In addition to her film work, she published several books and hosted a radio show to "prescribe" solutions for common figure flaws and dressing woes, often invoking the names of actresses she had dressed with similar figure and style problems. The promise was to increase women's knowledge of how to create their own signature "look" on par with their favorite, and allegedly equally imperfect, actresses. Claire MacCardell, one of America's premier designers of the mass-produced, casual "American" style emerging in the 1950s, took a similar approach in her book *What Shall I Wear?* by employing actresses as "models" of specific dressing styles and "looks," as did U.S. designer Elizabeth Hawes in her own series of how-to manuals. All three, however, addressed their readers as if they, too, were performers, characters needing to costume themselves appropriately and yet remarkably for their daily life appearances. "You need to know the role you play for your audience," MacCardell asserted, and "show off the clothes."[58]

Since then, an array of media have offered the masses advice on how to dress and how to *judge* Hollywood actresses relative to popular fashion. Leisure "sights"—film, television, music video, print publications, and fashion runways—have allowed popular fashion to evolve simultaneously from many different sources. The results are innumerable available looks, suited for different lifestyles, economic means, and body types. Indeed, when *In Style,* an offshoot of *People Weekly* covering "Celebrity+Beauty+Lifestyle+Fashion," ran a cover in October 1996 that asked, "Who's got the look?" the mystery was solved through a feature-by-feature list of the "best" physical attributes and clothing items of different film actresses. The breakdown of woman-centered commodities in the 1940s films of which Doane has spoken finds its contemporary placement in the fissuring instruction of how to look now, the piece-by-piece puzzling and purchasing of the best look for "the everywoman." That Elizabeth Hurley, a model attempting a film career, sat as the *In Style* issue's cover model (and did again for a special issue called "The Look" in fall 1999) further illustrates a late-1990s symbiosis of the American popular film and fashion industries.

Similarly, the redefinition of popular looks as being designer—not star—induced allows *In Style* to group celebrities according to what they are wearing: Halle Berry in the Missoni look; Gwyneth Paltrow in the Gucci look; Angela Bassett in the Escada look. Just as Christian Dior leapt to fame with his New Look in 1947, designers are being revealed in public consciousness as having "looks" of their own—styles ultimately brought to the public eye through their various celebrity clients. Thus emulators copy the designer's look, not that of the actress. As I have shown, this trajectory of film-actress-based to film-character-based, and then film-character-based to film-audience-based fashion trends derives from a complex network of cultural influences. Any signature "look" of an actress has become the celebrated "look" of a fashion designer or, just as likely, the "look" the audience "looks upon" as appropriate.[59]

The contemporary moment is one eager for Hollywood glamour but wary of its worth. Sharon Stone's applause for simplicity speaks to a delicate balance: to be praised, female film stars' manner of dress must meet certain criteria of aesthetic beauty and glitz while still suggesting an eye toward economy. Stone might have been even more materially familiar by wearing a T-shirt and leggings to the Oscars, but she would have then disappointed celebrity watchers such as Blackwell, who still seek a hint of Morin's "exquisite extravagance." In this way, Stone personifies how the role of the costume designer in manufacturing a "star image" has been subsumed by the fashion industry, mass merchandising, and the leveling of style through the "cheap copy." And in this as well we can contextualize Patty Fox's statement that opens this chapter. What *is* the popular look of Hollywood actresses today? By analyzing contemporary representations of popular actresses in popular discourse, the phenomenon of "reinvention," the migration between movie actress and runway model, and actress-related clothing merchandising for mass—often lower economic—markets, my reading of "Mr. Blackwell's Worst-Dressed List" and other modern celebrity fashion critiques reveals a complex but certain evolution in signature star styling. Indeed, if nothing else, the superior amount of media coverage of actresses' dress at each year's Academy Awards ceremony— from network and cable television shows to the popular press—suggests the relevance of reexamining Eckert's model of the film star "fashioned" for her mainstream audience; in other words, how the success of the Carole Lombard in Macy's window gave way to the public's delight in Sharon Stone in a Gap turtleneck.

Notes

I am grateful to Peter Wollen, Chon Noriega, Lyn Delliquadri, Irwin Epstein, Susan Reinhardt, and David Desser for their incomparable support of this project.

1. Patty Fox, *Star Style: Hollywood Legends as Fashion Icons* (Santa Monica, Calif.: Angel City, 1995), vii.

2. Charles Eckert, "The Carole Lombard in Macy's Window," *Quarterly Review of Film Studies* 3, no. 1 (1978): 1–23.

3. Janet Ozzard, "Fashion Flashback: Both On and Off the Screen Hollywood's Celebrities Often Set the Style," *W*, May 1996, n.p.

4. For more on Swanson's wardrobe, see Fox, *Star Style*, 10–19.

5. Mary Ann Doane, *The Desire to Desire: The Woman's Film of the 1940s* (Bloomington: Indiana University Press, 1987), 26.

6. Ibid., 24. For more on silent-era clothing display in film, see Maureen Turim, "Seduction and Elegance: The New Woman of Fashion in Silent Cinema," in *On Fashion*, ed. Shari Benstock and Suzanne Ferriss (New Brunswick, N.J.: Rutgers University Press, 1994).

7. Claudia Roth Pierpont, "The Strong Woman," *New Yorker*, 11 November 1996, 106ff.

8. For more on costuming during this era and shifts into the next, see Jane Gaines, "Costume and Narrative: How Dress Tells the Woman's Story," in *Fabrications: Costume and the Female Body*, ed. Jane Gaines and Charlotte Herzog (New York: Routledge, 1990), 180–228.

9. For more on each of these stars, see Fox, *Star Style*. Also, photographer and journalist Cecil Beaton, who was romantically involved with Garbo, offers a charming account of her dressing style sense in Cecil Beaton, *The Glass of Fashion* (Garden City, N.Y.: Doubleday, 1954), 235–39.

10. Charlotte Cornelia Herzog and Jane Marie Gaines, "Puffed Sleeves before Teatime: Joan Crawford, Adrian and Women Audiences," in *Stardom: Industry of Desire*, ed. Christine Gledhill (London: Routledge, 1991), 74–91.

11. Herzog also speaks of newsreels as fashion show films, extending back to 1909. Charlotte Herzog, "Powder Puff Promotion: The Fashion Show in Film," in *Fabrications: Costume and the Female Body*, ed. Jane Gaines and Charlotte Herzog (New York: Routledge, 1990), 134–59. For a thorough analysis of the literal commodities of glamour and display, see also Jeanine Basinger, *A Woman's View: How Hollywood Spoke to Women, 1930–1960* (Hanover, Conn.: Wesleyan University Press, 1993), 114–58.

12. For a discussion of costume designers' imperatives regarding characters' costumes and their mass consumption, see Jane Gaines, "Costume and Narrative: How Dress Tells the Woman's Story," in *Fabrications: Costume and the Female Body*, ed. Jane Gaines and Charlotte Herzog (New York: Routledge, 1990), 180–211.

13. Much has been written about all three of these actresses' "masculine" stylings. For a brief overview of these and other popular actresses in film's historical and a feminist cultural context, however, see Kathryn Weibel, *Mirror Mirror: Images of Women Reflected in Popular Culture* (Garden City, N.Y.: Anchor, 1977), 91–133.

14. Ibid., 212. Dior's design metaphor was the "inverted flower."

15. Francine Du Plessix Gray, "Prophets of Seduction," *New Yorker*, 4 November 1996, 86.

16. "Mammary madness" refers to Molly Haskell's several published tellings of this period. For more on the reception of these stars, as well as the "nonthreatening" quality of Monroe, see Weibel, *Mirror Mirror*, 123–24.

17. Valerie Carnes, "Icons of Popular Fashion," in *Icons of America*, ed. Ray B. Browne and Marshall Fishwick (Bowling Green, Ohio: Popular Press, 1978), 231.

18. Elizabeth Wilson, "Audrey Hepburn: Fashion, Film and the 50s," in *Women and*

Film: A Sight and Sound Reader, ed. Pam Cook and Philip Dodd (Philadelphia: Temple University Press, 1993), 40.

19. Brigid Keenan, *The Women We Wanted to Look Like* (London: Macmillan, 1977), 88; Alan Cartnal, "Bonnie, Clyde Style Creator Concentrates on Elegant Look," *Los Angeles Times,* 1 April 1970, 4.

20. See Rex Reed, *Travolta to Keaton* (New York: William Morrow, 1979), 217–22. During Keaton's interview with Reed, she seemed unaware of her visual impact when she announced, "I don't think I'll ever have [Farrah Fawcett-Majors's] public image. I'm an actress, not a fad. I don't think I stand out in a crowd" (218).

21. Carnes, "Icons of Popular Fashion," 229.

22. Ibid., 231.

23. For an overview of 1960s fashion, including Quant, see Nicholas Drake, ed., *The Sixties: A Decade in Vogue* (Englewood Cliffs, N.J.: Prentice Hall, 1988).

24. Carnes, "Icons of Popular Fashion," 234.

25. Lois W. Banner, *American Beauty* (New York: Alfred A. Knopf, 1983), 287.

26. Carnes, "Icons of Popular Fashion," 236. Levi-Strauss also won a Coty American Fashion Critics Award in 1971 for similar reasons. "Fashion Critics Honor Levis," *Los Angeles Times,* 17 June 1971, sec. IV, p. 20.

27. Banner, *American Beauty,* 287.

28. Carnes, "Icons of Popular Fashion," 237.

29. Interview with Edith Head in Mike Steen, *Hollywood Speaks: An Oral History* (New York: G. P. Putnam's Sons, 1974), 247–58. For more on Head's influence on dress styles, see Robert Gustafson, "The Power of the Screen: The Influence of Edith Head's Film Designs on the Retail Fashion Market," *Velvet Light Trap* 19 (1982): 8–15.

30. Banner, *American Beauty,* 289.

31. Mr. Blackwell and Vernon Patterson, *Mr. Blackwell's Worst: 30 Years of Fashion Fiascoes* (New York: Pharos, 1991), 3.

32. Keenan, *The Women We Wanted to Look Like,* 11.

33. Sandra Ley, *Fashion for Everyone: The Story of Ready-to-Wear, 1870's–1970's* (New York: Charles Scribner's Sons, 1975), 140–41; Keenan, *The Women We Wanted to Look Like,* 22. For more on the journalism style and the content of *Women's Wear Daily,* see Katie Kelly, *The Wonderful World of Women's Wear Daily* (New York: Saturday Review Press, 1972).

34. Blackwell and Patterson, *30 Years of Fashion Fiascoes,* 4.

35. Ibid., 5. It is important to note that Blackwell's list attempts a leveling line, instructing all women, famous or not, to embrace "fashion individuality" (or a personally suited look) and "reject false fashion images, Madison Avenue's latest advertising blitz, and what's considered 'in' and 'out.'" At the same time, however, Blackwell acknowledges his higher expectation—indeed, requirement—of celebrities to dress well. A far cry from the original best-dressed list, Blackwell's commentary grew increasingly biting over the years, and his best-dressed list became increasingly ignored. The adage "There's no such thing as bad publicity" has kept Blackwell's list part of the ever-bustling but increasingly tawdry American mass-media publicity machinery. Blackwell's campy critiques have served as a model for contemporary fashion reviews; as Leon Hall commented on the E! cable network's 1997 *Joan Rivers' Oscar Preview,* "Last year the styles were boring; there wasn't enough horror!"

36. Nancy Friday quoted in Anderson Jones, "Nancy Friday Explains: The Power of Television Beauty," *TV Guide,* 3–9 August 1996, 29. Also, in 1968, *TV Guide* printed a mock panel discussion that included Edith Head and Blackwell on late 1960s television fashion figures and celebrity. See Dick Hobson, "Do Stars Dress Well on TV?" *TV Guide,* 5 October 1968, 6–10.

37. Head in Steen, *Hollywood Speaks,* 252. Richard Dyer's *Stars* (London: BFI, 1979) also remains a useful aid for analyzing the complexity of star texts.

38. *People Weekly*'s annual "Best and Worst Dressed" and "50 Most Beautiful People" issues fall into this category as well.

39. Gaines, "Costume and Narrative," 200.

40. Rebecca Mead, "Don't Hate Them Because They're Beautiful," *New York,* 22 July 1996, 24.

41. "Multiplicity: With So Many Stars Showing Up at So Many Events, Designers Can't Help but Send in the Clones," *People Weekly,* 16 September 1996, 180–85.

42. Merle Ginsburg and Lisa Lockwood, "You Oughta Be in Pictures: The Hottest Romance in Hollywood Is the Love Affair between Fashion and the Stars," *W,* July 1996, 58.

43. Rene Chun, "The Hollywood Style Connection," *Mirabella,* March–April 1997, 58.

44. On the "makeover movie" in earlier incarnations, see Basinger, *A Woman's View,* 140–47.

45. For more on eighties and nineties fashion, including the internationalization of labels, see Elaine Feldman, *Fashions of a Decade: The 1990s* (New York: Facts on File, 1992).

46. Douglas Kellner provides a well-chronologized analysis of Madonna's fashion-ability in "Madonna, Fashion, and Identity," in *On Fashion,* ed. Shari Benstock and Suzanne Ferriss (New Brunswick, N.J.: Rutgers University Press, 1994), 159–82.

47. Valerie Steele quoted in Adam Platt, "The Untouchables," *Allure,* January 1997, 139. Also, following in the footsteps of Canadian *Fashion Television,* MTV has assisted the cohabitation of the music and fashion industries through fashionphile programming such as *House of Style* and *Fashionably Loud,* each intended to show what's hot and hip as worn by professional models (as opposed to musicians). The E! network has created similar programs devoted to what, and who, is "happening" in the fashion industry.

48. Quoted in Maureen Sajbel, "Evita Rules! Style Watchers Believe the Film Can Usher in a New Era of Power Glamour—with a Little Help from Madonna," *Los Angeles Times,* 27 November 1996, E1ff.

49. This contrasts with film-related merchandise created for children, which tends to arrive in stores prior to a film's release.

50. "Get That Evita Look: Madonna's Sizzling Retro Look Is Coming to a Mall Near You," *Star,* 7 January 1997, 24–25.

51. Fred Davis, *Fashion, Culture, and Identity* (Chicago: University of Chicago Press, 1992), 64.

52. David Ehrenstein, "The Elvis of Style: She's Hot, She's Sexy, She's Skinnier Than Ever. Audrey Hepburn Is . . . ," *Los Angeles Magazine,* November 1996, 109–13.

53. Edgar Morin, *The Stars,* trans. Richard Howard (New York: Grove, 1960), 48, 55. Also relevant is the rise of celebrity clothing lines; that is, the star *as* designer. These items, however, tend to be distributed through lower-middle-class venues such as Kmart, Sears, and home shopping television channels, and therefore aptly reveal the "down-scaling" of the fashion trade and the mass marketability of celebrity. Significantly, star designers are not necessarily expected to wear these products themselves.

54. Louise Farr, "Stone's Clothes Call: She May Be Dying at the Box Office but She Sure Looks Great," *W,* February 1997, 60. On the "humanizing" of couture through the employment of movie stars as models, see Ginsburg and Lockwood, "You Oughta Be in Pictures," 59.

55. Kenneth Battelle, who styled Babe Paley, Jacqueline Onassis, and Marilyn Monroe, was prompted to comment on Sharon Stone's self-determined ever (costume) changing look, stating, "Her life is a role, I guess." Quoted in Platt, "The Untouchables," 137. See also John Lahr, "The Big Picture: Whether Sharon Stone Wins an Oscar for *Casino* or Not, She Should Win One for the Best Role She's Created So Far—That of

Sharon Stone," *New Yorker,* 25 March 1997, 72–78. It should be noted as well that the performance for which Stone has received the most critical praise was in *Casino* (1995), a role that allowed her to wear an array of lavish costumes.

56. See, for instance, "The Look of Vera Wang," *In Style,* November 1996, 46–47.

57. *Excessory chic* is my term; it originates with the profligate use of accessories but also the material excesses of fashion of the 1980s; *Simple chic* comes from *In Style*'s "What's Hot Now: Secrets of Style '97" issue, January 1997.

58. Claire MacCardell, *What Shall I Wear? The What, Where, When and How Much of Fashion* (New York: Simon & Schuster, 1956), 92–93. See also Elizabeth Hawes's three books, *Why Is a Dress?* (New York: Viking, 1942), *Fashion Is Spinach* (New York: Grosse Random House, 1938), and *It's Still Spinach* (Boston: Little, Brown, 1954); and Edith Head's *The Dress Doctor* (Boston: Little, Brown, 1954) and *How to Dress for Success* (New York: Random House, 1967). For a couturier's angle, see Christian Dior, *Christian Dior's Little Dictionary of Fashion: A Guide to Dress Sense for Every Woman* (London: Cassel, 1954).

59. At press time, Gwyneth Paltrow's "fashion-ability" appears to be particularly reminiscent of Stone's.

9.

Hollywood Goes on Sale; or, What Do the Violet Eyes of Elizabeth Taylor Have to Do with the "Cinema of Attractions"?

Aida A. Hozić

Fortunately or unfortunately, Miss Taylor, sentiment went out of this business long ago.

Sol Siegel, head of MGM production, to
Elizabeth Taylor, actress, in 1959[1]

In the early 1980s, writes Greil Marcus in his "secret" history of the twentieth century, *Lipstick Traces*, Elizabeth Taylor threatened to sue a cable company that was about to air an unauthorized TV film about her life. "I am my own industry," she said in defense of her legal stance. "I am my own commodity."[2]

The statement caught Marcus's attention as the most apparent admission of self-commodification in recent show business history. But, coming from Elizabeth Taylor, the statement was also indicative of profound changes in Hollywood's relation to itself, its talent, and the world of consumption in the post-studio era. Long before she became the best friend of Michael Jackson, a name behind a fragrance line, a perpetual bride, and the world's most famous weight watcher—in short, long before she became her own industry and her own franchise—Elizabeth Taylor was an actress and, perhaps, the last relic of the old Hollywood studio system. Acquired by MGM in 1942, at the age of ten, she was one of the few child actors and actresses who made a smooth and uninterrupted transition into adult stardom. The public and the studio executives marveled at her transformation from a puppy-loving girl into a man-loving woman with no visible mishaps in her teenage years. She went to school in the Culver City studio, held her birthday parties on MGM's sound stages, and even met her first dates and husbands through studio publicists. What bothered others—the

205

studio's ownership of their lives, the feeling of being someone else's property—did not seem to bother Elizabeth Taylor. "It was like going to Disneyland every day," she said years later.[3] She appeared to be so perfectly adjusted to the movieland environment and so subsumed under the fictional projections of her own life that critics claimed she was a polyester artifact resembling the place of her creation. "Elizabeth Taylor in London or Ceylon or Texas or ancient Egypt or contemporary Manhattan is always pure Beverly Hills," wrote Foster Hirsch in a pictorial account of her life in the movies.[4] She stayed with MGM for seventeen and a half years and saw everyone—from Clark Gable to Ava Gardner to Esther Williams—leave before her. And yet, the last star on the studio roster and long its most dutiful daughter, Elizabeth Taylor was also the star whose world-famous violet eyes, caprice, and tenacity in loving the wrong men exposed all the limitations of the Hollywood studio system and precipitated its downfall. By falling in love with Richard Burton during the shooting of *Cleopatra* in the early 1960s and placing her own life in the forefront of the cinematic narrative, Elizabeth Taylor did not just bring 20th Century Fox to the brink of bankruptcy or turn her own life into an industry, she paved the way for a reversal of Hollywood's history from the "dream factory" of its Golden Age into a contemporary version of the "cinema of attractions" akin to motion pictures' earliest days.

In this essay, I recount the history of this reversal by pulling together several, seemingly disparate, threads of Hollywood's economic development in the post-*Cleopatra* period: the shift from production to distribution as the core activity of Hollywood studios, the changing importance of brand names and stars, the increased marginalization of films and other cultural products within the emerging global entertainment sector, and the unprecedented enthusiasm for digital technology and special effects in latter-day Hollywood. Whereas the key to these changes, I will suggest, has been the intense and continuous battle over brand names between Hollywood's producers and merchants, the somewhat paradoxical outcome of these changes has turned out to be the postmodern reinterpretation of what Gunning and Gaudreault, in their analysis of early cinema, have termed the "cinema of attractions."[5] I begin, therefore, with a discussion of the similarities between early motion pictures and contemporary Hollywood's attractions and then proceed to an analysis of the structural and contextual characteristics of these two periods that could have stimulated the development of similar cinematic styles and genres and defined their differences. Despite caveats that such historical parallels require great care, and that the limitations of economic determinism in the analysis of cinema can never be overstated, the comparison of these two periods can still be quite illuminating. The long and fascinating hegemony of narrative cinema and the just as fascinating tradition of textual analysis have allowed us to forget the extent to which movies are always commodities among other commodities inextricably entwined with the world of consumption: Elizabeth Taylor's reclaiming of the ownership of her violet eyes is an excellent reminder of this simple fact.

The Cinema of Attractions: Then and Now

Following the famous Brighton conference of 1978, where film scholars first had a chance to see a systematic presentation of the surviving fiction films made between 1900 and 1906, historians of the early cinema have been arguing over the dominant style of the prenickelodeon films.[6] In contrast to scholars who portray this period as the era of the teleological evolution of narrative cinema, the path toward film as a "higher art," Tom Gunning has suggested that the early motion pictures could be viewed as the "cinema of attractions": as self-conscious moments of spectacle deeply immersed in the emerging consumer culture of the early 1900s. Gunning proposes several definitions of *attractions*: they are shocking and discontinuous experiences of the phantasmagoric world of commodities and expressions of repressed—"utopian, uncanny, or fantastic"—aspects of modernity; they are willing ruptures of the self-enclosed fictional world that directly solicit viewers' attention; they are, by and large, exhibitionist performances—a wink of an eye, a recurring look at the camera, a striptease addressed at the spectator, a continuous display of magic tricks and effects.[7] The thread that runs through all these definitions is the idea that cinema is not an isolated diegetic universe but a porous and complex social institution in constant dialogue with its environment.

Whereas film scholars mostly contest the historical accuracy of Gunning's arguments, I am much more interested in the implicit and explicit openness of Gunning's cinema of attractions toward its social and economic context. The debate between "narrative" and "attraction" is laden with important theoretical disagreements—from differences in the conceptualization of industrial and aesthetic change as linear or punctual, teleological or nonteleological, to differences in understanding the role of a spectator and the mode of reception as governed by identification or distance, quiet voyeurism or excitement. The proponents of the "narrative" perspective see film history as the process of the enunciation of a new art form or, in economic terms, as the process of product differentiation. Over the years, the argument goes, film separated itself from other forms of entertainment—such as vaudeville, freak shows, and amusement parks—to become a self-sufficient and self-contained universe divided from its audiences and its surroundings by the "fourth wall" borrowed from theatrical tradition. From the perspective of the cinema of attractions, on the other hand, this process of abstraction has never been pure and complete; rather, it has been troubled and contentious. Both "attraction" and "narrative" continued to intermingle within single films, even in the feature-film era, and the cinema of attractions has found an extended life in genres such as pornography, musical comedies, and newsreels. Thus, according to Gunning, instead of thinking about "narrative" and "attraction" as mutually exclusive cinematic forms, we should think about them in terms of their relative dominance—within particular films and genres as well as over the course of the century-long history of film.[8]

Just as complex has been the cinema's relationship with the world of consumption. The study of film as the cinema of attractions, says Gunning, enables us to look at film from a broader perspective of developing consumer culture in which visual attractions—billboards, advertisements, department store displays, world's fairs—served as both ends in themselves (i.e., as entertainment) and means to incite consumption. At the turn of the century, films were projected onto billboards, shown in amusement parks, and displayed in department stores; they served as platforms for product promotion. The culture of modernity, writes Gunning, was a culture intent on "arous[ing] desire through aggressive visuality."[9] Cinema played an integral part in the cultivation of the American consumer culture and continued to intersect with the production of consumers throughout Hollywood's Golden Age. As historians Lary May and Lizabeth Cohen have shown, Hollywood was instrumental in the transformation of the United States from a frugal Victorian society into the land of mass consumption, and from a cacophonous world of immigrant neighborhoods into the nearly homogeneous country of Americans.[10] Similarly, Charles Eckert's studies of merchandising and tie-ins in the studio era have revealed the extent to which Hollywood's near monopoly over the concept of beauty influenced the development of fashion and cosmetics industries in the United States and touched the life of nearly every American woman.[11] Consequently, Hollywood producers developed a clear sense of their impact on average consumers: even as late as the 1950s, with their industry in disarray, they were still arguing that the U.S. government should support the export of American films as a means of promoting the nation's commercial interests abroad.[12]

However, as both Gunning and the scholars of the studio system would agree, the elements of spectacle that continued to linger through Hollywood movies as well as Hollywood's links with the world of consumption became subservient to film narrative in the studio era; as Gunning has put it, they went "underground."[13] Magic and tricks that once entertained audiences to no end became much less overt. Major studios were reluctant to use visible special effects in their A productions, so monsters, flying saucers, and utopian landscapes—generally regarded as inexpensive substitutes for stars or decently scripted film narratives—became trademarks of low-budget films and smaller and lesser studios. Product placement, merchandising, and tie-ins also maintained a semblance of invisibility in Hollywood's most important films. Eckert's studies of Hollywood's "plunge into the marketplace" and Charlotte Cornelia Herzog and Jane Marie Gaines's close reading of Joan Crawford's "puffed sleeves" in *Letty Lynton* point to a nearly seamless intertwining of films' narratives and characters with their commercial surroundings.[14]

And yet, following the collapse of the studio system, the American film industry in many ways reverted back to its pre-Hollywood days. Thanks to the multiplication of distribution channels and the increased reliance on merchandising and tie-ins, films have once again become transparent triggers of consumption, their pristine narrative form often visibly tarnished by displays of Nike shoes, Coca-Cola cans, Pizza Hut meals, and GM cars. Studio executives make no bones about the fact that movies are now "marketing events," and that their merchandising and licensing potential determines whether or not they will be made.[15] Producers change plots and story lines in order to maximize the number of characters suitable for toy manufacturing, and blockbuster films come close to crossing the line between being pure advertisements for movie paraphernalia and actual feature films. Even in terms of dollars and cents, theatrically distributed films are no longer the primary source of income for Hollywood studios: theater tickets now represent less than 15 percent of total consumer expenditures on filmed entertainment in the United States, and the $100 billion market for licensed merchandise, driven by sales of movie-related brands, is approximately ten times larger than global box-office revenue.[16] Dwarfed by sales of popcorn, M&Ms, and sodas in theater lobbies, translated into underwear and theme park rides, and transformed into franchising empires, film and TV products are rapidly losing their own distinct identities. As Sam Grogg, a former dean of the School of Filmmaking at the North Carolina School of the Arts in Winston-Salem would say, "All the movies nowadays lead to the Gift Shop."[17]

At the same time, a number of nonnarrative and nonfiction forms are beginning to intrude into "classic" Hollywood films or constitute their own distinct genres in direct competition with feature films. Over the past decade, special effects have become not just possible replacements for actors and stars but determinants of Hollywood's box-office performance. Animated characters and "morphed" or "composited" images are openly advertised as key attractions to the moviegoing audiences: in the hype of *Terminator 2*'s release, it was difficult to say whether Arnold Schwarzenegger or ILM's liquid robot had the greater audience-drawing power; discussions about *Forrest Gump* focused more on the "morality" of the digital imaging that enabled Tom Hanks to shake hands with President Nixon than on the film's dubious political message; and effects in films such as *Twister* and *Volcano* came close to completely overshadowing the movies' thin narrative plots. But simulation technology, which stands at the heart of Hollywood's transformation, does not limit itself to special effects, computer games, and digital environments. It spills over into urban areas, leisure parks, and the well-protected zones of consumption. Special-effects designers, computer animators, and software engineers are constructing theme park rides, imaginary submarines, and virtual-reality war games and placing them in theme parks and shopping malls around the world, from Los Angeles to Nagoya, Japan. Their purposes are both to entertain and to put potential consumers into familiar narratives and child-like situations, encouraging them to spend money along the way. As Michael Sorkin has perceptively written, "One of the main effects of Disneyfication is the substitution of recreation for work, the production of leisure according to the routines of the industry."[18]

Hollywood's colonization of our everyday lives also has its other side: the transformation of reality into spectacle. In a world in which direct transmission of a war is regarded as prime-time entertainment for the purposes of airtime advertising sales, we should probably not be surprised that the new reality-based genres are directly competing with feature films for viewers' attention. The serialized lives of the rich and famous, like the ones to which Elizabeth Taylor so stringently objects, and their even more populist counterparts—talk shows, courtroom television, and infotainment programs—are feeding the maw of TV and cable distribution much as newsreels and B movies once fed the theater chains of the major Hollywood studios. Their power, however, rests in both their ability to customize real-life events into prefabricated narratives and their alleged openness to audience participation. Unlike the closed and seemingly self-contained form of feature films, reality TV combines the emotional triggers of melodrama with calls for viewers' plebiscites on an entire gamut of issues—from sexual harassment, domestic violence, and child abuse to cross-dressing, body piercing, and the historical fact of the Holocaust.

Despite the possible or apparent cultural debasement of which Hollywood and the American media are so frequently accused, there is a certain openness in this plurality of entertainment forms, a certain appeal in the constant bickering of visual attractions that the world of cinema and the world of consumption have carried on throughout the twentieth century. However, it would be a mistake to ignore the significant changes that have taken place in the entertainment industry in that same period. The cinema may have come full circle, but the industry has incorporated a learning curve in its development. And as it transformed itself from a relatively small and decentralized business of technological enthusiasts, immigrant peddlers, and traveling exhibitors into the fastest-growing and one of the largest industrial sectors in the United States, it also transformed the attractions themselves.

What's Love Got to Do with It?

Rewind to Elizabeth Taylor and her violet eyes. On 19 October 1959, in the last days of the Hollywood studio system, Elizabeth Taylor signed a contract with 20th Century Fox to play the title role in a film called *Cleopatra*, based on a flimsy novel by an unknown Italian author, Carlo Mario Franzero.[19] Legend has it that Elizabeth Taylor jokingly requested one million dollars for her participation in the movie. The producers, eager to elevate the film from yet another Roman spectacle into a star-studded drama, took her request seriously and accepted. The fee made Elizabeth Taylor the first female star ever to command such an amount for a single movie. It also instantly increased the film's budget from two to six million dollars—one of the many miscalculations that doomed the production from its outset. In addition, Taylor insisted on a foreign location so that she could ensure the maximum tax break on her earnings registered through the company in Switzerland. The studio responded by setting the production first at London's Pinewood Studio, where the production could benefit from generous British subsidies, and then in Cinecitta studio in Rome, where the weather and availability of extras seemed more congenial to the producers' desire to create a credible imitation of Egypt.

In both London and Rome, the production was mired with problems: London fog turned out to be poor substitute for African sun; Taylor barely survived two life-threatening illnesses; a plague of Roman stray cats frequently ruined takes with their screeching; "slave girls" went on a strike provoked by the pinching of Italian technicians; the Italian Communist Party orchestrated a boycott of the production and accused 20th Century Fox of promoting racial segregation among *Cleopatra*'s dancers.[20] None of the problems, however, could even begin to compare with the greatest of them all—the love affair between costars Elizabeth Taylor and Richard Burton, whose double adultery provoked unprecedented public attention and official outrage. The Vatican condemned Taylor as an unfit mother and an erotic vagrant.[21] U.S. Congresswoman Iris Blitch accused Taylor of lowering the prestige of American women abroad and destroying U.S. relations with friendly countries, Italy in particular. The congresswoman requested that the Department of Justice declare Richard Burton and Elizabeth Taylor ineligible for reentry into the United States.[22] *Playhouse* magazine organized a plebiscite with a single question: Can you forgive Elizabeth Taylor? This was the public morality play of the decade, a prelude to John and Yoko and the suburban equivalent of the sexual revolution that was yet to come.

Cleopatra premiered in New York on 12 June 1963, five years after its producer, Walter Wanger, acquired the rights to Franzero's novel. For the occasion, director Joseph L. Mankiewicz cut ninety-six hours of footage—accumulated mostly as a cover-up for the poorly written and often nonexistent shooting script—into four hours and three minutes of the ultimate Hollywood kitsch, so bad that it could not even qualify as camp. No one seemed to care—for what people had come to see were not Antony and Cleopatra, but Richard Burton and Elizabeth Taylor. Even before the premiere, *Cleopatra* had become an assured box-office hit. The film's unprecedented publicity allowed Fox to extract exuberant guarantees from theater owners, close to fifteen million dollars, to ask for 70 percent of the gross instead of the usual 50 percent, and to raise the price of theater tickets threefold to the unbelievable five and a half dollars.[23] By the year's end, *Cleopatra* had earned twenty-six million dollars and had become the top-grossing film of 1963. The Academy of Motion Picture Arts and Sciences awarded it nine Oscar nominations. And yet, even as the greatest hit of the year, *Cleopatra* could not recuperate its costs, and it remains, to this day, one of the most expensive movies ever made. The debacle forced Darryl Zanuck to close down 20th Century Fox and sell its back lot to remain solvent. "It was desperate," said Zanuck's son Richard a few years later about the atmosphere at the studio in the aftermath of *Cleopatra*. "There were only about fifty people here—everyone else had been canned—and we just sat around looking at each other. . . . It's an awful thing to say, but things were so tight, we were trying to figure out ways how to get another janitor off the payroll."[24] It was not just the end of a studio—it was the end of an era.

It would be easy to dismiss *Cleopatra* as yet another Hollywood exercise in excess and mediocrity. But the significance of the film and the events that surrounded its ill-fated production was much greater than that: Taylor and Burton's love affair punctured the motion pictures' diegetic universe and brought to light an important shift in power relations within the American film industry.[25] The fiasco reverberated throughout the industry and, especially when compared with Benjamin and Krim's success in packaging independent productions at United Artists, revealed just how cumbersome, difficult, and ultimately useless studio control over production had become. The return of sentiment into "the business" ended the long period of producers' dominance in the motion picture industry, marked the beginning of the merchants' ascent to power in the entertainment sector, and indirectly ushered Hollywood into the age of synthetic thespians and digital technology. The merchants—distributors, financiers, agents—who have come to the dominate the industry in the aftermath of *Cleopatra* turned former studios into franchiselike media organizations that derive most of their profits from royalties and licensing fees and, therefore, place enormous emphasis on the purchase, development, and maintenance of rights to brand names and characters. As the 1995 Time Warner annual report openly acknowledged, the motto of the industry is that "brands build libraries, libraries build networks, networks build distribution, distribution builds brands."[26] Thus the proliferation of stars who regard themselves as "their own industries" finds its logical counterpart in the proliferation of special effects and animated characters as substitutes for actors and human talent. Therein lies the difference between the early moving images and the resurgent cinema of attractions: whereas early cinema, just like the consumer culture of its time, had an emancipatory potential in its promise of mass participation and perpetual novelty, the attractions of the new entertainment economy seem to be merely symbols of a hollowed-out industrial complex and its enormous commercial power.

In order to understand the full impact of this saga and its implications, it is important to remember that the critical issue here is not Hollywood per se but the instruments of social and economic control that it embodies. If we stop for a moment and look at the way in which Hollywood moguls governed their empire in the studio era, we will see that their power rested on two factors: occupation of space and occupation of privacy. The concentration of motion picture production in Hollywood and, even more important, the construction of film studios enabled motion picture producers to increase the speed and quantity of their production and to start standardizing their product. The star system, on the other hand, allowed them to communicate directly with their audiences and, therefore, to weaken the power of locally entrenched exhibitors.[27] However, due to the nature of the motion picture industry and its dependence on human talent, the control of Hollywood moguls over their "brand names" had a more perverse and exaggerated manifestation than in other industrial sectors.

The transformation of actors into stars entailed occupation of their privacy. Christine Gledhill writes that actors became stars only "when their off-screen life styles equal[ed] and surpass[ed] their acting ability in its importance."[28] Similarly, Richard deCordova notes that the star system developed only when "picture personalities" outgrew the textuality of their pictures.[29] But these excursions beyond the boundaries of a scripted text were never allowed to go too far: although producers eagerly exploited and generated the attention that surrounded the stars, they feared the erratic behavior of their assets and the autonomy that could stem from their individualized publicity. Hence the studio's control over stars and creative talent extended far beyond the standard economic mechanisms—restrictions on unionization, seven-year contracts, limitations on transfers from studio to studio—to encompass publicity, moral codes of conduct, and general adherence to the studio's prepackaged narrative assigned to each particular player in the industry. Convinced that only fiction could be truly manipulated, Hollywood moguls relied on diegesis not only in the production of their films but in the sustenance of their entire economic endeavor. To use Tino Balio's term, Hollywood producers created a "controlled institution" to match the controlled environments of their studios.[30]

The symbolic and physical departure of production from Hollywood's studio lots that started in the 1950s—the "hollowing out" of the "dream factory"—destroyed the "controlled institution" of the studio system. As *Cleopatra* so vividly demonstrates, the reintroduction of spatial distances into the industry—between Hollywood moguls and their crews on location around the world, between producers and their audiences, between labor and creative talent and studio management—undermined the ability of the studios to control the production process and eroded their more subtle instruments of power. Dispersion of production, labor problems, and the assertion of creative talent's power in the period between 1950 and 1970—both in the United States and overseas—created an impression among motion picture executives that the risks of the production process were far greater than its potential benefits. The spatial reorganization of production also made it less and less possible for motion picture producers to finish productions on time and under budget. Accumulated losses in production created an opportunity for distributors, financiers, and agents to fill the power vacuum and reorganize the film and entertainment industry in a way that would minimize their risks. Afraid of any additional losses that could result from production, the merchants have shifted the burden of production onto an increasing number of independent producers and developed a complex transnational web of relationships that effectively excludes filmmakers, and all those involved in the production side of the entertainment business, from fair participation in profits.[31] The horizontal integration of media companies, the presale arrangements between bankers and distributors, the simultaneous multiplication and conversion of distribution venues are all buffers created to protect middlemen and their earnings. They distance producers from their own works to such an extent that they ultimately have little or no control over them, and they intersperse layers and layers of products between consumers and the "original" product so that they have little or no choice but to purchase them: as discounted burgers at McDonald's, fruit juices at Giant, extra dollars on a Visa card, free miles on USAir, shoes at Foot Locker, or popcorn at Blockbuster.

Ironically, the loose contractual entity focused on acquisition, maintenance, and sales of intellectual property rights that stands at the core of contemporary merchant empire seems far more accommodating of human error, individual idiosyncrasies, and cultural heterogeneity than the studio system was. While products flow from one medium to another, it is difficult not to notice that, within the universe of the global entertainment companies, Lorena Bobbit is as much of a star as Madonna, Disney distributes Buñuel's *Belle de Jour,* Chinese and Taiwanese films pack U.S. cinemas, and the Lion King speaks with the voice of James Earl Jones. But, as is usually the case in Hollywood, appearances are deceptive. What connects these varied visual and social phenomena is not just their similar status as commodities—simulacra

among other simulacra in the constant process of symbolic exchange—
but the genuine and institutionalized flight from production that stands
behind their appearance.

Thus the decline of producers and the ascent of merchants bring
about an inversion of power relations in the entertainment industry,
turning it upside down and inside out. What was once inside, tightly
controlled by the studios and engulfed in their narratives (production,
labor, talent) is now externalized; what was once outside (a messy reality, outrageous behavior, emotional outbursts, pacified audiences) has
become the industry itself. The effects of this translation of the world
into an uninterrupted flow of attractions are different from those of
the "age of mechanical reproduction" that Walter Benjamin described
in the mid-1930s. When Benjamin wrote about film as the quintessen-
tial art of modernity—where "the sight of immediate reality has become an orchid in the land of technology"[32]—he was primarily concerned with the fact that film blurred the distinction between reality
and the image, between the original and its copy. Because mechanical
reproduction was inherent to film, the penetration of technology into
the reality was, according to Benjamin, so deep that technology itself
was no longer visible. What remained as art was the semblance of a reality more real than reality itself. The reproduction took the place of
the original—depriving the original of its "presence," of its existence
in time and space, of its tradition—and embarked upon a life of its
own. The "age of mechanical reproduction," Benjamin feared, was the
age of "mass participation," and film—whose audiences were critical,
but in an absentminded way—was particularly conducive to the "reproduction of masses." In the age of mechanical reproduction, the separation of art from reality was such that art absorbed reality and became a purpose unto itself. As such, as sheer *l'art pour l'art,* it perfectly
corresponded to the world in which war—the ultimate form of the
world's own self-alienation—had become an aesthetic phenomenon
par excellence.

Benjamin was writing under the assumption that originals still existed. And, indeed, contrary to many of Benjamin's darkest visions, the
age of mechanical reproduction actually increased the value of the
original, because the latter made mass reproduction possible. By contrast, the current reorganization of the entertainment industry transforms the original into the epiphenomenon of its alternate identities: it
is not film as the mechanical reproduction of reality that is relevant,
but film's permutation into consumer goods, travel options, and software programs. Film has become a by-product of financial trans-

actions, distribution deals, and technological advancement, and the distancing from production, artistry, and "reality" is so great that both reality and cultural products are ephemeral. One does not have to search too far for examples: Jane Austen's novels are sold with the label "now a major motion picture," just as consumer goods are advertised in magazines with the label "as seen on TV." The copies of the copy—for that is what ancillary products are in their essence—no longer increase the value of the original, they guarantee its authenticity and its continued existence.

The love affair between Elizabeth Taylor and Richard Burton that nearly destroyed 20th Century Fox and signaled a period of radical transformation in the American film industry represented an element of unscripted reality that burst into the tightly controlled environment of the Hollywood studio system. It was an act of emotional emancipation, both for the actors and for the audiences, similar in its potential effects to a character's walking out of the cinema screen and taking off his costume. The changes that have since taken place in the entertainment sector have diminished the impact of this rupture. The entertainment industry, to use once again an apt self-description of the Time Warner public relations department, now has the world as its stage and its audience.[33] There is no way out because we are all already in.

Conclusion: Lost in the House of Mirrors

"There is no film industry anymore, it's all entertainment," said Sam Goldwyn Jr. in 1994, as his company financed the distribution and exhibition of foreign and independent films with the worldwide franchise of a TV show called *American Gladiators*.[34] The blurring of the boundaries between different forms of entertainment, the transformation of films into consumer products, the merging of make-believe and real life—these are no longer accidental and playful fragments of postmodern media culture but the economic preconditions of the continued existence of the global entertainment sector. Thus, although Gunning may be right when he claims that the cinema of attractions constitutes the "forgotten future of our recent past," the overwhelming experience of contemporary visual attractions makes this memory somewhat less appealing.

According to Gunning, consumer culture's continuous imbrication with and exploitation of the cinema of attractions did not necessarily diminish its "fascinating and even liberating possibilities." On the contrary, its open-ended dialogue with the audience, its almost Brechtian insistence on interruptions and nonidentification, its meandering nonnarrative form—all contained elements of freedom common to both avant-garde film and Coney Island. Thus, in Gunning's view, the cinema of attractions undermined the traditional dichotomy of low and high culture and opened up the possibility for explorations of hidden pockets of modernity.

There is no doubt that some aspects of contemporary visual attractions—from video game arcades to MTV programs, Web site designs, satellite TV, and even (why not?)a stampede of digital rhinoceros in a TV commercial—provoke the joyous excitement and silent awe that we so readily identify with viewers' experience of early cinema. But new attractions also contain a new and paradoxical element perfectly visible in Elizabeth Taylor's assertion of property rights over her life—they are binding exactly because they seem so voluntary, and they are entrapments exactly because they appear liberating. In a world in which there is little but attractions left, in which intimacy has become a matter of public display, in which visual products are recycled through hundreds of distribution venues and ancillary markets, attractions are becoming as imprisoning as the narrative cinema they have displaced. With the ominous media enterprises lurking in the background, it is as if the plurality of visual lures that once characterized the cinema of attractions has been reduced to just one—the house of mirrors. Imagine, if Elizabeth Taylor were to get lost in it—as "her own industry, her own commodity"—she would see nothing but an endless reflection of her own violet eyes.

Notes

1. Quoted in Dick Sheppard, *Elizabeth: The Life and Career of Elizabeth Taylor* (New York: Doubleday, 1974).

2. Quoted in Greil Marcus, *Lipstick Traces: A Secret History of the Twentieth Century* (Cambridge: Harvard University Press, 1989), 106.

3. Quoted in Sheppard, *Elizabeth*, 1.

4. Foster Hirsch, *Elizabeth Taylor* (New York: Pyramid Communications, 1973), 12.

5. André Gaudreault and Tom Gunning introduced the term *cinema of attractions* at the 1985 Colloquium on Film and History at Cerisy. Their presentation was subsequently published as "Le Cinema des premier temps: un defi a historie du film?" in *Historie du Cinéma: Nouvelles Approches,* ed. Jacques Aumont, André Gaudreault, and Michel Marie (Paris: Publications de la Sorbonne, 1989). In this essay I rely primarily on the following texts: Tom Gunning, "The Cinema of Attractions: Early Film, Its Spectator and the Avant-Garde," and "Non-Continuity, Continuity, Discontinuity: A Theory of Genres in Early Films," both in *Early Cinema: Space, Frame, Narrative,* ed. Thomas Elsaesser (London: British Film Institute, 1990); Tom Gunning, *D. W. Griffith and the Origins of the American*

Narrative Film: The Early Years at Biograph (Urbana: University of Illinois Press, 1991); and, in particular, the rich and stimulating debate between Charles Musser and Tom Gunning published in *Yale Journal of Criticism* 7, no. 2 (1994): Tom Gunning, "The Whole Town's Gawking: Early Cinema and the Visual Experience of Modernity" (189–201); Charles Musser, "Rethinking Early Cinema: Cinema of Attractions and Narrativity" (203–33).

6. For an overview of the debates among historians of the early cinema, see Stephen Bottomore, "The First Twenty Years of French Cinema (Paris, 4–6 November 1993) and the Musser-Gunning Debate," *Historical Journal of Film, Radio and Television* 14, no. 2 (1994): 215–19.

7. Gunning, "The Whole Town's Gawking," 196–97; Gunning, "The Cinema of Attractions," 57.

8. Gunning, "The Whole Town's Gawking," 191.

9. Ibid., 194.

10. See Lary May, *Screening Out the Past: The Birth of Mass Culture and the Motion Picture Industry* (Chicago: University of Chicago Press, 1983); Lizabeth Cohen, *Making a New Deal: Industrial Workers in Chicago, 1919–1939* (New York: Cambridge University Press, 1990).

11. Charles Eckert, "The Carole Lombard in Macy's Window," in *Stardom: Industry of Desire,* ed. Christine Gledhill (London: Routledge, 1991), 30–39.

12. "From the point of view of national interest, a strong Hollywood also is important. Hollywood 'pix' have been recognized as ambassadors not only for democratic ideals, but for the general commerce of this country's varied industries from bathtubs to refrigerators." Editor Thomas M. Pryor, *Daily Variety,* 15 November 1961, quoted in U.S. Congress, House, Committee on Education and Labor, *Impact of Imports and Exports on American Employment, Hearings,* 87th Congress, 1st and 2d Sessions, 1962, 498.

13. Gunning, "The Cinema of Attractions," 57.

14. Eckert, "The Carole Lombard in Macy's Window"; Charlotte Cornelia Herzog and Jane Marie Gaines, "Puffed Sleeves before Teatime: Joan Crawford, Adrian and Women Audiences," in *Stardom: Industry of Desire,* ed. Christine Gledhill (London: Routledge, 1991), 74–91.

15. See, for instance, Bruce Handy, "101 Movie Tie-Ins: With Merchandising Money Rivaling Its Box-Office Take, Hollywood Is Saying, Attention Shoppers!" *Time,* 2 December 1996, 78–81.

16. For detailed analysis of consumer spending on leisure, see "Leisure Time," *Standard and Poor's Industry Surveys,* 6 April 1995, sec. 2, p. L18. Global retail sales of licensed merchandise crossed the $100 billion threshold in 1994, thanks to *Mighty Morphin Power Rangers, The Lion King,* and Looney Tunes. See Adam Sandler, "Mighty Rich Merchandise," *Variety,* 19 June 1995, 36.

17. Sam Grogg, from a talk given in Charlottesville, Virginia, organized by the Virginia Foundation for the Humanities, April 1994.

18. Michael Sorkin, "See You in Disneyland," in *Variations on a Theme Park: The New American City and the End of Public Space,* ed. Michael Sorkin (New York: Hill & Wang, 1992), 228.

19. Sheppard, *Elizabeth,* 243. For a vastly entertaining account of Elizabeth Taylor's participation in the *Cleopatra* debacle, see Harry Medved and Michael Medved, *The Hollywood Hall of Shame: The Most Expensive Flops in Movie History* (New York: Putnam, 1984).

20. Medved and Medved, *The Hollywood Hall of Shame.*

21. Sheppard, *Elizabeth,* 317.

22. Ibid.

23. Ibid., 329.

24. Richard Zanuck quoted in John Gregory Dunne, *The Studio* (New York: Farrar, Straus & Giroux, 1968), 14.

25. As Matthew Bernstein notes in his detailed study of Walter Wanger's career, *Walter Wanger, Hollywood Independent* (Berkeley: University of California Press, 1994), "The studio set forth the notion, which countless historians and biographers repeat, that *Cleopatra* ruined Fox. But in truth, Fox did itself in, and the film was its most convenient scapegoat" (343). By the time of the film's shooting in Italy, all the prerogatives of the studio system that had made 20th Century Fox into one of Hollywood's most successful companies were already falling apart. The lack of a shootable script, turf battles within the management, and location shooting exposed the pitfalls of Hollywood's "frenzied transition" in the post-studio era. Unable or unwilling to follow any of the ground rules of studio filmmaking, and yet still bureaucratically bound to the studio, protagonists of the *Cleopatra* saga found themselves at odds with each other and the studio system itself.

26. Time Warner, *Building Global Brands* (1995 annual report), 1.

27. The film industry was not an isolated case in this respect. As Susan Strasser has written in her wonderful study of early American marketing, manufacturers, burdened by enormous investments in their production facilities, could no longer "afford to be the passive factor of neoclassical economics or the relatively weak link in an old fashioned chain dominated by large wholesale merchants." Susan Strasser, *Satisfaction Guaranteed: The Making of the American Mass Market* (New York: Pantheon, 1989), 19. Fearing such dependence on the already powerful distributors, manufacturers "took their cue from a few industries, such as book publishing and patent medicines, where manufacturers courted customers directly" (19), and where patents and copyrights endowed them with a quasi-monopoly position in the market. The development of branded products such as Crisco shortening, Ivory soap, Kodak cameras, and Campbell's soup enabled the manufacturers to tilt the price elasticity in their favor: "The consumer who wanted no substitutes for Ivory soap or Steinway pianos would be unwilling to settle for another product just because it was cheaper" (25). By creating customers who would come to the store with clear ideas of what they desired, manufacturers were hoping to develop direct links with their customers so that they could bypass the seemingly omnipotent wholesalers and retailers.

28. Christine Gledhill, "Introduction," in *Stardom: Industry of Desire,* ed. Christine Gledhill (London: Routledge, 1991), xiv.

29. Richard deCordova, *Picture Personalities: The Emergence of the Star System in America* (Urbana: University of Illinois Press, 1990).

30. See Tino Balio, *Grand Design: Hollywood as a Modern Business Enterprise* (New York: Charles Scribner's Sons, 1993).

31. It is impossible here to do justice to the relationship between power and spatial organization of production, or to describe in detail the transition from producers' to merchants' dominance in the American economy. Although I devote all my attention to these issues in my dissertation, "The Rise of the Merchant Economy: Industrial Change in the American Film Industry" (University of Virginia, 1997), it may be important to note here that similar changes have also taken place in other national film industries and other industrial sectors. From Japan to India and to Europe, dispersion of production and worldwide centralization of distribution and finance have dramatically decreased the number of films produced and have come to threaten the survival of national film industries as we have known them. Consequently, the global entertainment industry no longer accumulates its profits by increasing the quantity or the quality of its products; rather, it recycles the same products through a number of distribution venues—an assemblage of large media companies that, much like Wal-Mart or Ikea or Pier 1 Imports (depending on the perceived level of sophistication of the audiences), dominate the mar-

kets by limiting our choices while offering a deceptive variety of "culturally diverse" products.

32. Walter Benjamin, "The Work of Art in the Age of Mechanical Reproduction," in *Illuminations* (New York: Schocken, 1968), 233.

33. Time Warner, 1990 annual report, 9.

34. Sam Goldwyn Jr., telephone interview with author, Los Angeles, January 1994.

10.

Consuming Doubts: Gender, Class, and Consumption in Ruby in Paradise and Clueless

Angela Curran

Can cinema spectators be critical? This topic has been the subject of much debate among film theorists. Taking consumption as a metaphor for the passive viewer, we can say that many contemporary film theorists, especially those grounded in Lacanian-Althuserian psychoanalysis, argue that narrative films create "consuming viewers," viewers who uncritically accept the social messages of the films' narratives. These messages are assumed to be socially conservative ones. These theorists also criticize narrative films for failing to engage viewers in reflection on social issues. They suggest that only nonnarrative cinema holds out the possibility for film to be socially critical. Along these lines, Laura Mulvey argues that classic Hollywood cinema, as a mass medium, is a tool that positions viewers to take on the dominant gender ideology.[1] Movies themselves, especially popular and commercially successful Hollywood-produced ones, are often criticized by philosophers and cultural critics alike as mere commodities rather than as an art form that has the potential to inspire viewers to struggle for social change and propose alternatives to a consuming lifestyle.

This critical view of mainstream narrative cinema has also been advanced by Frankfurt school philosophers Theodor Adorno and Max Horkheimer, who coined the term *culture industry* to refer to a vast complex of social institutions, including the film industry, dedicated to the domination of nature in the interest of commercial profit.[2] Unlike their Frankfurt school philosopher colleague Walter Benjamin, Adorno and Horkheimer were skeptical of the liberatory possibilities in mass-marketed art forms, and many readers have interpreted their attack on the culture industry to mean that cinema that is produced by the culture industry is mere escapist entertainment aimed at generating profits for the rich and powerful.[3] The only kind of art that escapes this control by the culture industry is avant-garde art. This art refuses to reproduce the viewer as consumer and challenges its audiences, who are "enlightened outsiders," to see the contradictions within consumer capitalism, showing them the possibilities for human freedom.

At the heart of these criticisms is the view that there is a basic distinction between "art" and "entertainment": films that qualify as "art" must withhold the traditional pleasures associated with mainstream narrative cinema, and instead challenge viewers to think about the possibilities for social change; films that count as mere "entertainment," on the other hand, provide pleasurable involvement through the conventional means of Hollywood narrative without helping the viewer to reflect on social issues. It is further assumed that every movie falls into one or the other, but not both, of these categories.[4]

In this chapter, I discuss two recent narrative films that challenge this view of the nature of film as a consumer product: *Ruby in Paradise* (Victor Nuñez, 1993), an interesting, independently produced film and Grand Jury Prize winner at the 1993 Sundance Film Festival; and *Clueless* (Amy Heckerling, 1995), a witty adaptation of *Emma*, Jane Austen's novel about self-delusion and notions of class and decorum fundamental to English society, transposed to a Beverly Hills high school in thrall to consumer culture. For some of us, it is much easier to see how *Ruby in Paradise* has a form and content that explores in a serious way the problems of consumer capitalism. In bringing these two films together in one discussion, however, I want to show how, in their own ways, both raise interesting questions about the role consumption plays in American society.

In addition, both films are of special interest in relation to the topic of feminism and consumption in that both show young women coming to adulthood in a society whose central concern is consuming. *Ruby* shows the special challenges that working-class women face in making a life in an economy structured around consumption. *Clueless* presents a parody of the consumption patterns of upper-class young women, calling into question the view, presented in advertisements for women's makeup and clothing, that control and self-expression come through active participation in gender-defined consumer practices.[5] I will demonstrate how the questions these films raise about American consumer culture also apply to the nature of film itself as a consumer product, showing the need for a third alternative to the "art" versus "entertainment" dichotomy that Adorno and Horkheimer present in their critique of consumer capitalism and art.

Figure 1. Publicity poster for *Ruby in Paradise*.

I begin by presenting my interpretations of the two films, then turn to some discussion of the larger issues of consumption that they raise.

Selling in Paradise

Ruby in Paradise tells the story of a young woman in her early twenties, Ruby Lee Gissing (Ashley Judd), who leaves her home in the mountains of east Tennessee in search of something new. The film begins with a rather startling scene in which we see a young woman driving away as her old life—which includes a man evidently furious about her unexpected departure—disappears in her rear window. This pretitle sequence is accompanied by a woman's voice (Sam Phillips) singing about a life in which "they sell us ourselves" and we are "raised on promises." Later we learn—through Ruby's first recording in her diary (entries from which are presented in the voice-over that runs through the film)—that she left Tennessee ("without getting beat up or pregnant") to forge a life on her own and to discover who she is and what she wants.

On her own, with just a high school education, Ruby relocates to Panama City, a beach town in northwestern Florida. Arriving at the beginning of the off-season in a town whose economy revolves around tourism, Ruby needs a job in order to survive. In spite of the seasonal downturn, Ruby is hired as a salesclerk by Mildred Chambers (Dorothy Lyman), the owner of a gift shop that sells souvenirs and beach accessories.

As the story develops, we see Ruby make friends with a coworker, Rochelle Bridges (Allison Dean), and record her thoughts about making it on her own for the first time in her life. Ruby's newfound freedom is threatened by Ricky, Mrs. Chambers's son, who manages the books for the store and sexually harasses the women employees. Despite warnings from Rochelle, Ruby has a brief affair with Ricky. Her decision to break off the affair soon after it has begun costs Ruby her job at the store when she refuses Ricky's demands that they get back together. Spurned again after showing up at Ruby's house, drunk and pleading for her affection, Ricky becomes violent, then tells her not to return to work. He then discredits Ruby with his mother.

While Ruby is out of work, the new man she has been seeing, Mike McCaslin (Todd Field), offers to support and take care of her, but she rejects his offer, getting by instead on a small loan from Rochelle. After many unsuccessful attempts to find another retail job, Ruby finds a low-rung job at a commercial laundry. Although the work is demanding, she is encouraged by two friendly coworkers,

Persefina (Felicia Hernández) and Wanda (Bobby Barnes), and she has at least managed to survive. Rochelle eventually tells Mrs. Chambers about the real circumstances surrounding Ruby's departure from the store, and Ruby gets her old job back, plus a promotion to assistant manager.

Bristling at Mike's criticism of her salesclerk job, which he calls meaningless, Ruby finds a growing gulf between the two of them and starts to see less of Mike. The movie ends with Ruby's having managed to survive through hard times, but leaving open the question of whether she will be able to find a meaningful life in the consumer milieu of Panama City.

We are introduced to life in Panama City through a series of shots that show that Ruby's new home is a place where the natural beauty of the ocean and beach is side by side with a great commercial sprawl of souvenir shops, strip malls, advertising signs, and topless bars. This juxtaposition of natural beauty and commercialism sets up one of the basic conflicts the film addresses: whether these two elements of Panama City can coexist in harmony with one another or whether the consumer capitalism that drives the economy of this resort town will in the end spoil its natural beauty and appeal.

The film examines this issue through the character of Ruby, whose job selling at the Beach Emporium makes her dependent on the system of consumer capitalism upon which the economy of Panama City is structured. We see that Ruby's vulnerable class position—working-class, financially unstable, just a high school graduate with no special skills—does not leave her with the option of removing herself from the consumer world, for her survival depends on it. Later on, when Ruby loses her job at the Beach Emporium, we see how degrading it is for her continually to apply for jobs and be rejected, and how the new job she finds—working at a commercial laundry—is even less desirable than her salesclerk job. Ruby must somehow, then, construct a life for herself that gets around her own dehumanization by the consumer system while she remains within the confines of that system.

Through Ruby, the film presents a strong critique of an elitism that suggests that a meaningful life can be found only outside the commercial world of Panama City. At the same time, the film highlights the special difficulties that life in consumer culture poses for working-class women like Ruby. The film suggests, therefore, a complex and interesting view of life in consumer society. The conflict between natural beauty and commercial development that *Ruby in Paradise* examines can also be seen as a metaphor for questions about the nature of film: Are serious "art" films the only alternative to "entertainment" movies, or is this view of film too simplistic to fit movies that, like *Ruby* itself, do not fit easily into just one of these two categories?

Ruby's dilemma in relation to the consumer system is represented in the film by the two male characters, Ricky and Mike, who also represent opposing versions of masculinity. One interesting aspect of the story is found in the striking differences between these two men, both in the way they treat Ruby and in their own relations to the consumer world of Panama City. Ricky is a wheeler-dealer type, an investor in stocks and real estate, believing that there is "no future in retailing." He is someone, Rochelle tells Ruby on Ruby's first day of work at the gift shop, who is able to "make money when all the signs are down." He gambles away his mother's money, resenting his need for his mother's financial backing even as he goes behind her back, at times, to make risky investments that may turn a profit but also could lose her money. Although Ruby rejects Ricky's kind of masculinity, she is tempted by his class position, which is superior to Ruby's own and something she might like herself to aspire to, to "move up" in the world. Against her better instincts, therefore, she agrees when he insists she go out with him, in spite of his mother's policy that Ricky not date store employees.

Ricky represents a kind of crass commercialism, associated with a generation of young entrepreneurs who have made fast money off of the commercial development of Panama City. The threat he poses to Ruby can also be seen as representative of the potential abuses Ruby may suffer at the hands of the commercial system. Ricky is basically out for himself, and he is willing to use other people as instruments to further his own interests. We see how this philosophy of self-interest comes across in his relationship with Ruby. When they have sex it is intense and passionate, but Ricky is clearly focused on his own pleasure, not Ruby's. The next day at work after their first night together, Ricky gives Ruby a Walkman—a symbol of technological progress—as a token of his affection, then demeans her by telling her to straighten the shelves and sweep the street. As Ruby leaves in the morning after their second night together at Ricky's place, she discovers a drawer filled with gift-wrapped Walkmans identical to the one Ricky gave her. Ruby has struggled to leave behind her old life of dominating men—hinted at in the opening scene of the film—yet she realizes that now her independence is threatened by Ricky. She vows to get away from him, and she breaks off her affair with him, saying, "I didn't come all this way to be your chippy."

Before she resolves to get away from Ricky, however, Ruby goes on a shoplifting spree at a local mall, going from store to store, stealing clothes, accessories, and CDs. Back home, she realizes that having these things does not, in fact, make her feel better, and she takes them, along with Ricky's Walkman gift, to a local charity drop box.

Most people, especially women living in today's consumer-oriented society, are familiar with Ruby's desire to acquire things to bolster her self-esteem. This is a message continually put out in commercials, such as the Charles Ritz ad, analyzed by Susan Douglas, in which a smartly dressed woman says, "I've discovered that it is easier to face the world when I like what I see in the mirror."[6] The film's shoplifting scene is striking, however, because it shows that if Ruby is to succeed in bolstering her self-esteem by acquiring commodities, she must steal, for as a financially unstable working-class woman, she does not have the money necessary for this kind of quick fix to the ego. Ruby's short-lived relationship with Ricky illustrates, then, that her independence is threatened should she attempt to better herself by associating with a man like Ricky. We also see how the promise of happiness through consumption is limited to people whose economic situations are better than Ruby's own precarious financial standing. Ruby's affair with Ricky is representative of the kinds of problems and abuses she faces from commercialism: it may, figuratively speaking, screw her over if she is not careful.

If Ricky represents a domineering, self-interested kind of masculinity, Mike is Ricky's opposite. Sensitive, cultured, and romantic, with a great-grandfather who helped settle Panama City, Mike's affections for Ruby are real and his courtship of her unhurried. A strong critic of the commercial development that is ruining the natural environment of Panama City, Mike once was active in trying to change things, but now chooses instead to shut himself off from the growing threat of commercialism that engulfs the area, practicing "low-impact living," the philosophy of "letting nature have a chance." With his criticisms of the commercial world in which Ruby makes a living and his own comfortable financial situation, Mike sees himself as offering Ruby an alternative to the selling game, which, he says to Ruby, "can't mean anything to you."[7]

One way that the movie surprises us is by introducing Mike as someone who, we hope, will be the man of Ruby's dreams, only to dash these hopes when we see the condescending judgments he makes about Ruby and her job. Although their occupations both appear to be similar—Mike works at a local nursery, and so, like Ruby, is in a kind of retail sales job—Mike is what economists call "downwardly mo-bile."[8] He has chosen to take a job that is not commensurate with what might be expected of someone from his educational and class background. In contrast, it is not easy for someone with Ruby's class and educational background to move up and out of her social and eco-nomic class. These differences between Ruby's and Mike's social and economic classes, as well as their personal and philosophical differ-ences, become apparent as their relationship develops.

One important scene brings out these differences by presenting Mike's criticisms of the mainstream movies that Ruby enjoys watch-ing. Mike insists they leave a fantasy science fiction movie playing at a local cineplex, even though Ruby is enjoying herself. He criticizes the film, saying that such a film "takes over the mind with fantasies that have nothing to do with being alive." Ruby agrees to leave, but she dis-agrees with him, saying, "It's just a movie." In response to Ruby's query, "What gives you the right to say?" about what others should want to watch, Mike responds, "Because it is so clear." Although Mike may not realize that his criticisms of commercial movies amount to elitism, Ruby recognizes that Mike's critique is not only aimed at the film, but is also a condescending judgment about her and what she finds pleasurable in movies.

Perhaps the most telling difference between Ruby and Mike is evi-dent in a scene in which they walk on the pier together at night after dinner. After this evening, they will stop seeing each other on a regular basis. Appreciating the beauty of the ocean scene at night, Ruby says, "No matter how much they screw it up, there is always the ocean." Mike in turn responds, "Yes, polluted and dying." Mike focuses on the commercial development that is threatening to ruin the ocean, whereas Ruby, while cognizant of this problem, is still able to appreciate the beauty in the beach setting. Mike's observations concerning the envi-ronmental destruction he sees around them ring true to Ruby, but she bristles at the condescension with which they are delivered. When she tells Mike to "please stop looking down at the rest of us," she exposes the class privilege that is at the basis of his own critique of the com-mercial development of Panama City.

Like Ricky, Mike offers Ruby the possibility of financial security, but the gender and class hierarchies he unconsciously accepts would limit Ruby's sense of self and her independence were she to accept his offer of support. Through the failure of their relationship, we also see the limitations of a "liberal" critique of commercialism and its effects on the environment that is not conscious of the position of privilege from which it is issued. Mike's critique of "action/fantasy" movies, in contrast to the pleasure Ruby takes in them, shows also that his character stands for an austere film aesthetics, suggesting that films that aim to please are "junk" not worth seeing. I shall return to discuss this point of difference between Ruby and Mike a bit later on.

If Ruby's relationships with the male characters in the story are disappointing, showing that she has yet to meet a man who can make her happy, she nonetheless meets working women who are inspiring role models for her own life. Mildred, like her son, may be in business to make money, and her store survives on the tourism that is threatening to overrun the area, but she shows compassion in her business dealings, hiring Ruby at the start of the off-season because she recognizes a "rage and fury in her from a long time ago." Mildred's own life has been hard; she has raised her son as a single mother, but she has managed to survive without losing her sense of empathy for people less fortunate. Ruby's friend and coworker Rochelle alerts Mildred to the real circumstances surrounding Ruby's departure from the store, helping her to get her job back and lending her some money so she can get by until her first paycheck. Wanda and Persefina, Ruby's coworkers at the laundry, are cheerful and supportive, encouraging her to persist at the job even as Persefina tells her, "Don't lose your mind." These women help Ruby to get by and offer possibilities for surviving the dehumanization of the business world in which they live and work.[9]

Narrative Closure and Social Criticism

It may feel like a victory that Ruby has managed to survive through it all, but when she gets her job back at the Beach Emporium it remains to be seen whether she can protect herself against her own commodification in the Panama City consumer society. As the story moves to a close, we get some mixed messages about whether Ruby's attempt to create a meaningful life for herself while selling beach accessories will be successful.

Shortly after Ruby's return to the Beach Emporium, Ricky makes an unsettling appearance, apologizing for his behavior and telling Ruby that, through therapy, he has become a "new man," renouncing sexual violence even as he continues to have a business-oriented mindset, saying enthusiastically, "Business is booming." This scene might suggest that Ricky (or someone equally as nasty) will reappear in Ruby's life, or it may just show Ricky humbled, if not changed, before her. But its effect is unsettling, reminding us of Ruby's past troubles at a time when she is just beginning to recover herself, and suggesting that perhaps more troubles are ahead for her. Ricky's reappearance also reminds us of the hazards that commercialism, in its worst form, poses for Ruby as she tries to create a meaningful life while working in retail sales.

On the other hand, this scene is immediately followed by one that shows both the importance to Ruby of finding beauty in her life and her ability to look critically at her own place in consumer society. Ruby wakes up in the morning before going to work and hears a beautiful song, sung by a young Indian woman passing by Ruby's bungalow apartment. This scene, in fact, takes us back to the beginning, when Ruby first arrived in Florida and heard this same young woman singing this song outside Ruby's motel room. This time, however, Ruby seeks out the young woman to learn more about the song. As the two share tea and cookies, they talk about leaving home to find a life with more financial security in Panama City. "Does that make it right?" Ruby asks her new friend, when the young woman says that the whole world dreams of coming to America for its material benefits and security. We see that the difficulties Ruby has lived through have not deadened her ability to question the American dream of abundant material possessions and consumption. Her appreciation of the song reminds us that Panama City is a place of both great natural beauty and commercial sprawl, and we are left feeling confident that Ruby will continue to find the beauty in this environment even in unexpected places.

What the film may fail to provide by its end, however, is the assurance that Ruby's willingness to try for a meaningful life in Panama City will ultimately be successful. This is illustrated in particular by the very last scenes in the movie. I suggest that the film's ending is purposively ambiguous, leaving us uncertain about whether Ruby will indeed be able to resist being reduced to a mere commodity in consumer society.[10] This ending is part of an aesthetics that keeps the audience aware of the problems for Ruby of life in consumer society.

In the final scenes, Ruby arrives for work in the morning; we see a faded "Step Up" sign on the front door of the shop as Ruby arrives, reminding us, somewhat ironically, that this job is supposed to be an advancement over the hard labor of the commercial laundry. She calls out, "Hi, everyone," as she enters the store. No one answers her, and the noise we hear is the sound from the streets. We see no one in the store, just the store merchandise, presented in a series of medium and long shots. The last shot is a close-up of a souvenir tray, one Ruby had admired earlier in the film, with a scene of a silhouetted young woman at the beach at the start of the day and the message "Paradise." Then the movie ends with the credits and another Sam Phillips song about surviving in a materialistic world by "trying to hold on to the earth." The final image as the credits finish, a shot of a sign reading "Welcome to Florida, the Sunshine State," repeats a scene from the very beginning of the film.

This ending leaves us with some mixed messages about Ruby's future life in Panama City. There is the suggestion that, with her return to retailing, Ruby will become a mere commodity glittering in an artificial paradise.[11] Right before leaving for work, Ruby writes in her diary, "Can we ever know our true desires?" "Where does caring come from?" "Why are all of us so often lonely and afraid?" The ending might be a kind of postmodern deconstruction of these questions, for with the repeat of the opening shot of the "Welcome to Florida" sign, we are reminded that Ruby went to Florida in search of a better life and to create her own identity. The image of the young woman on the reproduced image on the tray could be taken as a symbol of Ruby herself, as she had admired this tray at the retail convention she attended with Mildred.

This closing shot, focusing on a mass-produced media image of paradise, suggests that in a society focused on the acquisition of material goods, there is no possibility of finding one's true desires or real happiness, only mass-mediated versions of happiness, of the kind the tray represents. In this way the film ends on a pessimistic note, departing from the more optimistic vision of resisting commodification while remaining within the consumer value system, and presenting a kind of postmodern evacuation of all the political and personal options available for living a meaningful life in a materialist society.

But the ending also leaves us hopeful about Ruby's ability to craft a life for herself in Panama City. Before she leaves for work, we see that Ruby is continuing to write in her diary, taking time to reflect on the significance of the new life she has found. The questions she raises and her conversation with the young Indian singer show us that, despite her hardships, she has not lost her capacity for self-examination and empathy. The difficulties she has lived through have not deadened her ability to question the American dream of abundant material possessions and consumption. Ruby's own mood is positive and upbeat as she arrives for work. Although she has started to see less of Mike, we learn that Ruby has made her mark on him, for he is back working to try to change things, rather than just complaining about the problems he sees.

The last shots focusing on the consumer image of a day in paradise are a reminder of what Ruby is up against in her struggle to survive, even as there has been much to suggest that Ruby herself will be up for making her way through this challenge. She will continue to "play in the face of certain defeat," as the title character in Ralph Ellison's *Invisible Man* says, pondering his own need to withdraw from his underground and venture outside again to try to make a difference in the world, even as we have seen the invisible man's own hardships in trying to survive as a black man in a racist society.

What the ending of *Ruby in Paradise* fails to deliver, however, is the assurance that Ruby's attempts for a meaningful life in her consumer-oriented society will be successful. By refusing to provide an easy way out of the obstacles that Ruby must face, the ending is a realistic reminder of the problems of living in consumer society. By withholding a happy romantic ending, *Ruby* turns the audience's attention to the issue of trying to live meaningfully in a society geared toward consumption and material wealth. We are reminded of Ruby's past struggles and made aware of her vulnerability to future hardships in consumer society, even as we are also cognizant of Ruby's strength and determination to survive. When the final shot presents a repeat of the "Welcome to Florida" sign from the film's beginning, this may suggest that life in Panama City is circular, but it leaves us reflecting further on the issues of consumption, class, and gender that the movie raises but does not resolve.[12]

Film as Art or as Entertainment?

The concerns that *Ruby in Paradise* raises about consumer society can be understood as worries about film itself: Should film entertain and "sell" to "the masses" or should film be "art" that challenges viewers to think about life's big questions and important social issues? The issue of whether art should entertain or challenge viewers is the subject of an age-old debate in aesthetics. *Ruby* surprises by calling into question the very terms with which the debate has been framed.

As a low-budget ($350,000 to get it in the can), independently produced movie that played in the "art houses," not the cineplexes, we might expect *Ruby* to come down on the "art" side of the art/entertainment classification. Yet it does not fit easily or exclusively into this category. Nuñez shot the film in Super-16 (later blown up to 35mm) and used a high-speed film stock that produces a grainy quality not usually seen in glossy mainstream Hollywood films.[13] The narrative focuses on economic hardship and spurns the conventional happy romantic ending. But the cinematography is beautiful and visually appealing, drawing the eye in with its nuances of shading. The narrative is not that of a fast-paced "action" movie, but instead has a number of "dead time" close-up shots of Panama City and detailed scenery. Yet there is a narrative and a story that is told, one that is pleasurable and engaging, setting Nuñez's film apart from independent movies that eschew narrative in favor of avant-garde nonnarrative forms. The center of the movie is the luminous performance by Ashley Judd, but she is not presented as a mere object for male pleasure; often the camera looks *with* her, to see what she sees and to convey her point of view. With a form and content that do not easily fit into either of the traditional categories of art or entertainment, *Ruby in Paradise* shows that one traditional way of looking at film breaks down when applied to films like *Ruby* itself, suggesting the need for an alternative category.

We can also come to this conclusion by realizing that, through the character of Ruby, the film self-consciously takes on the art versus entertainment distinction central to Adorno and Horkheimer's critique of consumer capitalism and art. Mike's criticism of the science fiction fantasy movie Ruby enjoys aligns him aesthetically with Adorno and Horkheimer, for he says that the pleasure the story induces through its fantasy allows the movie to "take over your mind," suggesting that movies should exercise the audience's critical faculties, and that pleasurable engagement with a story stunts the viewer's capacity for critical reflection. This is similar to Adorno's view that Hollywood films are not complex enough to allow for individual interpretation. Rather, Adorno says, "the product prescribes every reaction" so that "the power of the culture industry's ideology is such that conformity has replaced consciousness."[14]

Ricky's character can be understood to represent the view that all that matters in film is commercial gain through pleasing "the masses," a view that Adorno and Horkheimer would criticize as consumer capitalism at its worst. Ruby rejects both the elitism that is implied by Mike's critique of pleasurable storytelling and the crass commercialism of Ricky's profit-oriented business dealings. From her character, therefore, we gain a useful critique of Adorno and Horkheimer's aesthetics, suggesting that a director can reject commercial gain as the primary goal of moviemaking without accepting the elitism that is at the basis of their distinction between avant-garde films and popular cinema forms.

Key to Ruby's own aesthetics is her act of writing in her diary. She does this both for the pleasure of thinking and reflecting and as a way to create order out of her daily events. Writing for Ruby, in other words, is both a pleasurable end in itself and a means to the end of understanding the significance of her life. In writing, Ruby "authors" or creates herself and her life by bringing to the fore details for further reflection, although there is also a sense in which her writing is without purpose, insofar as she writes simply for the pleasure of it. Another important aspect of Ruby's aesthetics is her interest in looking—at herself in the mirror, at the ocean, at her neighbor going fishing, at whatever is around her. This ability to look and observe, the film suggests, is a key aspect of her survival in the appearance-only consumer world of Panama City.

The film suggests an analogy, therefore, between Ruby and the artist, perhaps more specifically the film's director, Victor Nuñez himself. Just as Ruby's writing is one way in which she attempts to find beauty in consumer society, *Ruby* suggests that the film's director also aims to craft a film that expresses his aesthetic vision even as it speaks to the social realities of life in American society. Like Ruby, a film director like Nuñez can survive only if he can secure funding, yet this does not mean that either must "sell out" to consumer society in order to get by. At the same time, through the analogy made with Ruby and the artist, we are mindful of the hardships that face a filmmaker in today's profit-driven economy when he or she makes movies with meaningful subject matter and unconventional narratives.

In these ways, the film and the character of Ruby call for another approach to looking at film, one that is an alternative to the art/entertainment dichotomy with which I began this discussion.

Clueless: Parody as Social Criticism

Clueless, a witty social satire on conspicuous consumption in the lives of wealthy young women growing up in consumer-minded Beverly Hills society, examines some of the same issues as *Ruby in Paradise,* albeit from a radically different class perspective. Understanding the use of parody and imitation in *Clueless* is central to understanding how the film functions as a social criticism of consumer society. The story calls into question the consumer value system at the heart of upper-class Los Angeles by creating a parody of that society's manners and mores, even as it represents the story's protagonist as an engaging young woman who uses consumer practices as an area of self-expression. Anyone who has seen the 1996 screen adaptation of *Emma* (starring Gwyneth Paltrow) cannot, in fact, fail to see that *Clueless* is more successful in conveying the satire in Austen's critique of class-conscious Surrey society than is that more traditional rendering of Austen's story.

Figure 2. Publicity poster for *Clueless*.

Clueless is not only a parody of modern consumer society—by setting the story of Jane Austen's *Emma* in contemporary consumer society, the film pokes fun at the pretensions of "art" films that use the classics as their basis even as it shows that an appealing comedy about teenage girls can be highly effective in presenting the truth in Austen's critique of a status- and consumption-obsessed society.[15] *Clueless* is another example, therefore, of a film that addresses the nature of film as a consumer product and shows the need for an alternative to the art/entertainment dichotomy presented by Adorno and Horkheimer.

The protagonist of the story is Cher (Alicia Silverstone), a fifteen-year-old student at Bronson Alcott High School in Beverly Hills. Like Emma Woodhouse, she was left motherless as a baby and she has no real responsibilities other than to attend school and take care of her lawyer father, Mel (Dan Hedaya). Cher's primary amusement is shopping with her best friend Dionne (Stacey Dash), who, like Cher, is smart, wealthy, and beautiful; Dionne also happens to be black. Although the queen of her social universe, Cher has to contend with Josh (Paul Rudd), the stepson of one of her father's ex-wives, who between classes at a local college hangs around Cher's house reading Nietzsche while chiding Cher for her shallowness.

Cher's world is a small one, comprising the language, dress, rules of social conduct, and automobiles of an elite section of Los Angeles teendom. She says that her housekeeper from El Salvador speaks "Mexican," and she thinks that Bosnia is in the Middle East. Her debate class argument that Haitian immigrants should be given sanctuary in the United States rests on an analogy with the garden party she threw for her father's fiftieth birthday. She sees nothing wrong with having a dog-fur backpack.

Feeling "impotent and out of control" when her debating teacher, Mr. Hall (Wallace Shawn), refuses to raise her grade, Cher hatches a plan with Dionne to make him fall in love with another teacher. When the plan works, everyone's grades rise and Cher becomes the most popular student at the school.

Responding to Josh's criticisms that her world of the Galleria is self-interested and limited, Cher decides to give Tai (Brittany Murphy), a "clueless" newcomer at the high school, a makeover to prove to herself and Josh the social benefits of her fashion expertise. Under the tutelage of Cher and Dionne, Tai is soon catching the boys' eyes. Although Tai's own preference is for Travis, a sweet but spacey skateboarder, Cher attempts to match Tai with Elton, one of the most popular boys in the school.

The structure of Cher's universe starts to crumble, however, when Cher finds that Elton has fallen for her, not Tai. Cher's own romantic interest, Christian, a Luke Perry type, turns out to be gay. She fails her driver's test, even though she prepares for it by wearing her most responsible-looking outfit. When Tai says she has fallen for Josh, Cher reacts badly; then she realizes that she herself has fallen for Josh. Determined to show Josh that she is not just a "ditz with a credit card," she helps her social studies teacher, Miss Geist, organize assistance for the victims of a local environmental disaster, and gives away some of her own belongings in the process. While helping Josh and another lawyer prepare for one of her father's cases, she mismarks some documents. She thinks she has failed in Josh's estimation, but Josh instead professes his love for her. Tai and her first love, Travis, get together, and the movie ends with Cher catching the bridal bouquet at the wedding of Miss Geist and Mr. Hall.

Consumption as Narcissistic Liberation

It may be hard for some viewers to decide whether *Clueless* is a send-up or a celebration of a meaningless consuming lifestyle. One reviewer asserted that it "avoids significant social commentary by focusing instead on the trivial pursuits of a group of wealthy teenagers."[16] And Bloomingdale's made *Clueless* required viewing for junior buyers.[17] These responses to the film miss the fact that irony is a key element in its strategy of looking critically at Beverly Hills consumer society, which functions in the film as a microcosm of the American consuming lifestyle.

The film begins with a cheery "Kids in America" song and immaculately groomed young women and men indulging in wealthy Southern Californians' favorite pastimes: driving around in expense cars, shopping, and lounging by the pool. We then hear the voice-over of a young woman (Cher) say, "You're probably wondering if this is a Noxzema commercial or what." This beginning pokes fun at the artificial nature of commercial advertising, but it also makes us cognizant of the conventions of representation at work in the film. Next we hear Cher say, "But seriously, I have a way normal life for a teenage girl." Then we see her go to her computer and run a program that helps her pick an outfit for the day by matching the right skirt and top combination to a photo image of her body. David Bowie's hip song about consumption and style, "Fashion," plays in the background.

There is irony, of course, in the idea that it is "way" (i.e., totally) normal for a teenager to use a computer to help select her daily outfits, but this opening also lets us know that the film will not simply display images of beauty, wealth, and consumption currently in vogue (as the Bloomingdale's marketing department might suppose) but will deconstruct these images—that is, help us to understand the origins of these media representations of beauty and happiness and the roles these representations play in promoting consumption in our lives. It is not by accident, then, that the film starts with a reference to commercial advertising. Through the character of Cher, *Clueless* presents a parody of recent commercial advertising that suggests that shopping and consumption give women the power to take control of their lives. Through its satire of this advertising, the film calls into question the message of the advertisers that consumption is the means to self-expression and control, providing a potent criticism of the role that consumption plays in defining the "new woman" of the commercial advertising of the 1980s and 1990s.

This advertising has received critical attention recently from feminist media critic Susan Douglas. Feminists in the 1970s argued that conformity to mass-mediated images of femininity deprive women of their independence and autonomy. Douglas argues that advertisers coopted this feminist message with advertisements suggesting that women can, on the contrary, take control of their lives through a variety of consumer practices accessible to all who have the time and money to afford them. Douglas comments, "Turning on its head the feminist argument that the emphasis on beauty undermines women's ability to be taken seriously and control their lives, advertisers now assured women that control *comes* from cosmetics." Furthermore, women of the 1980s were, she says, "urged to take care of themselves, and to do so *for* themselves."[18] In this political atmosphere, "women's liberation metamorphosed into female narcissism"; "narcissism was more in for women than ever, and the ability to indulge oneself, pamper oneself, and focus at length on oneself without having to listen to the needy voices of others was the mark of upscale female achievement."[19] Douglas states further, "Though I write about what emerged in the 1980's in the past tense, I feel awkward doing so, because the ad strategies established then are still in high gear and we watch their efforts with sorrow, anger and empathy."[20]

Clueless presents as absurd the idea that consumption is the key to women's liberation by representing Cher as an extreme example of this thinking. Cher sees consumption, more specifically shopping, as a way for her to take control of her universe. There apparently is no problem that cannot be solved, to Cher's way of looking at her life, by shopping:

the local Galleria functions as a recreation place and a site for personal therapy. Disturbed that Mr. Hall will not raise her grade, she goes shopping all day with Dionne to "gather her thoughts" about what to do about this. When Tai is desolate that Elton does not care for her, Cher suggests that they all go to the mall and watch the new Christian Slater to forget about their troubles. Confused about her reaction to Tai's interest in Josh, Cher realizes that she herself is in love with Josh while she is walking through her neighborhood shopping area. Even in the depths of her confusion over Tai and Josh, she still wonders whether a store has the dress displayed in the window in her size.

The story challenges the view that conspicuous consumption is an exercise of choice and self-expression by highlighting the absurdity of the lengths to which the women characters are willing to go to achieve the right look. It is hard to miss the irony when Cher comments nonchalantly, for example, that her mother died because of "a freak accident during a routine liposuction," or not notice that something is radically wrong when Cher's main concern when she is mugged at gunpoint is that her designer Alaia dress not be ruined. Cher's wealth and her ability to consume are not represented as something to be envied and emulated, as in, for example, *Lifestyles of the Rich and Famous* (which also, by the way, has its own sense of fun about conspicuous consumption). Instead, the film makes good-humored satire of Cher's obsession with consumption, showing the folly in believing that enslavement to a life structured around consumption amounts to liberation.

The consuming habits and lifestyles of upper-class Los Angeles are also parodied through a number of visual details. Cher, Dionne, and Tai appear to be the only young women in their high school who have not had plastic surgery. Everywhere Cher goes in Beverly Hills, people are shown using cell phones, even when they are out dining and should instead be conversing with their dining partners. People are car obsessed to the extreme; parents like Mel buy cars for their teenagers even before they are old enough to drive legally. And the biggest scare for Cher is not being robbed at gunpoint, but the close encounter that she, Dionne, and Murray have with a Mack truck on the freeway while Dionne is learning to drive.

Rather than suggesting that self-centeredness is a good thing, as the advertisers suggest, narcissism comes under critical attention in the film's story line when Josh criticizes Cher for her self-interestedness. In response, Cher marshals her knowledge of cosmetics, clothes, and exercise videos to give Tai a makeover, claiming to be "doing good" by making Tai fashionable and popular. Although the story does not lead us to believe that Cher abandons her self-centeredness and obsession with shopping, by the end of the narrative some cracks have emerged in her way of thinking.

The film suggests that emulation of Cher's consumer practices and social rules is the means by which she comes to question these very practices. Tai's makeover works all too well. After being rescued from danger at the mall by Christian, Tai becomes the most popular girl in school; she then snubs Travis in order to impress her new friends. Dressed in a plaid ensemble identical in style to the ones that Cher and Dionne wear, Tai tries to enlist Cher's help in winning Josh. When Cher expresses her doubts about the wisdom of the match, Tai responds harshly, denouncing Cher as a "virgin who can't drive. " Of course, Tai is just parroting the accepted social hierarchies of their high school, but through seeing these views mirrored in Tai, Cher now sees the cruelty at the base of her own social universe.

Cher's perceptions of herself and others are mediated through a consumer rating system that confuses wealth and cost with individual self-worth. Her own views are quite muddled, but at times she express-es the view that superficial appearances, including wealth and material acquisitions, can be equated with a person's character and worth as an individual. She sees the designer clothes she wears and the Starbucks coffee she drinks as indicators of individual self-worth and good taste, not social privilege, and she sees Kmart hair extensions and "generic" brands not as indicators of income level but as signs of bad taste. This view begins to unravel for Cher when Elton tells her that his father's social standing makes him too good to go out with Tai. By seeing her own snobbishness come back at her in the form of Elton's judgment of Tai, Cher learns that there is more to self-worth than having the right clothes.

Another breakdown of Cher's worldview occurs when she realizes through her experiences with Elton, Christian, and Josh that there is more to attracting a boy than the right clothes and appearances. With Elton and Christian she learns that certain things are out of her control, and men aren't always what they appear to be. Her romantic interest in Josh prompts the biggest crack in her thinking, calling into question the value she places on shopping and making her feel selfish and shallow. She cannot use the strategies of the past, of dressing up and so on, on Josh without his seeing through her. Hence her attraction to Josh makes her rethink her values, if only just a bit, in order to win him.

Although Cher's "crisis" about her self-centeredness forms a cen-tral part of the narrative, the story leaves us thinking that Cher's views have been shaken but not radically altered by her love for Josh. This suggests that we need to consider whether Josh's own politics and his desire for "do-gooding" are presented as a serious alternative to Cher's consuming lifestyle. Are we to suppose that, through the character of Josh, the film presents an effective alternative to the consuming lifestyle that Cher embraces?

We can get one clue to the answer to that question by considering how *Clueless* adapts the characters from the original *Emma* story. In *Emma,* Mr. Knightley, the longtime family friend who becomes Emma's love interest, is clearly Emma's moral superior, showing her the cruelty at the base of her judgments and behavior toward other people, such as Miss Bates, the kindly but overly talkative "town spinster." In contrast, Josh is not presented as Cher's superior but more as her equal in intelligence and goodness. Cher's knowledge of *Hamlet,* for example, may be based on the Mel Gibson film, but this serves her well enough for her to correct Josh's pretentious girlfriend, who misquotes from the play. Cher's life may be structured around consumption and fashion, but she is able to see that the social rules she lives by are flawed when she sees these mirrored in Tai and Elton. Through her love for Josh, Cher is prompted to question her consuming lifestyle. But when Cher tries to "imitate" his "do-gooding"—for example, by giving away a small fraction of her hundreds of ensembles—the effect is comic rather than a serious suggestion of how to counter the problems of consumer capitalism.

Cher's imitation of Josh, in fact, serves as part of the film's send-up of Josh's own politics. Like the other characters in *Clueless* (e.g., the hippie-looking Travis Birkenstock, the scary litigator lawyer-father Mel, the verbally adept hipster Murray, the same-sex-oriented physical education teacher Miss Stoger, the gay Christian who knows how to dress and likes to shop), Josh is presented as a parody of a politically minded environmentalist who talks vaguely about making "a contribution" and listens to what Cher calls the "complaint rock" of the local college radio station. But he can articulate no effective alternative to Cher's consuming lifestyle other than watching the news on CNN and attending tree-planting meetings. Josh may see through Cher, but Cher is also perceptive when she questions how tree plantings by celebrities are effective in correcting the environmental problems of Los Angeles. "Why don't you just get a gardener to do it instead?" she quips. The movie does not, therefore, attempt to counter Cher's consuming lifestyle by presenting an effective alternative to it through Josh's character; rather, it presents Josh's vague liberal environmentalism as a view that itself comes under scrutiny.

Can Parody and Pleasure Be a Source of Social Criticism?

As *Clueless* moves to a close, the ending focuses on the romance theme, with the wedding of Cher's teachers and the final scene in which she catches the bridal bouquet. It may seem as if this ending takes the focus away from the social critique of consumption and places it on the future romantic bliss that is suggested when she catches the bouquet. Just as the movie begins, however, with an ironic reference to film conventions, so it ends in the same way.

After Josh and Cher acknowledge their love for one another and kiss, Cher is heard in voice-over saying, "Well you can guess what happened next," then the camera cuts to a wedding scene, suggesting (according to the typical Hollywood convention) that Cher and Josh live happily ever after. Next Cher is heard in voice-over disclaiming the suggestion: "As if! I'm only fifteen and this is California, not Kentucky." We then see that the wedding in question is that of Miss Geist and Mr. Hall. In a scene that pokes fun at gender stereotypes, at the wedding reception Josh, Murray, and Travis sit at one table worrying about the plans that Cher, Dionne, and Tai are making for their own weddings at the next table. Miss Stoger, the gung ho gym instructor, rushes up to say it is time for the bride to throw the bouquet, and the film ends with Cher catching the bouquet and kissing Josh.

This ending is very clever. Cher's disclaimer, "As if!" makes the romantic ending an ironic one. The film does not simply present the happy romantic ending, but suggests it, then uses pleasurable, but not hard-biting, satire to make fun of the viewer's expectation of such an ending for this movie. Like the opening shot, the ending makes us aware of the conventions that govern film narrative and representation, and so we recognize the artifice in ending a movie with a happy romantic union. At the same time, the film does not withhold from the viewer the pleasures of a happy romantic union between Josh and Cher, but reaches narrative closure through their happy coupling. In this way the ending presents a satire of Hollywood's need to end every romance narrative with a happy ending while also providing the viewer with the satisfaction and pleasure of seeing Cher and Josh happily together and the hint of their own future union.

The use of parody and pleasurable narrative conventions in *Clueless* raises some interesting questions about the film's effectiveness as social criticism. Can parody be an effective form of social critique? Does the pleasure viewers take in parody undermine the film's ability to focus viewers' attention on social criticism? Can a film like *Clueless,* which combines the pleasures of both parody and conventional narrative cinema, succeed as social criticism? Some background on the analysis and use of parody in literary theory and social criticism will be useful in helping to answer these questions.

Discussion of the importance of imitation and parody in art and literature has a long history. In his *Poetics,* Aristotle analyzed tragedy as a species of pleasurable imitation (mimesis) and argued that imitation is a basic human activity, one in which we take natural delight and through which we learn our first lessons (48b5–15). Aristotle also noted that we take pleasure in recognizing an imitation *as* an imitation, hence our own ability to recognize a work of art as an imitation as such is an important source of our pleasure in the work.

Parody and imitation as a form of social resistance have also been analyzed by social theorists. In Ralph Ellison's *Invisible Man,* the grandfather of the invisible man advises his grandson about how to get by as a young black man living in racist white southern society. He tells the invisible man he needs to "undo" the racist white men by "yes-Sir-ing" them to death, by being the perfect imitation of their idea of a subservient young black man. This strategy will make the invisible man conform to the letter but not the spirit of the racist stereotypes, making visible to the invisible man and to his white oppressors the role-playing and artifice required of him by the racist power structure. Along these same lines, postmodern feminists such as Luce Irigaray and Judith Butler have argued that imitation and parody have important roles to play in undermining oppressive gender stereotypes.[21]

Literary theorists have also looked at how parody functions in a literary context. In literary theory, parody is understood in a specific sense, as a device by means of which "the language, theme or style of an author or work is closely imitated for comic effect or in ridicule" *(Oxford English Dictionary).* Schopenhauer analyzed how literary parody achieves its comic effects as follows: "Parody substitutes for the incidents and words of a serious poem or drama insignificant low persons or trifling motives and actions. It subsumes the common place realities which it sets forth under the lofty conceptions given in the theme, under which in a certain respect they must come, while in other respects they are very incongruous."[22] Here a work of parody functions to deflate the pretensions of an original work, often to comic effect, by presenting a comic discrepancy between the literary work and its imitation. Along the same lines, Russian literary critic Mikhail Bakhtin has discussed extensively parody's use in literature as a device to disrupt accepted social dicta.[23] Central to a work of parody, according to Bakhtin, are its use/appropriation of other works and texts and its critique of the serious intentions and sacredness of the original works.

We can see that parody and imitation in all these different aspects are at work in *Clueless*. First, imitation functions within the story line as a means by which Cher comes to question her own social manners and mores. When Cher sees Tai imitating the social hierarchies Cher has taught her, such as by snubbing Travis, she sees the cruelty at the base of her own social clique. Cher wanted to give Tai a "makeover" so that she would fit more readily into the accepted social groups at her school, but she is forced to question her own judgment about these matters when she sees them rebound on her in the form of Elton's attitude toward Tai.

Next, in showing that Cher can learn to question her own values by looking at them mirrored in others, the movie sets up an analogy between the viewer and Cher: just as Cher comes to rethink her social mores through seeing them parroted back at her, *Clueless* suggests that viewers can learn to take a critical look at the role of consumption in their own society by seeing these practices imitated, albeit in excess fashion. What the viewer sees, after all, is an exaggerated imitation of a life replete with the cell phones, cars, and beauty regimes that figure prominently in a yuppie lifestyle. For viewers who do not have the wealth necessary for the kind of conspicuous consumption the film examines, the film shows, in a humorous way, that the lifestyles of the wealthy elite are not what they are cracked up to be, exposing the absurdity of a life structured around consumption and nothing else.

Third, in taking the story of *Emma* and transposing it to the contemporary teenage world of the Galleria, *Clueless* pokes fun at the pretensions of "art" films that use the classics as their basis. *Clueless* does not simply "adapt" the classic *Emma*, it presents a satire of the view that there is great distinction to be made between "high art" and "popular culture" by showing that the critical points made in *Emma* also ring true when presented in a film that deals with modern popular culture and consumer society. In this way *Clueless* functions as a parody in the way that Schopenhauer and Bakhtin describe, by deflating the pretensions associated with the sacred cows of the literary canon.

Here we can consider some possible limitations on this use of parody as a form of social criticism. Significantly, the film makes use of the pleasures of imitation and comedy to get its critical points across. The audience can take pleasure in recognizing the imitations the story presents and in seeing the humor in a life of mindless conformity to advertising ideals. The use of comedy and the appeal to viewing pleasure of

Clueless would disappoint critics like Adorno and Horkheimer, however, who would argue that the romance narrative and comic satire deflect the viewer's critical attention away from the issues of consumption the film examines. They would also fault it for failing to present any serious alternative to a life structured around consumption. In this way, they would argue, *Clueless* fails as a criticism of consumer capitalism.

From my perspective, this assessment is flawed. It relies on an unsupported assumption that movies that provide us with pleasure cannot also stimulate us to think critically about social problems. It also assumes that viewers are not capable of finding the escapades of young women in thrall to consumer culture both amusing and problematic. Finally, it suggests that viewers will be "seduced" by the pleasing images of the teenagers the movie presents and will not want to go beyond those images to think about the significance of the issues of consumer culture the film examines. All three of these assumptions are based on another: that viewers cannot be critical of what they see. On the contrary, the film suggests that viewers can enjoy recognizing the conventions at work in the narrative even as they take pleasure in the appearance of narrative closure through romantic union that the story provides.

These last points lead to some reflections on the way in which *Clueless,* through its form and content, suggests a need to rethink the art/entertainment dichotomy presented by Adorno and Horkheimer. This distinction relies on the view that pleasure and entertainment are incompatible with critical reflection on the social issues examined in the film. It also assumes that popular films like *Clueless* that have appealing characters and provide the traditional pleasures of narrative cinema, including romantic liaisons, cannot also be an important source of criticism about modern consumer society. On the contrary, I have suggested that this appealing comedy about wealthy young women succeeds in providing the truth in Austen's satire of a consumer society much more so than the more traditional "art house" rendering of *Emma* that came after it.

Clueless also provides a parody not just of consumer society but of film as a social institution with an accepted set of conventions and social history. My discussion of the ending is a case in point. Another example is found in the scene in which Christian arrives at Cher's house on Saturday night for what Cher hopes will be a hot date. Josh is at work with Mel and some other lawyers in the living room, preparing an important case of Mel's. Cher comes down from upstairs dressed to kill for her date with Christian. As she comes down the stairs, we hear the theme song from the schmaltzy romantic movie *Gigi* playing in the background. As he sees how beautiful Cher looks, Josh's expression sinks, suggesting his interest in Cher is more than big brotherly. This reference to *Gigi* clues us in on what will develop later between Cher and Josh, even as the film makes fun of itself as a romance story that is recycling the plot of its Hollywood forerunner. Rather than simply serving up a romance narrative for the viewer to take in, *Clueless* makes us aware of the conventions it is using as it provides the audience with a bit of the pleasure typically associated with the romance narrative.

In this way, *Clueless* suggests that a Hollywood film can both provoke critical reflection in the viewer and entertain with a pleasurable story that ends with a happy romantic union. Like *Ruby in Paradise*, *Clueless* is a film that challenges accepted views concerning the nature of film as a consumer product.

Conclusion

What can we learn about consumer society from these two movies? *Ruby in Paradise* departs in its form and content from the conventions of easily marketable movies, and it surprises the viewer by presenting a strong critique of an elitism that finds that quality (in movies or in life) can be found only outside the commercial mainstream. *Ruby* presents the problems with a life in which "we're all selling, forget what's inside," even as it reminds us that rejection of this system may be based on class privilege that many working women do not have. *Clueless*, on the other hand, comes nicely wrapped as an easy-to-take commercial film that provides a sharp critique of the messages about consumption and women's liberation featured in recent advertising campaigns. Through an interesting combination of parody and pleasure, it highlights the problems and incoherence of a view that equates superficial appearances with individual worth even as it amuses us with a witty story that is a satire of everything from exercise videos to movies themselves. Both films suggest that our relationship to the mass media today is not as simple as one might think.

These two movies, although different in their genres and narratives, suggest that film criticism that has been dominated by Adorno and Horkheimer's distinction between art and entertainment needs to be reexamined. *Ruby* suggests that independently made films with serious subject matter can still have appealing visual aesthetics and pleasurable stories to tell. It rejects an "art house" elitism that suggests that thought-provoking films appeal only to "enlightened outsiders," showing the importance of making movies that speak to working people's lives and experiences. *Clueless* shows us that social criticism need not be confined to independently made, avant-garde films, and that parody and pleasure can be a potent combination for social critique. Both movies suggest some new directions for thinking about film criticism and consumer culture.

Notes

Versions of this essay were read to a faculty group at the Race and Gender Resource Center at Bucknell University in October 1997; to an audience at the University of Texas, San Antonio, as part of Women's History Week, March 1998; and to Charles Sackrey's Theater and Economics class at Bucknell University. I am grateful to the audiences at these presentations for very helpful discussion. My thanks go to Jane Braaten for her insights on Adorno's aesthetics, and special thanks to James Clarke, Cynthia Freeland, and Tom Wartenberg for very helpful comments on a previous draft of this chapter.

1. Laura Mulvey, "Visual Pleasure and Narrative Cinema," *Screen* 16 (1975): 6–18 (reprinted in Laura Mulvey, *Visual and Other Pleasures* [Indianapolis: Indiana University Press, 1990]).

2. Theodor W. Adorno and Max Horkheimer, "The Culture Industry: Enlightenment as Mass Deception," in *Mass Communication and Society,* ed. James Curran, Michael Gurevitch, and Janet Woollacott (London: Edward Arnold, 1977). See also Theodor W. Adorno, "The Culture Industry Reconsidered," trans. Anson G. Rabinbach, *New German Critique* 6 (fall 1975): 12; Theodor W. Adorno, *Aesthetic Theory,* ed. Gretel Adorno and Rolf Tiedemann, trans. C. Lenhardt (London: Routledge & Kegan Paul, 1984), esp. 24–27; Miriam Hansen, "Introduction to Adorno: Transparencies on Film (1966)," *New German Critique* 24–25 (fall-winter 1981–82): 186–98.

3. See Walter Benjamin, "The Author as Producer," in *Understanding Brecht* (London: New Left, 1973); Walter Benjamin, "The Work of Art in the Age of Mechanical Reproduction," in *Illuminations,* ed. Hannah Arndt (New York: Harcourt Brace & World, 1968). On cinema as escapist entertainment, see, for example, Simon Frith, *Sound Effects: Youth, Leisure, and the Politics of Rock 'n' Roll* (New York: Pantheon, 1981), 43–46. But see also Lambert Zuidervaart, *Adorno's Aesthetic Theory: The Redemption of Illusion* (Cambridge: MIT Press, 1991). Zuidervaart argues that "the point of his [Adorno's] criticism is not to promote autonomous art and demote mass mediated art, but to see the dialectic within and between them as parts of the total system: 'Both bear the stigmata of capitalism, both contain elements of change. . . . Both are torn halves of an integral freedom, to which however they do not add up'" (31; he quotes from Adorno's letter of 18 March 1936 to Walter Benjamin).

4. Although this line of thinking has dominated film studies itself, it has been called into question by other theorists. One line of response comes from cultural studies, which has examined the ways in which viewers are able to structure interpretations of films that go "against the grain" of the films themselves. Cultural studies theorists suggest that films can be politically critical if viewers suppose they are such. I find that there are problems with this approach. Cultural studies theorists too often readily conclude that the social messages contained in narrative cinema are socially conservative ones, and then attribute to the viewer the tactic of "resisting" these messages. This approach too easily overlooks

the possibility that the film texts themselves may present subversive or challenging ideas. Thus in this essay I propose an alternative approach to narrative cinema (which I call a *rereading* strategy) that explores the possibility that narrative film texts themselves contain social critiques.

5. For an interesting feminist analysis of these advertising campaigns, see Susan J. Douglas, *Where the Girls Are: Growing Up Female with the Mass Media* (New York: Random House, 1995), 254.

6. Ibid.

7. Mike's relation to consumer society can be understood in terms of some themes from the *Odyssey* that are subtly invoked and reworked in the narrative. In a reversal of the hero epic, Ruby is the wanderer-hero, Odysseus, in search of her home, and the sea is invoked a number of times in the film as a metaphor for Ruby's journey of self-discovery and finding her home in the world. In a gender role reversal, Mike is Calypso, the goddess who prevented Odysseus from continuing his journey for seven years, keeping him against his will on her island paradise, and offering him the equivalent of immortality if he would stay with her. For the director's own view of Mike as a Calypso figure, see "Ruby on the Road: Mandhola Dargis Talks with Victor Nuñez," *Artforum,* November 1993, 64. I disagree, however, with Nuñez's own understanding of the character of Mike as representing a feminist perspective; I discuss this further below.

8. I thank Charles Sackrey for this way of putting the point.

9. There are a few hints in the movie that suggest that Ruby may also have an erotic interest in women. In one scene Ruby exchanges gazes with another young woman while sitting outside at a retailers' convention she and Mildred have attended. Ruby may just be looking at the vivacious young woman and wondering if she herself could ever feel so confident, or her look may be a gaze of erotic interest. The scene leaves this open. In another scene, while out of work, Ruby goes to a topless bar with the intent of applying for a job. She gazes intensely at the woman topless dancer who is performing, then has second thoughts about applying for the job. The manager asks her why she is there, and also informs her that women customers must be accompanied by men. This restriction is presumably aimed at preventing women from watching women perform. Here again there is a suggestion of women as an alternative erotic interest to men, but the story line does not follow this up.

10. My thanks to Tom Wartenberg for this way of explaining my reading of the film's ending.

11. For this reading of the film and an interesting comparison with Jane Campion's *The Piano,* see Bert Cardullo, "Rubies in Paradise," *Hudson Review* 47, no. 3 (1994): 437–44.

12. Here it is useful to compare the treatment of class and class differences in *Ruby in Paradise* with the way consumption and class are treated in another film about coming to adulthood, *Pretty in Pink* (John Hughes, 1986). That film is a story about an unlikely romance between Andie (Molly Ringwald), an unconventional young high school senior, and Blane (Andrew McCarthy), a popular high school "richie" from a very different social circle. The class differences between the characters threaten to end their relationship, but the story closes with a happy ending in which Andie and Blane are reunited and their commitment to the relationship reaffirmed. The message the viewer takes away from *Pretty in Pink* is that class and class differences are not, in the end, significant for the way in which one lives a life and the choices one has.

13. Godfrey Cheshire, "Victor Nuñez: Persistence in Paradise," *Film Comment* 30, no. 2 (1994): 10–16.

14. Adorno and Horkheimer, "The Culture Industry," 361; Adorno, "The Culture Industry Reconsidered," 17.

15. My thanks to Tom Wartenberg for his suggestion that parody can be a form of

social criticism and his suggestion that I develop the idea that *Clueless* functions in this way as a social criticism of consumption.

16. Tom Doherty, "Clueless Kids," *Cineaste* 21, no. 4 (1995): 14–17.

17. See Karen Schoemer and Yahlin Chang, "The Cult of Cute," *Newsweek*, 28 August 1995, 54–58.

18. Douglas, *Where the Girls Are,* 254, 245.

19. Ibid., 146.

20. Ibid., 247.

21. Luce Irigaray, *This Sex Which Is Not One,* trans. Catherine Porter (Ithaca, N.Y.: Cornell University Press, 1985); Judith Butler, *Gender Trouble: Feminism and the Subversion of Identity* (New York: Routledge, 1990).

22. Arthur Schopenhauer, in *The Philosophy of Laughter and Humor,* ed. John Morrell (Albany: State University of New York Press, 1992).

23. Mikhail Bakhtin, *Rabelais and His World,* trans. Helene Iswofsky (Bloomington: Indiana University Press, 1984); Mikhail Bakhtin, *The Dialogic Imagination,* ed. Michael Holquist, trans. by Caryl Emerson and Michael Holquist (Austin: University of Texas Press, 1981).

11.

(Un)Real Estate: Marketing Hollywood in the 1910s and 1920s

Jeffrey Charles and Jill Watts

> Briefly, he permitted himself a vision of his own future home—a palatial
> bungalow in distant Hollywood, with expensive cigars in elaborate hu-
> midors and costly gold tipped cigarettes in silver things on low tables.
> Harry Leon Wilson, *Merton of the Movies,* 1922

On a typically sunny California day in 1923, the successful director and
movie pioneer Mack Sennett, the powerful newspaperman and land developer Harry Chandler, and a host of luminaries from both the film
and local business communities gathered to celebrate the opening of the
city's latest subdivision, Hollywoodland. Although the ceremony itself
was a gala event, Chandler had pulled out all the marketing stops to ensure the success of the development. He had used the old developer's
trick of placing piles of bricks and lumber to create the illusion that lots
were selling fast and people were already building. And just in case the
star-studded opening failed to attract proper attention, Chandler had
made sure his development could not be ignored. He built a huge sign
advertising the subdivision: HOLLYWOODLAND. He lit the sign at night
with 4,200 lightbulbs, and it shone so brightly it could be seen several
miles out to sea.[1]

Despite Chandler's promotional tactics, the subdivision never really
flourished. Yet his grand marketing gesture, the brightly lit sign, became the development's lasting legacy, surviving as a beacon that symbolized not only a community, but also an industry and lifestyle for all
Americans to emulate. When the sign fell into disrepair in the 1940s,
workers removed the last four letters, and the sign's initial purpose was
forgotten. Nevertheless, its original designation, HOLLYWOODLAND,
needs to be revisited, for it points to the connections between land and

illusion that ultimately influenced American cinema, the film colony, and the consumption of its product.[2]

As many have observed, the cinematic experience alone made a powerful contribution to mass-market culture, its fantasies designed to promote consumer desire. But in the late 1910s and 1920s, the studios and public relations agencies increasingly realized that grounding cinematic illusions in a particular place, Hollywood, heightened the authenticity of what appeared on the screen. This increased the demand not just for movies, but for a vast array of consumer items and goods presented through film, ranging from cosmetics to bathroom fixtures, from household furnishings to even the land itself. As Carey McWilliams observed in the 1930s, "To vulgarize the concept, it has made possible the distillation of a pure essence, Hollywood, used to sell clothes, real estate, ideas, books, jewelry, furniture, cold creams, deodorants, and perfume."[3] The presentation and representation of Hollywood magnified and intensified the "glamour" so crucial to the audience's reception of the images on the screen. At the same time, of course, the place of Hollywood felt the impact of the industry that now dominated its local economy. Prior to the arrival of the film industry, realtors and developers manipulated spatial reality and staged elaborate spectacles to "sell" Hollywood. These local developers found natural allies among the film colonists actively creating "Tinseltown." This collaboration between movie agents and local promoters created a new form of commodified space—a type of "unreal estate."

The evolution of this connection between the town of Hollywood and its cinematic manifestations reveals several important aspects of Hollywood-based consumer culture in the 1910s and 1920s. Central to this affiliation was the constant interplay between Hollywood, the real place, and Hollywood, the filmic space, a symbiotic relationship that facilitated and promoted the marketing of both. From the beginning, the town, despite some grumbling from a few residents, actually thrived on the cult of celebrity and benefited directly from its fabricated reputation. Conversely, the movie industry realized its full potential as the text of film became increasingly tied to the context of place. In essence, both the town and the industry gained from the blurring of fantasy and reality, together relying heavily on spectacle and spectatorship to achieve their ultimate commercial ends. The two became dependent on the marketing and consumption of real and unreal visual space. Yet the mutually beneficial elements of this collaboration were short-lived. By the late twenties, the partnership between geographic place and cinematic space began to dissolve, and ultimately the unreal, the representation of the community, superseded the town itself.

Since its earliest incarnations, Hollywood has been the object of vigorous fantasy based on promotion. Like many Southern California communities, Hollywood was born out of real estate speculation, its first subdivision a product of the Southern California land "boom" of the 1880s. This boom originated partly from the new affordable rail transportation from the East, but mainly from the fervent promotional activities of agents and developers. Although land was seemingly Los Angeles's one marketable commodity, the boosters did not promote it, as they did in other regions, by focusing exclusively on material advantages—its agricultural richness or commercially lucrative location. For the most part, boosters concentrated on less tangible qualities, selling above all the climate—overstating its mildness and touting its healthful and spiritual endowments.[4] In Hollywood's case, the job of enticing buyers to a drought-prone area situated inconveniently far from downtown Los Angeles was first undertaken in 1886 by a developer from Ohio named Horace Wilcox. But Wilcox died before his marketing of Hollywood got off the ground, leaving the task to his wife Daieda. In 1894, she remarried and, as Daieda Beveridge, began attempts to develop the town as a refined and upscale suburb. In many ways, her vision encapsulated the Victorian ideals of midwestern town building. By 1904, Hollywood had banned alcohol, fireworks, and gambling. In addition, in an effort to attract respectable residents, Beveridge reportedly offered free land to religious groups who agreed to build churches in the community.[5]

But Daieda Beveridge soon encountered aggressive competition—a syndicate of Los Angeles's most powerful speculators and citizens, including H. J. Whitley, Moses Sherman, and Harry Chandler, who had also begun to invest in Hollywood property. As Beveridge and the syndicate battled for the spoils, they adopted strikingly similar tactics, even joining together to produce promotional literature extolling the area's hills, in reality dry and scrub covered, as a lush, tropical "California paradise." Their brochures claimed Hollywood possessed "a perfect climate—absolutely frostless" and bragged that it was "the only suburb commanding a view of the mountains, Los Angeles and the sea."[6]

At the outset, this marketing of Hollywood was virtually indistinguishable from that of hundreds of other Southern California boom communities. But the promotion of Hollywood soon took a unique turn. In 1900 an obscure French flower painter, Paul DeLongpre, began making the rounds of Los Angeles society, hoping to attract a patron. Daieda Beveridge encountered him at a party, liked his paintings, and, according to her good friend Edward Palmer, "when he [DeLongpre] talked in large figures and fine architecture Mrs. Beveridge became intrigued, and offered him three sixty five foot lots."[7] With help from Beveridge and her adversary, H. J. Whitley, DeLongpre built an elegant Moorish mansion, surrounded by elaborate gardens. These gardens reportedly provided inspiration for his numerous flower paintings, which he sold from his estate. Meanwhile, Beveridge used DeLongpre to market her vision of Hollywood as a place of culture and refinement, celebrating the fact that Hollywood was now home to a "world-renowned" artiste. The Whitley-Chandler-Sherman syndicate also exploited DeLongpre's presence, taking advantage of Sherman's new streetcar lines to run special excursions to the painter's home and gardens. In addition to taking a tour of the estate led by DeLongpre himself, patrons could purchase pictures of their trip taken by an on-site photographer, postcards offering various views of the house and gardens, and certainly, if they so desired, one of the artist's floral compositions. Most important, as they rode to and from the grounds, a guide treated them to a discourse on the joys and advantages of purchasing Hollywood real estate.[8]

These Hollywood real estate moguls sold land and houses by exploiting an early form of spectatorship and playing on the public's interest in celebrity, foreshadowing the advertising strategies used to market Hollywood and, later, Beverly Hills as the "home of the stars." As a result of the tours, postcards, and pamphlets distributed around the country by Hollywood boosters, DeLongpre became nationally renowned. Significantly, his house and gardens actually received more national attention than his flower paintings, the home regarded as an expression of his artistic persona:

> To say that the new habitation of the world's greatest portrayer of flowers is worthy of an artist, and a most fanciful one at that, but ill expresses the popular estimate of it. To fully appreciate this unique creation one must know Paul de Longpre. The versatile Frenchman is in sentiment and temperament a poet as well as an artist, and withal he is, in greater degree than most of his clan, a practical man of business. All these qualities have combined in the evolution of his home, which ranks to day as the greatest showplace in Southern California.[9]

Several of the postcards bore DeLongpre's portrait inset in the corner above the depiction of the home and gardens, a practice used later on postcards of movie stars' homes, which linked the commodified identity of the celebrity with that of geographic space.[10]

By the time the studios arrived in 1911, the promoters of Holly-wood had created an image of a respectable, high-toned, and prosper-ous suburb, and had even succeeded in attracting several other artistic celebrities, including composer Carrie Jacobs Bond (whose best-selling song "The End of a Perfect Day" was, it was frequently pointed out, written in the Hollywood Hotel). Bond was joined by author Owen Wister, famous for his novel *The Virginian,* Frank Baum of *Wizard of Oz* fame, and Elinor Glyn, who later wrote *It* and was another fre-quenter of the Hollywood Hotel. The area had become an artists' colony, but of a significantly distinct type. Perhaps because it was a tourist destination, Hollywood particularly attracted commercially conscious writers and musicians, who were willing to cross the line and produce for mass audiences.

Still, it was not Hollywood's carefully cultivated image or the pres-ence of other creative people that first attracted early filmmakers. Rather, the region's weather, its diversity of geography, its safe distance from New York's film industry disputes, and, importantly, its relatively inexpensive rental property drew the first film colonists to Hollywood. The common notion that movie people were unwelcome and were re-fused lodging in the area is belied, in part, by the enthusiastic greeting they received from realtors. In 1919, *Photoplay* recounted the arrival of Hollywood's first studio, the Nestor Film Company, run by David Horsley and Al Christie:

> Al was very enthusiastic about a certain piece of property which the
> agent finally showed him on Sunset Boulevard in Hollywood. . . .
> While the agent talked in glowing terms about the land, Al spied a
> decrepit looking old roadhouse on the corner of Gower Street. Al
> winked at his partner, made an excuse to walk around the block, and
> disappeared in the gate of the roadhouse. While the partner discussed
> front feet at so much per, Al made the acquaintance of Mrs. Blondeau
> who owned the old house on the corner. When Al came out of the
> house, he again looked at the front footage at so much per, rode back
> to Los Angeles in the real estate agent's car, and, as he went, whis-
> pered to his partner that he had leased the old roadhouse for three
> months at forty dollars a month.[11]

While the realtor had lost a sale, Mrs. Blondeau, a longtime resident of Hollywood, made a killing. The Nestor Film Company was soon fol-lowed by another; that one rented an adjacent lot Mrs. Blondeau owned, but this time for $240 a month.

Actually, film companies had been migrating to Southern California since 1909. At first the studios scattered across Los Angeles County—Biograph in Los Angeles proper, Kalem in Glendale, Selig in Edendale. In her discussion of this formative period, film historian Eileen Bowser observes that "all of Southern California was in the process of becoming 'Hollywood,' but that symbol was not yet born."[12] Hollywood could not have become even a symbolic construction, however, had not studios actually clustered together in the town itself. Although a number of prominent studios always remained outside Hollywood's precise borders, the concentration within a geographic area facilitated the development of a common identity as an industry and as a "colony."

During the 1910s, the infant film industry received eager assistance from real estate agents and local developers who were anxious to associate Hollywood with the film colony. Early on, developers had recognized the marketing potential presented by moviemakers. Additionally, the film colonists themselves provided consumers for the developers' product, because they needed not only somewhere to work but somewhere to live. Certainly, those dealing in land well knew that successful show people commonly invested in real estate, a practice well established in and around the New York area, where attorneys and investors offered in the pages of *Variety* to advise those in the theatrical profession on real estate speculation.[13] It is no surprise that by 1912 and 1913, the number and concentration of studios in Hollywood had increased rapidly. Universal, Famous Players-Lasky, Vitagraph, Kalem, and Triangle all leased or purchased lots in the community during that period. Harry Chandler, with large investments in and around Hollywood, was particularly influential in attracting film folks, packaging his leases with promises of low-interest loans for films and equipment and, even, in the case of Mack Sennett, for a home mortgage. Chandler, who also owned the powerful *Los Angeles Times,* began active promotion of the picture business in his paper and was the first to assign a regular columnist, Grace Kingsley, to cover the film industry.[14]

These promotional efforts were quickly and remarkably successful. Lots were sold; studios, homes, and businesses were built. Hollywood Boulevard rapidly developed into a fashionable shopping district, thanks to the business generated by studios. The film fans were soon flocking to the area to see "movieland." Local businesses were eager to accommodate them, and built new hotels and restaurants. By the late teens, as a result of the rise of the studios, Hollywood had been transformed from bucolic suburb to thriving city, becoming, as it had originally aspired to be with DeLongpre, a major tourist destination. By the end of the decade, guided tours of the environs resumed, with enterprising individuals conducting tourists and film fans to see the sights of what was quickly becoming the movie capital of the world. Studios themselves rapidly exploited this situation. After a brief time in Hollywood proper, Carl Laemmle relocated his Universal Studios just over the Hollywood Hills in the San Fernando Valley and offered visitors tours of his state-of-the-art studio, where patrons could see their favorite Hollywood movie artists at work. Laemmle, one of the originators of the star system, recognized that the system reached its greatest moneymaking potential when linked with real geographic space.[15]

Yet the cinema had dramatically changed the nature of artistic celebrity, and the Hollywood of Carl Laemmle and Cecil B. DeMille was far different from that of Paul DeLongpre. One indicator of that change appeared as early as 1915, in a *Photoplay* article by Grace Kingsley that was among the first to celebrate the new Hollywood context for the movies, their feature players, and the industry. In "Movie Royalty in California: Estates and Palatial Homes Bestowed on Photoplayers by Their Calling," Kingsley observed that while in the East, even settled actors merely had "an eating account in one hotel," but in California, the "photoplayers had *homes*." She described Hollywood as "housing more picture people than any other spot in the world" and proceeded to focus in great detail on the domestic lives of several of the stars, lavishing the most attention on the bungalow of Mary Pickford. "A house of rough Oregon pine, stained brown, with a wide inviting porch in front and a great sun parlor at the side," she wrote. "There is a white tiled kitchen at the rear of the house and here 'Little Mary' loves to dabble her white fingers in cakemaking whenever she has time."[16] Kingsley's article demonstrates the pivotal role fan magazines played in the development of movie stars as celebrities, creating both a sense of distance from the movie "royalty" and a perception of casual intimacy with the purportedly unaffected "Little Mary." The particular emphasis on the domestic context derived from writers' and editors' attempts to appeal to their vastly female readership.[17] It reified and reenforced the traditional domestic roles and image that Pickford delineated on the screen, making her seem all the more real to film audiences and even more visually consumable.

The interaction between spectatorship and the marketing of Hollywood was assuming a variety of forms, all attempting to suggest that consumption of a product might provide an intimate, domestic connection with a screen image. "Extend to your friends an invitation to meet with Miss Anita Stewart, photoplay star," read a 1915 advertisement in the *Motion Picture Supplement*. "At the proper moment introduce your friends [to Miss Stewart] through the medium of National Film Star spoons, which have masterpiece reproductions of the most prominent Photo Players."[18] One could "meet" Miss Stewart through her picture on a spoon, just as one could "meet" her on the screen in a provincial theater, and both of these meetings commodified the image of Miss Stewart, playing upon the tool of spectatorship. In the strictest sense, Anita Stewart left the screen and could be not only viewed but even possessed.

All the more potent, then, were articles on the actual home lives of the stars, situating the stars in the domestic space of Hollywood. Unlike the apparitional space on a film screen, here was a physical space that could be visited, a real place offering the possibility of a genuinely shared experience between star and audience. The existence of Hollywood as actual space where, fans knew, most movies were made and most stars lived their offscreen lives, complicated and deepened the culture of cinema. As Miriam Hansen argues, early films, and perhaps their viewers, had not yet resolved the tensions between the "realness" and the illusion of the cinematic image. Hansen points to films whose topic was the confusion caused by the misinterpretation of action on the screen as something that was really happening in the space of the theater. Such bewilderment was evident even in spectators' behavior. By the time studios moved to Hollywood, the tension between illusion and reality had been partially resolved by the development of a conventional cinematic narrative style that encouraged spectators to understand the pictures to be telling fictional stories. But, Hansen argues, there remained considerable ambiguity about the nature of film reality and room for a variety of responses to cinematic illusion.[19]

That Hollywood combined the unique with the ordinary helped shape spectator responses. By the close of the 1910s, Hollywood had established itself as a town of unusual distinction, housing the motion picture industry, its studio bosses, and those who worked for them. Most important, it had become home to its stars. Yet these stars challenged the popular image of the rootless, nomadic thespian, living out of a suitcase in hotels and apartments. Instead, Hollywood picture players were home owners, bound to the land. The fan magazines went to great lengths to assure their readers that the stars were, despite their wealth, in many ways normal town dwellers. Of course, residents of Hollywood had to put up with intersections and sidewalks blocked by film crews shooting their latest features. And, wrote one "living neighbor to the movies," there were those unusual sorts who practiced their craft late at night, like the couple who were either reciting lines or enacting real-life domestic squabbles when the wife shrieked, "You'll murder me—you'll murder me, you brute." But on the whole, film people were "the pleasantest sort of neighbors."[20]

Generally, fan magazines dismissed any rumors of the wilder side of the film colony. It was still represented as an idyllic community with "law-abiding" citizens and "beautiful houses along swell-shaded streets of pepper tress." Film director Lois Weber described Hollywood as "a very prosaic sort of place. Its streets are filled with shoe merchants, bank clerks, glass and paint store salesmen, drug clerks, hardware dealers, cafeteria waitresses, grocery men and tailors and the ordinary run of professional people and tradesmen found in any fast growing American suburb." In Weber's view, Hollywood was just a modest burg: "A girl looking for work in Hollywood is just as safe as she would be in Keokuk . . . asking the manager of the local dry goods store for a position as a sales girl."[21] According to the stars and fan magazines, Hollywood's biggest problem was not wildness and debauchery. Rather, through the advent of the movies, Hollywood by the late teens had become an instantly recognizable and celebrated geographic spot, so much so that some worried that the backdrop, although beautiful and varied, was quickly becoming "used up."[22]

The 1920s proved that such fears were unfounded as the film industry and the town of Hollywood experienced unprecedented growth. In the years between 1920 and 1924, the Los Angeles area added more than a million citizens, inaugurating a phenomenal expansion in real estate sales and development. This boom had many sources—oil prime among them—but as architectural historian Merry Ovnick contends, "the attracting image" was "the glamour, fun and excitement associated with Hollywood," which, "with its close link to the tastes of movie-goers, would find expression in unrestrainedly imaginative housing styles."[23] As Hollywood grew from 36,000 residents in 1920 to 165,000 residents in 1929, most set up households in the classic California bungalows that had sprouted along the thoroughfares and byways, but the area was beginning to boast a collection of unique architectural forms. In the Hollywood Hills, the remnants of Krotona, a theosophist colony, contained a variety of structures combining the influences of Eastern, Middle Eastern, and Old California designs. French provincial, Craftsman, English country, Arabic, and Far Eastern styles began to dot the area, especially on the hillsides and in the canyons.[24]

At the same time, a discernible shift occurred in the real domestic spaces occupied by Hollywood film colonists. This transformation commenced with the rise of the extravagant mansions built by stars and movie moguls in and around Hollywood. Where the stars and producers of the 1910s occupied smart California bungalows, those of the twenties, who saw their salaries skyrocket, inhabited elaborate and luxurious palaces. The industry elite provided prime targets for developers and speculators anxious to sell off their Hollywood parcels. Growing increasingly richer and with more and more disposable income, they not only attracted consumers to the area, they were consumers themselves. Magnates such as Louis B. Mayer became heavily involved in local real estate, using land deals to entice industry cooperation. Mary Pickford, Irving Thalberg, Harry Rapf, and Joe Schenck were at one time or another partners with him on choice real estate investments.[25]

Leading the way for the Hollywood elite were what one biographer has called "the most popular couple the world has ever known," Mary Pickford and Douglas Fairbanks.[26] Their decision in 1920 to settle prominently in the house that the press, with help from Fairbanks's publicity agent, named Pickfair was a brilliant public relations move that aided not only the couple and their studio but also Hollywood land barons. Pickfair was not in Hollywood proper; it was actually situated in Beverly Hills. But Doug and Mary's residence there eventually permitted Beverly Hills to be absorbed into the image of Hollywood, as a type of upscale suburb of the movie colony. The images of glamorous domesticity that emanated from photographs and newsreel footage obscured the less-than-acceptable origins of Pickford and Fairbanks's marriage, which had emerged from an adulterous affair, and ensured their continued celebrity. The architect for the large house was a stage designer, and the house functioned, in essence, as a set, where each public appearance was carefully scripted and prodigiously photographed.[27] Both in the pages of magazines and in newsreels in darkened theaters, fans were treated to images of Doug and Mary in the gardens, enjoying their gazebo, entertaining guests, and playing with their dogs. At the same time, shots of Pickfair's interior revealed the splendor in which they lived, the rooms decorated with tasteful, expensive, and elegant furnishings. Again, through the spectacle of domestic space, Hollywood communicated that Fairbanks and Pickford were both similar to and different from the rest of America, both real and unreal to their public. It successfully established the couple as American royalty, yet theirs was a royalty to which all could aspire.

Although Pickfair was Doug's gift to Mary (he had transformed his old hunting lodge into a genteel domestic space), in fact the house and its public image symbolized Pickford's mastery of real estate. Despite her cinematic image of docile womanhood, offscreen Pickford often broke with convention. She had cleverly negotiated with the studios for huge salary increases and in turn invested her earnings in real estate. During the 1920s, she emerged as one of the most successful land investors among the Hollywood elite. "Doug paid the bills, Mary bought the corner lots," said one niece, describing the financial arrangements during their marriage.[28] Pickford realized that, in this era and this community, image determined land value as much as location. She shrewdly managed all appearances from her home, carefully constructing an image for herself and Fairbanks that promoted their careers and their position in Hollywood's hierarchy.[29]

Even to Pickford, however, the public response to Pickfair was stunning. The home immediately became one of the most popular tourist destinations in Los Angeles. Although the house was rather inaccessible, weekend crowds grew so large that Fairbanks immediately had to build a formidable gate. One Sunday, Pickford was startled to hear the cries of a hot dog vendor who was hawking his wares from a trailer he had set up just outside Pickfair's entrance.[30]

With Pickfair, both the marketing of the place of Hollywood and the fans' response to this marketing had entered a new phase. The star system had been consolidated, and public relations agents better understood the nature of screen celebrity—that what appealed to the public was a "personality" that included contextual knowledge of offscreen activity. The industry came to value, as well, the importance of possessions in establishing "personality." Here the fan magazines helped enormously, lavishing attention on Gloria Swanson's opulent estate and huge wardrobe and Rudolph Valentino's romantic castle Falcon's Lair and chauffeur-driven Italian automobile. Just as onscreen signifiers—clothes, rooms, furnishings, cars—needed to be uniform to establish character clearly, so did offscreen possessions and homes, which functioned as extensions of the stars' cinematic personas.[31] As fan magazines and the film industry quickly learned, the screen images acquired greater potency if they were somehow "authenticated."[32] Fans were hungry for facts about the "real lives" of the stars, and they used this knowledge to clarify their viewing of the stars on the screen.

After Pickfair, then, there was a discernible shift in the construction of stars and their domestic places. In the 1910s, studios were careful to delineate many stars in a manner that conflicted with their fictionalized characters. Prior to the twenties, when Victorianism and traditional values held firm, film fans who read *Photoplay* discovered, for example, that onscreen flirt Ethel Clayton had "hundreds and hundreds and hundreds of books, that fill[ed] two bookcases ranged on the north and south sides of the living room" or that the "domestic spider web of the head vamp of the Pacific, Louise Glaum, very strangely resembles an innocent little bungalow grown over with dainty and unwicked vines."[33] Obviously, it was reassuring to know that Ethel Clayton was really a respectable young woman and that Louise Glaum was a dainty bungalow dweller rather than a sexually voracious man-killer. In fact, it let viewers know that "they were nothing like the characters they played onscreen" and made them personally less threatening and more marketable.

Such disjunctures were less effective in the twenties. After World War I, the mass market had come into its own, and American tastes and values underwent a transformation. Partly because of the rise of consumerism and the cult of materialism, opulent lifestyles were more enticing to audiences. With the twenties rebellion against Victorian values, screen characters who were good in the fictional film realm needed to project goodness in the real spaces, whereas those who were bad on screen were free to be bad at home. Little Mary Pickford, who had left one husband and secured a Nevada divorce to marry her lover, the all-American boy, Doug Fairbanks, had to project a vision of domesticity, posing in the doorway of Pickfair above the caption "Mrs. Douglas Fairbanks." On the other hand, Rudolph Valentino's Falcon's Lair projected an air of mysterious and brooding sensuality, its furnishings and design invoking images of danger and hypersexuality.

The desired effect of this public relations hype was lampooned in the popular novel *Merton of the Movies,* published in 1922 by Harry Leon Wilson, which was made into a Broadway play and then into a film in 1924. The central character, Merton Gill, a stock clerk and delivery boy in Simsbury, Illinois, spends most of his time lost in daydreams of becoming a rich and celebrated Hollywood dramatic actor. He is convinced by the films and fan magazines that he avidly consumes that his real talent is for the screen, and that one day he will find fame and fortune in Hollywood. After years of frugal saving, he does escape Simsbury for Hollywood. There, he struggles for his "art" until finally, penniless and hungry, he sneaks into a studio and makes his home on movie sets, his desperate condition ironically underscored by the artificial luxury of the elegant stage prop bed in which he sleeps. Just as Merton is about to starve, he is rescued by a movie stunt girl named Flips, who feeds and befriends him. She realizes that his acting is so bad that it constitutes a hilarious parody of the stars he imitates. Tricking him into filming a slapstick comedy that he thinks is a melodrama, she makes him into a star. Although he never quite realizes why he is funny, Merton becomes a matinee idol; he takes Flips as his wife, and at the end of the novel the two are securely ensconced in a "luxurious Hollywood bungalow, set among palms and climbing roses."[34]

This story, remade several times as a film, offers a clever send-up of the developing culture of Hollywood—its studios, wannabe movie actors, the stars, and their gullible fans. In Wilson's novel, Merton is a naive spectator, unable to discern the difference between fantasy and reality in film and Hollywood. It is clear that place plays an important role in Merton's confused aspirations, given that his visions of success depend upon his arriving in the geographic place of Hollywood and living in the domestic spaces that film colonists inhabit. But it is also clear that he is never able to distinguish between the reality of the place and the fictional Hollywood he has imbibed from film and magazines. In the end, *Merton of the Movies* emerges not only as a thinly veiled critique of Hollywood but as a sly indictment of the type of image-conscious consumerism that the film industry both thrived on and encouraged.

As the twenties proceeded, the place and space of the stars became more and more ostentatious. Even the films reflected this transformation. Whereas the sets and scenes of the films of the teens tended toward simplicity and often seemed ordinary, those of the twenties reflected the increasingly lavish and extravagant domestic lives of the stars. Lois Weber and several others began to rent and film in actual mansions in and around Hollywood. Merton and his dream bungalow represented an earlier Hollywood. In a remake of *Merton of the Movies*, *Show People* (1928), the aspiring greenhorn actress Peggy Pepper makes the signifier of success a lavish mansion with elaborate furnishings and attendant servants. Some have argued that such shifts in imagery reflected the twenties obsession with wealth and materialism, but it is also true that they mirrored a real change in the lifestyles of those who produced and acted in the movies of this period.

The widening gap between the real lives of the film audiences and the (un)real lives of the stars did not deter, but rather increased, the fans' obsession with movie actors and actresses. Their demand for information on and glimpses into the world of the stars actually increased. Hollywood promoters and developers, in alliance with studio bosses, intensified their efforts to exploit fans' desire to authenticate and consume information on their favorite movie celebrities. The practice of touring the stars' homes, with its promise of potential in-person meetings, had by the mid-1920s become a tourist ritual. Individual guides soon had to compete with businesses such as Golden State Auto

Tours, which, in 1923, advertised the "finest half-day tours out of Los Angeles," taking visitors

> past beautiful Echo Park and into Hollywood the capital of the moving picture world. Here you will see the studios of Wm. S. Hart, Wm. Fox, Jesse Lasky, Christie and others less important, giving you an opportunity of seeing the street scenes, glass-enclosed stages, etc. You will also pass the homes of some of the most noted film stars.[35]

One of the trips offered by Golden State Auto Tours concluded with a meal in the Universal Studios cafeteria, a chance to "have lunch with your favorite 'movie.'" (The popular use of the term *movie* to describe a film player indicated the depth to which the performer had become identified with and perceived of as the commodity itself.) Many of the other tours culminated with a visit to Pickfair.

Significantly for the physical development of Hollywood and its environs, it was not just the tourist business that tried to appeal to the possibilities of "real-life" association with the stars, but also the business of real estate. One of the early maps to the stars' homes in Beverly Hills was distributed by a realty firm hoping to sell lots in a neighboring development. British travel writers Jan Gordon and Cora Gordon described how one realtor tried to sell them land in the vicinity of Beverly Hills by stressing the "value of having the Fairbanks as neighbours." "You'll find them just lovely folks," he told them. When they actually arrived at the lot, they found that the Fairbanks house was just barely visible, several miles away.[36]

While tours attempted to fulfill the public's thirst for an insider view of the stars and assisted developers in their efforts to sell off plots in Tinseltown, not everyone in the film colony was pleased. Throughout the teens, some of Hollywood's most notable figures could be found in the city directory, but as their fame became increasingly married to their geographic and domestic space, their privacy diminished. In 1924, stars expressed outrage when they learned that the advertising firm of Lord and Thomas had published a guide with the addresses of sixty-five of Hollywood's most famous personalities.[37] Although this commodification of domestic space profited studios and land agents, the blending of public and private space angered many actors and actresses, increasingly forcing them to retreat behind stone walls and locked gates. Because fans were undeterred and continued to stream into Hollywood to seek out their film idols, the stars' attempts to isolate themselves only succeeded in making their images all the more distinct and, as a result, more desirable.

The hope of spotting the stars in their native habitat quickly became the object of fan magazine parody. In 1921, Adela Rogers St. John went "sightseeing the movies" on the "Hollywood Rubberneck Wagon" and recounted the guide's patter:

> Ladies and gentlemen we are now entering Hollywood, the native lair of the motion picture. We don't say you have to take your shoes off when stepping on this holy ground, but we do advise you to grease up the vertebrae in the good old neck, because any minute you may see Mary Pickford standing on some corner, or Bebe Daniels doing a Spanish dance on the sidewalk, or Katherine MacDonald smoking a cigarette.[38]

The "reality" of Hollywood had become as prone to manipulation as the screen image, and it generated its own fictions, where insider information extended the cinematic illusion. Hollywood's need to polish its image also accounted for an increasing focus on the homes of the stars. The industry and the town had been tainted by scandal in the years 1920–22. A number of drug-abuse revelations, culminating in Wally Reid's hospitalization and death, plus the unsolved murder of director William Taylor, and of course the Fatty Arbuckle case, led to books such as *The Sins of Hollywood,* a sensational exposé that argued the town made "Sodom look sick." "Ancient degenerates had to exercise a certain amount of prudence" but, protected by its financial power, "Moviedom's imagination had free play—unfettered, unrestrained it made the scarlet sins of Sodom and Babylon, of Rome and Pompeii fade into a pale yellow."[39]

Such criticism not only concerned movie moguls, who feared the fallout would result in the boycott of their product, but also worried the land barons. The tours, revealing the stars to be living in respectable circumstances, counteracted to some degree the rumors regarding Hollywood's depraved state. Beverly Hills, already a fashionable suburb and made more so by Pickfair, offered a publicly prominent escape from the now fully urbanized den of iniquity that was Hollywood proper. Yet, in another sense, the city's blemishes may not have been as much of a deterrent as business leaders first feared; in fact, scandal may have created more curiosity regarding Hollywood and its stars. As the extravagant architecture of the homes they built in Hollywood and Beverly Hills reveals, stars and industry leaders had no intention of retreating to domestic innocence, or of abandoning the public relations that occasionally obscured the public's sense of local realities. If nothing else, they recognized that suggestion of scandalous excess fit the demands of stardom during the roaring twenties. The fact that the tours and maps to the stars' homes became hot commodities during this era, actually proliferating even after the scandals of the early twenties, indicates that, if anything, the public's appetite had only been whetted.

The theatricality of the stars' homes invited participants to experience voyeuristically the lives of their screen idols. The gaze of the tourists, viewing the residential settings of the stars, increasingly corresponded to the gaze of filmgoers. Exempted by the spectacle of these homes from normal codes of conduct, tourists were encouraged to peek into and even stare at private domestic spaces. Like film audiences, the tourists asserted a claim on the space they ogled, "appropriating" it as a vicarious possession.[40] They had been well tutored in spectatorship in theaters, but the tours made the cinematic imagery seem just a little more real and the real lives of the stars seem more fantastic. As in the time of DeLongpre, at the end of the tours there were postcards and pictures to be bought that would serve as visual reminders and additional verification of the authenticity of the experience.

As it developed in the early twenties, touring the stars' homes was an intensely gendered experience, with women constituting the bulk of tour "audiences" and reportedly expressing the most interest in the feminine-related domestic spaces of the stars. As Laura Mulvey, Mary Ann Doane, and others point out, the construction of gender relations is inherent in cinematic viewing. In their view, the male-dominated film industry depicts women as the "object" of the male spectator's voyeurism, perpetuating women's subordination by encouraging men to possess and control the female image. The fact that women are also spectators does not alter the gender hierarchy reproduced by films because women are encouraged to project themselves into the female characters that are to be possessed. As an extension of this notion, women become acquisitions, and the consumerism inherent in the movies tends to oppress rather than empower them as spectators.[41]

Little in the marketing of stars' homes challenges this interpretation of the repressive nature of cinematic culture. Fan magazines did not celebrate Gloria Swanson's accomplishments as a successful single woman whose earnings permitted her to purchase one of Hollywood's most splendid estates. Rather, they portrayed her as a social climber whose marriage to a count represented her attempt to achieve the nobility that would legitimate her wealth. Even Mary Pickford, although a brilliant businesswoman, received little attention for her savvy investment strategies, garnering the most attention as "America's Sweetheart" and as Doug's wife.[42] Pickfair was photographed room by room, showing the refinement of Little Mary's domestic touches. This publicity and commentary by the magazines encouraged fans, especially women, to interpret the domestic spaces of their stars in a way that did not threaten male domination or woman's traditional role in the home. Presumably, the fans were to find contentment in their own domestic spheres just as their female movie counterparts supposedly did in real life. When female tourists gazed upon the homes of Hollywood's successful women photoplayers, they were not to see the resulting wealth of working women but rather to project themselves into the ideal domestic space.

But one did not have to come to Hollywood to participate in the commodification of the stars' home lives. Behind the excessive detailing of the estates and material possessions of celebrities was the obvious attempt to provide models for domestic consumption. Just in case those lessons had not been absorbed after more than a decade of glimpses into the stars' homes, *Photoplay* made them explicit in "How the Stars Make Their Homes Attractive," an article that appeared in 1929. "It is true that we all can't have as beautiful and elaborate homes as those of the film celebs," the piece read. "But we can, with bright linens and a few pots of paint, make many of our dull rooms gay and livable."[43] Although many anecdotal reports of the impacts of this type of marketing exist, and one historian has suggested that the publicity surrounding actors' homes was responsible for the popularity of the Tudor and small-scale beaux arts Italianate styles across the country, the actual reception of this message in the hinterlands is difficult to trace. Several firms marketed plan books based on Hollywood architecture. One company encouraged do-it-yourself builders to "select the home you've dreamed about," allowing them to choose from Spanish and English styles, bungalows, or "Two Story Homes De Lux," all replicas of "Hollywood's Newest Homes."[44] Those who took advantage of these opportunities could bring the physical space of Hollywood, in a form, to their own neighborhood, no matter how distant they were from Tinseltown.

Closer to home, Hollywood spectacle clearly influenced the local residential architecture of Los Angeles, where, during the twenties, tract house developments were filled with such "Hollywood set touches" as half-timbering and rustic doors with strap hinges. Given the impact that Hollywood and its stars had on these mass-market houses, it is not surprising that the American Institute of Architects invited Mary Pickford to address them in 1926; her topic was "Spanish Architecture, Ideal for the California Home." Pickford's urging was unnecessary, as the heavily mythologized Hispanic heritage was already deeply influencing California architecture, having been given an enormous popular boost by her husband in his 1920 film *The Mark of Zorro.*[45]

For nearly everyone involved in California real estate, from architects to land speculators, ties to Hollywood paid off. Beverly Hills benefited from its close association with Hollywood, at times becoming almost indistinguishable from the nearby town. Meanwhile, local businessmen, among them prominent film magnates, rushed to cash in. The towns of Sherman and Lankershim renamed themselves West Hollywood and North Hollywood, respectively. Hobart J. Whitley, one of the original developers of Hollywood, now used Hollywood stars to advertise his developments in the San Fernando Valley. Cecil B. DeMille publicized the community he had planned from the ground up, Fernangeles, by giving away tickets to the opening of *The Ten Commandments* and by making an ostentatious appearance at the development's opening in stereotypical director's garb of khaki and knee-high boots.[46]

Although these satellites of the film colony were early indicators that the geographic boundaries of Hollywood were beginning to dissolve, the town remained central in the construction of the industry's identity and, as a result, continued to maintain, in the eyes of speculators, a distinct marketability. Furthermore, the commingling of film people and the real estate industry indicated the close alliance that evolved between the movie bosses and the land developers.

Hollywoodland, with its star-studded opening and spectacular sign, represents a high point in this affiliation. Strangely, despite Hollywoodland's movie lineage, its promotional brochure made no mention of its fabulous associations, simply promising investors a "delightful residential district free from the turmoil and congestion of the busy city . . . combining the luxury of modern conveniences with the splendid outdoor sports and recreational advantages of the hills." (It also promised that evergreens, firs, cedars, pines, redwoods, sycamores, and other native California trees would be planted in profusion, and that "the beautiful hillslopes of Hollywoodland will take on the added charm of the Woodland.") Given the subdivision's name and the sign, reminiscent of the searchlights that by 1923 were found at every movie premiere, it is likely that the brochure's authors believed that the connection with the stars needed no more emphasis. Further, in widely publicized plans, Mack Sennett proposed to build a fabulous two-million-dollar castle on the hilltop above the sign. He reportedly planned to offer Hollywood tourists a glimpse into his bedroom and bath for a fee. In theory and probably partly in jest, Sennett thus proposed to take the spectacle of touring even further, allowing the public actually to enter his private space.[47]

But even as developers and filmmakers unveiled Hollywood's latest subdivision, with hopes of it becoming another Beverly Hills, some distressing trends had already begun to appear. By this time both the city and the industry had grown alarmed at the numbers of young men and women who, attracted by the images of glamour and excitement, arrived in town looking to become stars themselves. Undoubtedly, local business leaders were most worried about the general problem of order, as unemployed Hollywood hopefuls wandered the streets. The main thrust of their published concerns, however, particularly after the scandals involving Arbuckle and Taylor, was the fate of young women. As a result, mixed messages about the town of Hollywood began to be disseminated. On the one hand, fan magazines and industry publications continued to stress the possibilities of refinement, glamour, and wealth, and local town leaders depicted Hollywood as a "city of homes and churches," where stars contributed more to charities than to scandals. In these versions Hollywood remained a highly desirable place to live and work.

But at the same time, both groups were active in attempts to discourage any more migration to the area, downplaying its opportunities. *Photoplay* continually published articles with titles like "Don't Go to Hollywood" and ran a long series by Adela Rogers St. John about the tragic consequences of such trips titled "The Port of Missing Girls." In 1923, the Hollywood Chamber of Commerce inaugurated a campaign to curb "unrestrained immigration of movie aspirants," telling those who still dared, "Come well provided with Money and bring your Mother." Such slogans inadvertently played into the hands of critics who wrote luridly of the "sheiks" ensnaring the "butterflies of the boulevard, driven there, as if by magic, from their peaceful if monotonous homes over in Iowa, Missouri, Ohio, Kansas, Texas and Colorado attracted by the glare of film life and vain hopes of achieving fame and glory 'just like others did' . . . now they are like broken reeds. They present a sorry spectacle, indeed."[48]

Attempts at town boosterism had by the mid-1920s mingled with efforts to discourage any more settlement in the area, a mixed message that indicated strains between the geographic space of Hollywood and the film industry. Gradually, the film industry began to sever its physical connection with Hollywood. The disintegration of the relationship stemmed from several forces. Feeling the pressure of censorship and increased scrutiny of their activities, members of the film industry had to limit any associations that would call their reputations into question. As Hollywood became flooded with seekers of fortune and fame, it increasingly assumed the sordid characteristics of the place denounced in 1930s fiction, what Nathanael West described as a "dream dump," marked by failure and unfulfilled hopes.[49] The departure of the stars to other areas had already begun and would continue to accelerate as residence in Hollywood became less and less an indicator of success and more associated with dreams deferred.

Soon the studios followed, their move dictated as much by financial and spatial concerns as by the decline in the area's reputation. In the late twenties, the film industry was jolted by the coming of sound, which had a significant impact on the art of filmmaking, actually requiring an alteration in the physical settings in which movies were made. Directors no longer had the freedom to film at any location, and the process required "quiet on the set." Many stars and moviemakers were unable to make this transition. Mack Sennett, whose Keystone Kops had blocked other traffic as they filmed their frantic chases down Hollywood's main streets, was one victim. By the late twenties he was bankrupt, and his dream home above the Hollywood sign was never constructed. Studios were forced to construct large soundstages and elaborate back lots where they could safely shoot outdoors without the interference of real-life noises. Its blocks congested and overbuilt in the initial boom of the movies' arrival, the city of Hollywood could not meet the studios' needs for growing space, compelling moviemakers to search for larger places and spaces on which they could build their monstrous stages and sets. By 1929, most of the studios had left. One observer wrote in *Photoplay*: "It scarcely seems possible even to those who remember that only a few years ago these deserted studios were gay and busy. . . . It was romance and glorious dreams were being woven for all the world. That was yesterday. Now the old Hollywood land marks are going and there is little today to suggest the Hollywood that was."[50]

Although the studios and stars left Hollywood behind, they also took it with them. By the late twenties, anywhere the film industry's elite could be found, there was Hollywood. It was, as famous Hollywood columnist Louella Parsons put it, "a state of mind."[51] Hollywood still signified glamour and excitement, but it was no longer defined by geography. It became, in may ways, as fixed in unreal space as the films it produced.

And what of the community that gave Hollywood its name? The

departure of the film colony severely undermined the construction of the town's identity as well as its economic prospects. In many ways, Hollywood lingered, a shell of its former self. Those who remained were aspirants, the local businesspeople, and, as Carey McWilliams has observed, "the 'workers' of the industry; the craftsmen, the white collar office workers, the skilled and unskilled laborers."[52] With the advent of the Depression, the town was even harder hit. The thriving downtown of shops, restaurants, and hotels around Hollywood Boulevard went into decline, never again to experience the height of its early-twenties prosperity. What became obvious was that the campaigns that linked the name Hollywood to the movie industry had been a phenomenal success in every respect but one: they had failed to ensure the long-term prosperity of the local community.

The major reason for this failure, of course, was that the selling of Hollywood had always been more about the interests of the movie industry than about the interests of local boosters. The early industry benefited from the economies of concentration, and the affiliation with a single name allowed them to "sell" the context of the industry in a way that benefited their product. The area of Hollywood, its own reputation previously established by the California climate and lifestyle, proved a perfect "fit" with films' promotion of leisure and glamour. Once the town had outlived its usefulness and lost some of its appeal, the industry moved out.

Nevertheless, the town of Hollywood did not surrender its claim to the title of film capital of the world. It remained entrenched in filmgoers' consciousness as the geographic place where films were created and stars resided. Tours of the area's sites continued, although increasingly focusing not on the present but on monuments to the movie industry's glorious past. Above all, there remained the sign in the hills, a potent symbol of the merged identities of the town and the movies, and a tribute to both the real and the unreal Hollywood.

Notes

1. Gregg Williams, *Hollywoodland, Established 1923* (Los Angeles: Papavasilpoulos, 1992), 6–9.

2. Ibid.

3. Carey McWilliams, *Southern California: An Island on the Land* (Santa Barbara, Calif.: Peregrine Smith, 1973), 339.

4. Ibid., 96–112; Norman Klein, "The Sunshine Strategy: Buying and Selling the Fantasy of Los Angeles," in *Twentieth Century Los Angeles: Power, Promotion, and*

Social Conflict, ed. Norman Klein and Martin J. Schiesl (Claremont, Calif.: Regina, 1990), 1–38.

5. Bruce Torrence, *Hollywood: The First 100 Years* (Hollywood, Calif.: Hollywood Chamber of Commerce, 1979), 25, 49–50.

6. "Hollywood—Ocean View Tract," advertising brochure, 1903, box 39, California Ephemera Collection, Special Collections, University of California, Los Angeles.

7. Edwin O. Palmer, *A History of Hollywood* (Hollywood, Calif.: Edwin O. Palmer, 1938), 110.

8. Ibid., 114–15.

9. Moses King, "A California Paradise—Home Gardens and Studio of Paul de Longpre: The Pre-eminent Flower Artist—Hollywood Superb Suburb of Los Angeles," pamphlet, n.d., box 39, California Ephemera File, Special Collections, University of California, Los Angeles.

10. Postcards of DeLongpre and movie actors' homes in box 10, John and Jane Adams Postcard Collection, Special Collections, San Diego State University.

11. Pat Dowling, "Who Started Hollywood Anyway," *Photoplay,* June 1919, 92–93.

12. Eileen Bowser, *The Transformation of Cinema, 1907–1908* (New York: Charles Scribner's Sons, 1990), 161.

13. On real estate development and "show business" in the New York area, see Betsy Blackmar, "Uptown Real Estate and the Creation of Times Square," in *Inventing Times Square: Commerce and Culture at the Crossroads of the World,* ed. William R. Taylor (New York: Russell Sage Foundation, 1991), 51–65; advertisements, *Variety,* 4 May 1917, 30, and 11 May 1917, 124.

14. Robert Gottlieb and Irene Wolt, *Thinking Big: The Story of the Los Angeles Times, Its Publishers and Their Influence on Southern California* (New York: G. P. Putnam's Sons, 1977), 146–47.

15. John Drinkwater, *The Life and Adventures of Carl Laemmle* (New York: G. P. Putnam's Sons, 1931), 181–85; "They've Come to Open University City," *Los Angeles Times,* 15 March 1915, sec. II, p. 4.

16. Grace Kingsley, "Movie Royalty in California: Estates and Palatial Homes Bestowed on Photoplayers by their Calling," *Photoplay,* June 1915, 123–27.

17. Kathryn H. Fuller, *At the Picture Show: Small-Town Audiences and the Creation of Movie Fan Culture* (Washington, D.C.: Smithsonian Institution Press, 1996), 116–18.

18. Advertisement, *Motion Picture Supplement,* March 1915, 68.

19. Miriam Hansen, *Babel and Babylon: Spectatorship in American Silent Film* (Cambridge: Harvard University Press, 1991), 23–42.

20. Mary Dickerson Donahey, "Living Neighbor to the Movies: Adventures of a Home in Movieland," *Photoplay,* February 1916, 63–69.

21. Claire Windsor Collection Scrapbook 2, 1921–22, Film and Theater Arts Library, Special Collections, University of Southern California.

22. "The Hidden Glory of California," *Photoplay,* June 1919, 28–34.

23. Merry Ovnick, *Los Angeles: The End of the Rainbow* (Los Angeles: Balcony, 1994), 168.

24. Ibid., 160–63.

25. Charles Higham, *Merchant of Dreams: Louis B. Mayer, M.G.M. and the Secret Hollywood* (New York: Donald I. Fine, 1990), 59, 104.

26. Booton Herndon, *Mary Pickford and Douglas Fairbanks: The Most Popular Couple the World Has Ever Known* (New York: W. W. Norton, 1977).

27. Charles Lockwood, *Dream Palaces: Hollywood at Home* (New York: Viking, 1981), 101–23.

28. Quoted in Scott Eyman, *Mary Pickford: America's Sweetheart* (New York: Donald I. Fine, 1990), 167.

29. Herndon, *Mary Pickford and Douglas Fairbanks,* 123–37.

30. Grace Kingsley, "When Hollywood Was a Pasture," *Photoplay,* June 1927, 32–34, 140.

31. On Swanson and Valentino, see Lockwood, *Dream Palaces,* 2–14, 124–27. On the star system and "personality," see Jib Fowles, *Starstruck: Celebrity Performers and the American Public* (Washington, D.C.: Smithsonian Institution Press, 1992), 30–32.

32. On authenticity and celebrity, see Joshua Gamson, *Claims to Fame: Celebrity in Contemporary America* (Berkeley: University of California Press, 1994), 137–39.

33. Elsie Vance, "Ethel Clayton at Home," *Photoplay,* January 1915, 126; "Some Palaces the Fans Built," *Photoplay,* June 1917, 77.

34. Harry Leon Wilson, *Merton of the Movies* (New York: Grosset & Dunlap, 1922), 330.

35. "Sight-Seeing in Southern California via Golden State Auto Tours," pamphlet, Goodman Collection, Special Collections, University of California, San Diego.

36. "Beverly Hills Street Map with a Key to the Homes of Motion Picture Celebrities and Other Notables Compiled by J. F. Sullivan, Sales Manager and Jack Conant, Assistant Sales Manager of Geo. E. Read, Inc.," Beverly Hills, Calif., 1926; Jan Gordon and Cora Gordon, *Star-Dust in Hollywood* (London: George G. Harrap, 1930), 54–57.

37. Bruce Henstell, *Sunshine and Wealth: Los Angeles in the Twenties and Thirties* (San Francisco: Chronicle, 1984), 83.

38. Adela Rogers St. John, "Sightseeing the Movies on the Hollywood Rubberneck Wagon," *Photoplay,* April 1921, 30–31, 109.

39. *The Sins of Hollywood: A Group of Stories of Actual Happenings Reported and Written by a Hollywood Newspaperman* (Los Angeles: Hollywood Publishing, 1922), 73.

40. Relevant here are discussions of both tourism and film spectatorship. On tourism, see John Urry, *Consuming Places* (New York: Routledge, 1995), 7–9; on the voyeurism of a film audience, see John Ellis, *Visible Fictions: Cinema, Television, Video* (New York: Routledge, 1992), 49–51; on space and film spectatorship, see Barbara Bowman, *Master Space: Film Images of Capra, Lubitsch, Sternberg, and Wyler* (Westport, Conn.: Greenwood, 1992), 3–15.

41. Laura Mulvey, "Visual Pleasure and Narrative Cinema," *Screen* 16 (autumn 1977): 6–18; Mary Ann Doane, "The Economy of Desire: The Commodity Form in/of the Cinema," in *Movies and Mass Culture,* ed. John Belton (New Brunswick, N.J.: Rutgers University Press, 1996), 119–34; Hansen, *Babel and Babylon,* 84–89, 245–53.

42. Richard Koszarski, *An Evening's Entertainment: The Age of the Silent Feature Picture 1915–1928* (New York: Charles Scribner's Sons, 1990), 266–68, 293–96.

43. Lois Shirley, "How the Stars Make Their Homes Attractive," *Photoplay,* April 1929, 69.

44. Advertisement, *House Beautiful,* January 1930, 105.

45. Ovnick, *Los Angeles,* 170–72, 194.

46. Charles Higham, *Cecil B. DeMille* (New York: Charles Scribner's Sons, 1973), 124.

47. S. H. Woodruff Company, "Hollywoodland," brochure, 1923, Special Collections, California State Historical Library, Sacramento; Lockwood, *Dream Palaces,* 78–79.

48. Jack Richmond, *Hollywood: The City of a Thousand Dreams: The Graveyard of a Thousand Hopes, Facts and Fancies of Filmdom for the Movies Sake and for Movie Aspirants* (Los Angeles: n.p., 1928), 28. Booster publications included Laurance Hill and Silas E. Snyder, *Can Anything Good Come Out of Hollywood?* (Hollywood: Snyder, 1923); Laurence A. Hughes, ed., *The Truth about the Movies: By the Stars* (Hollywood: Hollywood Publishers, 1924). The Adela Rogers St. John series ran in *Photoplay* from February to July 1927.

49. On thirties novelists, see David Fine, *Los Angeles in Fiction: A Collection of Essays* (Albuquerque: University of New Mexico Press, 1995).

50. Marquis Busby, "Ghostly Studios of Yesterday," *Photoplay,* November 1929, 42.

51. Louella Parsons, *The Gay Illiterate* (Garden City, N.Y.: Garden City, 1945), 41.

52. McWilliams, *Southern California,* 331.

12.
Lights, Camera, Faction: (Re)Producing "Los Angeles" at Universal's CityWalk

Josh Stenger

Los Angeles became a city through the act of seeing and its industrial transmission all over the world. Because so many pictures were shot in L.A., we were seeing its streets, its ocean and desert, its cars, trees, and light. Before ordinary people ever dreamed of traveling vacations, L.A. was the ideal place to go. . . .

. . . People in L.A. think in scenes and give you lines; the city is a daytime talk-show. Its great urban and civic problems may slip past if it plays well.

David Thomson, "Uneasy Street," 1994[1]

Los Angeles . . . Keep The Dream Alive!
billboard in Los Angeles, 1994

"The Classics Last Forever"

Over the past sixty or seventy years, Los Angeles and the "L.A." lifestyle have become a familiar cultural mythology, one marked by affluence, fame, beauty, health, and leisure. This lifestyle, and the landscape that serves as its setting, was originally promoted as early as the late 1800s by civic boosters hoping to attract well-to-do New England and midwestern residents (and their money) to the developing city. The "imagery, motifs, values and legends" initially popularized during the booster era, according to Mike Davis, were on the one hand "endlessly reproduced by Hollywood" and on the other "incorporated into the ersatz landscape of suburban southern California."[2] This remains the case even today, where the production of "Los Angeles" is at once undertaken by the film industry, architects, and urban planners alike. To be sure, both materially, at the level of its built environment, and ideologically, at the level of its cultural mythology, Los Angeles has for more than one hundred years promoted itself as a singular form of urban fantasia. As the film industry began to play a defining role in the production and distribution of that mythology, it became increasingly difficult to distinguish L.A.'s cultural geography from that of its cinematic doppelgänger.

Baudrillard, for whom the city must have first seemed a triumphant mental playground, calls L.A. "nothing more than an immense script and a perpetual motion picture."[3] This script, as it were, is dominated by spectacle and illusion; it functions largely as a reminder that to live in Los Angeles is to live according to the metaphors made available by the film industry. Inside this place of "pleasure domes decreed," Davis argues, the perspective of the L.A. resident is, like the projected image, depthless and inauthentic: "To move to Lotusland is to sever connection with national reality, to lose historical and experiential footing, to surrender critical distance, and to submerge oneself in spectacle and fraud."[4] Economically, culturally, and psychologically invested in its celluloid self-image, Los Angeles, as Baudrillard and Davis would have it, is sorely lacking an authentic urban identity.

Although its tremendous cultural-industrial complex seems relentlessly committed to producing and disseminating an image of the city as an American Elysium, the reality of Los Angeles for many of its residents is quite stark, as Davis, among others, is quick to point out: "Decades of systematic under-investment in housing and urban infrastructure, combined with grotesque subsidies for speculators, permissive zoning for commercial development, the absence of effective regional planning, and ludicrously low property taxes for the wealthy have ensured an erosion of the quality of life for the middle classes in older suburbs as well as for the inner-city poor."[5] In their efforts to make the city "the entertainment capital of the world," L.A. and its leadership have too often turned a blind eye to genuine urban reform. Seeing itself as a kind of postmodern Eden, L.A. has historically relied on a cultural and sociospatial politics of urban spectacle and symbolic erasure.

Ongoing efforts to safeguard the hegemony of its cinematic past insinuate themselves into the city's landscape, as if to remind residents and tourists alike that Hollywood both stars in and produces the only true "L.A. story." Indeed, movies in general, and those set in and concerned with the city in particular, have told and retold the glamorous story of Los Angeles to great effect. But this is changing.[6] And although the area's host of theme parks and its image of perpetual springtime draw millions of visitors annually, the fantasy of L.A. is often clung to most dearly, most desperately, by those who make their lives and livelihoods there. Signs like the one mentioned above—"Los Angeles . . . Keep the Dream Alive!"—at once hint at a dire situation and yet continue to conflate "city" and "fantasy" as a viable rhetorical strategy for community building.[7]

While the dream may be fading, recovery efforts remain, with few exceptions, entrenched in the project of reproducing existing social and material relations and class divisions through a policy of what Davis calls "spatial apartheid."[8] Like the high-profile Hollywood Redevelopment Project, Universal's CityWalk is one of the most notable among several plans to revitalize areas of the city.[9] Sitting astride the Universal City foothills, CityWalk is both a structural and a symbolic link between the Universal Studios theme park and Cineplex Odeon's eighteen-theater multiplex, working to funnel visitors and their money through Universal City's spectacular entertainment complex. A one-story, two-"block" collage of restaurants and eclectic boutiquelike stores, CityWalk aims to capture at the level of its architecture the essence of a utopian, Hollywood-inspired Los Angeles. More important, however, because it is so imbricated in film culture and history, CityWalk collapses Los Angeles's history into film history, both of which end up commodified by this synthetic Main Street cum theme park.

If CityWalk were merely a shopping mall, it would hardly pass notice. Uncannily out of the way and small by mall standards, CityWalk lacks the convenience and usefulness one normally associates with malls. However, attached to Universal Studios and one of L.A.'s largest multiplex theaters, this 1,500-foot-long strip is able to promote Los Angeles's movie-made mythology to an estimated eight to ten million visitors a year.[10] In many ways, the place resists classification: part mall, part theme park, part homage to the silver screen, and *all* insistently "Los Angeles," CityWalk is, more than anything, a spectacle. Considering it as such, I mean to invoke Guy Debord's description of the spectacle and the process by which it organizes social relations around it:

> The spectacle appears at once as society itself, as a part of society and as a means of unification. As a part of society, it is that sector where all attention, all consciousness, converges. Being isolated—and precisely for that reason—this sector is the locus of illusion and false consciousness; the unity it imposes is merely the official language of

generalized separation. The spectacle is not a collection of images; rather, it is a social relationship between people that is mediated by images.[11]

In claiming to offer "Los Angeles" to shoppers, visitors, tourists, and moviegoers alike—the distinctions among these different roles already becoming blurry—CityWalk and the Universal complex imply that the city itself can be experienced only through the twin discourses of Hollywood film and consumerism, cementing the bonds that join spectacle, conspicuous consumption, and the availability of "L.A." as a navigable and a safely lived experience. Although it may seem perhaps too local a phenomenon to merit such close scrutiny, CityWalk—with "sequels" already in the works in Orlando, Florida, and Osaka, Japan— is in fact at the front guard of a new phase of consumer culture, a phase in which the conventional shopping mall is rebuilt as entertainment complex. By so effectively combining tropes of the mall, the theme park, and film culture, CityWalk is ushering in—along with other hybrid consumer spaces such as Planet Hollywood, the Hollywood-Highland project on Hollywood Boulevard, and Disney and Warner Bros. stores— a multivalent consumer space wherein shoppers, by default, play the additional roles of moviegoers and tourists.

One might say, after Jameson, that CityWalk wears its postmodernism on its sleeve, enthusiastically and unironically editing together yesterday and tomorrow, cinema and city. Nostalgia is a powerful marketing tool, and at CityWalk it is, in many ways, the organizing principle of what retailers and designers call the "corporate dress" of the place. Designed as a "high-tech facsimile of Los Angeles city streets," CityWalk simulates a halcyon retrospective of the L.A. experience.[12] From the futuristic facades to the well-aged vintage neon signs recovered from the 1940s and 1950s, CityWalk strikes a somewhat schizophrenic balance between an imagined past and a hoped-for future. It carefully folds local vernacular architecture into Hollywood imagery and iconography, as if to proclaim the end of any manifest distinction between urban geography and retail fantasy.

At CityWalk, L.A.'s past is reducible to Hollywood's Golden Age, both of which are in turn offered up as neatly packaged commodities. Despite the ineluctable fact that most of the available wares are rather kitschy souvenirs and other forms of consumer ephemera, CityWalk continues to promote itself as a vehicle for historical (and retail) continuity. In the central courtyard, for instance, this message is made clear: mannequins of Groucho Marx, Humphrey Bogart, Carole Lombard, and Frankenstein's monster—all holding cups of coffee—stand atop an old-seeming Maxwell House billboard whose caption neatly conflates product placement, Hollywood history, the marketability of movie stars, and the prevailing ethos of the entire mall area: "The Classics Last Forever."

A Westside Story

As one maps the way CityWalk's head architect, Jon Jerde, and his team worked with Universal, neighbors, and store owners to re-create L.A., one sees that the primary strategy is to reproduce the affluent Westside and beach communities, drawing connections to the entertainment industry, affluence, and cultural capital, all of which are overrepresented in these sections of the city. Wondering whether, if "served only the choicest cuts of the real city, [visitors] would still come away malnourished," collaborating architect Craig Hodgetts considers the mall's process of geographic selection to be intimately linked with consumption, but, like a gourmet meal, one that sacrifices substance to presentation: "There's a predisposition to having an easy, bite-size piece of reality which does not challenge you . . . a kind of secondhand reality that's predigested."[13]

A tour through CityWalk helps to illustrate the point. Beginning at the Cineplex Odeon entrance (one of only three points of entry or

Figure 1. "The Classics Last Forever": CityWalk's "Los Angeles" is a shrewd combination of set design, film history, star power, and product placement.

exit—there is also one in the courtyard that leads into the central parking structure and one at the other end that connects CityWalk to Universal Studios), one starts off at the beach, so to speak, as the experience is framed first by a reproduction of a fishing boat outside the upscale Gladstone's 4 Fish, known to natives of the city from its original restaurant overhanging the Pacific Ocean at the intersection of Sunset Boulevard and Pacific Coast Highway.[14] At Gladstone's, boasts CityWalk's on-line publicity, one can enjoy "a truly California beach experience. . . . If you didn't know better, you'd swear that you're at the beach. But how can that be—you just drove up the hill to get to Universal CityWalk. Well, there it is—sand, palm trees, Beach Boys music, weight lifting contests, beach activities." Things are simpler at CityWalk, apparently; just "relax under the swaying palm trees on a real sand beach and watch the world go by" (or rather, "go buy"): it is, after all, "the perfect place for a quick bite and a cool drink before or after a movie."[15] Almost charming in its lack of self-consciousness, the suggestion that the "truly California beach experience" can be had twenty miles inland on top of a hill in the San Fernando Valley certainly gives one pause.

Moving into the strip of stores and restaurants, one arrives quickly at the open-air rotunda that acts as a corner joint to CityWalk. Here there is a high concentration of still more trendy restaurants for those visitors who might not like seafood or the "California beach experience": Tony Roma's, B.B. King's Blues Club, KWGB (World's Greatest Burgers), Wizardz Magic Club and Dinner Theater, and the Country Star Hollywood, which "provides patrons with the total country music experience through top-of-the-line visual, interactive innovations." Secondarily, the CityWalk Web site notes almost in passing that the restaurant also features "great bar-b-que."[16] If shopping is not foregrounded on the Cineplex end of the strip, dinner-before-a-movie stands in as the dominant form of consumption.[17] Down the strip is Wolfgang Puck's California Pizza, a nod to the Southland's favorite celebrity restaurateur. A veritable explosion of color and style, Wolfgang Puck's not only signifies the quintessence of "California cuisine," it alludes to Puck's other posh oceanside restaurants, like Granita in Malibu and Chinois on Main in Santa Monica, and, of course, to Spago in Beverly Hills.[18]

In the courtyard, one also finds CityWalk's now-famous computerized water show/fountain, built into the ground and programmed to "dance" a number of choreographed routines. Again, "cultured" residents of the area should recognize this as the handiwork of WET (Water Entertainment Technology) Design Company, the company that built the celebrated fountain at the Los Angeles Music Center—the eastern-most reference to L.A.'s topography at CityWalk. Presumably, despite its proximity to Skid Row, the Music Center—which includes the Dorothy Chandler Pavilion, the Mark Taper Forum, and the Ahmanson Theatre—has a strong enough connotative tie to high culture to gain representation here, if only through the oblique allusion of the water fountain.

Rounding the corner, patrons encounter other direct references to the "good" parts of Los Angeles. A UCLA Extension Center—whose facade mimics the brickwork adorning the original campus's signature building, Royce Hall—offers a number of film and media courses and reminds the crowd that education is a prerequisite of upwardly mobile consumption.[19] While most visitors probably have little cause to "use" the continuing-education center in the way they "use" the other shops, they can find, two doors down, the UCLA Spirit Shop, which allows visitors a more context-appropriate way to experience the university—by purchasing UCLA-inscribed mementos. Inside, the Spirit Shop displays a freely adapted landscape view of the actual campus, the same view one would have walking out of the student store in Ackerman Union. UCLA's presence at CityWalk is an important one, if only because it asks visitors to consider the absence of cross-town rival USC. Although USC's notoriously wealthy and fiercely loyal alumni would seem to make a USC Spirit Shop welcome if not outright de rigueur, CityWalk's architectural Westside bias would suffer considerably by referencing that part of Los Angeles—South-Central, Watts, Bell Gardens, the nucleus of the Los Angeles riots—in short, black, poor, dangerous, Other. UCLA, surrounded by moneyed communities like Westwood, Bel Air, Beverly Hills, and Brentwood, on the other hand, evokes that right-side-of-the-tracks feeling so crucial to feel-good consumerism.

Still less-obvious clues about CityWalk's architectural biases pepper the structure's facades, such as the front end of an old Cadillac that is driving out of the Hollywood FreeZway storefront. The other end is wedged into the side of the Hard Rock Cafe a few miles away at the Beverly Center, even as a second Hard Rock has opened just on the other side of the Cineplex Odeon at Universal.[20] Meanwhile, stores like Things from Another World and Wizardz contribute to a feeling of magic and fantasy, reminding visitors that CityWalk is both "L.A." and "not-L.A." Other establishments, such as Captain Coconuts, Surf City Squeeze, Malibu Ranch (which specializes in surfwear *and* country attire!), and Island Nut Company intone a "tropical" beach and ocean image so as to heighten CityWalk's association with L.A.'s fabled coastline. The entire structure also evokes head architect Jon Jerde's other major local architectural achievement, the Westside Pavilion, a more subtle resonance meant to solidify CityWalk's connection to up-scale mall culture.

As important as this connection is, so too is the way CityWalk capitalizes on the local corporate history of Cineplex Odeon to strengthen its association both with the "right" parts of town and with the right kind of theater chain. Beyond simply providing a place to see movies, the Universal Cineplex offers its role in L.A.'s cinematic past to the recipe, one that is itself wrapped up in conspicuous consumption and high-end theater building. Debuting in Los Angeles in 1982 when it opened a fourteen-screen multiplex at the Beverly Center, Cineplex spent the eighties acquiring footholds in premier theater locations. Buying and restoring theaters such as the Fairfax and the Brentwood in 1985,[21] what was then Cineplex Odeon established itself both as a major presence in movie-loving West L.A. and as a conservator of local entertainment history, something MCA and Universal Studios could already claim.

Especially after the 1992 civil unrest garnered some rather unfavorable international publicity for the city, re-creating L.A. as a safe, desirable, and containable consumer space looked to be as challenging as it would be profitable. In order to recuperate the city's tarnished image in the name of upscale consumerism and moviegoing, CityWalk obviously had to evince a "narrative quality" even as it edited rather drastically the text of the city.[22] Anyone who has ever spent time in Los Angeles will notice immediately that CityWalk evokes a highly particularized sense of the Southland, a spatial contrivance that the architecture proudly foregrounds rather than de-emphasizes. Incorporating its class politics into the mall's mise-en-scène, CityWalk reflects a beautified version of L.A.'s architectural vernacular, even as that vernacular is framed as a model of failed social harmony that can be restored only through privatization and thematization.

As a commodity, the "City" in CityWalk is most fully accessible and most recognizable to the affluent. To be sure, CityWalk's is a semiotics of exclusivity, one that is read most fluently by members of the middle- and upper-middle classes. As I argued earlier, at the level of its architecture, CityWalk reproduces the same social and spatial divisions that exist throughout the city by reducing Los Angeles to a kind of geographic narrative of its high-rent Westside communities. L.A. is distilled down to a series of high-priced consumer metonymies in which one can "sample the pleasures of the city without the aftertaste of urban decay."²³ Such a statement belies one of the fundamental contradictions on which CityWalk is built and that it struggles to conceal: most local visitors to CityWalk don't live in, don't work in, and certainly don't shop in parts of town where they would normally encounter "the aftertaste of urban decay." For those who can afford to shop there, the L.A.-as-paradise that CityWalk purports to regain was never really lost to begin with. By offering an image of safety to a demographic whose penchant for security-through-privacy has made the gated community a staple of local neighborhood planning, the mall simply amplifies the perceived threat of heterogeneity generally, and of class difference specifically.

CityWalk, according to Jerde's description, "attracts a real ethnic mix. There are faces of all colors, eyes of all shapes. It may be a walled city on top of the hill, but its drawbridge is always down and a racially diverse crowd streams across it."²⁴ Although the crowds are always multicultural and multiracial at Universal—it's hard to imagine anyplace that draws more than ten million visitors annually not to be—an early MCA survey of CityWalk's patrons indicated that nearly three-fourths of them come from the San Fernando Valley and the foothill and canyon communities that link the Valley and the city: "a multi-ethnic [but primarily] middle- to upper-class crowd."²⁵ Jerde is fast becoming the most recent in a long tradition of unique Los Angeles architects. In both theory and practice, approach and design, Jerde can at times, like L.A. itself, embody massive conceptual contradictions. Seeming at once visionary and reactionary, Jerde describes L.A.'s polyethnic and multicultural population as a source of a rich diversity, but also as a kind of bizarre, if atomized, network of exotic and potentially lucrative otherness:

> Probably L.A.'s greatest asset is our tremendous ethnic population. And what we already have, entwining with the downtown and all around it, are some of the greatest existing *theme parks* you ever saw. There's a Chinatown. There's a Little Tokyo and Olvera Street. There's all these wonderful things that are all standard one-liners. They're all sort of separate, but they could easily be linked, woven into the downtown. So people that would be the users of these attractions, these districts, would now become the inhabitants and users of the downtown.²⁶

While Jerde may wax egalitarian here, arguing that *all* cultures and spaces are potential sites for further thematization and commodification, one nonetheless senses that at CityWalk, the road from ethnic panacea to racial and economic pariah is a short one. Built to keep out, or at best to be uninviting to, such overdetermined social groups as the homeless and young African Americans, CityWalk and the adjoining Universal Cineplex take pains to erase all traces of true urbanism. For instance, while on the premises, patrons are, if necessary, reminded by security that "non-commercial expressive behavior," such as wearing a baseball cap backward (signifying, apparently, membership in a gang and thus an imminent threat to other visitors), is grounds for removal.[27] An anonymous restaurant manager puts matters in perspective: "There's a very high-level clientele up here. . . . It's not cheap to eat at Gladstone's. The stores aren't cheap either. You have to pay for parking. All that deters the trouble-making crowd."[28]

The Universal Cineplex plays its part, as well. Although it drew fire from urban activists, filmmakers, and film fans alike, in 1993 alone the multiplex refused to exhibit John Singleton's *Poetic Justice* during its opening weekend, because executives feared young black moviegoers would disrupt the atmosphere, and declined even to book the Hughes brothers' *Menace II Society* or Mario Van Peebles's *Posse*. Such instances have become something of a thorn in MCA's side, as its selective marketing strategies' implicit discrimination becomes increasingly and ironically transparent.[29]

Despite the fact that MCA wants no trouble from young African American moviegoers, it nevertheless spent $200 million in 1996 to acquire a 50 percent share in Interscope Records, "one of the most successful start-up record companies ever." Interscope—whose notorious reputation for producing controversial "gangsta rap" caused Time Warner to dump the label in the wake of an organized anti-rap campaign just six months before MCA's buyout—has become synonymous with the stereotype of the same urban black youth culture MCA fears will invade CityWalk to see the "wrong" movies. Still, the company apparently could not resist the profit potential to be realized from the same demographic.[30]

The official comment from Cineplex Odeon regarding its decision about *Poetic Justice* made front-page news; it also made insidiously plain the measures the theater was prepared to take to ensure a virtually homogeneous consumer experience: "Our film programmers in Los Angeles are ensuring that the theater is programmed with an upscale demographic to make sure that CityWalk's environment is kept safe with a family atmosphere."[31] Inside Universal's carefully engineered social utopia, "family," "upscale," and "safe" become interchangeable. Such business practices, however, have obviously severe ramifications for filmmakers whose work does not conform to "appropriate" community standards. In 1987, for instance, the Universal Cineplex hosted nearly forty thousand moviegoers on its opening weekend alone, and attendance has not slowed down since. Whereas most multiplex theaters are anchored by shopping malls these days, Universal Cineplex, turning this equation on its head, proved such a powerful magnet that MCA decided to build CityWalk just for good measure.[32] Given that multiplex theaters of this scale command a considerable market share in the exhibition industry, it seems nearly impossible for black filmmakers even to gain "equal access" to the screen.[33]

Films about the inner city are about as unwelcome as architectural reminders of any neighborhood one wouldn't find in an Aaron Spelling serial—namely, the cinematic L.A. the world (supposedly) knows and loves. Sharon Zukin has written that in postmodern cities like Los Angeles, "the forging of a metropolis out of many private jurisdictions has challenged the primacy of public space as an organizing principle of social life." Rather, privatized "consumer" space becomes the "organizing principle." The geographic concentration of such spaces gives rise to what Zukin calls "new patterns of regional specialization [that] reflect the selective location of highly skilled and highly valued economic activities. . . . These concentrations enable places to capitalize on their initial advantage."[34] Accordingly, CityWalk, while "capitalizing

Figure 2. Excess Hollywood: Wolfgang Puck's California Pizza's three-dimensional facade shows California cuisine to be, just like Hollywood, cartoonishly alive.

on its initial advantage" afforded by its ties to Universal Studios and the Cineplex Odeon, is able, or rather obliged, to invoke a new, idealized L.A., both to stimulate and to authorize forms of "highly valued economic activity"—among them, shopping, moviegoing, and tourism.

CityWalk simultaneously aligns itself with and distinguishes itself from other outdoor, streetlike shopping spaces in middle- and upper-middle-class L.A., such as Santa Monica's Third Street Promenade, Venice Beach's Ocean Front Walk, Pasadena's Old Town, Hollywood's Melrose Avenue, and Beverly Hills's Rodeo Drive. In the process, it presents itself as a familiar yet distinctive consumer space, activating the same kind of consumer euphoria as these other sites (which is arguably protracted by its proximity to the theme park and movie theaters). Yet it goes one step further: by alluding to these and other prime consumer-cultural venues, CityWalk lays claim to solving the problems of both safety and consolidation, offering the entire consumer-cultural vastness of the sprawling "upscale" shopping districts in one convenient, sheriff-patrolled street, a "cinematic" or "televisual" version of Los Angeles that has been "recorded and dismembered and then edited back together into a fantasy world where Koreatown is next to Van Nuys and Griffith Park is somewhere between Torrance and Santa Monica."[35] There exists a more selective spatial logic, however. Of these locales, for instance, only Griffith Park's famous Hollywood sign and Santa Monica's Third Street and beachfront have the kind of cachet to be represented at CityWalk.

Street Cleaning

From its deliberately hyperbolic architecture to its visually frenetic decor, CityWalk feels rather like a theme park, a hyperreal cartoon of Los Angeles iconography. Yet, just as Disneyland balances the sensory bombardment of Fantasyland with the comparative calm of Main Street USA, so too is CityWalk able to combine flash and fantasy with a sense of the familiar. Thus, for instance, visitors find Wizardz Magic Club and Dinner Theater—a two-story imaginarium dedicated to illusion and sleight of hand—right across the "street" from the Upstart Crow bookstore and coffeehouse, where they can browse for light reading material or opt for a relatively quiet, even semiprivate latte at one of the outdoor tables. On one side of the street is the decadent, the "magical"; on the other, the "neighborhood" sidewalk café and bookstore. By grafting these two different styles and atmospheres onto a single, shared built environment, mall designers are able to fabricate a kind of symbolic unity between the visual (even visceral) appeal of the spectacular and the everybody-knows-your-name comfort of the town square. Together, these render the experience of CityWalk-as-street not only safe, but outright enjoyable.

Critics, say CityWalk's proponents, take the place too seriously; CityWalk is not insidious, it's just about fun. Indeed, the whole place may be artificial, but "the fun is authentic," the "pleasure is real."[36] Such defenses are commonplace, and they constitute an argument that frames critiques of such places as being not only out of proportion, but joyless. The question remains, however: Just what is the source of this authentic and allegedly holistic pleasure? As Robin Wood reminds us, "Pleasure in itself is patently ideological."[37] Thus it is worth examining more closely just how important the multiple significations of the same space function to construct a kind of visual, emotional, and geographic narrative of "place." Indeed, much of the enjoyment that visitors experience derives from their trying to decipher the various codes superimposed on one another in this densely packed visual space that is at once Main Street, theme park, shopping mall, recombinant L.A., and Hollywood pastiche. In other words, such an examination must attempt to interpret just why CityWalk has struck a nerve in tourists and Angelenos alike.

On one level, CityWalk and the adjacent Cineplex Odeon multiplex are able to draw several million local residents annually not simply because of their glitz and glamour, of which there is plenty, but also because, even as it suggests itself as a kind of "body double" for the real L.A., the strip of shops and restaurants is deliberately reminiscent of a small-town Main Street. Despite the inevitable weekend and evening crowds, there is in fact something surprisingly peaceful about walking around CityWalk early on a weekday morning when the usually ubiquitous white noise of the freeway—one is never far from one in L.A., after all—is thankfully undetectable, the matinee fans have yet to arrive for the early show, and the stores themselves are just opening to the public. To be sure, at the right time and without the crowds, one feels almost like a flaneur strolling through a nineteenth-century arcade of fantastic facades. The feeling is not accidental, of course; "in this world of film, [storefronts] are larger than life," built at one-and-a-half scale, meant to convey a sense of invitation, inhabitability, and grandiosity all at once.[38]

There is something subtly different about the stores' facades that exists apart from their kaleidoscopic visual appeal: the sheer artifice of the storefronts, one discovers, comes at the expense of the all-too-familiar glass-walled facade; that is, storefronts are not organized around window displays in the same way conventional mall shops or even stand-alone stores are. Because stores on city streets must accommodate the drive-by window-shopper as well as the erstwhile pedestrian, shop windows are often stretched across the length of the stores' facades so as to afford motorists a glance inside.[39] Meanwhile, even though traffic speed is not an issue in the shopping mall, stores almost always devote their front walls to merchandise displays or large-pane glass to provide maximum interior visibility, the logic apparently being that there is nothing else for potential customers to look at while in the mall except what stores have to sell. CityWalk, however, does not conform to this design trope; there are window displays, to be sure, but they are not intended to compete with, distract from, or constitute the overall visual pleasure of the place. As a result, although one may very well shop at the stores there— most do, of course—one feels as if CityWalk is designed less for shopping than for experiencing. For Jon Jerde, building CityWalk was, in fact, "like designing experience. . . . People enjoy the changing spaces, the strong geometric qualities—it is a sequential plan of orchestrated events."[40]

Such an "experience" can never exist fully outside consumption, however. Certainly, evoking Main Street means also fulfilling the "most important" function of Main Street—namely, "retailing."[41] As both civic square and commercial center, Main Street has always combined shopping with being a public citizen. Walt Disney took this dual function to its extreme when he built Main Street USA (designed to resemble his hometown of Marceline, Missouri) as the entranceway to Disneyland; it is impossible to think of Main Street today without thinking of Disneyland, which in turn is to think about the thematization and commodification of public space. In his book-length study of Main Streets in American small towns, Richard Francaviglia points out that "Disney's abiding faith in material progress helps explain why Main Street is such a popular icon: it is typically American in that it features the material culture of prosperity as the underpinnings of economic security and community strength."[42] Thanks to mall developers and designers, who almost always incorporate the basic spatial logic of Main Street into mall architecture, the imbrication of Main Street, communal American idealism, and consumerism exist today as part of our everyday built environment.

Because its stock-in-trade is L.A.'s cultural mythology, which it at once draws on and strengthens, CityWalk requires that visitors be able to "read" the narrative it creates out of stucco and neon. By eliciting a

strong aura of the fantastic and the pleasurable, the architectural design works to create a shared sense of story and event among visitors.
For residents especially, one imagines that the narrative experience that
CityWalk encourages most is the recovery of an idyllic Los Angeles; the
Main Street image invokes a powerful sense of nostalgia, a throwback
to a more innocent time—the 1980s, for instance!—when the fantasy
of L.A. as a paradise by the sea still had some purchase among residents. As Norman Klein writes of the place and its role in reclaiming
the Southland of a bygone era: "From every direction, the fractious facades project innocence, like bits of a Spielberg movie about the late,
great city of Los Angeles. It is a very charming elegy."[43]

Although it is more likely that CityWalk's planners think of the
mall as a recovery (if not a sequel) of a lost L.A., rather than an
"elegy," in positioning CityWalk as a kind of Main Street in a city that
is notoriously decentralized, they have assured that part of CityWalk's
narrative content works to reinstill a sense of community built on a
myth of common space and shared identity through active consumption. How successfully CityWalk makes available a sense of ownership
to the L.A. residents who visit is a problematic issue, for it is only
through a kind of semiotic contortionism that CityWalk manages to
make locals feel as if they are simultaneously "right at home" and
tourists in their own backyard.

It is precisely the fact that CityWalk "masquerades" as a public
space for rebuilding community that has prompted Mike Davis—at
once L.A.'s fiercest advocate and most acerbic critic—to call CityWalk
"an ominous parallel universe . . . the moral equivalent of the neutron
bomb."[44] CityWalk, purporting to reinvigorate L.A.'s beleaguered sense
of (comm)unity, instead participates in the reaffirmation of community
tensions surrounding racial, cultural, and, especially, class difference.
By Davis's own description, "'community' in Los Angeles means homogeneity of race, class and, especially, home values."[45] The organization
into small (sub)urban enclaves of the middle, upper-middle, and upper
classes reinforces an already potent fear of the Other, who is seen
through a "demonological lens."[46] The logic of spatial constructions in
the city being one primarily informed by the privileging of clear divisions, this fear of the Other is most visible, perhaps because it is almost
impossible to take for granted, in public and has been manifested in the
city's decades-long campaign to eradicate public space. After one peels
back the Main Street "layer" of CityWalk, then, one sees the way the
mall similarly works to reclaim the city street in the name of those who
desire, indeed demand, safe shopping and dining. If the image of Main

Street has a semiotic shortcoming, it is that it has no direct connection to the daily lived experience of Angelenos, for whom *street* has a distinct set of connotations, very few of which are positive.

The perceived threat of heterogeneity in the public sphere, especially in the street, has become acute in cities like L.A., in which social and spatial interaction between classes remains shockingly infrequent.[47] The most common type of such public "interactions"—driving—remains conveniently spatially contained; the reign of the automobile across the horizontal sprawl of the Southland allows one to limit one's public exposure to the semiprivate confines of one's car. If this description of Los Angeles sounds alarmist, one might consider the not entirely unironic fact that CityWalk's grand opening came just thirteen months after the aftermath of the verdicts in the trial of the police officers accused of beating Rodney King.[48] Having watched itself burn for three days and nights only a year before, L.A. welcomed the grand opening of CityWalk, whose arrival surely seemed like salt in the wounds of the thousands of residents whose lives were directly affected either by the "riots" specifically or, more generally, by the systematic urban neglect that seems almost a matter of public policy in Los Angeles. The sluggish and ineffectual Rebuild L.A. (RLA) public works program headed by former Olympic Commissioner Peter Uberoth to help the South-Central communities recover was quickly and with much publicity upstaged by MCA's answer to the problem in the form of CityWalk. The message: if the real city can't fix things, the entertainment industry can, and will.[49]

Publicizing CityWalk as a remedy for the "real" dangers of the street—crime, poverty, homelessness, drug abuse, not to mention those forms of assault on person and property specifically tailored to L.A.'s auto-mobility, such as drive-by shootings and carjacking—planners at entertainment giant MCA, which owns CityWalk, believe that "people will keep coming to CityWalk, in part because of its relative safety compared to real Los Angeles streets."[50] Indeed, CityWalk "sought to act like a new brand of town square. Hollywood Boulevard with a child-proof cap. A sanitized Venice Beach for a populace grown weary of looking over its shoulders."[51] Speaking of Venice Beach in particular, one of the city's most historic and heterogeneous public spaces, then president of MCA Lawrence Spungin put matters in perspective, lamenting: "Take Venice Beach. . . . there's somebody on every street corner with a 'Work for Food' sign. It's not fun anymore."[52] Such a statement smacks of a barely concealed contempt for the homeless who have settled in Venice (which is its own municipality), not, as

Spungin would have us believe, to disturb the crowds of fun seekers so much as to avoid the LAPD's systematic efforts to drive them out of downtown.[53] Spungin's remark rather deftly juxtaposes several of CityWalk's central motifs: pleasure for pleasure's sake ("not fun anymore"), the truly public street as an uncontrollable space ("somebody on every corner"), and the erasure of labor under the mandate of a hegemonic consumerism ("will work for food"). To be a "street person" is to be always already marked as outside the consumer culture, and thus to be scorned.

Given the acknowledged sense of fear attached to the urban experience, then, one might ask of CityWalk, whose design is "more akin to urban planning than shopping mall design,"[54] whether or not there is a danger, or at least a commercial liability, in reproducing the text of the city even in such an expurgated version. It should be noted, however, that CityWalk exploits such anxieties even as it rewrites them as new sources for consumer desires. The dual rhetorics of fear and desire provide a framework through which CityWalk can articulate itself as a space that offers not only escape from the reality of Los Angeles (and therefore from crisis) but a new and improved simulation of the city available for both material and visual consumption.

While the architecture is staggering and the storefronts cartoonishly alive, the primary image of desire that is abstracted from the urban topos and grafted onto CityWalk is that of the street, albeit a restless, uncomfortable amalgam of the city street and the small-town Main Street. Indeed, with the exception of the central role that film plays throughout the Universal entertainment complex, CityWalk's simulation of the street is of far greater rhetorical and ideological consequence than virtually any other thematic component, for, as I have suggested above, in the most automobile-dependent city in America, if not the world, the street remains primarily something one *views* rather than something one *experiences*.[55] CityWalk renders, even at the level of its name, a version of city life in which experiencing the city as a pedestrian (potential consumer) rather than as a driver or passenger (worker) is not only safe but desirable.

In a city where residents are notoriously reluctant to walk and fiercely devoted to their cars, evoking the pleasure of foot travel and the street is neither easy nor unproblematic. To guarantee its success, CityWalk had to effect a wholesale symbolic inversion of the perceived stigma attached to those experiences. This was accomplished on one important level through the location of the structure atop the foothills of Universal City, whose primary access roads—Lankershim Boulevard

Figure 3. Nobody walks in L.A.: CityWalk promotes itself as a cure for the dangers of "real" city streets, offering pedestrian shopping along its carefully engineered, palm tree–lined streets.

and the Hollywood Freeway—are somewhat distant, making CityWalk virtually impossible to reach without an automobile and all but ensuring the absence of those for whom walking is a necessity or form of survival rather than an option. Still, defending the "public" nature of CityWalk, project manager David Froelich was reported in the *Los Angeles Times* as making the following argument: "CityWalk is a real city street, he said, not an amusement park. He points out there's no entry fee. If you didn't want to pay the $6 parking fee, you could even take a bus to Universal City and catch a studio tram to CityWalk. But [as *Times* staff writer Doug Smith observed] most of those who packed into the two-block street . . . took the escalator down from the parking structure."[56]

An important function of CityWalk's distancing from the street, along with its labyrinthine parking structures, high-profile security guards and sheriff's deputies, and impeccably maintained physical plant, is to act as a kind of packaging for the city-as-commodity, a safety seal of sorts, meant to eliminate all forms of potential contamination. Exploiting consumer desire for both purity and security, CityWalk sanctions walking in *this* street by purifying it of, and protecting it from, all forms of exterior threat.[57] Despite CityWalk's efforts to protect its borders, so to speak, violent reality has found its way inside on several occasions—most notoriously in a brutal double homicide on Mother's Day of 1995.[58]

Still, other commercial districts, one feels, like downtown's largely Hispanic Broadway area and the aforementioned Venice Beach—areas that are at once more socioeconomically and more ethnically diverse, and that are more in the tradition of the open-air bazaar—are light years away from the foothills of Universal City. The phalanx of personnel charged with maintaining the CityWalk grounds succeeds primarily in reinforcing the ignominiousness of the truly public street, exaggerating distinctions between some binaries (such as dirty and clean, public and private, threatening and nonthreatening) while blurring distinctions between others (tourist and local, architecture and set design, cinematic and geographic Los Angeles). Whether or not one spends money becomes increasingly irrelevant; the experience is consumed by all at the level of the gaze and, significantly, at the expense of other native markets throughout the city.

This politics of discrimination is claimed as an advantage for the consumer. In the end, the streetlike atmosphere of CityWalk is only that, street*like*. Characterized by closure, safety, purity, and cleanliness, this is the street of the anticarnival. Crowd control and invisible yet eerily present modes of surveillance work to create a sense of obedience and play a key role in transforming the street into a fishbowl. One local architect, Doug Suisman, has commented on the fact that the structure works to ensure a passive disposition from the time the visitor reaches the front door: "Everyone has to pass through a gate. . . . at a very subtle level, that puts you in a passive role."[59] Other "subtleties" continue this effect, like the two black-steel stairwell towers that ascend four or five stories high but lead nowhere. One guard I spoke with called these the "teasers" because "everyone wants to know about them." Although unstaffed, the twin staircases located at different ends of the walkway command attention, a reminder that someone might be, and in fact probably is, watching.

One of the most stifling effects of such measures can be appreciated only when matched against the larger structure's spectacularity. Because it offers itself as spectacle, CityWalk positions its visitors as spectators and observers, never participants or spectacles in their own right. Even the "street performers"—many of whom, as many local L.A. residents recognize, originally began performing in other, more "open" spaces, such as Westwood Village, Venice Beach, and Santa Monica's Third Street Promenade—must audition in order to gain permission to perform in what CityWalk's administrators aver is truly a space for all people. As one journalist has remarked of making street performers and public artists audition, "This place is run by a movie company; they believe in that sort of thing."[60] The point is not at all trivial; the performers at CityWalk function more as traditional "players" or outright actors, yet another way of circumscribing the visitor's role as spectator, shopper, tourist, moviegoer—above all, consumer.

With the full weight of institutional authority, the structure itself, so painstakingly constructed as spectacular, gives the sense that the visitor-as-consumer is merely an interloper welcome to watch for a while. In arguing that the mall takes pains to impart a sense of passivity to its patrons, I am not suggesting that everyone "experiences" CityWalk the same way. Just as meaning is produced by readers and film spectators in a variety of ways, so too do mall strollers construct their own unique experiences of the space. The point that must not be lost, however, is that the meticulously maintained environment and everyone from the architects and designers to the security guards and landscape artists work to minimize the kind of creative license one might bring to bear on the place during a leisurely walk down CityWalk's street. One of the primary strategies deployed to authorize certain experiences within the mall is the careful conflation of "city" with "cinema," a spatial and design logic wherein visitors experience L.A.—for better and worse—as "just a movie."

Consuming the Gaze

In *America,* Jean Baudrillard, with Los Angeles specifically in mind, writes:

> The American city seems to have stepped right out of the movies. To grasp its secret, you should not, then, begin with the city and move inwards to the screen; you should begin with the screen and move outwards to the city. It is there that cinema does not assume an exceptional form, but simply invests the streets and the entire town with a mythical atmosphere.[61]

I have intimated on several occasions that the city of Los Angeles imagines itself, largely, through the movies. Like the Hollywood sign and the Walk of Fame, monuments to the industry proliferate throughout the city. The profound influence of the film industry on Southern California's culture has been inscribed onto its very map: Fox Hills, Studio City, Century City, Culver City, Universal City, Hollywood—in each of these is the legacy of illusion writ large across the L.A. landscape. CityWalk continues in the tradition of Hollywood to write an Edenic story of a Los Angeles without problems, and thus its functional linkage between Universal Studios tours and Cineplex Odeon takes on great magnitude. It is of no small consequence that Jerde's architectural strategy took on these dimensions:

> CityWalk is bland, almost invisible, when viewed from the outside. Inside it's a different story. . . . [Jerde's] crew set out to fashion a three-dimensional equivalent of a movie about Los Angeles—the city you came here to love but could never find. They chose not to provide exact replicas of L.A. locales like City Hall or the San Fernando Mission, but to evoke L.A.[62]

Jerde's goal to "fashion a three-dimensional equivalent of a movie about Los Angeles" marks an important remove from reality; significantly, the architect wanted to fashion not the equivalent of L.A. (or part thereof) but the equivalent of a movie about L.A., essentially consummating the relationships among CityWalk, the movie industry, and the cultural mythology of L.A. they each promote. CityWalk is offered to Los Angeles and the millions who come to visit it each year as proof positive that a safe, clean, convenient city, although impossible to attain through local public policy changes and the restructuring of social and material relations, can be delivered by an entertainment corporation. The effect, according to Norman Klein, is that CityWalk's synthetic urban experience "has something of the relationship to the real city that a petting zoo has to nature."[63]

Certainly, as much as it is about Los Angeles, CityWalk is also about the movies. Of course, one of CityWalk's points, finally, is that there is no substantive difference to be made between the two. By linking itself architecturally and semiotically to Hollywood film, CityWalk is able to reassert "the movies" as synecdoche for "Los Angeles." CityWalk even "reads" like a Hollywood blockbuster: it characteristically sacrifices content and character to spectacle and "plot" (paradise restored). Indeed, despite a strong supporting cast of stores and restaurants, its main attractions, Los Angeles and the movies, are offered as the essence of the CityWalk experience. CityWalk clearly imparts the sense that L.A.'s cultural mythology is best preserved in an upscale, consumption-driven media environment.

It is worth noting here that CityWalk has revived an old tradition in Los Angeles architecture. As Maggie Valentine recalls in the title of her book-length study of the movie theaters designed by S. Charles Lee, when it comes to L.A. architecture and movie culture, "the show starts on the sidewalk."[64] At CityWalk, where in many ways the show

Figure 4. Fantasy for sale: Wizardz and stores like it evoke a primarily visual appeal while representing "Los Angeles" as reducible to a series of spectacles and consumer spaces organized around the shared history of Hollywood film.

is the sidewalk, facades and other visual stimuli play key supporting roles in creating the spectacle. On the one hand, the complex reproduces all the glamour and hype associated with Hollywood's grand movie palaces, such as the Chinese and the Egyptian, which were "designed as fantasies to help transport viewers into the make-believe world of films."[65] On the other hand, however, CityWalk continues a specific architectural trend that originated in L.A. in the 1920s, wherein businesses were built to look like what they sold. Ranging from the Van de Kamp bakeries and restaurants shaped like windmills to the Brown Derby restaurant (of which the Universal Hard Rock Cafe is oddly reminiscent), many of these structures were designed not by architects, but by Hollywood set designers who found that such architecture "proved to be a particularly effective form of advertising—a three-dimensional billboard."[66] In a classic case of form following function, CityWalk re-creates itself as a "three-dimensional billboard" for the city, as well as for the film industry's central role in sustaining L.A.'s culture and economy.

This emphasis on design is no accident, nor is it without functionality, for CityWalk's links to movie culture and the film industry, combined with the mall's hyperkinetic architecture, transform the primary act of consumption into a visual event. CityWalk makes the image of "Los Angeles" available, and thus most consumable, through its visual economy. As a result, "shopping" and "watching" become virtually indistinguishable at CityWalk, whose architecture and design activate traditionally cinematic modes of spectatorship. In capitalizing on the convergence of tourism, moviegoing, and mall shopping, CityWalk casts visitors in the role of what Anne Friedberg calls the "consumer-spectator," whose speculative desires define the available experience.[67] From an oversized, midnight-blue King Kong that hangs above the walkway, connected by a large neon pole, to the bronzed candy wrappers embedded in the concrete underfoot, CityWalk's designers clearly put a premium on creating things to see. At CityWalk, in other words, the credo of the beleaguered shopper seems less a sign of annoyance than the sine qua non of the whole experience: everyone here is "just looking"!

Although CityWalk may purport to be a mall, the fact remains that it is not the kind of mall that any self-respecting shopper would consider as a place to do serious shopping. Indeed, it boasts a scant twenty to twenty-five stores at any given time, and instead of being anchored by major department stores, it is connected to a multiplex and a theme park.[68] Exploiting at every turn the marketability of film in

general and of Universal pictures specifically, the mall presents itself as
a three-dimensional cinematic space that can be penetrated and actively
explored by consumer-spectators. Corridor walls are adorned with
movie posters, and the ubiquitous Muzak plays only sound tracks from
Universal-released pictures. Stores such as Out-Takes, moreover, liter-
alize the metaphor by allowing shoppers to pose against a blue screen
and have their images digitally grafted onto still images from their favorite films, literally projecting them into the screen space of the
movies, if only momentarily. The mall's next-door neighbor, Universal
Studios Hollywood, similarly sells the movies as an inhabitable space.
This motif is crucial to CityWalk's overall success; in the process of
making the movies seem tangible and inhabitable, so too, through its
collapse of L.A. into Hollywood film, does CityWalk make its version
of "Los Angeles" seem tangible and inhabitable.

Conclusion

Describing the "New Hollywood," Thomas Schatz has written, "Competing successfully in today's high-stakes entertainment marketplace requires an operation that is not only well financed and productive, but
also diversified and well coordinated." He also points out that since the
1930s, MCA has established itself as a "clear industry leader in terms
of diversification."[69] CityWalk certainly has proven itself a successful
brainchild of the ever-expanding entertainment corporation. Its success
has not been lost on heady MCA executives, either. "Using clips from
Boris Karloff and Steven Spielberg films," MCA, in the name of diversification through expansion, unveiled in 1996 a highly anticipated and
controversial plan to spend twenty-five years and 2 billion dollars doubling the size of the Universal Entertainment Hollywood complex.[70]

Initially, plans included adding nearly six million feet of new
venues—hotels, shops, a new "family-oriented" theme park, studio
and production space, office space, and the like—and slightly more
than that in new parking space. In less than two years after announcing the original proposal, however, Universal and MCA bowed to pressures from adjacent home owners and city council members and
agreed to reduce the projected expansion by 40 percent and cut back
construction time to fifteen years. MCA is proceeding with plans to
add more than three million square feet of new commercial, production, and office space; the first wave of development will include the
opening of CityWalk 2000, a 250,000-square-foot addition to the existing pedestrian mall. Universal has a history of fighting neighborhood
groups over the noise created by outdoor attractions at the Universal

Studios theme park, an issue it has chosen to address in an unorthodox two-pronged strategy: first, the aforementioned reduction in proposed expansion; second, the recent acquisition of more than two dozen residential parcels on streets abutting its property.[71] Although the short-term purpose of acquiring such land seems to be to provide a buffer of potentially acquiescent home owners between Universal's property and that of aggravated home owners, one wonders how long it will be before MCA proposes to incorporate residential homes and apartment complexes into its massive cinematic playground.

In the final analysis, CityWalk may indeed become a prototype "city" for the twenty-first century, a franchised or corporate-owned community designed, according to Jon Jerde, to "realize the fantasies of the local population."[72] A fellow architect also waxes rhapsodic about a future world populated by CityWalks: "Every city in the world is going to want one of these. . . . For years, places like London and San Francisco have fretted that they would end up being converted to theme parks—while L.A. fretted that it would never become a city at all but remain a sort of gigantic, characterless, roadside attraction. Turnabout is fair play. What MCA has done . . . is turn a theme park on the hill *into a real city.*"[73] Such a view is problematic, of course. For instance, one might apply to CityWalk Michael Sorkin's criticism of Disneyland: "[It] invokes an urbanism without producing a city . . . produces a kind of aura-stripped hypercity, a city with billions of citizens (all who would consume) but no residents. Physicalized yet conceptual, it's the utopia of transience, a place where everyone is just passing through."[74] According to the "just passing through" logic of CityWalk, visitors are led to believe that the problems of Los Angeles are always already someone else's responsibility.

Aside from drawing consumer dollars away from other shopping areas and tourist attractions in the city, CityWalk exacts a major ideological toll on efforts to strengthen the area's embattled sense of community. Norman Klein warns of the kind of future awaiting cities that continue to promote (spatial) enclavism, (economic) privatization, and (cultural) thematization at the expense of building ties between communities of different complexions and classes: "The future promises more pedestrian-friendly environments modeled on theme-park mall variations of real city streets. They will have to be policed intensively, or at least have complex surveillance, not to prevent crime necessarily, but rather to shield us from what may be a few blocks away."[75] Los Angeles seems perpetually in need of substantive, proactive urban reform. As (re)development becomes more and more the province of private investors, however, such reform seems likely to reproduce or even exacerbate existing divisions and tensions. Distilling L.A.'s urban geography into a celluloid playground, and casting its patrons in the role of postmodern consumer-spectators, CityWalk obliterates the manifold realities of the city, reducing its cultural, geographic, and historical diversity to a rather homogeneous city upon a hill whose terrain is defined more and more in terms of sales and scripts.

Notes

1. David Thomson, "Uneasy Street," in *Sex, Death and God in L.A.*, ed. David Reid (Los Angeles: University of California Press, 1994), 325, 327.

2. Mike Davis, *City of Quartz: Excavating the Future in Los Angeles* (New York: Vintage, 1992), 20. For more detailed discussion of the booster era, see Davis, 17–30, or Kevin Starr, *Inventing the Dream: California through the Progressive Era* (Oxford: Oxford University Press, 1985).

3. Jean Baudrillard, *Simulacra and Simulation,* trans. Shield Faria Glaser (Ann Arbor: University of Michigan Press, 1994), 13.

4. Davis, *City of Quartz,* 18.

5. Ibid., 7.

6. A partial list of films set in and about Los Angeles from the past ten or fifteen years evidences the trouble even the film industry has had representing the city as a Pacific paradise. Whereas some films, such as *Down and Out in Beverly Hills* (1986) and *Pretty Woman* (1990), continued to render L.A. as a fairy tale waiting to happen, many others challenged such depictions. Dystopic science fiction/cyberpunk films such as *The Terminator* and *Terminator 2: Judgment Day* (1984, 1991), *Blade Runner* (1982), *Demolition Man* (1993), *Strange Days* (1995), and *John Carpenter's Escape from L.A.* (1996) have imagined L.A. as the model of a cold, cruel near future dominated by technology, surveillance, and bitter disputes between social classes as well as between humans and machines/computers. Meanwhile, films like *Colors* (1988) helped (despite that film's own racial conservatism) to establish a new genre spearheaded by young African American filmmakers who began to offer what to them were more realistic versions of what life is like in Los Angeles: *Boyz N the Hood* (1991), *Menace II Society* (1993), and *Poetic Justice* (1993) gave a new face—both urban and human—to Los Angeles film. Still others, like *L.A. Story* (1991) and *The Player* (1992), satirized the stereotypical L.A. that other films seemed to be perpetually reproducing. Films such as *Grand Canyon* (1991), *Short Cuts* (1993), and *Falling Down* (1993) used the city to map social relations and their (forbidden) hybridization and spatial integration, as well as the tragedies and dangers of anonymity and urban stress. Finally, films like *Who Framed Roger Rabbit* (1988), *The Two Jakes* (1990), and *L.A. Confidential* (1997) continued to be centrally concerned with Los Angeles history but refused to offer any kind of "paradise-by-the-sea" narrative of the city.

Perhaps no better (or worse) example exists than the otherwise forgettable *Last Action Hero* (1993), which can be read as a recent Hollywood reassertion of L.A. as a utopian space. The cartoonish white-collar crime world of sun-drenched L.A., where bullets only stun and all women come equipped with skintight latex, is matched against the foreboding menace of a perpetually dark New York, where single mothers struggle to keep their children safe from the harm that lurks around every corner. In the *Last Action Hero*, L.A. is a purely fantastic space; the city is the movie, the movie is the city. New

York, on the other hand, is L.A.'s evil twin, embodying reality and all of its concomitant flaws.

7. This sign appeared on Venice Boulevard shortly after the Northridge earthquake of 17 January 1994. The billboard stood sentry over the section of the overcrowded boulevard that had been designated a detour route for those who would normally have spent their daily downtown commute safely crammed into a traffic jam twenty feet above the street level on the then-collapsed Santa Monica Freeway. The billboard stoically faced downtown, staring down at the drivers on their homeward commute out of the city's nucleus and into the seemingly infinite suburbia that surrounds Los Angeles. As a manifest symbol of the city's semiotic damage control, the sign worked to counteract the growing unease of commuters who, until the earthquake, had never really been forced to descend from the freeways into the nether regions of the city. Rather, many had for years on end driven dutifully from home to work and back again without ever having seen the indigence and lack that dominate much of the city's landscape. Although the sign did not bother to go into details about exactly what the "dream" is, the onus of keeping it alive clearly fell on the driver.

8. Davis, *City of Quartz,* 230.

9. I should take this opportunity to remind the reader that, like much work dealing with contemporary issues, this essay is always in a sense swimming upstream—it is, in other words, always conscious of, and bound by, the rapidly evolving nature of its subject matter. My research on Los Angeles and projects like CityWalk has yielded one important truism: the city is a restless place, and often within a short time span the order of things changes dramatically. This essay focuses most directly on L.A. and CityWalk during the mid-1990s; although I have updated my research through early 1999, the urban landscape simply moves faster than most printing presses. Consequently, I encourage the interested reader to continue along with the caveat that nothing about the landscape and architecture of consumer culture under postmodernism is constant. To wit, additional urban renewal and redevelopment programs have been proceeding apace with the construction, the opening, and, by now, the safely described success of Universal's CityWalk. Several such programs that are planned, under way, or completed include development in Canoga Park, Pershing Square, Downtown's Grand Central Market, Culver City, Venice Beach (Ocean Front Walk), and Olvera Street. Most of these efforts rely on federal funds designed to subsidize recovery efforts from the Northridge earthquake of 1994.

Without a doubt, however, the most singularly important renewal program has been the L.A. Community Redevelopment Agency's (CRA) designation of the Hollywood Redevelopment Project (HRP). Approved in 1986 but only recently garnering widespread national attention, the Hollywood Redevelopment Project is a thirty-year development program that encompasses more than 1,100 acres of residential and commercial properties. It affects more than 37,000 residents who, combined, speak more than eighty languages, making the HRP the most populated and heterogeneous redevelopment effort ever undertaken by the CRA—the agency responsible for administering all government-funded urban renewal programs in Los Angeles. Evelyn De Wolfe, "Developers Hope to Recapture Old Hollywood Glitter," *Los Angeles Times,* 8 March 1987, 1, 6. At a staggering cost of $922 million, the HRP is also the most expensive redevelopment project in city history. The HRP is especially relevant to this essay because, like CityWalk, it marks a wide-scale effort (undertaken simultaneously by city planners and private investors) to intertwine further Hollywood film culture and Los Angeles's cultural geography. See also Duke Helfland, "Hollywood: Is It Ready for Its Close-Up?" *Los Angeles Times,* 10 November 1996, A1; Nicolai Ouroussoff, "Could It Be Magic—Again?" *Los Angeles Times,* 23 November 1997, F6; Robert A. Jones, "Waiting for Life on the Boulevard," *Los Angeles Times,* 19 April 1998, B1; Greg Goldin, "MALL-YWOOD," *L.A. Weekly,* 18–24 December 1998, 30–32ff.

Although CityWalk—unlike, say, the HRP—was not designed to rejuvenate a slug-gish economy, it has set a new standard for projects whose goals are to do just that. Not insignificantly, the planners of these projects more often than not measure design ap-proaches and expectations against CityWalk's example. To varying degrees, they re-produce the enclavism and sociospatial hostility toward public space embodied not only at CityWalk but around the city.

Notably, the only major commercial planning project whose priorities involve differ-entiating itself from CityWalk is the Olvera Street renewal project. Vivien Bonzo, president of the Olvera Street Merchants Association, has remarked: "We don't want to turn it into a Universal Studios [next door to CityWalk]. . . . We want it to be real. We want to pro-mote the [historical] qualities that are inherent here." Quoted in Tommy Li, "Merchants, City Hope to Revive Prosperous Past of Olvera Street," *Los Angeles Times,* 14 August 1994, 3. Olvera Street, touted as L.A.'s "first street," is populated primarily by mer-chants of Mexican and Central American cultural products. Add to this the fact that Olvera Street is in the heart of downtown L.A., and one does not need to push the area's connection to racial and ethnic (and geographic) otherness too far to deduce that per-haps its desire to remain "real" has been responsible for its decline in popularity among a consumer population conditioned to be skeptical of both the area and its inhabitants.

10. Although shopping malls historically have a failure rate of less than 1 percent, CityWalk has what might be the closest thing to a surefire profit margin; built deliberately to connect two already popular attractions, CityWalk benefits at once from the 2.5 mil-lion locals who visit the complex to see movies and concerts at the Universal Cineplex and the adjacent Universal Amphitheatre annually, from the 4.5 million tourists who come for the Universal Studios tours, and from the more than a million residents who come specifically to visit the shopping area. In this essay, I am concerned primarily with the roughly 3.5 million people who reside locally.

11. Guy Debord, *The Society of the Spectacle,* trans. Donald Nicholson-Smith (New York: Zone, 1994), 12.

12. Patrice Apodaca, "MCA's CityWalk Has 'em Strolling in the Aisles," *Los Angeles Times,* 12 June 1993, D1.

13. Quoted in Amy Wallace, "Like It's So L.A.! Not Really," *Los Angeles Times,* 29 February 1992, A1.

14. Not coincidentally, the other end of CityWalk also relies on metaphors of the ocean: a large wave tank in front of the Current Wave, a store full of miscellaneous trendy items, also draws a connection to the Pacific.

15. See Universal CityWalk's home page at http://www.mca.com/citywalk.

16. Ibid.

17. According to the CityWalk Web site, CityWalk and the Cineplex Odeon even offer a Cinema Concierge Club that allows frequent moviegoers to get priority seating at any CityWalk restaurant if they are on their way to a movie.

18. Wolfgang Puck's has, in the past five years or so, become its own trendy California cuisine chain. Like its original location at CityWalk, other sites continue to associate the chain's titular owner with the glitz of Hollywood and the pomp of upscale shopping neighborhoods—West Hollywood's Sunset Village and Santa Monica's Third Street Promenade, for instance.

19. Doug Smith, in "CityWalk Opens at Universal Entertainment," (*Los Angeles Times,* 25 May 1993, B1), reports that the UCLA Extension Center, the Upstart Crow (CityWalk's bookstore), and the Nature Co. were specifically requested by local home owners and agreed to by CityWalk's planners.

20. Ibid. The new Hard Rock Cafe is not meant to be considered officially part of CityWalk. Instead, planners note, it is the first new anchor of a proposed expansion that will add more than 250,000 square feet to CityWalk in an addition to be called CityWalk 2000.

21. Douglas Gomery, *Shared Pleasures: A History of Movie Presentation in the United States* (Madison: University of Wisconsin Press, 1992), 107–8; for an extended discussion on the history of Cineplex, see 105–14. Recent years have seen the Brentwood multiplex close in the face of redevelopment projects in West L.A.

22. Norman Klein, "A Glittery Bit of Urban Make-Believe," *Los Angeles Times*, 18 July 1993, B17.

23. Aaron Curtiss, "At CityWalk, the Real City Intrudes on the 'Fake One,'" *Los Angeles Times*, 13 August 1994, B1.

24. Quoted in Aaron Latham, "The Walk in L.A.," *New York Times*, 11 September 1994, sec. 5, p. 27.

25. Suzan Ayscough and Judy Brennan, "Will Movie Meccas Do the Right Thing?" *Variety*, 12 July 1993, 69.

26. Quoted in Allison Silver, "Jon Jerde: Pioneering Architect Who Put 'Experience' into Downtowns," *Los Angeles Times*, 20 December 1998, M3, emphasis added.

27. Norman Klein, "The Price of Safety at the Mall," *Los Angeles Times*, 28 November, 1993, B15. On the topic of targeting specific groups as potential troublemakers—among them "panhandlers" and teens of color—former MCA president Lawrence Spungin has remarked: "We are not making a demographic selection. . . . We are making sure that people who come here behave in a certain way." Quoted in David Wharton, "Walk on the Mild Side," *Los Angeles Times*, 27 May 1994, 10.

28. Quoted in Ayscough and Brennan, "Will Movie Meccas Do the Right Thing?" 69.

29. It is worth noting here that in October 1998, Cineplex Odeon participated with several other area theaters in Hollywood in hosting the second annual Los Angeles International Film Festival, which featured, among other things, an extensive roster of Latino films. I would argue that such participation is not necessarily a harbinger of a kinder, gentler CityWalk, but rather that such a decision is commensurate with the complex's ongoing efforts to attach itself to certain middle- and upper-middle-class forms of leisure and consumption. In a city such as L.A., hosting an international film festival is likely to be more about reaping good publicity and healthy box-office receipts than about ushering in a new racial politics.

30. Chuck Philips, "MCA Offers $200 Million to Acquire a 50% Stake in Interscope Records," *Los Angeles Times*, 19 January 1996, D1. See also a letter to the editor by William Chitwood, "Perspective on Corporate Responsibility, Still Peddling Filth for Profit," *Los Angeles Times*, 19 January 1997, B17.

31. Quoted in Carla Hall, "Theater Chain's Action Triggers Cries of Racism," *Los Angeles Times*, 25 July 1993, A1.

32. Gomery, *Shared Pleasures*, 110.

33. Ayscough and Brennan, "Will Movie Meccas Do the Right Thing?" 69.

34. Sharon Zukin, *Landscapes of Power: From Detroit to Disneyworld* (Los Angeles: University of California Press, 1991), 218, 13.

35. Curtiss, "At CityWalk the Real City Intrudes," B1.

36. Latham, "The Walk in L.A.," sec. 5, p. 27; Herbert Muschamp, "Who Should Define a City?" *New York Times*, 15 August 1993, sec. 2, p. 32.

37. Robin Wood, "Papering the Cracks: Fantasy and Ideology in the Reagan Era," in *Movies and Mass Culture*, ed. John Belton (New Brunswick, N.J.: Rutgers University Press, 1996), 205.

38. Donald Shillingburg, "Entertainment Drives Retail," *Architectural Record*, August 1992, 86.

39. Interestingly, over the past several years, a number of strip malls in communities such as the San Fernando Valley and West L.A. have inverted this design trope. Since the high-profile looting during the 1992 riots, many businesses are literally turning their backs to the street. Rather than boasting paned-glass facades, many new buildings minimize or completely eliminate street-side windows. Again, this is usually couched in the

rhetoric of community building, as such businesses gladly sacrifice whatever incidental business they may have attracted from random passersby in order to effect a sense of "neighborhood." Those who live nearby know what is inside these "corner stores" already, and those ne'er-do-wells from outside the area who might mean harm to such places will have a harder time gaining access.

For fuller discussions of the history of retail architecture and design in Los Angeles, see Sam Hall Kaplan, *L.A. Lost and Found: An Architectural History of Los Angeles* (New York: Crown, 1987); Richard Longstreth, *City Center to Regional Mall: Architecture, the Automobile, and Retailing in Los Angeles, 1920–1950* (Cambridge: MIT Press, 1997).

40. Quoted in Shillingburg, "Entertainment Drives Retail," 86.

41. Richard V. Francaviglia, *Main Street Revisited: Time, Space, and Image Building in Small Town America* (Iowa City: Iowa University Press, 1996), xix.

42. Ibid., 164. For an extended discussion on Disney's Main Street USA and on the "malling" of Main Street, see Francaviglia's chapter 3, "Image Building and Main Street."

43. Klein, "A Glittery Bit of Urban Make-Believe," B17.

44. Quoted in Nancy Spiller, "There's No There Here, Either," *Mother Jones,* January/February 1993, 14.

45. Davis, *City of Quartz,* 153.

46. Ibid., 224.

47. New York City, on one important level, serves as a counterexample to Los Angeles. Its primarily vertical integration creates opportunities (necessities) for frequent interactions among people from every socioeconomic class and racial and ethnic background. The "street" in New York City does not evince the same sense of opprobrium and dread as it does in Los Angeles. Downtown L.A. is perhaps the best example of this fear enacted at the level of architecture. Fredric Jameson's discussion of the Bonaventure Hotel and its structural "border control" in *Postmodernism, or the Cultural Logic of Late Capitalism* (Durham, N.C.: Duke University Press, 1984) is now a landmark model for interpreting spatial constructions as cultural texts. Davis elaborates on other structural components of the downtown business sector, which draws thousands of commuters from the wealthiest communities around it, even while the area has been economically deracinated. Massive parking garages are located immediately across from key freeway off-ramps to shuttle workers quickly into the protected space of the workplace, and the cores of downtown superstructures and skyscrapers are connected by what Davis describes as "ramparts and elevated pedways" to minimize further the need for workers to descend completely to street level. Remarking further on the culture of the workplace community, Davis notes, "In contrast to the mean streets outside . . . [enclosed and secured] parking structures [of the downtown office buildings] incorporate beautifully landscaped microparks, and one even boasts a food court, picnic area, and historical exhibit." Mike Davis, "Fortress Los Angeles," in *Variations on a Theme Park: The New American City and the End of Public Space,* ed. Michael Sorkin (New York: Hill & Wang, 1992), 159, 163.

48. It is also worth noting a similarly ironic historical coincidence: Walt Disney formally opened Disneyland to the pubic almost a year to the day after the completion of the Watts Towers; although the towers did not become an emblem of the vitality and enduring spirit of the predominantly African American community of Watts overnight, they have, in the wake of the 1965 Watts riots and now the 1992 "civil unrest," become an icon of a Los Angeles culturally and geographically distinct and distant from the thematized versions that seem to ring the city.

49. If CityWalk's high-profile opening did not offer enough of a contrast to more traditional forms of urban renewal such as those undertaken by the RLA, one need only look to the Hollywood Redevelopment Project, which had been approved in 1986 by the Community Redevelopment Agency. The HRP represents, at a cost to the city of almost

one billion dollars, a thirty-year commitment by the city to revitalize Hollywood as the capital of the entertainment industry. The operating budgets of similar CRA-funded redevelopment projects designed to respond more directly to infrastructural and economic damage sustained by communities during the 1992 civil unrest were dwarfed by the dizzying price tag approved by the CRA to stimulate growth of the retail, commercial, and entertainment-industrial sectors of Hollywood.

50. Patrice Apodaca, "High Hopes for High-Tech CityWalk Retail," *Los Angeles Times,* 8 June 1993, 12.

51. Wharton, "A Walk on the Mild Side," 10.

52. Quoted in Wallace, "Like It's So L.A.!" A1.

53. Because Venice is its own municipality, the Los Angeles Police Department has no jurisdiction there. Like other parts of the larger L.A. area—such as Universal City and West Hollywood—Venice is patrolled by L.A. County Sheriff's officers. For an enlightening review of the various techniques employed by the L.A. city government and police department in handling the homeless population downtown, see Davis, *City of Quartz,* chap. 4.

54. Shillingburg, "Entertainment Drives Retail," 86.

55. Anne Friedberg, in *Window Shopping: Cinema and the Postmodern* (Berkeley: University of California Press, 1993), discusses the "mobilized" gaze and the "virtual" gaze, remarking in the opening of her preface, "Living in Southern California, one learns rapidly about machines which mobilize the gaze; the lessons of the everyday are learned through an automobile windshield" (xi). Her ideas about the "mobilized" gaze bear directly on the way the millions of Los Angeles County residents who rely on some form of automotive transportation experience their environments as being always reminiscent of a kind of cinematic spectatorship.

56. Smith, "CityWalk Opens at Universal Entertainment," B1. Although CityWalk is clearly not a "real city street" as Froelich contends, it did engage the city of Los Angeles and its Metropolitan Transit Authority (MTA) in a very real battle over the city's future plans for constructing the Red Line of its new subway system, Metro Rail. The Red Line is fast becoming the "entertainment express." As of early 1999, more than $2 billion had been spent on almost seven miles of track connecting downtown's Pershing Square and Convention Center with Hollywood Boulevard (with scheduled stops at Hollywood and Western, Hollywood and Vine, and Hollywood and Highland). From Hollywood, the Red Line will continue northwest to Universal City and on into North Hollywood, providing tourists with arterial access to the city's corridor of film-related theme parks and attractions. Greg Goldin, "Why Hollywood Boulevard Is Sinking," *L.A. Weekly,* 14 October 1994, 11–12ff; Hugo Martin, "MTA Raises Curtain on Movie Glitz," *Los Angeles Times,* 15 September 1998, B1.

Seeming to acknowledge the greater profitability of increased access, especially in light of plans to expand the complex over the next decade, MCA went the rounds with MTA for more than a year, trying to negotiate a complete restructuring of the MTA's Red Line Lankershim station. MCA wanted the city to reconsider the route and move the Lankershim depot a half mile closer to Universal Studios/CityWalk/Cineplex Odeon. After spending millions of dollars lobbying everyone from the mayor's office to the federal government, MCA appears to have rewritten the map of the city's "public" transportation system by working out a compromise that will share expenses for a stop on Lankershim Boulevard. MTA agreed to add entrances and exits to both sides (previously, these were to be only on the west side—MCA's property abuts the east side) of the street at a cost of $2 million, to expand Lankershim Boulevard and build new on- and off-ramps to the Hollywood Freeway at a cost of $4 million, and to shrink plans for a massive parking structure (turning that detail over to MCA, which is free to charge for the privilege to park there). MCA, who sold the city adjacent property for the station at a price of $8.3 million, will build a $20 million "people mover" system that will shuttle visitors from the Metro Rail station to the top of the hill. Hugo Martin, "2 Sides Near Compromise on CityWalk Red Line Link," *Los Angeles Times*, 23 February 1994, B1; Nick Patsauoras, "MTA Deal with MCA Sells Out the Public," *Los Angeles Times*, 20 March 1994, B19.

57. Susan Willis, in *A Primer for Daily Life: Is There More to Life Than Shopping?* (New York: Routledge, 1991), provides an interesting discussion on the ideological function of the value consumers in late capitalism place on such things as packaging, purity, and hygiene (see especially her chapter "Unwrapping Use-Value").

58. Arguing that the infamous "Mother's Day murders" were "family related" and therefore could have happened anywhere, CityWalk proponent Richard Kahlenberg's "Despite Recent Killings, CityWalk Remains a Safe Spot," *Los Angeles Times*, 4 June 1995, B17, signals the potentially disastrous impact that "bad press" describing a double murder can have on CityWalk, where advocates clearly depend on believing in the site's safety and impregnability.

59. Quoted in Wharton, "A Walk on the Mild Side," 10.

60. Latham, "The Walk in L.A.," sec. 5, p. 27.

61. Jean Baudrillard, *America*, trans. Chris Turner (London: Verso, 1989), 56.

62. Richard Kahlenberg, "The City on the Hill," *Los Angeles Times*, 23 May 1993, B15.

63. Klein, "A Glittery Bit of Urban Make-Believe," B17.

64. Maggie Valentine, *The Show Starts on the Sidewalk: An Architectural History of the Movie Theatre* (New Haven, Conn.: Yale University Press, 1994).

65. Kaplan, *L.A. Lost and Found*, 90.

66. Ibid., 90–92, 95.

67. Friedberg, *Window Shopping*, 4.

68. Although shopping may not be the primary experience at CityWalk, enough money circulates to make the mall quite profitable. It is important to note that MCA rents store space at a rate of four to seven dollars per square foot, nearly double the rate of every other mall in the area. Apodaca, "High Hopes for High-Tech CityWalk," 12.

69. Thomas Schatz, "The New Hollywood," in *Film Theory Goes to the Movies*, ed. Jim Collins, Hilary Radner, and Ava Preacher Collins (New York: Routledge, 1993), 29, 13.

70. Barry Stavro, "Universal Studios Unveils 25-Year Expansion Plan," *Los Angeles Times*, 16 January 1997, B1.

71. David Robb and Jeffrey Daniels, "Universal to Scale Back Valley Expansion by 40%," *Hollywood Reporter*, 3 July 1997; Diane Wedner, "Valley Perspective, Valley Voices," *Los Angeles Times*, 8 November 1998, B17.

72. Quoted in Klein, "A Glittery Bit of Urban Make-Believe," B17.

73. Kahlenberg, "The City on the Hill," B-15, emphasis added.

74. Michael Sorkin, "See You in Disneyland," in *Variations on a Theme Park: The New American City and the End of Public Space*, ed. Michael Sorkin (New York: Hill & Wang, 1992), 231.

75. Norman Klein, "Salvaging Suburbia," *Los Angeles Times*, 15 November 1998, M1.

13.
Shopping Esprit: Pretty Woman's Deflection of Social Criticism

Thomas E. Wartenberg

A central bone of contention among theorists of film is whether mainstream narrative film supports oppressive social relationships. Although contemporary film theorists have generally answered this question affirmatively, resistance to this global criticism of narrative film has recently been growing.[1] Increasingly, theorists are calling attention to both the narrative structures of individual films and the possibility of alternative interpretations in an attempt to show the inadequacies of totalizing theories of film.[2] As salutary as such detailed analyses of particular films have been, they have tended to avoid the question of how films can embody social and/or political criticism through their narratives. Even more significantly, they have failed to see that narrative films embody many elements that can conflict with, and even contradict, the films' overall sociopolitical messages.

This essay presents one example of a film with a complex sociopolitical agenda that can be understood only through a careful examination of its narrative structure and representational strategies. *Pretty Woman* (1990) is an example of what I call "an unlikely couple film," that is, a film about a romantic relationship between two people whom society views as inappropriate for one another.[3] In this film, a street prostitute, Vivian Ward (Julia Roberts), falls in love with a very wealthy and powerful corporate takeover specialist, Edward Lewis (Richard Gere). Edward's wealth transforms Vivian into an appropriate partner for a wealthy capitalist. Edward, on the other hand, is also transformed by Vivian from an obsessive corporate raider—with no place for intimate relationships in his life—into a "capitalist with a heart" who values the joy he has found through his love for this woman.

On the face of it, then, this story of the successful formation of an unlikely couple embodies a critique of American capitalism for awarding positions of privilege to those who do not deserve them. The narrative of Vivian's ascent from a street prostitute to Edward's romantic partner can be seen to demonstrate that it is a mistake to view class distinctions as reflecting individuals' inner worth as human beings. Vivian is a better, more genuine human being, according to the film, than the wealthy women with whom Edward is acquainted, and she therefore deserves the class ascent that Edward provides for her. Similarly, Edward's transformation from a corporate raider into a partner in Morse Industries—the very firm he was poised to dismantle—functions to criticize a capitalist system gone wild. As a result of Vivian's caring treatment, Edward realizes that his obsession with work is really motivated by his deep psychological wounds. By becoming a partner in Morse Industries, Edward channels his energies into a constructive form of capitalist enterprise. The film thus seems to embody critiques of masculinity and capitalism in its contemporary Cinderella story of two unlikely partners finding each other despite the social differences that hinder their search.

Although this account of *Pretty Woman* recognizes that the film's narrative has the potential to develop a wide-ranging critique of post-Reagan American capitalism, it fails to see that the film employs a range of narrative and representational strategies and techniques that contain and limit the critical possibilities inherent in its unlikely couple story. That is, although the film taps into a general hostility toward capitalist greed prevalent at the time of its making, it deflects the egalitarian thrust of its critique by advocating the legitimacy of both a "natural" social elite and a "kinder" form of capitalism. As a result, rather than making a significant criticism of America in the post-Reagan age, *Pretty Woman* celebrates this America as the "land of dreams," a phrase that the film self-consciously employs to characterize Hollywood, the scene of both its story and its creation.

Central to *Pretty Woman*'s containment of the critical thrust of its narrative is its use of shopping. The scenes of Vivian/Julia Roberts on Rodeo Drive are some of the most memorable in the film, as evidenced, for example, by their appearance in *Romy and Michele's High School Reunion* (1997)—both literally and as the subject of the girls' discussion. The issue this raises—and that will form the focus of this essay—is exactly what about *Pretty Woman*'s depiction of shopping deflects the film from making a significant critique of capitalism and masculinity.

Transformation as Critique

The first question that needs to be discussed is why one might take *Pretty Woman,* a mainstream Hollywood movie, to have any critical potential at all. To answer this, we need to look at *Pygmalion,* Anthony Asquith's 1938 film based on Bernard Shaw's play of the same name, for *Pretty Woman* adapts the narrative of *Pygmalion* to America in the 1990s.[4] As in *Pretty Woman,* the central subject of the earlier unlikely couple film is the transformation of a woman into a lady through the agency of an upper-class man. However, *Pygmalion* uses that transformation as a means for making a twofold social critique. Not only does Eliza Doolittle's (Wendy Hiller) ability to pass as an aristocrat show that the aristocrats' presumption of their biological superiority is unfounded, the understanding of class that emerges from Henry Higgins's (Leslie Howard) "experiment" shows that Higgins himself— *the* man of science—has just as irrational a view of his own superiority as does the aristocracy. The film makes the democratic point that neither the aristocrat nor the scientist has a justifiable claim to being superior to other human beings; the biology of the former is no more a justification of their social privilege than is the superior knowledge of the latter.

Pygmalion's criticism of the pretensions of the aristocracy involves its presentation of Eliza's transformation from a flower girl into a person capable of passing as a duchess. Eliza is able to pass as a member of the aristocracy because Higgins has taught her the social habits that mark members of that class, most centrally and famously those of speech. The story of the flower girl's transformation into a lady "fit for a king" criticizes the pretension characteristic of aristocrats that their class privilege is deserved. The film presents this privilege as just that, something that enables certain people to view themselves as better than others. It locates the real source of that privilege not in biology but in the social realm, that is, in the habitual behaviors, verbal and otherwise, through which the privileged distinguish themselves from others.

The film is able to unmask the pretensions of the aristocracy by means of its narrative of Eliza's social ascent because her ability to pass as an aristocrat shows that aristocrats are not inherently superior to other people, for Higgins's experiment has transformed Eliza into one of "them." This demonstrates that all a poor person like Eliza lacks is appropriate training; once she has received it, she actually conducts herself with a more authentic aristocratic bearing than do the real aristocrats. According to this portion of the film's narrative, class is not a measure of an inborn difference among people, but simply the result of the different training given people of different classes.

Pygmalion does not rest content with making a criticism of the pretensions of the aristocracy, however, but turns its critical eye back toward Higgins, the one who engineered the experiment in the first place. In a series of scenes that follow Eliza's triumph, Higgins is himself exposed as laboring under pretensions that allow him to see himself as better than others. Unlike those of the aristocracy, Higgins's pretensions are grounded in his scientific knowledge rather than any biological inheritance. But despite the factual basis for Higgins's assumption of his own superiority to others—he is, after all, a master linguist—the film criticizes his attitude as a masculinist failure to acknowledge his own need for those others.

Higgins's reactions following Eliza's victory demonstrate that his sense of his own superiority is really a moral failing. When Higgins and his friend Colonel Pickering fail to appreciate how much of "their" success is due to Eliza's efforts and skills, she leaves them. After they find her again, Eliza attempts to explain to Higgins how he has offended her. As part of her explanation, she tells Pickering that she owes her real education to him rather than to Higgins, her apparent mentor. Indeed, rather than understanding learning how to speak to be the means of her class ascent, Eliza explains that she sees things quite differently than the young girl who first came to Higgins's home asking to be taught how to speak "proper":

> It [being taught proper pronunciation] was just like learning to dance in the fashionable way: there was nothing more than that in it. But do you know what began my real education? . . . Your calling me Miss Doolittle that day when I first came to Wimpole Street. That was the beginning of self-respect for me. . . . You see, really and truly, apart from the things anyone can pick up (the dressing and the proper way of speaking, and so on), the difference between a lady and a flower girl is not how she behaves, but how she's treated. I shall always be a flower girl to Professor Higgins, because he always treats me as a flower girl, and always will: but I know I can be a lady to you, because you always treat me as a lady, and always will.[5]

Although this speech is ostensibly addressed to Pickering, its real audience is Higgins. Eliza is not simply telling him that he does not have an accurate understanding of how class operates—that it is how others treat one, not how one speaks, that establishes one's class position— she is also telling him that his continual belittling of her marks a serious moral failing.

As the scene continues, the significance of this latter observation is brought home, for Higgins is shown to be unable to drop his sense of his own superiority to Eliza in order to accept the intimacy that she offers him. In response to her demand that he treat her differently, Higgins can only respond with statements that assert his independence from her, such as, "If you come back I shall treat you just as I have always treated you. I can't change my nature and I don't intend to change my manners."[6]

The film thus exposes the important psychological function that Higgins's commitment to scientific objectivity, with its ideal of the dispassionate pursuit of truth, plays in his life: it allows him to maintain a pretense of independence and autonomy that lets him deny how important Eliza has become to him. Behind Higgins's commitment to science lies a failure to acknowledge his need for Eliza, his dependence upon her.

From *Pygmalion*'s point of view, then, the total devotion of *men* of science like Higgins to their research is a masculinist strategy for denying their fundamental condition as human beings, for seeing themselves as different from, and superior to, the rest of humankind. Unlike others, men of science claim that they do not need others, that their pursuit of truth sets them above the simple feelings, such as love and caring, through which people acknowledge their need for and dependency upon one another for their own happiness. But this flight from what I shall call our *finitude* as human beings is presented by the film as a real weakness of Higgins and his ilk, for it is based on their inability to accept the fact that they, too, need other people in order to achieve genuine fulfillment as human beings.[7]

This sketch of an interpretation of *Pygmalion* indicates the critical possibilities inherent in this unlikely couple film.[8] On the one hand, the film uses an ascent narrative to criticize the aristocratic belief in the legitimacy of class distinctions; on the other, the failure of the man of science to see that his own masculinist assumption of superiority is equally unfounded allows the film to criticize a use of scientific knowledge as an alternative grounding for class (and gender) hierarchy. With this dual thrust, *Pygmalion* stands as a radical critique of social hierarchy in general.

A Shopping Lesson

Pretty Woman updates the *Pygmalion* story to the context of American society in the post-Reagan era. Henry Higgins, the master linguist, has become Edward Lewis, a corporate takeover specialist modeled on the likes of Michael Milliken; Eliza Doolittle has become Vivian Ward, a street prostitute; and Higgins's bet that Eliza can pass as a duchess has been transformed into Edward's desire that Vivian pass for his girl-friend. Instead of the privileged aristocrats in Higgins's social milieu, Edward's social world consists of superwealthy American capitalists and their consorts.

Narratively, *Pretty Woman* tells the story of Vivian's ascent from a street prostitute into an upper-class woman through her relationship with Edward. Edward wants Vivian to pass as his girlfriend so that she can accompany him to a variety of social gatherings that he needs to attend while he is in Los Angeles for a week engineering the takeover of Morse Industries. Her success at appearing to be Edward's girlfriend allows Vivian actually to become his girlfriend by the end of the week the two spend together. Like Eliza Doolittle, Vivian ascends through her ability to pass as a member of the upper class.

The main narrative difference between the two films is that, unlike Higgins and Eliza, Edward and Vivian form a couple at the end of the film.[9] This is because Edward, unlike Higgins, has learned something from his relationship with his unlikely partner. Although Edward's obsession with his work is just as total as Higgins's commitment to his, Edward is changed by his interaction with Vivian. He comes to see that his obsessive commitment to his work is really a quest for dominance, one that shuts him off from genuine human relationships. Because Edward undergoes such a transformation, he can then acknowledge his own dependence on, and need for, Vivian, so that he and Vivian can remain together in an upbeat romantic resolution.

As a mainstream, Disney-produced romantic comedy, *Pretty Woman* might seem an unlikely candidate for a film with an agenda of serious social criticism. And, in fact, it does not include any significant critique of hierarchy. Yet the film does share with *Pygmalion* the basic narrative structure that allowed the earlier film to develop a trenchant critique of British society between the two great European wars. So what needs to be explained is how *Pretty Woman* is able to blunt the egalitarian elements in its narrative and end up celebrating the power of great wealth.

An important factor in *Pretty Woman*'s celebration of wealth is its substitution of clothes for language as the perceptual marker of class difference. Instead of criticizing the assumption of the rich that exter-

nal signs such as clothes are an adequate means for justifying class differences among women, *Pretty Woman* accepts the validity of that assumption in order to justify Vivian's superiority to the rich themselves.
As a result, the film deflects the egalitarian implications of its own criticism of Edward's wealthy cohort.

Pretty Woman's containment of the critical implications of its ascent
narrative emerges with paradigmatic clarity, then, in a three-sequence
narrative that focuses on shopping. In what follows, I will look closely at
the three sequences while asking how this use of shopping and clothing
as a sign of class identity for women transforms the egalitarian thrust of
the film's *Pygmalion*-like narrative into a celebration of wealth.

The first sequence shows how shopping regulates class distinctions by keeping the markers of class out of the hands of the "wrong"
people. Vivian has been given a large sum of money by Edward in
order to buy clothes that are more suitable for his companion than the
hooker's outfit she was wearing when she first picked him up. On the
"morning after," still wearing her hooker's costume and accompanied
by the sound of the song "Wild Women" on the soundtrack, Vivian
enters a chic Rodeo Drive boutique intent on buying the clothes she
needs. But a disdainful saleswoman virtually throws her out the door,
telling the astounded Vivian, "I don't think we have anything for you.
You're obviously in the wrong place. Please leave." Vivian's appearance makes her an unwelcome client in this elite boutique even though
she waves in the face of the saleswoman the money Edward has given
her to purchase clothes. Her appearance—the very clothes she is wearing but wants to replace with those she is buying—is viewed by the

Figure 1. Vivian tries to shop on Rodeo Drive in *Pretty Woman*.

saleswomen as a sign of her inappropriateness as a client in their boutique, money notwithstanding.

This sequence demonstrates that more is at stake in shopping in a capitalist society than simply the satisfaction of our basic human needs. It presents shopping as an activity that creates and reinforces our identities as individuals belonging to certain classes.[10] Not only does shopping determine our identities in this way, it also allows others to "read" our identities from our appearance. So when Vivian transgresses the rules by stepping out of her class position and entering the elite boutique on Rodeo Drive, the salespeople inform her that she does not belong there, for they see themselves as having to resolve the contradiction between her appearance and her presence in their store. In so doing, the saleswomen police Vivian's transgression of the established borders of class identity.

But it is not just the borders between different class identities that these saleswomen police when they prohibit transgressions such as Vivian's, for the film presents the rich as taking the ability to shop in certain stores as establishing a person's worth as a human being. Vivian's rejection by the saleswomen on Rodeo Drive is thus more than simply a prohibition of her shopping in these elite boutiques: it is a sign of their belief that she is not worthy of so doing, that she is less deserving as a human being than are their clients. The saleswomen here express a view of society analogous to that held by the British aristocracy: there are certain people who are better than others and who deserve their social privilege.

But another important thematic element surfaces here, for viewers experience the saleswomen's treatment of Vivian as *morally wrong*. Even if she is a hooker, Vivian does not deserve the rude treatment dished out to her at the boutique. As we shall see, this element of the film's narrative, one that links it to the fairy tale Cinderella, plays an important role in the film's containment of any egalitarian implications.

The introduction of this moral perspective transforms the film's clear perception of how shopping enforces class identities in American society. This is accomplished through the introduction of another variable into the equation in the next shopping sequence—Vivian's beauty—that links the film directly to Cinderella's famous glass slipper. Because she is so beautiful, the film claims, Vivian really *is* a suitable customer for the fancy boutiques on Rodeo Drive. By presenting women's physical appearance as a marker of their character, the film presents an alternative justification for class privilege among women. The problem with American society, according to *Pretty Woman*, is not that it has class divisions, but that they are made on an inappropriate basis.

The film begins to present this alternative understanding of the social and moral significance of shopping in a sequence that occurs after Bernard Thompson (Hector Elizondo), the manager of the Beverly Wilshire Hotel, where Edward and Vivian are staying, intercedes on Vivian's behalf after she has returned from her first venture on Rodeo Drive distraught. Thompson calls a friend at a clothing store and explains Vivian's situation to her. As a result, when Vivian enters this store, she is treated courteously and is able to purchase the dress she needs.

The payoff occurs in the next scene, when Edward returns to the hotel to pick up Vivian, who is to accompany him to an important dinner with the Morses. The film shows him entering the bar where he told her to meet him and looking around, unable to find her. After showing Edward in a long shot as he enters the bar, the camera then cuts to a medium shot taken from behind as he looks around the room, trying to find Vivian. The camera retreats once again to a long shot of Edward turning to leave the bar. Looking from behind Edward's back, however, we see that the woman sitting at the bar in a tasteful and elegant black cocktail dress is Vivian. When Edward turns, the camera brings Vivian into focus, mirroring the process of Edward's recognition of her. The impact of this recognition is emphasized in a series of shot/reverse-shot close-ups of them as they notice both each other and their noticing of each other. As she walks up to him, she says, "You're late," to which he responds, "You're stunning." Her response—"You're forgiven"—ends

Figure 2. Edward finally recognizes Vivian.

their interaction as they walk out of the bar arm in arm, the perfect couple.

This second shopping sequence establishes Vivian's right to shop on Rodeo Drive. The film suggests that she has a more natural right to shop there than many of the rich women who do so as a matter of course. That right is established by how she looks in the clothes she has bought. They look as if they had been designed for her—as we know they actually were. Because Vivian's beauty makes her a suitable wearer of this type of clothing, the film presents her as deserving to wear it.

The central claim of this scene is that Vivian deserves to be wealthy, albeit in a way that distinguishes her from those pretenders who habituate Rodeo Drive's boutiques. Her worthiness of class elevation depends on a series of equivalences. The crucial visual point that establishes this claim is that Vivian has the type of beauty that makes it fitting that she wear clothes sold in the exclusive and trendy boutiques lining Rodeo Drive. The stylish clothes available at these stores are not suitable for every woman. Not everyone can wear them, for they suit only a select few. Those whom they suit are those who appear beautiful when wearing them. But beauty is not simply a natural fact about women, according to the film. It is presented as revealing a real hierarchy among women. Those who, like Vivian, are beautiful deserve to have the social privileges that allow them to wear the clothes that suit their beauty.

Pretty Woman thus establishes Vivian's worthiness by means of a subtle visual strategy. First, Vivian's beauty is presented as a sign of her worth as an individual; then, because clothes are used to signify class, the fittingness of boutique clothing to bring out her beauty establishes that she really should wear them; finally, this means that she deserves to be wealthy, for beauty is the "natural" basis for social privilege among women. In this sense, it is misleading to speak of *Pretty Woman*'s presenting a *transformation* of Vivian's character. It would be more accurate to see the film as depicting a process through which Vivian's upper-class identity is brought forth from its merely implicit existence into a fully explicit one.[11]

But why does *Pretty Woman*'s substitution of clothes for language result in the containment of the critical implications of its *Pygmalion*-inspired plot? A first answer is that it represents beauty as a natural fact about women that legitimates a social hierarchy among them. This use of beauty entails a very different view of class than that of *Pygmalion,* one that relies on a trope from the story of Cinderella. Where the earlier film depicts Eliza's ability to pass as a member of the upper class as evidence that there is no legitimacy to class distinctions, Vivian's ability to pass is taken as evidence of her being a member of a legitimate upper class—as opposed to the wealthy impostors who now occupy that position—just as Cinderella's beauty justifies her ascent rather than the ascent of her sisters. Rather than pursuing the egalitarian implications of its criticism of the pretensions of the wealthy that their privilege is deserved, *Pretty Woman* uses Vivian's appearance to propose an alternative basis for women's class privilege: their physical appearance. An egalitarian social critique of class has been replaced with a view of an authentic aristocracy based upon appearance—at least among women.

That this really is *Pretty Woman*'s view of class becomes evident only in the film's final shopping sequence. This sequence takes place on the following day, when Edward expresses his surprise that Vivian didn't buy more clothes with the money he gave her. She explains that she didn't find shopping much fun because the salespeople treated her badly: "They were mean to me," she complains. Edward explains that "stores are never nice to people. They're nice to credit cards."

To rectify the situation, Edward takes Vivian to a boutique on Rodeo Drive himself. Although his ostensible goal is to get her a wardrobe suitable for her role as his companion, he has a deeper purpose in mind as well: Edward wants Vivian to gain a greater sense of self-worth from being catered to, hand and foot, by the salespeople in this store. To this end, Edward calls over Mr. Hollister, the manager of the store, and tells him point-blank that they "are going to be spending an obscene amount of money" in the store and that they will require a lot of people "sucking up" to them because that is what they like.

Vivian's experience of shopping is now radically different from the one she had during her first venture onto Rodeo Drive. Indeed, it functions as a moral corrective to her earlier slight. With at least four people attending to her, she has fun trying on different outfits. Her pleasure is emphasized by the strains of Roy Orbison's hit song "Pretty Woman," which accompanies her throughout the rest of this sequence, indicating that she has now become the "pretty woman" of the song's title. (The song tells of a man's fantasy that a pretty woman he sees on the street does not simply bypass him, but actually turns around and walks back to him. Vivian now qualifies as the sort of woman about whom a man can have this fantasy.) Her appearance totally transformed by the clothes she has acquired, Vivian is now a Cinderella waiting for her prince's final recognition.

After she leaves the store, Vivian walks along Rodeo Drive, a

Figure 3. "Pretty Woman" on Rodeo Drive.

"new woman." In a reverse tracking shot, the film focuses on Vivian, now wearing a long white dress, high heels, and long white gloves, her appearance totally transformed. Vivian's transformation is also registered in her bodily comportment, although the film does not thematize this, for she carries herself with greater composure and restraint than she did when dressed as a hooker. As she walks along the street, men turn to look at her. When they do, they no longer look at her with the leering gaze of unmediated sexual desire, as they did when she first entered the hotel with Edward, for Vivian is no longer a "wild woman." Instead, Vivian has now become a "pretty woman"—that is, her tasteful attire sublimates her sexuality in a way that conforms to the standards of upper-class taste.[12]

At this point, the film shows Vivian returning to the store in which she earlier was demeaned. She goes up to the saleswoman who treated her badly and reminds her of what she did. After making sure that the woman works on commission, Vivian shows her all the packages she is carrying, saying, "Big mistake. Big. Huge. I have to go shopping now." This incident functions as a sort of synecdoche for Vivian's class elevation at Edward's hands, for her return to the Rodeo Drive boutique signals an important consequence of that elevation: it *rectifies* the moral wrongs she suffered, including the one incurred earlier at the hands of the saleswomen. As a result, the pleasure viewers are meant to take in her flaunting her newly acquired wardrobe stems from a recognition that shopping has compensated her for the ill-treatment she received. The inclusion of this "moral rectification" scenario transforms the film's *Pygmalion*-like plot into a real Cinderella story that casts a different light on Vivian's ascent. Instead of portraying that ascent as a criticism of the injustice of the American class structure, this scene redresses wrongs Vivian has suffered and hence signifies her assumption of her rightful place. Because Edward's wealth has made this possible, viewers are asked to accept class hierarchy willingly as the necessary means for moral adjudication.

This final shopping spree ends with Vivian collapsed in a stuffed chair in her hotel room with a self-satisfied smile on her face. In fact, her shopping has satisfied her in more ways than she could have anticipated. Not only has she acquired a wardrobe that will allow her to pass as a woman from the appropriate class to be Edward's girlfriend, she has come into possession of a different sense of herself and her worth as a human being. Having all those salespeople make an elaborate fuss over her has affected her sense of who she is and how she can expect to be treated. She has now come to see herself as a worthwhile human being in a way that she didn't when she was thrown out of the first store at which she attempted to shop. Edward's wealth has allowed her to be treated in a manner that makes her think of herself as deserving the special treatment she received as a result of possessing that wealth.[13]

Edward's take on all this is important to understand, for it might seem odd that he has chosen to employ this tactic of showering Vivian with attention, of having people "suck up" to her. But Edward is clear about what it means to him. Throughout the film, he is portrayed as doing things not because he wants to, but in order to show others explicitly that he has the money to pay for the best that is available. So, to choose one highly symbolic example that the film emphasizes, he always stays in the penthouse, with its balcony, despite his fear of heights, in order to provide others with a clear visual marker of his extraordinary wealth. Money, for Edward, is a means of asserting his own power over others. And this is just what he wants Vivian to learn: that when she has money at her command, people will treat her as she deserves to be treated.

Thus *Pretty Woman*'s use of a narrative of class ascent achieves a result very different from *Pygmalion*'s. The earlier film uses the narrative of class ascent to criticize the English class structure. *Pretty Woman* uses the same narrative structure to criticize only the fact that American society grants privileged status to the wrong women. There are those who naturally deserve to be privileged, the film asserts through its tale about a shopping spree that brings forth a "pretty woman," and they are members of a natural elite, not the false elite of America's wealthy women. *Pretty Woman* accomplishes this deflection of the egalitarian implications of its narrative by reintroducing the basic pretense of the English aristocracy—that class distinctions have a natural basis—only the "natural" factor that grounds the distinction between the classes, at least for women, is physical beauty. Vivian's beauty justifies her ascent into the upper class, for it makes her genuinely superior to others, in the film's view, who only wear expensive clothes because they are able to afford them.[14]

Shopping, then, plays a fundamental role in *Pretty Woman*'s assertion of this view of class among women. By showing how clothes change Vivian's appearance and establish her as beautiful, the three shopping sequences establish the appropriate social position for her as a woman. Thus, *Pretty Woman*'s transposition of the location of a woman's transformation from the drawing room to the shopping mall changes the critical bite of the narrative of social ascent. Instead of implying that all people deserve the privileges reserved for the elite, the story now grounds a rather limited criticism of rich women as lacking the natural beauty that characterizes women in the real social elite.

Difference Re-Viewed

My discussion so far has emphasized how *Pretty Woman*'s use of shopping as a vehicle for class ascent contains the critical implications of the narrative of class ascent it shares with *Pygmalion*. This containment turns a democratic critique of social elites into an affirmation of an alternative basis for social privilege. In order to justify this view of the film, I will now show that *Pretty Woman* does actually contain the elements for a potentially egalitarian narrative that gets subsumed and subverted by the narrative of Vivian's ascent.

Early on, *Pretty Woman* presents Vivian as able to be more direct and genuine with Edward than the members of his milieu because she is working-class. This suggests that Vivian is herself more authentic and less artificial than the wealthy who constitute Edward's circle. The film thus embodies a moral critique of the rich, one that is contained by the film's subsequent affirmation of Vivian as a member of a legitimate social elite.

Edward expects people to suck up to him. This is his normal way of interacting with people, for his world is populated by those whose livelihoods depend on him in one way or another. All of these people—from his business associate Philip Stuckey (Jason Alexander) to the hotel manager, Bernard Thompson—are willing to prostitute themselves before Edward because their own livelihoods depend on his being satisfied with their manner of interacting with him. But it is not just people in his business milieu who treat Edward this way: the women in his social group are all too willing to prostitute themselves before him in hopes of snagging him for a husband. Because these women want something from Edward, they flatter him and even allow him to treat them inconsiderately.

The irony of the early scenes is that the film's actual prostitute, Vivian, does not prostitute herself in front of Edward, but treats him more like an equal than does anyone else. Indeed, it is Vivian's lack of guile that intrigues Edward and makes him want to learn more about her.

From their first meeting, Edward and Vivian do not relate to each other in terms that one would expect in a typical prostitute-client relationship. Edward stops to get directions in his fancy car—identified by Vivian as a Lotus Esprit. Vivian approaches the car, hoping to get at least one hundred dollars to help pay her rent. When Edward asks for directions, she first tells him that it will cost him five dollars, and then, in response to his indignation, she raises the price to ten. When he agrees to pay but asks for change for a twenty, Vivian promptly enters the car, takes the bill, and tells him that, for that amount, she'll show him personally.

The way that Vivian addresses Edward violates his assumption that other human beings are simply there to be ordered about by him. In contrast to the subservient attitude Edward demands and gets from his flunkies—what we see him characterize as "sucking up" in the third shopping sequence—Vivian approaches him as an equal, someone to be challenged. In part, this is because she is not in a position to expect more from him than some money for the rent. She has no reason to view him as a possible partner, someone who needs to be flattered and played up to as part of a seduction. To a certain extent, this is because of her own character as an individual, as someone who is still "innocent" despite her social situation. As a result, she interacts with him genuinely instead of simply flattering him. Because Vivian does not treat Edward in the way he has become accustomed to being treated, she forces him to consider exactly who she is.

In its early scenes, then, *Pretty Woman* presents a very different understanding of class from that apparent in the shopping sequences as discussed above. Here, the class difference between Edward and Vivian is presented as enhancing, rather than detracting from, their relationship. The film does this by showing how class status affects the manner in which people interact with one another. Because she is an outsider and cannot realistically hope to have a "relationship" with Edward, Vivian does not react to him through the network of social expectations that affects the manner in which most women of his class do. Although we might expect this working woman to be deferential to this obviously wealthy man, Vivian violates our expectations—and his. Her lack of deference, her willingness to treat him as just an ordinary guy, first allows Edward to see Vivian as more than a young prostitute and to move beyond an understanding of who she could be for him that is determined exclusively by her profession.

In these early scenes, then, *Pretty Woman* presents a critique of post-Reagan America's upper class. The rich are shown to be a set of sycophants who are more accurately described as prostitutes than the real prostitute at the center of the film. Their desire for more money and prestige makes their social interactions into manipulative scenarios whose intended outcome is only the enhancement of their position. From this perspective, Vivian's straightforward and down-to-earth manner gives her a moral authority that is lacking in the wealthy women and men who surround Edward. The film thereby suggests that life among the superrich is not all that it might seem, that there are deep moral failings among this group of people, so that even a street prostitute has a more authentic approach to life than they do.

Capitalism Re-Formed

So far, I have argued that *Pretty Woman* seeks to limit the critical potential of both its ascent narrative and its view of the wealthy as sycophants in two ways. First, it uses shopping to present a woman's physical appearance as the basis for a legitimate set of class privileges among women. Second, by treating Vivian's ascent as a rectification of moral wrongs, it asks its audience to accept hierarchy as necessary for redressing moral imbalances. But what about Edward's transformation? After all, I have claimed that *Pretty Woman*'s central departure from *Pygmalion* is its presentation of Edward as transformed by his relationship with Vivian. Doesn't the film use this narrative element to criticize the masculinist assumptions that have guided Edward's commitment to his career and thereby achieve a vantage point from which to criticize hierarchy?

Once again, *Pretty Woman* transforms the terms in which this narrative element is presented so as to contain its critical potential. Instead of developing Edward's acknowledgment of his own finitude as a human being into a significant criticism of masculinism, the film presents it as leading to an affirmation of class privilege, albeit on a different basis from that conceived by Edward's rich associates, for whom wealth is the only measure.

From the beginning, *Pretty Woman* presents Edward as someone who needs to be saved. He is clearly out of touch with the roots of his own obsession with corporate takeovers. Vivian's ability to show him how to return to his hotel is clearly symbolic of the role that she will play in his life: she will show him the way, that is, help him see that he has been dominated by a psychological compulsion that has robbed his life of its true potential.[15]

Edward's problem, we learn in the course of his intimate confessions to Vivian, is that his father deserted the family when Edward was young. His need to take over companies and destroy them, we are led to understand, stems from his anger at his father. The victory that he wins when he takes over and dismembers a company—his father's being the first—is that he corrects a moral imbalance by punishing an offender, even if only in his imagination. Of course, such victories are really Pyrrhic, for they don't provide Edward with what he really needs: an affirmation of the moral rightness of the world through a sense of his connectedness with other people, most notably his father.

In important respects, *Pretty Woman* presents Edward as having a masculinist sense of self in terms that are very similar to those of *Pygmalion*'s presentation of Higgins. Although Higgins is a man of science and not a finance capitalist, both of these men see themselves as better than other people. Their superiority is demonstrated by their adherence to particular projects: linguistics in Higgins's case, the acquisition of wealth and power in Edward's. Each of them also engages in this behavior, from the point of view of the respective films, as a way of denying his needs as a human being in an attempt to create himself as a person who needs no one else, who is totally autonomous.

Yet despite its presentation of a masculinist avoidance of the acknowledgment of one's finitude as a human being, *Pretty Woman* does not develop this narrative strand into a significant criticism of capitalism. Instead, the moral terms that it uses to characterize Edward's life as a takeover specialist as well as his transformation into a more traditional capitalist undercut the potential force of this criticism and present a more traditional capitalist elite as truly deserving of their social privilege.

An important step in Edward's transformation is his seeing that his acquisition of the Morses' company would be a morally destructive act that would not bring about the moral rectification he seeks. He comes to see that the Morses take pride in their company and that their fight to keep control of it has a different source than his desire to acquire it. Whereas he experiences the struggle through the lens of his moral quest to punish "bad fathers," the Morses see themselves as actually doing good for humanity through their firm and the goods it produces.

By presenting Edward as learning to make an important moral distinction between activities based on destructive impulses and those based on constructive impulses, *Pretty Woman* once again contains the egalitarian consequences of its narrative. The film asks us to accept the idea that there is a significant moral difference between finance capitalism, whose goal the film presents as the destruction of the firms acquired and thus the punishment of their owners, and more traditional capitalism, whose goal the film presents as the production of goods that satisfy human needs.

But such a distinction is inadequate to the moral complexities of capitalism. Indeed, the film's choice of arms manufacture as its example of productive activity seems a disingenuous hint by its makers that the distinction between productive and destructive activity cannot withstand critical scrutiny. Nonetheless, we need to understand exactly why a morally principled distinction between corporate raiding and running a family firm is unsustainable.

To begin with, the film's portrayal of the Morses as major players in the defense industry is implausible. Any firm with major Department of Defense contracts, as Morse Industries is alleged to have, cannot be family owned, for, as Tom Riddell pointed out in 1985, "defense contracting for the last twenty-five years has been concentrated in the largest firms."[16] The sorts of players he had in mind were Lockheed, Boeing, United Technologies, McDonnell Douglas, and Grumman, the five largest defense contractors in 1975.[17] Although a mom-and-pop or, in this case, pop-and-son operation might have a role as a minor subcontractor within the defense industry, no such firm could possibly go toe-to-toe with the multinationals and win.

The film resorts to such an unrealistic option because it wants to do two things: on the one hand, endorse the growing critique of the Reagan era's vast increase in inequities in wealth; on the other, contain the scope of that critique, applying it only to the *excesses* of that era rather than to the existence of wealth and social hierarchy per se. To succeed at this balancing act, the film has to exhume an acceptable alternative to the corporate raider to stand as the sign of the kinder, gentler nation America seemed to hope it could become.

The film compounds these problems when Edward attempts to explain his epiphany to Vivian. He wants to tell her that he has come to understand that his profession has nothing noble about it, that he can no longer engage in it as a means of improving the world by doling out appropriate punishment to the wicked. He makes this point by means of a rather complex joke in which he equates himself with Vivian by telling her that he has realized that "we both screw people for money." This equation of the corporate takeover specialist with the real prostitute takes place through an equivocation on the meaning of *screw*. Whereas Vivian screws people in the sense of having sexual intercourse with them, Edward only screws them in the sense of "to mistreat or exploit through extortion, trickery, or unfair actions."[18] Edward's attempt to assert a moral equivalence between his and Vivian's professions depends upon this equivocation. Although Vivian does "screw" people— that is, has sex with them—she does not mistreat them. Edward's self-critique is articulated in a form that compromises Vivian's integrity.

These two examples illustrate how the terms that *Pretty Woman* uses to tell its story contain its critical social implications. Edward's transformation from a corporate raider into a more traditional capitalist is supposed to embody Edward's recognition that his commitment to his career as a corporate raider was founded on unresolved psychological problems stemming from his father's desertion. But the very terms that the film uses to present this segment of its narrative undercut the possibility of using it to make a broader social criticism of capitalism, masculinism, and social hierarchy.[19]

Conclusion

I began this chapter by contrasting two ways of thinking about narrative film and structures of domination and oppression. In the body of the essay itself, I have looked in some detail at the narrative of *Pretty Woman*. My goal has been to show the complexity of the film's politics. I have argued that *Pretty Woman*, not least because of its glorification of shopping, deflects its own critique of wealth in post-Reagan America into a justification of an idealized earlier form of a capitalist elite. In this respect, *Pretty Woman* is very different from its inspiration, *Pygmalion*, a film with which it shares a basic narrative structure. Whereas *Pygmalion* makes an important and deep criticism of social hierarchy of British society, *Pretty Woman* strives to undermine the critical potential of that very narrative structure. As my discussion of the differences between these two films has shown, it is only through a careful examination of the specific nature of *Pretty Woman*'s narrative and representational structures that it is possible to understand its political perspective.

The lesson that I would draw from this is that it is a mistake to assume that the political significance of a film can be anticipated from its basic structure. Films with similar narratives can have different political effects as a result of their specific representational structures. As we have seen, prioritizing shopping as a means of establishing legitimate class privilege allows *Pretty Woman* to limit the potentially democratic critique inherent in its own narrative.

Notes

Material for this chapter was drawn from my book *Unlikely Couples: Movie Romance as Social Criticism* (Boulder, Colo.: Westview, 1999).

1. For one statement of the "global" view, see Laura Mulvey, *Visual and Other Pleasures* (Bloomington: Indiana University Press, 1989).

2. The attempts come from a number of different directions. Within philosophy, this view is exemplified by cognitivist film theory. For various examples of this approach, see David Bordwell and Noël Carroll, *Post-Theory: Reconstructing Film Studies* (Madison: University of Wisconsin Press, 1996).

3. For discussions of other unlikely couple films, see Thomas E. Wartenberg, "But Would You Want Your Daughter to Marry One? The Representation of Race and Racism in *Guess Who's Coming to Dinner*," *Journal of Social Philosophy* 25 (June 1994): 99–130; Thomas E. Wartenberg, "An Unlikely Couple: The Significance of Difference in *White Palace*," in *Philosophy and Film,* ed. Cynthia A. Freeland and Thomas E. Wartenberg (New York: Routledge, 1995), 161–79; Thomas E. Wartenberg, *Unlikely Couples: Movie Romance as Social Criticism* (Boulder, Colo.: Westview, 1999).

4. Kathleen Rowe, in *The Unruly Woman: Gender and the Genres of Laughter* (Austin: University of Texas Press, 1995), 198, argues that *Pretty Woman* is based on the Cinderella myth rather than the Pygmalion story. As will become clear, I see the film as involving a unique merger of both these predecessors.

5. George Bernard Shaw, *Pygmalion,* in *The Complete Screenplays of Bernard Shaw,* ed. Bernard F. Dukore (Athens: University of Georgia Press, 1980), 267–68.

6. Ibid., 269.

7. In his reading of *It Happened One Night* (1934), Stanley Cavell raises the issue of human finitude. However, Cavell does not see the failure to acknowledge one's finitude as linked to a masculinist desire for preserving one's sense of independence from others, a view that *Pygmalion* asserts. Stanley Cavell, *Pursuits of Happiness: The Hollywood Comedy of Remarriage* (Cambridge: Harvard University Press, 1981). Here I ignore the film's ending, which departs from the play's.

8. For a more extended interpretation of *Pygmalion*'s social criticism, see Wartenberg, *Unlikely Couples,* chap. 2.

9. In her interesting essay "Pretty Is as Pretty Does: Free Enterprise and the Marriage Plot," in *Film Theory Goes to Hollywood,* ed. Jim Collins, Hilary Radner, and Ava Preacher Collins (New York: Routledge, 1993), Hilary Radner discusses how *Pretty Woman* departs from the standard "marriage plot," arguing, among other things, that sexual experience functions as a replacement for virginity as a marker of women's value. For a critique of her view, see Wartenberg, *Unlikely Couples,* chap. 4.

10. It is worth noting that clothes are not the only means that the film uses to represent class; Vivian's bodily comportment serves as another signifier of class. In the early

scenes, Vivian gestures in a wild manner, throwing her limbs about in a way that indicates a certain lack of restraint. Once her wardrobe has been transformed, Vivian's bodily comportment is also changed, and she conducts herself in a more restrained and tightly controlled manner.

11. Lapsley and Westlake make a similar point. See Robert Lapsley and Michael Westlake, "From *Casablanca* to *Pretty Woman*: The Politics of Romance," *Screen* 33, no. 1 (1992): 27–49.

12. This scene exemplifies the film's portrayal of different "male gazes," the idea that men do not see all women as fitting into a single mold.

13. Vivian's transformation parallel's Eliza's claim that she was transformed by Pickering's treating her like a lady. However, it is important to see how different the meanings of the two transformations are in the contexts of the two films.

14. It is too simple to say that the film represents beauty as a class marker for women and wealth as a class marker for men. Edward's beauty is also important to the film's representational strategy. It is also worth reemphasizing that beauty, although based in biological characteristics, is a socially constructed norm that varies from society to society and from social group to social group.

15. The film here gives a reductive explanation of the evils of capitalism, treating them as explicable in terms of Edward's psychological problems.

16. Tom Riddell, "Concentration and Inefficiency in the Defense Sector: Policy Options," *Journal of Economic Issues* 19, no. 2 (1985): 452.

17. Tom Gervasi, *America's War Machine: The Pursuit of Global Dominance* (New York: Grove, 1984), 332. The recent merger of Boeing and McDonnell Douglas has reduced this number to four.

18. *Merriam-Webster's Collegiate Dictionary*, 10th ed. (Springfield, Mass.: Merriam-Webster, 1993), 1049.

19. Limitations of space prohibit me from comparing the significance of Edward's acceptance of Vivian as his wife-to-be to Higgins's rejection of Eliza's overtures. A fuller discussion would have to emphasize how Edward, unlike Higgins, comes to appreciate what a woman has done for him, thereby challenging his masculinist assumption of superiority and completeness.

14.

A Wild Child Goes Shopping: Naturalizing Commodities and Commodifying Nature in Nell

Larry W. Riggs and Paula Willoquet-Maricondi

Only those who buy and sell truly exist.

Fortune, 1986[1]

Nature as Constructed Artifact

Despite its pretense of exploring the interface between nature and culture, the 1994 "wild-child" film *Nell* repeats the logic of a Coors or Jeep commercial. This ostensible discovery and study of an adult "wild child" really takes no risk of violating liberal capitalist orthodoxy or of breaking out of Hollywood's servility to that orthodoxy. Ending with an orgy of suburban banality, presented as a fruitful integration of nature and culture, the film reiterates, in the guise of "family values," the acceptance of scientific-technological discipline that mainstream American media artifacts nearly always endorse. In this film, one is never outside the culture of consumption. In fact, we will argue, the film identifies the consumption of processed commodities in general, and of commodified cinema in particular, with intelligent consciousness itself. *Nell* relentlessly repeats the message that its viewers have internalized, and been internalized by, technology and commodities.

The recent television commercials that we have in mind here are those wherein the more or less traditional use of the attractions of the bucolic to enhance commodities is intensified by the increasing size of commodities and people relative to the elements of their "natural" settings. The Coors "Tap the Rockies" commercials are typical, in that miniaturized mountains serve as the equivalent of a playing field for gigantic athletes, disguised as ordinary people, who play football and basketball among the peaks. "Tap the Rockies," of course, is both a beer-hall pun and a statement of the core intent of extractive capitalism.

The commercial slogan says, in effect, that the Rockies have no intrinsic value. Even as "scenery," or recreational territory, they have no value until they have been brought into service as decor, or backdrop and raw material, for the consumption of a manufactured commodity. Moreover, Coors makes a virtue of its transformation of Rocky Mountain water into its beer. Thus a Rocky Mountain high is achieved by the commodification of water, and the water naturalizes the commercial product. The miniaturization of the mountains expresses their insignificance compared with the act of drinking—and, by implication, of brewing—Coors. Any pleasure in the given world is, literally, dwarfed by the pleasure afforded by commodities. Capitalism is the regime of "added value," and the commodity comes into existence when value—in the form of profitability—is added to what was there before capitalist activity. It is the technologically sophisticated extraction and transformation of preproductive material that nourishes, educates, and entertains the "smart consumer."

This "genre" of commercials has recently evolved beyond the "Tap the Rockies" stage: recently, commercials for Jeep Cherokee have shown features of the natural world—mountains and waterfalls, for example—contained *within* the automobile. Thus we have moved from exploiting the attractions of nature-as-landscape as a setting for commodities—through the gigantism of the commodity relative to its natural frame—to the commodity as *container* of the natural. The commodity is now the *world* wherein commodities, including "nature," will be experienced. By clear implication, there is no world outside commodities. Not only has nature become the setting and the occasion for acts of consumption, but nature itself can exist only as a consumable commodity. It is thanks to the bounty of technological production, not to nature's bounty, that life is possible, and good. This is the world that *Nell,* like the commercials, conditions us to perceive as uniquely real. Images of commodities replace the world.[2]

Another important element in these commercials, and in *Nell,* is the assertion that happy social connections, as well as opportunities for enjoyable solitude, are created and preserved by manufactured commodities. Coors is relentlessly associated with team sports and with the exuberant expenditure of energy by groups of young, attractive athletes. If we "play the game," imagining that these people are actually "high" in the Rockies (perhaps in two senses of the term) then we surely must assume that they and the beer were transported there—perhaps in Jeep Cherokees! The solitary adventurer in the more recent commercial explores—with the help of commodities such as an industrially manufactured kayak—the "pristine" landscapes contained within his Cherokee. He seems to have been *transported* both literally and symbolically, or even spiritually. The social connections developed as *Nell* unfolds, and celebrated in a picnic at the film's close, are entirely dependent on commodities, including four-wheel-drive vehicles and processed food. Here, as in the commercials, nature can have value only as a "recreation area."

And this is just what the "nature" inhabited by Nell actually is. The lake on whose shore Nell and her mother have lived is obviously a human-made one. This observation, confirmed by the film's credits, defines this ostensibly natural place as itself a manufactured simulation: the location for the film is Fontana Dam in Nantahala National Forest, North Carolina. The lake is an artifact of the Tennessee Valley Authority. The human-made recreation area is, in fact, a result of nature's conversion into both an accessory of the productive system and a consumable commodity whose existence occasions the consumption of other commodities: four-wheel-drive vehicles and fishing tackle, for example. The sheer ubiquity of commodities as dramatized in commercials—cars on Arctic ice floes, beer cans and basketballs on mountaintops, fjords and waterfalls inside cars—states that they and the system producing them are universal and irresistible. This also disguises technological power over nature as personal pleasure. Experience itself is a commodity having its source in production. The "story" of Nell is that of inescapable obedience to the law of consumption, and it disguises that obedience as emancipation into the world of happy social connections and intelligent awareness. In *Nell,* as in the latest Jeep commercial, the commodity *is* the setting. Not only is mechanized productivity the means to provide abundance for all without political restructuring, it is also the means of realizing the pastoral myth. Of course, pastoral has always implied a "civilized" life in the country. Indeed, pastoral has always been, essentially, a picnic.

Like her home, Nell herself is not really wild. She is, at most, feral, and the fascination of the feral may well be that it permits defining "nature" as a defective form of the civilized. The film tells us, in effect, that Nell needs the same kind of *development*—of value added—that "improved" the area that became Fontana Dam, and indeed the entire "backward" region whose "value," in capitalist terms, was enhanced by the Tennessee Valley Authority. It has been argued that advertising's most important function is to keep industrial power constantly on display, to reiterate endlessly that industrial production is our environment.[3] It might be argued that this is a key function of the media in general. *Nell* certainly performs it. Moreover, it is not going too far to say that the fabricated "nature" of the Fontana Dam recreation area has much in common with a cinematic set. Not only technology in general, but also cinema in particular is being naturalized in *Nell*.

What is being displayed here is power—technological, political, and cultural—disguised as beneficent abundance. Any opposition to this power, any exception to desire for its beneficence, is represented as solitary, naive, and *deluded*. This mainstream cultural overkill defines resistance to integration as both misguided and impossible. As Kaja Silverman says in her essay on another wild-child film, *Kaspar Hauser*, the threat of nonparticipation by any individual is intolerable to the dominant system, so any such threat must be represented as both crazy and futile.[4] The systemic preventive against such a threat is the inculcated fear of cultural exclusion. *Nell*'s constantly repeated refrain is that society, as mediated by technology and commodities, offers needed help, as well as nourishment, to otherwise sadly isolated individuals. Technology, which is personified in the film by the simultaneously motherly, sexually attractive, and scientifically brilliant Dr. Paula Olsen, is power to help. Resistance to that power is disqualified as both perverse and futile.

So, the "nature" here is literally a socially and technologically constructed artifact. In a sense, the setting of the film is hardly more real than the film itself. That the lake is, in "reality," an artifact of the Tennessee Valley Authority seems perfect: Nell's gradual, painful "progress" into fitness for inclusion in a picnic admirably reflects the TVA's mission to bring civilized amenities and economic growth to an "underdeveloped" region. The artificial lake eloquently expresses the American myth of technological enhancement of nature, of value added through economic development. Fishing, picnics, and camping combine with the production of electricity to define this "land of many uses." Of course, the fishing is not done for the purpose of obtaining necessary food. The food is provided by the grocery store in town.[5] In a very real sense, Nell herself has always been at a picnic, although it has been a defective one: her food has always been brought to her from town. Until her "rescue" by society, a rescue whose fundamental instruments are science and its technological devices, her picnic has been a sad and isolated one.

Nell's lake is linked to the foundational American belief that democracy and social justice can be achieved through the technological transformation of the land and the resulting abolition of scarcity. The story's progress is measured by the arrival of ever more, and larger, vehicles in Nell's domain. Michel de Certeau's perception that stories traverse and organize spaces, or domesticate them, seems quite relevant here.[6] In fact, in *Nell,* the story is *about* the penetration and organization of space by people who are inextricably entangled with their commodified means of surveillance, transportation, and communication.

This "machine in the garden" trickery has always been a delusive resolution of the real contradictions of industrial society—a fantasized combination, disseminated by the commercial media, of two fundamental myths about America into a myth about America's unique ability, through commodity production, to resolve all contradictions.[7] The machine-in-the-garden myth is reiterated as a seeming synthesis of the myths of America as a pastoral land immune to the corruptions of European urban civilization and as a land where unlimited economic development is possible. The human-made lake/recreation area is a perfect concrete example of the attempt to realize this synthesis. At least since the mid-nineteenth century, American cultural products have attempted to reconcile the commitment to technological progress and economic development with the pastoral ideal that is also central to American mythology.[8] The ritual, almost obsessive, visual representation of natural or pastoral settings as being enhanced by the presence of machines, or of manufactured commodities, attempts to persuade that this tension can be resolved *through* technological development. Commodity production and consumption are represented as the means to resolve all conflicts and contradictions. We must accept the machine's presence in the garden as appropriate and desirable in order to experience economic development as necessary and beneficent. Commodification must be seen as always an enhancement.

To this placement of all activity within the commodity, *Nell* adds the implication that the commodity is also *within us:* even Nell has always been dependent for nourishment on commodified food brought to her from the town. She survives by taking in processed groceries. The fact that Nell has never been to town does not make her existence an alternative to the life of towns. She is not an exception to the Law that all must have its source in the "value-added" production system. In fact, the film seems to argue, we ourselves, like Nell, are nothing more than added value. We are nourished by processed foods; therefore, we are products. The "nature" to which we travel for recreation is also a product, and the commodities that mediate our interaction with "nature" and each other are products. Thus nature is neither a source nor, in its remnants, a compensation for our loss of an unmediated relation with it. The fabricated nature to which we turn for relief from city life is itself a product of technological production. As Jean Baudrillard puts it, supermarkets and shopping malls pose as "a new-found nature of prodigious fecundity."[9] This is a clear denial that society is, in fact, made from nonhuman, nonsocial materials.[10] According to the ideology endorsed by this film, *there are no* nonhuman, non-social materials. Another tenet of this ideology, of course, is that the unlimited invasion of nature by commodities is permissible—indeed, it is desirable. The circle is closed. There is no space outside the regime of the commodity.

Commodity Consumption as Enlightenment

The film's story is about the explicit containment of Nell within the circle of commodities. At the exact chronological and thematic center of the film is a scene that makes this agenda discernible. This key scene, which forces us, as spectators, to acknowledge our complicity in Nell's "progress," is her emergence into the *light* of day. Nell has heretofore emerged from her house only at night. Her emergence into the light ties together intelligence, cinema, pleasure, and the consumption of commodities. Jerry Lovell, the physician who has taken partial responsibility for Nell, lures her outside by feeding her popcorn, which the print on the bag declares to be "Smartfood." Once he has gotten her outside and expressing desire for the popcorn, Jerry says that Nell is ready to watch movies. Nell's humiliating emergence into "enlightenment"—she jumps like a dog or a sea lion for the popcorn—prefigures her lustful "shopping spree" during her first trip to town and prepares the way for her literally painful introduction into modern, rational, ruptured vision that will begin in earnest when she slams into a glass wall while running toward a "vision" of her dead twin. Nell must join us in accepting recruitment into the light. What Silverman calls the "terrible fall" into separation and lack is here represented as inevitable, as constitutive of our subjectivity as spectators, and as required for access to pleasure and knowledge.[11] Perception and thought are organized socially, or technologically.[12] Every screen is a mirror, and every mirror is a window through which *surveillance* is practiced. Being smart is linked to spectatorship—to the movies. Intelligence, then, is another product. More subtly, it is linked to being watched. What Silverman calls a fall is advertised by *Nell* as a *rise*. This, too, is in keeping with the machine-in-the-garden myth: integral to the myth is the assumption that technology will liberate the mind.[13]

Modern vision is predatory.[14] This is not the participatory, directly sensuous vision of Nell at night, but vision connected with a style of knowledge that is inseparable from the optical technologies developed to enhance that style.[15] It is the vision experienced by us, as spectators, and it is the vision brought into Nell's habitat by the film, and by us. We are integrated into this kind of vision by the opening shot, in which the camera and, therefore, we are soaring over the forest. The film will open the forest to "our" masterful, inquisitorial gaze. Our consumeristic, spectatorial vision, aboard its technological transport, moves through the world of phenomena like a whale through a cloud of krill. However, as Nell's shattering encounter with the transparent wall suggests, this predatory vision separates us from the very visual experiences we "take in." Nell must learn to experience her sense of unity with the world, symbolized by her twin, whom she thinks she sees on the other side of the screen, as an illusion.

The "popcorn scene," at the end of which Jerry says, "She's discovered popcorn, now she can go to the movies," links the film's major thematic elements: commodities, knowledge, nourishment, and the movies. In fact, we would argue, the scene synthesizes, as if they were inseparable, the consumption of commodities, the attainment of "smartness," and meaningful existence in the world of spectatorship and surveillance. It also makes Nell both a fully exposed object of vision, which she has been for us all along, and a person who vociferously demands a commodity. She is, therefore, just like us: we are, after all, at the movies, consuming Nell—and *Nell*—visually; perhaps we are even munching "Smartfood." The character Nell and the film itself are commodities. Heretofore, Nell has consumed unconsciously and at a low level. Now, she is explicitly on her way to joining us as smart, sophisticated consumers of information, as well as of popcorn. Hollywood's usual nervous excess in endorsing the dominant conception of things shows here: as is so often the case, we have a film that simultaneously dramatizes the superiority of the world of commodity consumption over an alternative and denies that there could be, or ever was, an alternative. This recalls Max Horkheimer and Theodor Adorno's seminal essay "The Culture Industry," in which they say that the enemy always being "fought" in mainstream media products is the enemy long-since defeated: the truly independent thinker.[16] In fact, the truly independent, or unintegrated, thinker is not allowed to exist, or ever to have existed, in mainstream cultural products.

Not long after this crucial scene, where Nell explicitly becomes a consumer, she literally *goes shopping*. Between the popcorn scene and the "shopping spree," Jerry and Paula have had an argument—while doing the dishes in a suburban home/high-tech houseboat—and Nell, traumatized by the fight, has begged them to make up. Here, the three have become an incipient family. Their departure for town is immediately preceded by Paula's dressing Nell and fixing her hair. Nell's reaction suggests that there is an innate, but as yet undeveloped, love of primping in her; the long-hidden wild child is ecstatically being prepared to be seen. Her ecstasy is prolonged by her first ride in a car: as the three drive through the woods, Nell is "transported" by the speed-enhanced movement of the trees. In town, they stop first at the sheriff's office, perhaps to remind us that this story is unfolding under the auspices of the Law. Next, they go to the grocery store, where the camera sensuously pans over fresh fruit, mostly apples. Temptation is obviously suggested here, and it is linked with the theme of emergence into the light of knowledge. However, the film has thoroughly disqualified Nell's original habitat as either a garden or a paradise: she and her mother have always been nourished by commodities, and Nell's way of life has been systematically represented as grim. The happy family is represented as a group of consumers of commodified transportation and food. They both take in and are contained by commodities.

Here, Nell is shown to have an almost innate impulse to consume commodities. That need parallels her allegedly innate need to look good: once she has seen Paula put some items in the cart, Nell begins grabbing whole armfuls. Significantly, she goes straight to the baby food and baby bottles. Here, the gradually emerging theme of family values is further developed. Commodities are linked to reproduction and family life as well as to nourishment. By producing in Nell a new consumer, Jerry and Paula are already involved in reproduction: they are meeting every couple's obligation to reproduce the commodity-consuming way of life. In this sequence of scenes, then, Nell is initiated into repeating the childlike demand that a man and woman be a couple, into producing herself for display, and into being attracted by displayed commodities. She is becoming an accessory of the social processes of (re)production. Moreover, if Anne Friedberg is correct in seeing shopping as a powerful metaphor for spectatorship, then this scene reinforces the film's identification of us with Nell's "development" into intelligent life.[17]

Lewis Mumford once said that the technological cornucopia is a magnificent bribe to make us forget what has been lost through technological development.[18] *Nell* subtly substitutes processed commodities for nature's bounty, as it erases nature as a source of nourishment and rewarding emotional experience. In fact, the film's narrative development is a circle of technology and commodities that is complete, and closed, from the beginning. The extended helicopter shot that opens the film implicitly structures nature not only as a landscape—itself always a cultural artifact—but as a landscape *created* by the most technologically advanced aerial photography. Therefore, there is a machine in this particular "garden," or forest, from the beginning. The forest itself exists for us as an artifact of that machine. Furthermore, we, as subjects of the gaze perusing the landscape from the fully "naturalized" vantage point of the helicopter, are also artifacts of the optical technology being deployed. The opening shot assumes, and intends to install, a desire in us for penetration and exploration of the space it unveils. We, and the garden, are actually *in the machine*: the images and our awareness of them are produced and contained by the cinematic apparatus. The world of commodities is represented as the world of intelligent consciousness; our own intelligent consciousness is to be experienced as an artifact, a commodity. Naturalization—what Paul Shepard calls "indigenization"—of the culture of exploitation is clearly exemplified here.[19]

Vision and Language as Salvation

Representations of nature as "beautiful" landscape are usually references to prior representations. In this case, our aerial arrival in Nell's habitat is reminiscent of the audience's introduction into the "primeval" jungle in *Greystoke: The Legend of Tarzan,* of countless *National Geographic* and Discovery Channel nature documentaries, and of the use of helicopters to enhance "real" experiences of the Grand Canyon, the Hawaiian Islands, and other natural sites commodified as touristic "packages." Consciousness created by cameras mounted on helicopters is integral, now, to our idea of "nature." Our very sense of what nature *is* is inseparable from its invasion by technology and from our freedom to soar powerfully over it. Here, the technology itself is invisible to us, the more securely to attach us to it; it is as if the images we see were unmediated, or as if our sense of sight itself were a function of technological devices. Reality, now, is not merely a visual construct but a construct of optical technologies. This is the real "ocularcentrism" of our culture.[20] The physical, sensual eye is an accessory of optical apparatuses. We are the subjectivity indispensable to, and produced by, cinema. The hegemony of this *cyborg* eye is inextricably linked to the aesthetic of open—and now aerial—views. The long history of optics, which ties the theory of perspective to the practice of cinema and links the Cartesian updating of Platonic philosophy with filmic lighting as the invisible medium of realism, has bound our idea of knowledge inextricably to our identification with cameras. Our desire to see puts the machine in the garden and thus rationalizes economic development. From the beginning, we are committed; our complicity is enforced. We "see" nature as already a culturally appropriated artifact. The essence of the story being told in *Nell* is that we *already know* the story; we inhabit it, and it inhabits us.

The distinction between nature and landscape has been erased, for us, by the ubiquity of commodities. A nature revealed to us, or constructed for us, by technology and filled with commodities is, like a theme park, a simulacrum, even if we are physically there. Our sense of what is real is thus inseparable from technology and commodification. At the same time, the space explored in the film is defined, from the beginning, as one that is destined to come under the control of science, technology, and commodities. In fact, the successful assertion of this control *is* the story.

Having quickly established "our" ultra-high-tech consciousness, the film shows us the garden's penetration, on the ground, by a relatively low-tech motorbike. We are already implicated in the assumption that we are superior to what happens on the ground. Accompanied by Nell's keening gibberish and intercut with her dressing of her dead mother, the motorbike's noisy progress makes us accomplices in this deadly penetration. We return to our more gratifying sense of omniscient presence when the arrival of the young man on the motorbike is shown to us in a way that defines us as "already there": the shot of his arrival is taken from an angle that makes it clear that the camera is there ahead of him. We are already trapped into the circle of cinematic pleasure: we are condemned to enjoy identification both with the characters and with the medium. We penetrate and investigate, but we also see in a way that is defined for us as already fully comprehensive. Again, we already know the "story." The fact that we are not in a pristine environment, but rather in a merely backward and archaic one, is emphasized by the high-button shoes Nell is putting on her mother's feet as well as by the motorbike. Implicitly, things have already been improved by our arrival, which is permitted by the cinematic apparatus. Also, we are given the enjoyable sense of being everywhere.

Cinema is an artficial perceptual discipline, but we experience it as lucid omniscience. As an optical technology, cinema is allied with the panopticist, photological, *photocratic* essence of modernity.[21] Mastery of mysterious, undomesticated spaces—first by sight, then by colonization—is part of modernity's essence. The inspiring, far-reaching view is possible only because of the technology of aerial photography.[22] Thus, in the very beginning, cinema is identified not only with but as the liberated, free-ranging mind. We are securely tied here to the complex of motives and technology that is the movies.

The boy on the motorbike is named Billy Fisher, and he is bringing supplies from the town to Nell's now-dead mother. His name connects him with the men in the story who will later fish in the lake next to which Nell lives. The substitution of a recreational and commodity-oriented conception of nature for the idea that nature is a nourishing and revered mother is emphasized by the fishing—probably for stocked fish!—and by the fact that Nell's mother has always depended on processed commodities brought to her by motor vehicle. Billy Fisher's arrival prefigures the shopping spree that will later accelerate Nell's integration into the dominant culture. From the beginning, however, commodity consumption is fundamental: Billy takes money from a purse, placed for him outside the house, as he carries the groceries in.

In addition to the technologically assisted eye and the commodified recreation area, in the beginning of *Nell* is also the biblical Word, or Law. Nell's seemingly prelinguistic gibberish later turns out to be composed substantially of fragments from the Bible. The wild child, it turns out, speaks in the very voice of the dominant cultural system. Nell's biblical babbling further defines her habitat as a distinctly post-Edenic garden and justifies the deployment of some extremely sophisticated technology to penetrate the mysteries of her "speech." In fact, the man and woman whose evolution into a couple and a family eventually becomes the film's central preoccupation are brought together by this mystery. The scientific elucidation of Nell recalls Francis Bacon's foundational definition of science as the "Inquisition" that will force Nature to speak her secrets, and that thus assumes that Nature's "secrets" are encoded, however deeply and obscurely, in our language.[23] Here, those "secrets" turn out to be confirmation of what we already "know."

The film's careful economy both presents and rigidly controls the threat represented by Nell's apparent "wildness." The first indication that she exists at all comes when Billy Fisher hears a wail from Nell, a sound that we are surely intended to think of as a "call of the wild." Then Jerry, a doctor who is presented to us as unconventional and hostile to institutions, is brought to the house in the woods by the sheriff. The man who is destined to be tempted by Nell's world arrives in that world accompanied by a representative of the Law. The threat of wildness is thus already neutralized, as it will be again later, by the discovery of a huge Bible in the house. The sheriff's call to Jerry to "get back to civilization" is followed by Jerry's wistful, curious reentry into the house. There he sees Nell, who is shown to him and to us in a pose that contrives simultaneously to suggest sex, childbirth, and a chimpanzee.

This vision of "wild" femaleness is immediately domesticated: Jerry falls backward when Nell slams a door in his face. In falling, he sees a large, old Bible. He and we are safe: in the beginning is the Word. In the Bible, Jerry finds a note from Nell's mother that says, "Stranger, the Lord led you here." Jerry says to the sheriff, "*You* led me here." The linkage of biblical and social Law is clear. The Law, in fact, is never absent, in this story. The mention of the Lord gives Jerry the opportunity to say that the last time he saw the Lord was in church, at his wedding, "and look how that turned out."

The film thus ends this opening sequence, and forecloses any possibility of escape from conventionality, by denying that Jerry is really an unorthodox man: at first "staged" as an opponent of institutionalized cultural norms, Jerry is normalized as thoroughly as Nell will be. Damaged by childhood loneliness and a failed marriage, he is, just like Nell, precisely *not* what we were very briefly invited—tempted?—to see in him. He and Nell do not share a true participatory awareness of the given world, or a legitimate wish for such awareness; what they share is the need to be integrated into society. Jerry is lost, wounded, bitter, and isolated. He is not independent of social connections; he is in pain because he lacks such connections. Like Nell, he needs to be saved by the helpful network of contacts that technology and commodities will supply. "Officially, this creature does not exist," the sheriff says to Jerry just after they've "discovered" Nell. The film sets as a problem— and an illusion—that anyone might exist outside the beneficent network of legal, social, and technological connections.

Since medieval Christianity declared war on the sacred groves of European paganism, hostility to the wild forest has been a key element in Western ideology.[24] Nell's woods are negated as a tempting pantheistic paradise by the cinematic apparatus; by the presence of the motorbike, of the packaged food, and of the sheriff; and by the Bible. In case that is not enough, the sheriff announces at the end of this first visit that the old lady owned, and Nell now owns, "half these woods." So what briefly appeared to be a remnant of the forest primeval turns out to be the outer suburbs. It is already divided into properties. As he and the sheriff leave, Jerry turns and says, "That's one seriously disturbed lady." He is referring to Nell, but he is looking at the lake and woods. From this point on, wildness and *craziness* will be virtually synonymous in the film. In fact, the existence of wildness will not be permitted, except as synonymous with defectiveness. Thus, to the extent that it is allowed to exist, "wildness" is just an archaic, defective version of civilization that needs, and calls out inarticulately for, the therapeutic technological ministrations of "advanced" culture.

Technology and Commodity as Beneficent Mother

Jerry immediately appeals to the knowledge and technology located in the city, at the college, for help with the "seriously disturbed" Nell. This appeal occasions the advent of the female scientist: Dr. Paula Olsen is introduced as the subject of a panoptical gaze and as the deployer of powerful knowledge and technology. She embodies the help that Nell and Jerry have been alleged to need. Moreover, in the scene where Jerry consults Dr. Olsen, Nell is implicitly identified with autism, her seeming wildness thereby again reduced to mere defectiveness. The character of Dr. Olsen provides another opportunity for the film to deliver the message that we live within a definitively closed cultural circle: the power of the dominant ideology, as employed and imposed by its agents, is independent of those agents' biological sex. Dr. Olsen deploys a sophisticated technology of "helpful" surveillance, thus demasculinizing the dominant gaze without in any way compromising its dominance.

We first see Dr. Olsen as a kind of omniscient presence: she is observing, through one-way glass, a woman, presumably some kind of therapist, interacting with a violently autistic child. Not only is Dr. Olsen observing without being seen by her subjects, but her reflection in the glass is visible to us as a kind of beneficent spirit overarching the scene of scientific observation. Surveillance and "benevolent" knowledge will be Dr. Olsen's "signature" throughout the film. As a spectator who is invisible to those she watches, she is identified with us.

Machinery is traditionally associated with masculine aggressiveness. Dr. Olsen, however, is presented as quite willing to be aggressive, although she is female. For example, the houseboat in which she penetrates Nell's domain, with its phallic arrow-shaped wake on the lake and its high-tech apparatus, is clearly a "masculine" symbol of mobility and scientific sophistication. This female "master" is the triumph of the regime of the commodified artifact. The female figure, who once symbolized Nature, now wields the powerful, penetrating technological apparatus. At the same time, the houseboat symbolizes the synthesis of home, workplace, and recreation. It is a comprehensive symbol of commodity culture, like a fully modern suburban home or an ultra-high-tech warship. By showing us an aerial shot of the houseboat looking like a penetrating arrow, the film associates the boat's aggressive, quasi-military potential with the beneficence of Dr. Olsen's expertise. Placing this floating listening and observing device under the command of a woman facilitates the film's representation of technology as a better mother than nature. Moreover, the arrival of the houseboat subtly emphasizes the fact that the lake is actually a recreation reservoir. One of Dr. Olsen's first acts at the lake is to put on a bathing suit and dive into the water.

Paula Olsen, with her knowledge, acquired in the city, will naturalize technological intervention in Nell's life. Dr. Olsen's field of expertise is, interestingly, linguistics; this qualifies her to repair the damage done by Nell's natural mother, whose distorted speech Nell has learned. The technological mother, or the woman deploying the high technology of science, will set right the situation created by the biological mother. "The things people do to their kids," Dr. Olsen laments early in her association with Nell. Knowledge, which the film associates with the high-rise city where the college is located, is an indispensable additive to "nature." Specifically, linguistic expertise, combined with the fact that Nell's gibberish sounds to us like a desperate, painful *effort* to communicate, authorizes this invasive intervention. It also links the technology with *communication,* repeatedly identified by the film as a beneficent social imperative. The Law, personified by the sheriff, led Jerry to Nell. Now, technologically assisted Knowledge will take over her integration into society. Jerry and Paula are going to study Nell, which will entail subjecting her to constant surveillance, in order to interpret her speech, to understand what she is *trying* to say. Nell will be integrated into the world of meaningful discourse. The idea that this surveillance and integration are imperative is emphasized by the fact that three months of observation of Nell have been ordered by a judge. The linkage of knowledge, communication, technology, and law is again underscored by the film.

Technology, and the claim that it both embodies and creates knowledge, reinforces advertising as a display of the power and beneficence of capitalism. Dr. Olsen is tightly linked to both knowledge, or intelligence, and high-tech commodities. In fact, it is through her character that knowledge and technology are dramatized as synonymous. Her irresistibility as a scientific authority complements and reinforces the irresistibility of the film's basic ideological position. Not only is Dr. Olsen making "movies"—or videos—of Nell, in the name of science, but we are watching a movie about this scientific rescue. The physical "transcendence" that the soaring opening shot invited us to feel is now linked, through Dr. Olsen, with superior knowledge as metaphysical transcendence. In *Nell*, not only is the system of commodity production a better source of nourishment than "Mother" Nature, but Dr. Olsen is both a technologically masterful female and a better mother than Nell's defective biological one.

Once technology has been naturalized by association with femaleness, a family can be formed. In fact, once Dr. Olsen's houseboat and Jerry's low-tech pup tent have been installed near Nell's house, the film's focus becomes Paula and Jerry's development as a romantic couple. "Dr. Olsen" becomes "Paula" when the potential for a romantic attraction becomes evident. Technologically sophisticated commodities are placed at the heart of sexual attraction and, ultimately, of reproduction. In a sense, what the family reproduces is the commodity-based economy and the technological transcendentalism, or "technological sublime," essential to American mythology.[25] Technology is represented as embodying mind and therefore as having transcendental, metaphysical power.

The fact that, in this case, the typically "masculine" apparatus of scientific rationalism is wielded by a woman universalizes the ideology and works to blur further any possible distinction between nature, usually gendered as "feminine," and culture. We have seen that the film makes technology, not "Mother" Nature, the source of nourishment, comfort, and meaningful knowledge; now we see that a female can competently deploy culture's most sophisticated tools. Dr. Olsen's femaleness will also permit the connection of commodities and technology with the reproductive couple. Family values are among the ostensible imperatives in terms of which the ideology is expressed and validated. The male/female division of labor, and of status, is reversed, or erased, in *Nell*. The uncoupling of technological mastery from gender, or the uncoupling of the gender traits associated with such mastery from biological sex, seems to reiterate the myth that conflicts and contradictions can be resolved *through* technological development.

In a sense, *Nell* is about the economic and technological *development* of women. To have a female scientist as the agent who brings the machine to the heart of the forest fully naturalizes the penetration of nature by machinery. The female figure, who long symbolized nature, now wields the apparatus that penetrates and erases nature. That this is a penetration is, as we have said, emphasized by the houseboat's arrow-like wake. The idea that there is or should be nature untouched by technological artifacts is identified by the story of Nell with the oppression of females, with their entrapment in a low-tech, unintelligent domesticity. Erasing gender distinctions works here to erase any legitimate boundary around the regime of the commodity.

So scrupulous is this film in its repression of any potential resistance to its message that both the narrative and the cinematography work to calm the fear that might be aroused by the technologically sophisticated female, even as they assert her presence. In their first encounter, behind Olsen's panoptical screen, Dr. Olsen and Jerry are filmed with comforting ambiguity: although he is seeking *her* scientific expertise and advice, *she* is seated, while he is looming above her. Later, when she arrives in the town on her way to see Nell, Dr. Olsen is wearing rather masculine clothes and carrying what looks very much like an Indiana Jones hat. She will never be shown *wearing* the hat, however. Interestingly, at the time of Dr. Olsen's arrival, the sheriff's wife is having an episode of hysteria. The technologically sophisticated—*almost masculine*—female is proposed by this juxtaposition as the antidote for female craziness, for *hysteria*. Too low a level of material consumption and technological mastery is women's problem, the film suggests. Paula at one point reproaches Jerry for thinking that "Nell's natural habitat is a primitive cabin in the heart of a forest." Presumably, we are intended to find the intensely technologized suburban home/houseboat more "natural." The forest is associated with a "primitive" stage of civilization, one where the oppression of women is obvious. We are encouraged to accept the implicit proposition that the "advanced" civilization represented by the sophisticated technology of communication and scientific surveillance has eliminated oppression. The solution to all problems is a greater abundance of commodities.

The story gradually becomes a comfortingly familiar one to consumers of Hollywood fare: after, and no doubt partly because of, their initial conflict, which gives rise to some updated Tracy-Hepburn-style repartee, Jerry and Dr. Olsen—who, as we have noted, becomes "Paula"—will fall in love, marry, and have a child. In fact, Nell, when it is her turn to incarnate us within the story, becomes a spectator of their relationship and begins explicitly to demand that they become a couple. The relationship between Jerry and Paula, which will become a romantic and reproductive one, develops because of sophisticated knowledge and technology. Nell's defectiveness creates the need for Paula's expertise. Paula becomes the carrier of the Enlightenment/Jeffersonian assumption that knowledge always creates power for the good. Her connection with skyscrapers, technology, and science, traditionally associated with masculinity,[26] has the effect of universalizing masculine values and legitimating that universalization. The erotic/competitive relation between Jerry and Paula attaches them to the system; their struggle for control of the apparatus ties them to it. The couple is the solution to the problem represented by isolation; indeed, the couple is represented as necessary to make civilization work and to reproduce and spread its beneficence. Once the "Nell project" is under way, the heretofore low-tech Jerry is shown searching a computerized database for information on "Children of the Wild." Despite their apparent conflicts, he and Paula are already partners. The pretense of a serious story about wildness and civilization evaporates into another Hollywood romance. Nell turns out to be someone who wants to be part of a nuclear family! Indeed, she functions as a romantic stimulant and a go-between. Perhaps her most serious defect, all along, was having been reared by a single parent.

Female Desire and the Naturalization of Cultural Reproduction

Remixing the gender characteristics that work for the perpetuation of technological capitalism is hardly liberating. Redistributing gender traits—and their social functions—between the sexes, as is done here between Paula and Jerry, is actually part of the cultural/political reproductive process. Normative gender roles serve to keep individuals— especially those assigned powerful roles, of course—from perceiving the need for real social change.[27] The gender characteristics continue to be defined in relation to the deployment of the dominant apparatus. It hardly matters who is driving the Jeep to the final picnic—or piloting the technology-packed houseboat. Masculinity is not just a "trait," or set of traits, characterizing individuals. It is part of a system of social relations of power. The "masculine" functions associated with exploitation, and with an aggressively invasive knowledge apparatus, remain materializations of power regardless of who deploys them. Paula, who, inevitably, serves as the agent of a male mentor, deploys a comprehensive techno-epistemological hegemony. Al Paley, Paula's clearly iconic mentor, with his aquiline profile, beard, and seeming gift for prophecy, helps us believe that we, and the film, can have things every way at once: his presence reassures us that the advent of the scientific woman does not destroy the familiar patriarchal social order.

By deploying the surveillance technology, Paula takes over what is often referred to as the "male gaze." Her clearly phallic television camera is placed inside Nell's house. She and Jerry, despite their superficial conflict, share the desire to learn Nell's language. Paula's apparatus, however, is higher-tech than his. Paula is the voyeur/authority who both intervenes when she suspects an erotic charge in Jerry's relation to Nell and becomes interested in him herself, through the typically masculine workings of triangular desire.[28] Both Nell and Jerry become objects of

Paula's desire, knowledge, and control. In fact, the story ties the ignition of a sexual spark between Jerry and Paula to their assertion of technological power over Nell. Paula, in particular, seems to be seduced by watching a scene in which Nell is physically affectionate toward Jerry, whom she takes to be her "guardian angel." The act of watching, in which we, of course, are literally participating, is represented as sexually arousing. *Nell* is a movie, and movies are erotic aids that are produced by a very sophisticated technological process. Perhaps the idea of forming a family with Jerry is already occurring to Paula; perhaps the desire to prevent him from succumbing to what the film subtly defines as a quasi-incestuous temptation by Nell is part of Paula's motivation. In any case, the *voyeuse* is seduced by what she is *watching,* as we are.

Soon, we learn that both Jerry and Paula were lonely as children: he, an only child, envied a neighborhood family with seven children; Paula's father left her and her mother when Paula was thirteen. Thus the lack of a "satisfactory" family life and of sufficient social connections is shared by all three main characters. Sadness and alienation are implicitly treated as equivalents of Jimmy Stewart's bad dream in *It's a Wonderful Life.* Family formation and a high level of consumption are the antidotes. The formation of a new reproductive family would fill the lack that is felt by Jerry and Paula and imposed on Nell. In fact, Jerry and Paula have first to force Nell to feel lonely in order to "integrate" her. She must dream the bad dream of exclusion before she can feel lonely and needful of social connections. Nell must be made to stop experiencing the presence of her dead twin.

The first explicitly erotic moment between Jerry and Paula occurs as they are standing on the houseboat watching Nell swimming, naked, in the lake. Again, watching is linked to the experience of sexual arousal. Part of what creates the erotic charge here is shared voyeuristic pleasure. Paula is actually watching Jerry, who is watching Nell. He says, "We shouldn't be watching this," thus suggesting the voyeuristic nature of their pleasure. Paula clearly suspects that Jerry desires Nell. During the course of this scene, Jerry's attention rather suddenly and arbitrarily shifts from Nell to Paula. It is as if Paula's questions about his attitude toward Nell had served to discipline him, to remind him that spontaneous unity with the phenomenal world is illusory and wrong. It is at this point that Nell, unbeknownst to Paula and Jerry, swims to the boat and watches *them.* Now, Nell joins us spectators, and Paula and Jerry have become the film's focus. Paula and Jerry's evolution into a couple and a family is represented, through our association with Nell, as the fulfillment of *our desire.* It is also at this critical point that Jerry plays, on the houseboat's stereo system, Patsy Cline's recording of "Crazy." The lyrics of the song link craziness with loneliness, and Nell's exposure to this media artifact signals that her integration into the culture of pervasive need has begun in earnest.

Shortly after this scene, Nell realizes that the Bible has disappeared from her house. She is thrown into a panic, showing us that even the "wild" woman is sensitive to the danger of living outside the Law. This reinforces Paula's suggestion to Jerry that any desire on his part for union with Nell would be entirely illegitimate. In fact, this panic over the possible absence of the Law is closely associated by the narrative with the arrival of Billy Fisher and another sexually rapacious young man on motorbikes. The potential problem of undisciplined desire is symbolically resolved by a scene in which Nell's pagan, nymphlike joy in swimming, and in ecstatic union with her dead twin, is domesticated by a kind of baptism. With Paula presiding, in a white robe, Jerry, looking exactly like Johnny Weissmuller in a Tarzan movie and wearing a prominent cross on a necklace, gets into the water with Nell. This is all designed to show Nell—and Paula, no doubt—that Jerry is harmless. It can be read as a ritual castration or as a ritual reiteration of Christianity's triumph over pagan animism. It is, more obviously, the formation of an orthodox family, with the technologically sophisticated woman, wearing the robe of authority and purity, serving as mother authority to Nell and as wife authority to Jerry. The lake, already a commodified artifact, as we have seen, now becomes a baptismal font; thus it, like Jerry and Nell, is cleansed of any tempting pagan vestiges.

It is clear, we believe, that Nell serves as an example of what Julianne Pidduck calls the "1990's Hollywood fatal femme."[29] Because she is "crazy," "wild," and incompletely domesticated or integrated into sexual orthodoxy, and because she seems to be a temptation for Jerry, Nell can, despite her simplicity, be connected with "femmes fatales" from throughout Hollywood's history. Pidduck's point is that recent Hollywood films have often featured women who threatened the viability of "white, affluent, suburban families."[30] Certainly, the redemption of the middle-class nuclear family is on the agenda in *Nell*. Moreover, this film resolves the nervousness about changes in gender roles that Pidduck sees in the films she analyzes by incorporating the knowledgeable, competent professional woman *into* the suburban wife and mother. As in the old myth about the improvement of the garden by the machine, we have *Nell* asserting that a new degree of mastery for women can enhance the family without fundamentally changing it. Paula Olsen is given, under Al the Prophet's benevolent supervision, the power of "naming, narrative,"[31] because she does not threaten to narrate anything but the same old story. The woman is empowered only as a quasi-technological extension and confirmation of cultural, institutional power. Moreover, by desiring that Jerry and Paula be a couple, the wild child/pagan femme fatale becomes the precursor of the daughter they will soon have. Cultural reproduction will be naturalized by association with natural reproduction, and the battle over Nell's fate turns out to be foreplay.

As Paul Shepard has pointed out, commerce and skyscrapers are associated with male gods.[32] Olsen is constantly connected with these. All the authority figures in the film explicitly link law, technology, and social control with helping, nurturing fellowship. Nature, which Nell both represents and negates, is synonymous with lonely isolation. Al Paley exemplifies the American tradition of metaphysical justifications for technological development. With his aquiline profile and his stellar reputation as a scientist, Al is clearly intended to suggest a prophet. Indeed, from Paula's first nearly worshipful consultation with him about Nell, he predicts the "inevitable" course of events. This is another element in the film that suggests to us that the story is already known, that it is implicit in the system of meanings in which we have our own meaningful existence. Al is able to prophesy because, in the world of commodities, all is mass production, or reiteration. The sense of inevitability in these events is made explicit when Al says, "We can't turn the clock back." Again, the idea that there might be an alternative to the high-tech city is treated as a regressive, infantile fantasy. Nell's vestigially participatory/animist consciousness is consistently represented as childish, regressive, hallucinating, and isolated.

The family picnic that closes the story celebrates the fact that there never was a real challenge to the established order. Nell, who briefly appeared to be an extradiscursive, panerotic menace, has literally called Jerry and Paula into conventional couplehood. Her "regressive," animistic union with her twin has "developed" into a sort of maiden aunt's solicitude for Jerry and Paula's daughter. In reproducing themselves, Jerry and Paula have reproduced the dominant cultural values. They are a family, and we are spectators; family and spectators are engendered by technology. In fact, in the last scene, Paula and Jerry stand in for us by watching Nell one last time. The ride to the picnic—with Paula driving—makes us fully comfortable with the vehicular invasion of Nell's world, and therefore with ourselves. It is also a final endorsement of the "constructive" redistribution of gender prerogatives. Nothing, in fact, is threatened by the advent of the technologically masterful female.

Nostalgia as Commodity

As always, the real threat, the threat never allowed to appear, is that there will be resistance to the "light" and the commodity, that there will be effective nonparticipation, that the story will not be experienced as already told and known. Silverman's recognition that the signifying order, which confers meaning, accepts no obligation to represent the given world and instinctual reality as they really are is apposite here.[33] Technological culture has no fear of female competence or of female desire as long as both are structured "appropriately." The true fear is that the *desire* for technological competence and for a high level of material consumption will die out. No such possibility is glimpsed in *Nell*. Being *at* the movies, like being *in* the movies, is a form of social solidarity that tightens the dominant chains of meaningful social association.

The picnic/feast at the end of the film improves on the meager supplies brought by Billy Fisher at the beginning, as the middle-class recreational vehicles replace the minimal, scruffy, low-tech motorbike. This is added value indeed! Billy Fisher's arrival opened the narrative, and Jerry and the sheriff are *fishing* in the human-made lake at the end. The course of the story also makes clear, though implicit, that this story is told in a normative discourse: it expresses a social Law. Here, again, the presence of the sheriff at the scene of the discovery of Nell and at the picnic is crucial. This Law, the Law of social connections enacted and reproduced by technology and commodity consumption, is disguised as a story. Obedience to the Law is thus doubly disguised: we see the characters experiencing the picnic as a pleasure, and we experience watching them as pleasure and knowledge.

To obey the Law is to consume "Smartfood." It is well to remember that our own experience is an act of obedience to the Law. We, too, are consuming a commodity that has been produced by the combination of technology and commercialism. De Certeau, who calls reading the fundamental aspect of consumption, would surely include watching cinema among the acts of reading whereby we interpret our way into obedience.[34]

Just as the film's beginning reiterates that our experience of nature is dependent on advanced optical and cinematic technology, the ending reminds us that our idea of what nature is and our contact with it are inseparable from the automobile. In the end, as in the beginning, there is no Nature; there are only higher- and lower-tech artifacts, well-made and defective products, greater and lesser abundance of commodities. The alternatives are the motorbike and the station wagon, Nell's distorted gibberish and Paula's technologically assisted linguistics, Jerry's pup tent and Paula's floating suburban home/scientific information center, Nell's literally benighted life and the cinematic "light of day" and of intelligence. As Guy Debord has it, the industrial economy has transformed the world, but only into a world of economy.[35] We are left to identify with a technologically generated family of spectators nourished by "Smartfood." Moreover, owning "half these woods," Nell is, and always was, *rich*. Her discovery and rescue have revealed the wealth her backward life prevented her from enjoying. Here, again, is the implicit analogy between Nell and the area "developed" by the TVA. A wealth of resources is "released" by the integration of undeveloped regions and people into the regime of the commodity. As a bonus, because of its invasion by benevolent "experts," Nell's "primitive cabin in the woods" has become a picnic haven for smart, happy families.

A final point of crucial importance is that, at the end of the film, we are invited to conclude that Nell has become capable of nostalgia. She is now sufficiently enlightened to experience her dead twin as *not there*. Her final, sad glance over the lake, a glance doubled by the new family's nostalgic glance at her, seals her inclusion in the society whose consumption of commodities can be understood as compensation for the loss of organic connections with nature. Of course, as we have seen, the film also delivers the message that such connections never really existed, or that they were simply inferior versions of the much more intelligent connections now mediated for us by commodities. Nostalgia itself is a commodity whose "added value" depends on its linkage to the message that the past was not as we, in our nostalgic moments, pretend to remember it. Fredric Jameson has said that the function of the media is "to help us forget."[36] This is perhaps true, but, in a sense, Jameson's statement is not subtle enough to account for media products like *Nell*: commercial media products substitute nostalgia for real memory. Nostalgia is commodified memory, which "helps" us forget that there was ever anything but an earlier stage of commodity consumption to remember. The commodity is experience already lost, as it occurs, to commercial motivations; it is experience fabricated by a technological production process that is itself produced and driven by those commercial motivations. A Hollywood film, therefore, is perhaps the archetypal commodity: film and other media make us forget that there could be experience, a world to be experienced, and memory of that experience outside the commodified circle. The affluent suburban family, of course, iconized relentlessly by Hollywood since World War II, is the most efficient device yet *produced* for the consumption of commodities. Nostalgia is the mood that defines both experiences and the memory of them as commodified products.

This final scene of *Nell* encourages us to experience our momentary nostalgia for a more natural life as a comfortable luxury that only our commodity-based culture can provide. This subtly normative story more or less forces us to think that the real past was laborious, lonely, deluded, and dumb. There is no past allowed, except an earlier and less satisfactory stage of economic development. Nature is just undeveloped property, untapped resources. The production of commodities provides us with everything, including the opportunity to dream of a more "natural" life. The very space in which we can indulge in such dreams is engineered and maintained for us by the Tennessee Valley Authority and its ilk. The recreation area is Edenland, a theme park, and, even as we enjoy it, we must enact the dominant social imperative. We are tourists, the land is a playground, and play requires the appropriate commodified accoutrements. In fact, like the picnickers, and like the frolicsome nature consumers in the television commercials, we have a rather nostalgic way of experiencing the *present:* our experience is mediated—indeed, it is both permitted and separated from us—by commodities. The film's ending shows us yet another normative reflection of ourselves: Jerry and Paula are spectators; they are watching Nell and their little girl playing. Being a family, like being smart, is associated with spectatorship. The film's characters have been engendered by cinematic technology. As spectators, *we* are engendered by that technology. Our awareness is permitted and conditioned by it. We can feel all-knowing, on the condition that we accept the orthodox version of things as the only valid one: it's still *a Wonderful Life!* And don't you *forget* it.

Notes

1. Quoted from a 1986 issue of *Fortune* magazine by Anne Friedberg in her discussion of the marketing of "commodity-experiences" in *Window Shopping: Cinema and the Postmodern* (Berkeley: University of California Press, 1993), 115.

2. Kaja Silverman, *The Threshold of the Visible World* (New York: Routledge, 1996), 197.

3. Max Horkheimer and Theodor Adorno, *The Dialectic of Enlightenment,* trans. John Cumming (New York: Continuum, 1993).

4. Kaja Silverman, "Kaspar Hauser's 'Terrible Fall' into Narrative," *New German Critique* 24–25 (1981–82): 79.

5. On the commodification of nature, see Rebecca Solnit's excellent analysis, *Savage Dreams: A Journey into the Hidden Wars of the American West* (San Francisco: Sierra Club Books, 1994), particularly the chapter "Framing the View."

6. Michel de Certeau, *The Practice of Everyday Life* (Berkeley: University of California Press, 1984), 115.

7. Leo Marx, *The Machine in the Garden: Technology and the Pastoral Ideal in America* (Oxford: Oxford University Press, 1964).

8. Ibid., 6.

9. Jean Baudrillard, *Jean Baudrillard's Selected Writings*, ed. Mark Poster (Stanford, Calif.: Stanford University Press, 1988), 30.

10. Bruno Latour, *We Have Never Been Modern*, trans. Catherine Porter (Cambridge: Harvard University Press, 1993), 54.

11. Silverman, "Kaspar Hauser's 'Terrible Fall,'" 74.

12. Ibid., 77.

13. Marx, *The Machine in the Garden*, 35.

14. Michel de Certeau, "The Madness of Vision," *Enclitic* 7, no. 1 (1983): 26.

15. For a discussion of "participating consciousness," wherein no radical separation exists between subject and object, see Morris Berman, *The Reenchantment of the World* (Ithaca, N.Y.: Cornell University Press, 1981).

16. Horkheimer and Adorno, *The Dialectic of Enlightenment*, 149.

17. Friedberg, *Window Shopping*, 122.

18. Lewis Mumford cited in Jerry Mander, *In the Absence of the Sacred: The Failure of Technology and the Survival of the Indian Nations* (San Francisco: Sierra Club Books, 1991), 29.

19. Paul Shepard, *Man in the Landscape: A Historic View of the Esthetics of Nature* (College Station: Texas A&M University Press, 1991), xxvii.

20. See David Michael Levin, ed., *Modernity and the Hegemony of Vision* (Berkeley: University of California Press, 1993).

21. Luce Irigaray, *Speculum de l'autre femme* (Paris: Les Editions de Minuit, 1974).

22. See Paul Virilio, *War and Cinema: The Logistics of Perception*, trans. Patrick Camiller (London: Verso, 1989).

23. Larry W. Riggs, *Resistance to Culture in Molière, Laclos, Flaubert, and Camus: A Post-Modernist Approach* (Lewiston: Edwin Mellen, 1992), 34. See also Carolyn Merchant, *The Death of Nature: Women, Ecology, and the Scientific Revolution* (San Francisco: HarperCollins, 1989).

24. See Lynn White Jr., "The Historical Roots of Our Ecological Crisis," *Science*, 10 March 1967, 1203–7 (reprinted in *The Ecocriticism Reader: Landmarks in Literary Ecology*, ed. Cheryll Glotfelty and Harold Fromm [Athens: University of Georgia Press, 1996], 3–14).

25. Marx, *The Machine in the Garden*, 217.

26. Ibid., 109.

27. R. W. Connell, *Masculinities* (Berkeley: University of California Press, 1995), 25.

28. René Girard, *Deceit, Desire and the Novel: Self and Other in Literary Structure* (Baltimore: Johns Hopkins University Press, 1965).

29. Julianne Pidduck, "The 1990's Hollywood Fatal Femme: (Dis)Figuring Feminism, Family, Irony, Violence," *CineAction* 38 (1995): 64–72.

30. Ibid., 66.

31. Ibid., 69.

32. Shepard, *Man in the Landscape*, 109.

33. Silverman, "Kaspar Hauser's 'Terrible Fall,'" 82.

34. De Certeau, *The Practice of Everyday Life*, 167.

35. Guy Debord, *The Society of the Spectacle* (Detroit, Mich.: Black & Red, 1983).

36. Fredric Jameson, "Postmodernism and Consumer Society," in *The Anti-Aesthetic: Essays on Postmodern Culture*, ed. Hal Foster (Port Townsend, Wash.: Bay, 1983), 125.

Contributors

Heather Addison is a Ph.D. candidate in film studies at the University of Kansas. She is currently working on her dissertation, "Hollywood and the Reducing Craze of the 1920s," and her forthcoming publications include "Children's Films in the 1990s," an essay in *Film Genre 2000.*

Sarah Berry is assistant professor of media studies and production at the College of Staten Island, City University of New York. She is the author of *Screen Style: Fashion and Femininity in 1930s Hollywood* (Minnesota, 2000) and has published essays on film, television, and cultural studies. She also designs and produces educational multimedia.

Jeffrey Charles is assistant professor of history at California State University, San Marcos. He is the author of *Service Clubs in American Society: Rotary, Kiwanis, and Lions.*

Angela Curran is assistant professor of philosophy at Mount Holyoke College, specializing in ancient Greek philosophy, aesthetics, and philosophy of film. Her work in aesthetics currently focuses on feminism and film and on developing an account of critical spectatorship, including the role that emotions play in thinking about characters in film and tragedy.

David Desser is professor of cinema studies at the University of Illinois, Urbana-Champaign. He has authored and edited numerous books, including studies of Japanese cinema, Chinese cinema, Jews in American cinema, and the films of John Huston, and has published more than forty essays in scholarly books and journals.

Rebecca L. Epstein is a doctoral candidate in the Department of Film and Television at the University of California, Los Angeles. She conducts

355

research on topics of twentieth-century American popular culture and is writing her dissertation on the role of food in Hollywood gangster films.

Cynthia Felando received a Ph.D. from the Film and Television Department of the University of California, Los Angeles. Her dissertation, "Searching for the Fountain of Youth: Popular American Cinema in the 1920s," earned UCLA's Mary Wollstonecraft Award. She is currently the senior programmer for the Santa Barbara International Film Festival, and she lectures on the subjects of film and television. She was a major contributor to the reference book *Women Filmmakers and Their Films* and contributed an entry on Rudolph Valentino for the forthcoming *Oxford Companion to United States History.*

Aida A. Hozić holds a degree in comparative literature and philosophy from the University of Sarajevo, Bosnia and Herzegovina; a master's degree in international affairs from The Johns Hopkins University; and a Ph.D. in political economy from the University of Virginia. Her dissertation, "Rise of the Merchant Empire: Industrial Change in the American Film Industry," focuses on the conflict between producers and merchants (distributors, financiers, agents) in the American film industry and the increasing dominance of the latter in the post-studio period. She is now assistant professor in the Department of Politics at Ithaca College.

Garth S. Jowett is professor of communication at the University of Houston. He is the author of *Film: The Democratic Art* and the co-author of *Movies as Mass Communication* (with James Linton) and *Propaganda and Persuasion* (with Victoria O'Donnell). His most recent book is *Children and the Movies: Media Power and the Payne Fund Controversy* (with Ian Jarvie and Katherine H. Fuller). He serves as the series editor for the Sage Foundations of Popular Culture Series and (with Kenneth Short) as advisory editor for the Cambridge University Press History of Mass Communications Series.

Larry W. Riggs is professor of French and former director of interdisciplinary studies at Butler University. His publications include *Resistance to Culture in Molière, Laclos, Flaubert, and Camus: A Post-Modernist Approach* as well as essays in the *Romanic Review, Romance Languages Annual, Literature/Interpretation/Theory,* and *Literature/Film Quarterly.*

Sara Ross is visiting assistant professor of electronic media and film at Southern Methodist University. She is nearing completion of her dissertation on the flapper character in Hollywood films of the 1920s.

David Slayden is associate professor of media studies, advertising, and integrated marketing communications at the University of Colorado at Boulder. He is coeditor of *Hate Speech* and *Soundbite Culture: The Death of Discourse in a Wired World* (with Rita Kirk Whillock) and has published on issues of culture and society, focusing on politics, representation, identity, and technology. He is currently working on a book on image and authenticity in commercial culture.

Josh Stenger is currently a Ph.D. candidate in the Department of English at Syracuse University. His recent work focuses on the reciprocal relationship between the cultural geography of Los Angeles and Hollywood film history.

Gaylyn Studlar is professor of film studies and English at the University of Michigan, Ann Arbor, where she also directs the Program in Film and Video Studies. Her recent publications include the coedited volumes *Titanic: Anatomy of a Blockbuster* (with Kevin Sandler) and *Visions of the East: Orientalism in Film* (with Matthew Bernstein). She is currently working on a social history of American women and Hollywood cinema.

Thomas E. Wartenberg is the author of *Unlikely Couples: Movie Romance as Social Criticism* and *The Forms of Power: From Domination to Transformation* and the coeditor of *Philosophy and Film*. He is the editor of the Westview Press series Thinking through Cinema: The Philosophy of Film. He teaches philosophy and film at Mount Holyoke College.

Jill Watts is associate professor of history at California State University, San Marcos. She is the author of *God, Harlem U.S.A.: The Father Divine Story* and has just completed an interpretative biography of the life and work of Mae West.

Barbara Wilinsky is visiting assistant professor in the Department of Media Arts at the University of Arizona. She is currently working on a history of the growing popularity of art-film theaters in the United States in the years immediately following World War II.

Paula Willoquet-Maricondi is lecturer in interdisciplinary studies at Butler University. She writes on European and American film, literature, and ecological issues. She is coediting (with Mary Alemany Galway) a collection of essays on Peter Greenaway. Her essay on Greenaway's and Aimé Césaire's treatment of *The Tempest* was published in *Reading the Earth: New Directions in the Study of Literature and Environment,* and she is currently working on a book that explores the ecological dimensions of Greenaway's artistic productions.

Rick Worland is associate professor of cinema at Southern Methodist University. His research has focused on popular film and television in the post–World War II era in relation to U.S. social and political history. He has published in *Cinema Journal, Journal of Film and Video, Science-Fiction Studies,* and *Journal of Popular Film and Television.*

Index